Economic Freedom of the World

2001 Annual Report

James Gwartney
Florida State University

and

Robert Lawson
Capital University

with

Walter Park
American University

and

Charles Skipton
Florida State University

authors of this book have worked independently and opinions expressed by them are, therefore, their
own, and do not necessarily reflect the opinions of the members or the trustees of The Fraser Institute.

Cover designed by Brian Creswick @ GoggleBox

Canadian Cataloguing in Publication Data

Gwartney, James D.
  Economic freedom of the world ... report

  ISSN 1482-471X

  1. Economic history--1990- --Periodicals.   2. Economic indicators--Periodicals.
I. Fraser Institute (Vancouver, B.C.)   II. Title

HB95G93   330.9'005   C97-302072-5

TABLE OF CONTENTS

ACKNOWLEDGMENTS

As with previous editions of *Economic Freedom of the World*, we owe a debt to many people. Without the assistance and guidance of both Mike Walker and Milton Friedman, this project would never have gotten off of the ground. Mike organized the Fraser Institute/Liberty Fund conference series that provided the foundation for our measure of economic freedom. He also edited several of the conference volumes and provided both input and encouragement throughout. Milton Friedman's criticisms and suggested modifications shaped the research design of the project.

The institutes of the Economic Freedom Network again provided invaluable support for this report. They helped verify information and supplied us with missing data. Their use of the index in their respective countries has been nothing short of astounding. We have all the respect in the world for these freedom fighters operating in sometimes hostile environments.

Kathy Makinen at the DeVoe L. Moore Center of Florida State University assisted with data gathering and calculations. Fred McMahon and Chris Schlegel at The Fraser Institute did an excellent job of coordinating the data management and publication of the book. We are sorry for the loss of Dexter Samida, who has left The Fraser Institute and is currently studying in South Korea. Dexter's tireless work to convert the index to a database system paid huge dividends by saving us literally dozens of hours of labor. We wish him all the luck in his future endeavors.

James Gwartney

Robert Lawson

ABOUT THE AUTHORS

James D. Gwartney is Professor of Economics and Policy Sciences at Florida State University. He has a doctoral degree in economics from the University of Washington. Along with Richard Stroup and Russell Sobel, James Gwartney is author of *Economics: Private and Public Choice* (Harcourt Brace). This text, now in its ninth edition, has been used by more than one million students in the last two decades. A member of the Mont Pelerin Society, during 1993/1994, Professor Gwartney taught at the Central European University in Prague, Czech Republic. He has recently concluded a two-year tenure as Chief Economist at the Joint Economic Committee of Congress. He has published in the leading journals of professional economics, including *Public Choice, American Economic Review, Journal of Political Economy, Industrial and Labor Relations Review, Cato Journal* and *Southern Economic Journal.*

Robert A. Lawson is Associate Professor and currently serves as the George H. Moor Chair of Business and Economics at Capital University in Columbus, Ohio. A native of Cincinnati, he earned his B.S. in economics from the Honors Tutorial College at Ohio University in 1988 and his M.S. (1991) and Ph.D. (1992) in economics from Florida State University. He is a Senior Research Advisor for the Buckeye Institute for Public Policy Solutions, Adjunct Scholar for the Mackinac Institute, and Faculty Affiliate for the DeVoe Moore Policy Sciences Center at Florida State University. He has published articles in several journals, including *Public Choice, Journal of Labor Research, Asian Economic Review, Cato Journal, Journal of Institutional and Theoretical Economics,* and *Journal of Public Finance and Public Choice.*

ABOUT THE CONTRIBUTORS

Charles Skipton is a doctoral candidate in economics at Florida State University. His dissertation topic is international trade. During 1999 and 2000, he served as Staff Economist for the Joint Economic Committee of the United States Congress.

Walter Park is Associate Professor of Economics at American University in Washington, DC. He earned his B.A. at the University of Toronto, his M.Phil. at Oxford University, and his Ph.D. at Yale. He has published numerous articles on research and development, patents, and intellectual property rights in journals such as *Research Policy, Economic Letters, Economic Inquiry,* and *Journal of Economics and Finance.*

ABOUT THE PARTICIPATING INSTITUTES

CO-PUBLISHERS OF *ECONOMIC FREEDOM OF THE WORLD*

ACER, Albania

The Albanian Center for Economic Research is a public-policy institute that focuses on research and advocacy activities. In addition to providing policy makers and academics with applied economic research, it works to build public understanding of economic development issues. (E-mail: zefi@qske.tirana.al)

African Research Center for Public Policy and Market Process, Kenya

The African Research Center for Public Policy and Market Process, Kenya, is the first research centre founded in Africa by the African Educational Foundation for Public Policy and Market Process, an independent educational organization registered in the United States. The primary mission of the Center and the Foundation is to promote ideas about free markets and voluntary associations in Africa. The Center conducts research on all aspects of free markets, voluntary association, and individual liberty, and publishes the results to as wide an audience as possible. The Center also organizes seminars and conferences to examine liberty and enterprise in Africa. (E-mail: kimenyi@kippra.or.ke)

Association for Liberal Thinking, Turkey

The Association for Liberal Thinking is a non-profit, non-governmental organization seeking to introduce the liberal democratic tradition into Turkey. The Association promotes the understanding and acceptance of ideas like liberty, justice, peace, human rights, equality, and tolerance. It also encourages academic writing on liberal themes to help the Turkish people assess contemporary domestic and international changes and attempts to find effective solutions to Turkey's problems within liberal thought. The Association for Liberal Thinking is not involved in day-to-day politics and has no direct links to any political party or movement. Instead, as an independent intellectual group, it aims to set broader political agendas so as to contribute to the liberalization of Turkey in economics and politics. (E-mail: liberal@ada.net.tr)

Association pour la Liberté Economique et le Progrès Social (ALEPS), France

ALEPS promotes the idea of free markets generating social progress. It connects French liberal intellectuals with the global scientific community. Thanks to its permanent contacts with various prestigious foreign institutes, in 1990 ALEPS published "Manifeste de l'Europe pour les Européens," signed by 600 faculties from 28 countries.

The economic collapse of central planning and the disappearance of totalitarian regimes in Eastern Europe has not solved all social problems. A post-socialist society has still to be set up, both in Eastern Europe as well as in Western countries such as France, where 40 years of the welfare state have led to mass unemployment, fiscal oppression, an explosive expansion of social security, an increase in poverty and inequality, and a loss of moral virtues and spiritual values. ALEPS provides the political and intellectual push towards this necessary revival.

Cato Institute, United States of America

Founded in 1977, the Cato Institute is a research foundation dedicated to broadening debate about public policy to include more options consistent with the traditional American principles of limited government, individual liberty, free markets, and peace. To that end, the Institute strives to achieve greater involvement by the intelligent, concerned lay public in questions of policy and the proper role of government through an extensive program of publications and seminars. (E-mail: ivasquez@cato.org)

Center for the Dissemination of Economic Knowledge (CEDICE), Venezuela

CEDICE is a non-partisan, non-profit, private association dedicated to the research and promotion of philosophical, economic, political, and social thinking that focuses on individual initiative and a better understanding of the free-market system and free and responsible societies. To this end, CEDICE operates a library and bookstore, publishes the series, *Venezuela Today,* and other studies, provides economic training for journalists, and conducts special events and community programs. (E-mail: hfaria@newton.iesa.edu.ve)

Center for the New Europe, Belgium

The Center for the New Europe is a European research institute, based in Brussels, that promotes a market economy, personal liberty, and creativity and responsibility in an ordered society. CNE is founded on the belief that European integration can work only in a society led by a spirit of democratic capitalism. The Center develops policy alternatives, encourages economic growth and deregulation, seeks new market-based solutions for social and environmental concerns, and promotes individual freedom, choice and responsibility.

Center for Policy Research, Sri Lanka

The Center for Policy Research (CPR) is a non-partisan advocacy and policy-research institute dedicated to fostering democracy and promoting free enterprise. As part of its philosophy, CPR actively takes positions on the reform of critical policies and aggressively lobbies key decision-makers in the country. (E-mail: mmoragoda@eureka.lk)

The Center for Research and Communication, Philippines

The Center for Research and Communication (CRC) has, since 1967, conducted research and published works on domestic and international economic and political issues that affect the Asia-Pacific region. It provides forums for discussion and debate among academicians, businessmen, civil officials, and representatives of other sectors that shape public opinion and chart the course of policies. CRC is the main research arm of the University of Asia and the Pacific in Metro Manila, Philippines, and currently serves as the Secretariat of the Asia Pacific Economic Cooperation (APEC) Business Advisory Council. (E-mail: hbasilio@info.com.ph)

Centre for Civil Society, India

The Centre for Civil Society is an independent, non-profit, research and educational organization inaugurated on August 15, 1997 and devoted to improving the quality of life for all citizens of India. The CCS maintains that, having earlier attained their political independence from an alien state, the Indian people must now seek economic, social, and cultural independence from the Indian state. This can work from two directions simultaneously: a "mortar" program of building or rebuilding the institutions of civil society and a "hammer" program of readjusting the size and scope of the political society. The CCS conducts monthly dialogues on topical issues to introduce classical liberal philosophy and market-based solutions into public debate. It has published *Agenda for Change*, a volume in 17 chapters that outlines policy reforms for the Indian government, Israel Kirzner's *How Markets Work*, and *Self-Regulation in the*

Civil Society, edited by Ashok Desai. It organizes Liberty and Society seminars for college students and journalists. (E-mail: parth@ccsindia.org; website: www.siliconindia.com/civil)

Centro de Investigacion y Estudios Legales (CITEL), Peru

CITEL was organized in 1989. Its principal field is the economic analysis of law. To that end, it conducts research on different legal institutions, publishes books, and organizes seminars and colloquia. (E-mail: eghersi@computextos.com.pe)

Centro de Investigaciones Académicas (CIVILIZAR), Colombia

The Centro de Investigaciones Académicas is a private, non-profit, economic and social research organization. Established in 1996, the Centro is affiliated with the Sergio Arboleda University of Bogata. It is dedicated to the scientific study of economic and social topics and defends individual liberty, which it recognizes as a basic principle to guide programs of research and education. The Centro supports research and publishes studies on economic, social, and legal issues in order to promote Colombian economic growth and human development. (E-mail: usa5008@latino.net.co)

Centro de Investigaciones Económicas Nacionales, Guatemala

CIEN, the Center for Research on the National Economy, was established in Guatemala in 1982. It is a private, non-partisan, not-for-profit public-policy institute, funded by the sale of its books and periodical publications, income from conferences and seminars, and the support it receives from its members and the public. The Center's program is devoted to the technical study of economic and social problems that impede the stable development of the nation. Its members, staff, research associates, and supporters share the principles of a social order of free and responsible individuals interacting through a market economy functioning within the rule of law. (E-mail: curizarh@cien.org.gt)

Centro de Investigaciones sobre la Libre Empresa, A.C., Mexico

The Centro de Investigaciones sobre la Libre Empresa (CISLE) is a non-profit, educational and public-policy organization founded in 1984. Its aim is to defend and promote the ideals of free trade and free enterprise in all areas of society and it maintains that the fundamental source of well-being and the wealth of nations is a sound institutional order that guarantees competition, private ownership, and open markets. CISLE's activities are financed by a select group of generous donors. (E-mail: Ceninves@mail.infolatina.com.mx)

Centro Einaudi, Italy

The Centro di Ricerca e Documentazione "Luigi Einaudi" was founded in 1963 in Turin, Italy, as a free association of businessmen and young intellectuals to foster individual freedom and autonomy, economic competition and the free market. The Centro is an independent, non-profit institute financed by contributions from individuals and corporations, by the sale of its publications, and by specific research commissions. The Centro carries on research activities, trains young scholars and researchers, organizes seminars, conferences and lectures, and publishes monographs, books and periodicals, including: the quarterly journal, *Biblioteca della libertà*; *Rapporto sull'economia globale e l'Italia* (Report on the global economy and Italy); *Rapporto sul risparmio e sui risparmiatori in Italia* (Report on the savings and the savers in Italy).

Centrum im. Adama Smitha, Poland

The Centrum im. Adama Smitha, Poland (the Adam Smith Research Centre) is a private, non-partisan, non-profit, public-policy institute. It was founded in 1989 and was the first such institute in Poland and in Eastern Europe. The ASRC promotes a free and fair market economy, participatory democracy, and a virtuous society. Its activities in research and development, education, and publishing cover almost all important issues within the areas of economy and social life. The ASRC acts as a guardian of economic freedom in Poland. More than 50 experts are associated with the ASRC. (E-mail: adam.smith@adam-smith.pl; website: http://www.adam-smith.pl)

The Estonian Institute for Open Society Research

The Estonian Institute for Open Society Research was established in 1993 as an independent non-profit public-policy research institute. EIOSR's research and public-communication programs focus on the key issues of Estonian social and political development: building a free-market economy and open civil society; enhancing social stability and integration of minority groups; and promoting Estonia's integration into European and world structures. EIOSR's first effort was the Estonian translation of Milton Friedman's *Capitalism and Freedom* in early 1994. Current EIOSR projects include promoting the idea of philanthropy to local businesses and elaborating future scenarios concerning the integration of the Russian minority into Estonian society. (E-mail: volli@lin2.tpu.ee)

The F.A. Hayek Foundation, Slovak Republic

The F.A. Hayek Foundation is an independent and non-partisan, non-profit organization that provides a forum for the exchange of opinions among scholars, businessmen, and policy-makers on the causes of, and solutions to, economic, social, and political problems. It proposes practical reforms of the economy, education, social security, and legislation as the Slovak Republic is transformed into an open society. Education of high-school and university students is a large part of its activities. The F.A. Hayek Foundation promotes classical liberalism, which was virtually absent until 1989: market economy, reduced role of the government, rule of law and individual choice, responsibilities and rights to life, liberty, and property. (E-mail: hayek@changenet.sk; website: www.hayek.sk)

The Fraser Institute, Canada

The Fraser Institute is an independent Canadian economic and social research and educational organization. It has as its objective the redirection of public attention to the role of competitive markets in providing for the well-being of Canadians. Where markets work, the Institute's interest lies in trying to discover prospects for improvement. Where markets do not work, its interest lies in finding the reasons. Where competitive markets have been replaced by government control, the interest of the Institute lies in documenting objectively the nature of the improvement or deterioration resulting from government intervention. The work of the Institute is assisted by an Editorial Advisory Board of internationally renowned economists. The Fraser Institute is a national, federally chartered, non-profit organization financed by the sale of its publications and the tax-deductible contributions of its members. (E-mail: info@fraserinstitute.ca; website: www.fraserinstitute.ca)

The Free Market Foundation of Southern Africa

The Free Market Foundation of Southern Africa was established in 1975 to promote economic freedom. The FMF sponsors and conducts research, conferences, lectures, training programs and lobbying efforts in support of the free market. Its funding comes from membership subscriptions, project sponsorships, and income from sales and fees. (E-mail: fmf@jhb.lia.net)

Fundación Economía y Desarrollo, Inc., Dominican Republic

The Fundación Economía y Desarrollo, Inc. (FEyD) is a private non-profit organization dedicated to fostering competitive markets, private enterprise, and strategies that promote economic development. To meet its objectives, FEyD has several regular publications in the most important newspapers in the country. It also produces a one-hour television program called "Triálogo," which is broadcast three times a week and explains studies of the performance of the Dominican economy and its sectors. (E-mail: feyd03@tricom.net)

Fundación Libertad, Panama

Fundación Libertad, Panama, is a recently-formed, non-profit foundation engaged in the promotion and development of liberty, individual choice, and voluntary cooperation and in the reduction of government. Fundación Libertad was founded by members of professional and business organizations promoting free enterprise and democracy because the existing organizations could not fully address issues affecting the freedom of the common citizen, particularly the increasing discretionary power of the state and the proliferation of legislation fostering discrimination and establishing privileges, all of which are contrary to the spirit of democratic capitalism. Fundación Libertad has drawn initial support from sister organizations such as Centro de Divulgación del Conocimiento Económico (CEDICE) in Caracas, Venezuela, and the Centro de Investigación y Estudios Nacionales (CIEN) in Guatemala. (E-mail: Roberto Brenes: diablo@pty.com; Carlos E. González: cg@pananet.com.)

Fundación Libertad, Democracia y Desarrollo, Bolivia

The Fundación Libertad, Democracia y Desarrollo (FULIDED) is a non-profit organization founded by citizens interested in promoting democracy and freedom. The purpose of the Foundation is to investigate and analyze issues that have economic, political, or social impact on the free market and private initiative. Through seminars, debates, and publications, FULIDED seeks to reflect Bolivia's participation in the global economy. (E-mail: fulided@cainco.org.bo)

Hong Kong Centre for Economic Research

The Hong Kong Centre for Economic Research is an educational, charitable trust established in 1987 to promote the free market in Hong Kong by fostering public understanding of economic affairs and developing alternative policies for government. The Centre publishes authoritative research studies and is widely recognized as the leading free-market think-tank in Asia. It has been influential in persuading public opinion and the government in Hong Kong to liberalize telecommunications, open up air-cargo handling franchises, privatize public housing, adopt a fully funded provident scheme instead of a pay-as-you-go pension scheme, remove the legally sanctioned fixing of deposit interest rates by banks, and adopt market mechanisms for protecting the environment. (E-mail: asiu@econ.hku.hk)

Institute for Advanced Strategic and Political Studies, Israel

The mission of the Institute for Advanced Strategic and Political Studies is to develop policies in economics, strategic studies, and politics that will bring about limited government in domestic affairs and the balance of power in strategic planning. The Institute's Division for Economic Policy Research (DEPR) publishes *Policy Studies* in both English and Hebrew, while the Division for Research in Strategy and Politics produces a series of documents in strategic studies and another in politics. (E-mail: iaspsdc@aol.com)

The Institute for Economic Freedom, Bahamas

The Institute for Economic Freedom is an independent, non-political, non-profit institute that promotes economic growth, employment, and entrepreneurial activity. It believes that this can best be achieved with a free market economy and a decent society—one that embraces the rule of law, the right of private property, the free exchange of property and services, and the individual virtues of self-control, commitment, and good will. (E-mail: joanmt@bahamas.net.bs)

Institute for Market Economics, Bulgaria

Established in 1993, IME is the first independent economic think-tank in Bulgaria. It is a private, registered, non-profit corporation that receives international support and is widely respected for its expertise. IME designs and promotes solutions to the problems that Bulgaria is facing in its transition to a market economy, provides independent assessment and analysis of the government's economic policies, and supports an exchange of views on market economics and relevant policy issues. (E-mail: svetla@ime.bg)

The Institute of Economic Affairs, United Kingdom

The IEA's mission is to improve public understanding of the foundations of a free and harmonious society by expounding and analyzing the role of markets in solving economic and social problems, and bringing the results of that work to the attention of those who influence thinking. The IEA achieves its mission by a high-quality publishing program; conferences, seminars and lectures on a range of subjects; outreach to school and college students; brokering media introductions and appearances; and other related activities. Incorporated in 1955 by the late Sir Antony Fisher, the IEA is an educational charity, limited by guarantee. It is independent of any political party or group, and is financed by sales of publications, conference fees, and voluntary donations. (E-mail: crobinson@iea.org.uk)

The Institute of Economic Affairs, Ghana

The Institute of Economic Affairs (IEA), Ghana was founded in October 1989 as an independent, non-governmental institution dedicated to the establishment and strengthening of a market economy and a democratic, free, and open society. It considers improvements in the legal, social, and political institutions as necessary conditions for sustained economic growth and human development. The IEA supports research and promotes and publishes studies on important economic, socio-political, and legal issues in order to enhance understanding of public policy. (E-mail: iea@ghana.com)

Institute of Economic Analysis, Russia

The Institute of Economic Analysis is a macroeconomic research institute that analyzes the current economic situation and policies and provides expert analysis of acts, programs, and current economic policy. It will offer advice to Russian government bodies, enterprises, and organizations and prepares and publishes scientific, research, and methodological economic literature. It also conducts seminars, conferences, and symposia on economic topics. The Institute is an independent, non-governmental, non-political, non-profit research centre that works closely with leading Russian and international research centres. Its research focuses on macroeconomic, budget, and social policies. (E-mail: ieamos@glasnet.ru)

Institute of Economic Studies, Iceland

The Institute of Economic Studies was founded in 1989. It operates within the Department of Economics in the Faculty of Economics and Business Administration at the University of Iceland. From the outset, the Institute has been active in carrying out applied research projects commissioned by private and public clients ranging from small Icelandic interest groups to the Nordic Investment Bank to the governments of Iceland, Denmark, and the Faroe Islands. More recently, funded by research grants, the Institute has taken on large-scale applied research projects with substantial analytical content and economic research. (E-mail: tthh@rhi.hi.is)

The Institute of Economics, Croatia

The Institute of Economics, Zagreb, established in 1939, is a major scientific and research institution for the study of economic processes and the application of contemporary theories in economics. The Institute's objective is the economic and social advance of Croatia. Research encompasses both macro-economics and micro-economics, policy issues (including specialized areas such as business economics), current economic trends, methods of economic analysis, development of human resources, spatial and regional economics, international economics and technological development, and investment project planning. Researchers from both inside and outside the Institute work together on research projects. The Institute employs 40 full-time researchers, the majority of whom have completed specialized training courses in foreign countries. Results of the Institute's research activities are published in books, reports and studies as well as in scientific journals. The Institute maintains close contact with international organizations, professional associations, institutes, and universities. (E-mail: zbaletic@eizg.hr)

Institute of Macroeconomic Analysis and Development, Slovenia

The Institute of Macroeconomic Analysis and Development (IMAD) is a part of the Ministry of Economic Relations and Development. It does the key analysis for annual memoranda on economic policy and it coordinated the preparation of the Strategy of Economic Development of Slovenia and its Strategy for Accession to the European Union. Its activities also include analyses of current macroeconomic trends and of social, regional, and institutional development; simulations and evaluations of economic and developmental measures; development of methodological tools and information systems. The Institute has around 50 employees, two-thirds of whom are specialists. Its publications, *Slovenian Economic Mirror* and its Spring and Autumn Reports, are translated into English and distributed to a large international audience. IMAD also publishes the international *Journal for Institutional Innovation, Development, and Transition* (IB Review) and holds an annual conference on Institutions in Transition. (E-mail: rotija.kmet@gov.si)

Institute of Public Affairs, Australia

Established in 1943, the IPA is Australia's oldest and largest private-sector think-tank. Its aim is to foster prosperity and full employment, the rule of law, democratic freedoms, security from crime and invasion, and high standards in education and family life for the Australian people. To identify and promote the best means of securing these values, the IPA undertakes research, organizes seminars, and publishes widely. (E-mail: ipa@ipa.org.au)

Instituto Ecuatoriano de Economia Politica, Ecuador

The Instituto Ecuatoriano de Economia Politica (IEEP) is a private, independent, non-profit institution that defends and promotes the classical liberal ideals of individual liberty, free markets, limited government, property rights, and the rule of law. The IEEP achieves its mission through publications, seminars, and workshops that debate socio-economic and political issues. The IEEP's funding comes from voluntary donations, membership subscriptions, and income from sales of its publications. (E-mail: dampuero@ecua.net.ec)

Instituto Liberal do Rio de Janiero, Brazil

Instituto Liberal was founded to persuade Brazilians of the advantages of a liberal order. It is a non-profit institution supported by donations and the sponsorship of private individuals and corporations. Its by-laws provide for a Board of Trustees and forbid any political or sectarian affiliations. The institute publishes books, organizes seminars, and elaborates policy papers on subjects related to public policy. (E-mail: ilrj@gbl.com.br)

Instituto Libertad y Desarrollo, Chile

Libertad y Desarrollo is a private think-tank wholly independent of any religious, political, financial, or governmental groups. It is committed to the free market and to political and economic freedom. It publishes studies and analyses of public-policy issues. (E-mail: ega@chilesat.net)

Instituto para la Libertad y el Analisis de Politicas, Costa Rica

The Institute for Liberty and Public Policy Analysis (INLAP) is a non-profit, non-partisan organization, created to defend and promote individual liberty through analysis of public policy and educational activities. Its specific objectives are (1) to increase awareness of the moral foundations of liberty and to promote liberty as an individual right necessary to achieve the highest levels of economic and human development; and (2) to foster changes in social organization and public policies by influencing the thinking of policy-makers, community leaders, and citizens.

INLAP produces timely analyses of proposed laws, decrees, and regulations, and its recommendations provide guidance for elected officials who seek to achieve greater individual liberty and creativity and a more productive economy. Detailed studies of well-meant public policies that ultimately have adverse effects are conducted. The Institute's studies and recommendations are published in books, journals, and newspapers, appear as position papers and bulletins, and are also available via the Internet. (E-mail: riggo@attglobal.net)

The Korea Center for Free Enterprise

The Center for Free Enterprise (CFE) is a foundation committed to promoting free enterprise, limited government, freedom and individual responsibility, the rule of law and restraint of violence. Funded by the members of the Federation of Korean Industries (FKI), The CFE was founded as a non-profit, independent foundation on April 1, 1997, at a time of economic crisis in Korean society. The CFE has concentrated on championing a free economy through books and reports on public policies, statistics, and analyses. In workshops and policy forums, the CFE has put forward alternatives to policies proposed as solutions for issues facing Korean society. (E-mail: yooys@cfe.org)

Liberales Institut, Germany

The Liberales Institut (Liberty Institute), based in Potsdam, is the think-tank of the Friedrich-Naumann-Foundation. It spreads free-market ideas through the publication of classical liberal literature, the analysis of current political trends, and the promotion of research. The Institute organizes conferences and workshops to stimulate an intellectual exchange among liberals around the world. (E-mail: LibInst@fnst.org)

Liberales Institut, Switzerland

The Liberales Institut is a forum where the basic values and concepts of a free society can be discussed and questioned. The Institute's aim is the establishment of free markets as the best way towards the goals of openness, diversity, and autonomy. The Liberales Institut is not associated with any political party. Through publications, discussion forums, and seminars, the Institute seeks to develop and disseminate classical liberal ideas. (E-mail: libinst@bluewin.ch)

Liberální Institut, Czech Republic

The Liberal Institute is an independent, non-profit organization for the development and application of classical liberal ideas: individual rights, private property, rule of law, self-regulating markets, and delineated government functions. It is financed by its various activities and by donations from individuals and private corporations. (E-mail: michal.uryc@libinst.cz; website: www.libinst.cz)

Lithuanian Free Market Institute, Lithuania

The Lithuanian Free Market Institute (LFMI) is an independent, non-profit organization founded in 1990 to promote economic liberalism based on individual freedom and responsibility, free markets, and limited government. The LFMI's staff studies economic policy, develops reform packages, drafts and evaluates legislation, submits policy recommendations to the legislative and executive levels of government, and undertakes public education. LFMI's activities also include sociological surveys, publications, conferences, workshops, and lectures. LFMI has addressed economic reform: it promoted the idea of a currency board and provided decisive input to the Law on Litas Credibility, led the creation of the legal and institutional framework for the securities market, and initiated the policy-making process on private pension insurance through pension funds. LFMI's recommendations were adopted in legislation on commercial banks, the Bank of Lithuania, privatization, credit unions, insurance, and foreign investment. LFMI influenced the improvement of company and bankruptcy law. The Institute has also developed a proposal for tax and budget reform and its proposals were adopted in policy debates on income taxation, real estate tax, and inheritance and gift taxes. (E-mail: vaida@lrinka.lt; website: www.FreeMa.org)

Making Our Economy Right (MOER), Bangladesh

MOER (Making Our Economy Right), founded in 1991, is the country's lone free-market institute and continues to struggle to promote free-market capitalism despite all odds. The concept of individual freedom and free markets determining the supply of goods, services and capital is little understood in Bangladesh. For the past 50 years or so, Fabian socialism and doctrines of Karl Marx were the basis of our economy, part of the legacy remaining when Britain left India in 1947 and divided it into Pakistan and India. In 1971, Pakistan further split into two nations, Pakistan and Bangladesh. MOER contact person: Nizam Ahmad. (E-mail: nizam@bdmail.net)

The New Zealand Business Roundtable

The New Zealand Business Roundtable is made up of the chief executives of about 60 of New Zealand's largest businesses. Its aim is to contribute to the development of sound public policies that reflect New Zealand's overall interests. It has been a prominent supporter of the country's economic liberalization. (E-mail: 100405.1547@compuserve.com)

The Open Republic, Ireland

The Open Republic proposes open markets, individual freedom, voluntary action, the rule of law and religion as the means to make Ireland and all other countries better places to live and work. It opposes state control of industry and services and believes that state direction of economies and societies is the prime cause of corruption, poverty, and tyranny in the world. The Open Republic is Ireland's only source of policy and analysis oriented towards individual rights and open-markets. It evaluates public policy and proposes open-market, open-society solutions to Ireland's economic and social problems. (E-mail: pmacdonnell@openrepublic.org; website: www.openrepublic.org)

Szazadveg Institute, Hungary

The Szazadveg Institute is a non-profit organization performing political and economic research, advisory and training activities. This think-tank is independent of the government or any political parties and has been operating as a foundation since its establishment in 1990. Szazadveg publishes the results of its research to the public at large and also provides professional services to economic institutions, political and civil organizations, political parties, and the government. (E-mail: stumpf@bsp.mtapti.hu)

TIGRA®, Austria

TIGRA® is a non-partisan, international think-tank with headquarters in Salzburg. It was founded to study and advance effective and efficient economic policies. TIGRA® organizes workshops and publishes papers and reports ("From analysis to action!"). TIGRA® is a network of experts who can provide effective market solutions to policy makers. Special emphasis is put on knowledge management, governance, monitoring the scope and quality of regulations (cutting red tape), and setting benchmarks. (E-mail: tigra@austria.vg)

Timbro, Sweden

Timbro is a Swedish think-tank that encourages public opinion to favor free enterprise, a free economy, and a free society. Timbro publishes books, papers, reports, and the magazine, *Smedjan*. It also arranges seminars and establishes networks among people. Founded in 1978, Timbro is owned by the Swedish Free Enterprise Foundation, which has as its principals a large number of Swedish companies and organizations. (E-mail: mattiasb@timbro.se)

The Ukrainian Center for Independent Political Research

The Ukrainian Center for Independent Political Research was established in early 1991 as a non-profit, non-partisan, and non-governmental research institution that would increase awareness of democracy among the Ukrainian people and analyze domestic and international politics and security. The UCIPR is politically independent; it does not accept any funding from either the state or any political party. The UCIPR publishes books and research papers on Ukraine's domestic and foreign policy, the economy in transition, security, relations with neighboring states, the Crimean dilemma, interethnic relations, and the freedom of the news media. The Center has hosted a number of national and international conferences and workshops. (E-mail: kam@political.kiev.ua)

D'Letzeburger Land, Luxembourg (e-mail: letzlan@pt.lu)**; The Institute for Development of Economics and Finance, Indonesia** (e-mail: indef@indo.net.id)**; Liberty Network (LINE), Denmark** (e-mail: psj@line.dk); and **Bureau d'Analyse d'Ingenierie et de Logiciels (BAILO), Ivory Coast** (e-mail: bailo@globeaccess.net) are also members of the Economic Freedom Network.

Economic Freedom of the World

2001 Annual Report

EXECUTIVE SUMMARY

- This is the fifth edition of *Economic Freedom of the World*. Chapter 1 of this report updates the data from the earlier editions and presents an economic freedom index for 123 countries for 1999. Exhibit 1-1 shows the 21 components used to construct the index.

- In 1999, Hong Kong remained in first place with a rating of 9.4 (out of 10), followed closely by Singapore at 9.3. New Zealand ranked 3, the United Kingdom 4, and the United States 5. Australia, Ireland, Switzerland, Luxembourg, and the Netherlands round out the top ten. The rankings of other large economies include Canada (13), Germany (15), Japan (20), Italy (24), France (34), Taiwan (38), Mexico (62), China (81), India (92), Brazil (96), and Russia (117). Myanmar, Algeria, the Democratic Republic of Congo, Guinea-Bissau, and Sierra Leone rated lowest among the 123 countries for which data were available. See Exhibit 1-2.

- The economic freedom index is shown to correlate positively with measures of income per capita, economic growth, the United Nations Human Development Index, and longevity. It correlates negatively with indexes of corruption and poverty. Exhibits 1-4 through 1-9 illustrate these relationships.

- Chapter 2 uses survey data to supplement the objective components of the main index and develops a more comprehensive index of economic freedom for 58 countries. This more de-

tailed index integrates a number of factors that, until now, have either been omitted or poorly reflected in the economic freedom index. Specifically, it provides a more accurate reflection of cross-country differences in the freedom to contract and compete in business activities and labor markets. The more comprehensive index is constructed for 58 rather than 123 countries because of limitations in the data. See Exhibit 2-8 for the more comprehensive ratings. Exhibit 2-9 compares the more comprehensive index with the economic freedom index for 123 countries described in chapter 1.

- Chapter 3 constructs a Trade Openness Index for the period from 1980 to 1999 using selected components of the economic freedom index. See Exhibits 3-1 and 3-2. This chapter investigates the linkage between the openness of international trade and income levels and growth rates. See Exhibits 3-3 through 3-6.

- Chapter 4 discusses how to measure the strength of protection of property rights in *ideas*. Such a measure could be used for academic research, policy evaluation, or comparisons of intellectual property regimes across countries and over time. Chapter 4 focuses on quantifying the level of *patent rights* protection.

- Chapter 5 presents detailed Country Reports with component, area and overall ratings and rankings for all the countries in the data set from 1970 to 1999.

CHAPTER 1: ECONOMIC FREEDOM OF THE WORLD

INTRODUCTION

More than a decade ago, Michael Walker, the Executive Director of the Fraser Institute of Vancouver, British Columbia, and Nobel laureate Milton Friedman organized a series of conferences with the objective of clearly defining and measuring economic freedom. They were able to attract some of the world's leading economists, including Gary Becker, Douglass North, Peter Bauer, and Assar Lindbeck, to participate in the series and provide input for the study. These conferences eventually led to the publishing of *Economic Freedom of the World: 1975-1995* (which we wrote with Walter Block) and the organizing of the Economic Freedom Network, a group of institutes, in over fifty countries, seeking to develop the best possible measure of economic freedom. Since then, we have published *Economic Freedom of the World: 1997 Annual Report, Economic Freedom of the World: 1998/ 1999 Interim Report,* and *Economic Freedom of the World: 2000 Report.*[1] This report represents a continuation of these efforts.

In his foreword to *Economic Freedom of the World: 1975-1995*, Milton Friedman indicated that the indexes presented in that publication had brought the quest for an objective measure of economic freedom to a "temporary conclusion." Amplifying on this statement, Professor Friedman indicated that subsequent studies would "surely make revised editions necessary, both to bring the indexes of economic freedom up-to-date and to incorporate the additional understanding that will be generated." The measures developed in this publication are indicative of this evolutionary process. They reflect improved knowledge about how to measure economic freedom and the development of a more complete set of data for the achievement of that purpose. They represent movement to a new level.

The core ingredients of economic freedom are personal choice, protection of private property, and freedom of exchange. Individuals have economic freedom when the following conditions exist: (a) their property acquired without the use of force, fraud, or theft is protected from physical invasions by others and (b) they are free to use, exchange, or give their property to another as long as their actions do not violate the identical rights of others. Like a compass, this concept of economic freedom has directed our work.

No index of this sort is perfect. There are numerous trade-offs necessary along the way. For instance, the desire to cover a large number of countries means that we can include in the index only those types of infringements that occur widely and systematically across countries and only those for which the data can be relatively easily obtained. This approach means that many violations of economic freedom that occur in an idiosyncratic manner cannot be included in the index. Regulatory policy, in particular, is both complex and subtle and, therefore, difficult to measure.

For the first time, *Economic Freedom of the World* contains chapters devoted to particular topics. Chapter 2 will present a more detailed economic freedom index for a smaller set of countries. This index includes ratings for 58 nations and includes measures of economic freedom in labor markets and other areas that the main economic freedom index cannot measure effectively. Chapter 3 takes a closer look at economic freedom in the area of trade policy and presents a Trade Openness Index based on some of the components of the economic freedom index presented in this volume. Chapter 4, by Walter Park of American University, presents an index of patent rights and represents the beginning of our investigation of intellectual property rights more generally.

The main purpose of this edition of *Economic Freedom of the World* is to present the updated economic freedom ratings through the most recent period. The focus was to get the most current data available in this report. Nevertheless, often data from 1998 or, in rare cases, from 1997 were used when data for 1999 were not yet available. Chapter 5 presents Country Tables with the component data and ratings, area ratings, and summary economic freedom ratings.

Below is a review of the basic methodology of the economic freedom index, and a discussion of some of the changes made to the index in this edition.

METHODOLOGY OF THE INDEX

From the very beginning, our goal was the development of an objective measure of economic freedom rather than an index based on subjective assessments and "judgment calls." Therefore, our index is founded upon objective components that reflect the presence (or absence) of economic freedom–components that can be derived for a large number of countries from regularly published sources. This method will make it possible both to calculate the index for earlier time periods and to update it regularly. We also wanted to combine the components into a summary index in a sound, objective manner. While it is impossible to eliminate all subjectivity, our goal is to reduce, to the extent possible, judgment calls on the part of the authors.[2]

As Exhibit 1-1 illustrates, the index comprises 21 components designed to identify the consistency of institutional arrangements and policies with economic freedom in seven major areas. The seven areas covered by the index are as follows: (I) size of government, (II) economic structure and use of markets, (III) monetary policy and price stability, (IV) freedom to use alternative currencies, (V) legal structure and security of private ownership, (VI) freedom to trade with foreigners, and (VII) freedom of exchange in capital markets.

Areas I and II are indicators of *reliance on markets* rather than the political process (large government expenditures, state-operated enterprises, price controls, and discriminatory taxes) to allocate resources and determine the distribution of income. Areas III and IV reflect the availability of *sound money.* Area V focuses on the *legal security of property rights and the enforcement of contracts.* Area VI indicates the consistency of policies with *free trade.* Area VII is a measure of the degree to which markets are used to allocate capital. Reliance on markets, sound money, legal protection of property rights, free trade, and market allocation of capital are important elements of economic freedom captured by the index. We recognize that economic freedom is heterogeneous and highly complex: no single statistic will be able to capture its many facets fully and accurately. However, the index outlined in Exhibit 1-1 does encompass key ingredients of the concept.

We have been forced to make a few changes to the structure of the index in this edition and two components have been dropped. One component in Area V–Viability of Contracts–had to be dropped because the data source stopped reporting it. A second component–Percent of International Trade Covered by Non-tariff Trade Restraints (VI b i in the previous structure)–was eliminated because its data source no longer exists. The weights in Area VI were adjusted to distribute this component's weight among the remaining five components in that area.[3]

In total, 123 nations are included in this study. However, as the result of incomplete data or other factors (e.g., the split up of Czechoslovakia), we were only able to derive summary ratings for 122 in 1995, 116 in 1990, 112 in 1985, 108 in 1980, 83 in 1975, and 57 in 1970. After the data were assembled for each of the 21 components of the index, the ratings were calculated on a 0-to-10 scale. Higher ratings are indicative of institutions and policies more consistent with economic freedom.

The ratings for many of the 21 components in the index reflect various categorical characteristics; while others are based on continuous data. Countries with categorical characteristics more consistent with economic freedom are given higher ratings. For example, countries with few government enterprises

Exhibit 1-1: Components of Index of Economic Freedom

I   **Size of Government: Consumption, Transfers, and Subsidies**   **[11.0%]**

    a   General Government Consumption Expenditures as a Percentage of Total Consumption   (50%)

    b   Transfers and Subsidies as a Percentage of GDP   (50%)

II   **Structure of the Economy and Use of Markets** (*Production and allocation via governmental*   **[14.2%]**
and political mandates rather than private enterprises and markets)

    a   Government Enterprises and Investment as a Percentage of the Economy   (32.7%)

    b   Price Controls: Extent to which Businesses Are Free to Set Their Own Prices   (33.5%)

    c   Top Marginal Tax Rate (*and income threshold at which it applies*)   (25.0%)

    d   The Use of Conscripts to Obtain Military Personnel   (8.8%)

III   **Monetary Policy and Price Stability** (*Protection of money as a store of value and medium of exchange*)   **[9.2%]**

    a   Average Annual Growth Rate of the Money Supply during the Last Five Years   (34.9%)
minus the Growth Rate of Real GDP during the Last 10 Years

    b   Standard Deviation of the Annual Inflation Rate during the Last Five Years   (32.6%)

    c   Annual Inflation Rate during the Most Recent Year   (32.5%)

IV   **Freedom to Use Alternative Currencies** (*Freedom of access to alternative currencies*)   **[14.6%]**

    a   Freedom of Citizens to Own Foreign Currency Bank Accounts Domestically and Abroad   (50%)

    b   Difference between the Official Exchange Rate and the Black Market Rate   (50%)

V   **Legal Structure and Property Rights** (*Security of property rights and viability of contracts*)   **[16.6%]**

    a   Legal Security of Private Ownership Rights (*Risk of confiscation*)   (50.0%)

    b   Rule of Law: Legal Institutions, Including Access to a Nondiscriminatory Judiciary,   (50.0%)
That Are Supportive of the Principles of Rule of Law

VI   **International Exchange: Freedom to Trade with Foreigners**   **[17.1%]**

    a   Taxes on International Trade

        i   Revenue from Taxes on International Trade as a Percent of Exports plus Imports   (28.2%)

        ii   Mean Tariff Rate   (29.4%)

        iii   Standard Deviation of Tariff Rates   (28.4%)

    b   Actual Size of Trade Sector Compared to the Expected Size   (14.0%)

VII   **Freedom of Exchange in Capital and Financial Markets**   **[17.2%]**

    a   Ownership of Banks: Percentage of Deposits Held in Privately Owned Banks   (27.1%)

    b   Extension of Credit: Percentage of Credit Extended to Private Sector   (21.2%)

    c   Interest Rate Controls and Regulations that Lead to Negative Interest Rates   (24.7%)

    d   Restrictions on the Freedom of Citizens to Engage in Capital Transactions with Foreigners   (27.1%)

Note: The numbers in parentheses, *e.g.* (27.1%), indicate the weights used to derive the area rating. The numbers in bold in the brackets, *e.g.* **[17.2%]**, indicate the percentage weight allocated to each area when the summary rating was derived. These weights are derived by principal component analysis.

are given higher ratings than those with widespread use of such enterprises. Similarly, countries where price controls are absent (or apply in only a few markets) are given higher ratings than countries where these controls are extensively applied.

Depending on whether higher values are indicative of more or less economic freedom, alternative formulas are used to transform the 11 continuous variables to a 0-to-10 scale. When higher values are indicative of more economic freedom, the formula used to derive the 0-to-10 ratings is: $(V_i - V_{min}) / (V_{max} - V_{min})$ multiplied by 10. V_i is the country's actual value for the component, V_{max} the maximum value for a country during the 1990 base year, and V_{min} the minimum base-year value for the component. This formula is used to derive the ratings for all years. A country's rating will be close to 10 when its value for the component is near the base-year maximum. In contrast, the rating will be near 0 when the observation for a country is near the base-year minimum. As the actual values exceed the base-year minimum by larger and larger amounts, ratings will rise from 0 toward 10. Whenever the actual value for the component is equal to, or greater than, the base-year maximum, a rating of 10 is assigned. When the actual value is equal to or less than the base-year minimum, the rating is 0.

Higher actual values are often indicative of less economic freedom. Inflation and size of the transfer sector provide examples. Increases in these variables reflect reductions in economic freedom. When higher values for a component are indicative of less economic freedom, the formula used to derive the 0-to-10 ratings is: $(V_{max} - V_i) / (V_{max} - V_{min})$ multiplied by 10. This formula will assign higher ratings to countries with actual values closer to the base-year minimum. In some cases, component values of 0 represent an ideal—a benchmark that should be required for a rating of 10. For example, a 0 mean tariff rate and a 0 rate of inflation (perfect price stability) are benchmark outcomes representing maximum economic freedom. When 0 represents an ideal benchmark value, this value was included as V_{min} in the formula even if no country actually achieved this ideal during the base year. In some cases where extreme component values are present (for example, a 10,000% rate of inflation), V_{max} is constrained at a level

clearly warranting a rating of 0 even if this was not the maximum observed value during the base year. If this method had not been employed, extreme observations would have created such a large range that the ratings would have been concentrated near 10. The precise formula used to derive the 0-to-10 ratings for each component is presented in the section, Explanatory Notes and Data Sources, at the end of this chapter (page 14).

The procedures used to convert the continuous component values to the 0-to-10 ratings have two important characteristics. First, if all (or most) countries improve (or regress) with the passage of time, the ratings will reflect the change. Second, the distribution of the country ratings along the 0-to-10 scale closely reflects the distribution of the actual values among the countries.

Principal component analysis was used to determine the weight given to each component in the construction of the area index. This procedure partitions the variance of a set of variables and uses it to determine the linear combination—the weights—of these variables that maximizes the variation of the newly constructed principal component. In effect, the newly constructed principal component—an area rating, for example—is the variable that captures the variation of the underlying components most fully. It is an objective method of combining a set of variables into a single variable that best reflects the original data. The procedure is particularly appropriate when several sub-components measure different elements of a principal component. This is precisely the case with our index. Economic theory is a road map indicating components that are likely to capture various elements of a broader area (a principal component). In turn, principal component analysis indicates the permissibility of grouping components together and the weights most appropriate to combine a set of sub-components into a principal component. The component weights derived by this procedure are shown in parentheses in Exhibit 1-1; e.g., (50%). The same procedure was also used to derive the weights for the area components in the construction of what we will refer to as the summary index. These weights for each of the seven areas in Exhibit 1-1 are presented in bold-face type and enclosed within brackets; e.g., [11.0%]. The next section in this chapter looks at some of the basic results.

ECONOMIC FREEDOM OF THE WORLD IN THE 1990S

Exhibit 1-2 shows the summary economic freedom ratings for 1999, sorted from highest to lowest.[4] As in the past, Hong Kong topped the list, followed closely by Singapore. New Zealand ranked 3, the United Kingdom 4, and the United States 5. Australia, Ireland, Switzerland, Luxembourg, and the Netherlands round out the top ten. The rankings of other large economies include Canada (13), Germany (15), Japan (20), Italy (24), France (34), Taiwan (38), Mexico (62), China (81), India (92), Brazil (96), and Russia (117). Myanmar, Algeria, the Democratic Republic of Congo, Guinea-Bissau, and Sierra Leone rated lowest among the 123 countries for which data were available.

Some have charged that Hong Kong's economy is dominated by a small number of rich and powerful families that are able to manipulate economic affairs for personal benefit. Like other countries, Hong Kong undoubtedly has powerful elites. However, its openness to business and trade make it difficult to stifle the competitive process. Along with Singapore, Hong Kong is one of the world's most open economies. Competition is intense and the latest innovative products and technologies are available at economical prices. During the 1960s and 1970s, growth of the manufacturing sector transformed Hong Kong from a poor, less-developed, country into a high-income industrial power. The dynamic process continued during the 1980s and 1990s, as Hong Kong moved from a manufacturing-based economy to one based on high technology, finance, service, and trade. Hong Kong's economy is characterized by business entrepreneurship, a high level of employment, income mobility, and a relatively modest degree of income inequality. These are attributes of a free and dynamic economy. Of course, economic freedom should not be taken for granted. This is certainly true for an economy politically tied to a mother nation that is much less free. Hong Kong faces an uncertain future but, at least for now, it continues to be the freest economy in the world.

Exhibit 1-3 shows the summary ratings for 1990. In 1990 the top rated countries were Hong Kong (1), Singapore (2), the United States (3), Switzerland, the United Kingdom and Canada (tied for 4). Myanmar and Russia were at the bottom of the list.

There were many interesting changes during the 1990s. Several countries improved both their ratings and rankings substantially. For example, Ireland's rating rose from 7.3 in 1990 to 8.5 in 1999. During the same period, its ranking jumped from 22 to 6. Many Latin American countries, including Argentina, Bolivia, El Salvador, Nicaragua, and Peru were also among those registering substantial improvement.

As the economic freedom of some improved, the rankings of others declined. Canada dropped from 4 in 1990 to 13 in 1999. Venezuela and Mexico both fell considerably, and Indonesia tumbled from 33 to 72 during the decade.

ECONOMIC FREEDOM AND MEASURES OF SOCIAL PROGRESS

Although the economic freedom index has been designed as a measurement of economic freedom in its own right, we recognize the interest in how the index correlates with other measures of human well-being. Exhibit 1-4 shows the relationship between the 1999 Economic Freedom Index (EFI) and the level of GDP per capita (measured in 1998 purchasing power parity US dollars). The countries were grouped into quintiles for easy comparison. The relationship between the economic freedom rating and income is quite striking. More economic freedom is strongly related with higher levels of income. Exhibit 1-5 shows the same economic freedom quintiles with the rate of economic growth since 1990. The general pattern repeats itself.[5]

The economic freedom index has been useful in many other contexts besides examinations of income and economic growth. The next set of exhibits examines the simple relationships between the economic freedom index and other measures of social progress. Exhibit 1-6 shows the economic freedom quintiles with the Corruption

Exhibit 1-2: Summary Ratings for 1999

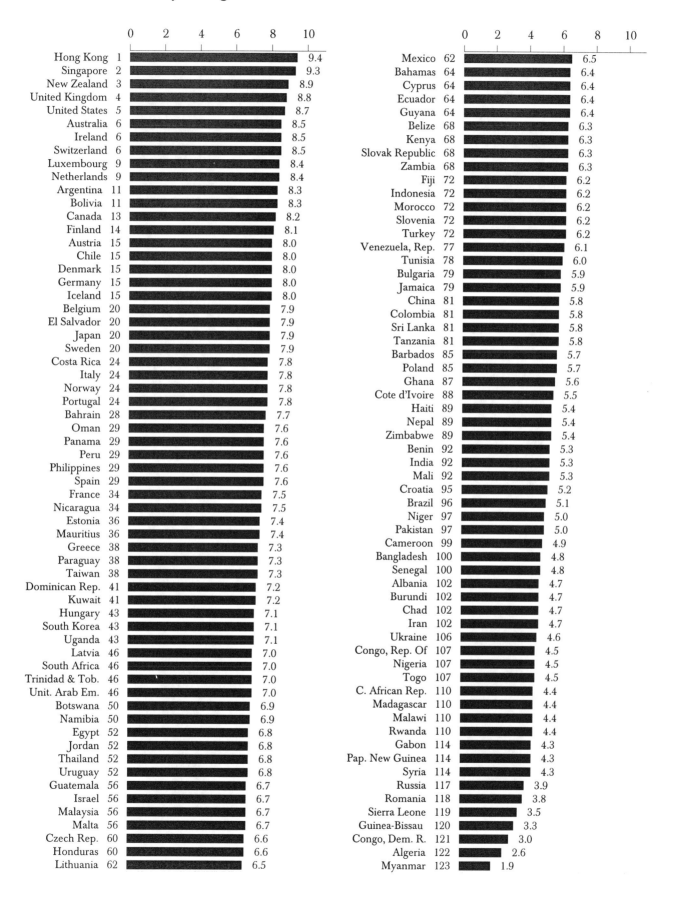

Hong Kong	1	9.4
Singapore	2	9.3
New Zealand	3	8.9
United Kingdom	4	8.8
United States	5	8.7
Australia	6	8.5
Ireland	6	8.5
Switzerland	6	8.5
Luxembourg	9	8.4
Netherlands	9	8.4
Argentina	11	8.3
Bolivia	11	8.3
Canada	13	8.2
Finland	14	8.1
Austria	15	8.0
Chile	15	8.0
Denmark	15	8.0
Germany	15	8.0
Iceland	15	8.0
Belgium	20	7.9
El Salvador	20	7.9
Japan	20	7.9
Sweden	20	7.9
Costa Rica	24	7.8
Italy	24	7.8
Norway	24	7.8
Portugal	24	7.8
Bahrain	28	7.7
Oman	29	7.6
Panama	29	7.6
Peru	29	7.6
Philippines	29	7.6
Spain	29	7.6
France	34	7.5
Nicaragua	34	7.5
Estonia	36	7.4
Mauritius	36	7.4
Greece	38	7.3
Paraguay	38	7.3
Taiwan	38	7.3
Dominican Rep.	41	7.2
Kuwait	41	7.2
Hungary	43	7.1
South Korea	43	7.1
Uganda	43	7.1
Latvia	46	7.0
South Africa	46	7.0
Trinidad & Tob.	46	7.0
Unit. Arab Em.	46	7.0
Botswana	50	6.9
Namibia	50	6.9
Egypt	52	6.8
Jordan	52	6.8
Thailand	52	6.8
Uruguay	52	6.8
Guatemala	56	6.7
Israel	56	6.7
Malaysia	56	6.7
Malta	56	6.7
Czech Rep.	60	6.6
Honduras	60	6.6
Lithuania	62	6.5

Mexico	62	6.5
Bahamas	64	6.4
Cyprus	64	6.4
Ecuador	64	6.4
Guyana	64	6.4
Belize	68	6.3
Kenya	68	6.3
Slovak Republic	68	6.3
Zambia	68	6.3
Fiji	72	6.2
Indonesia	72	6.2
Morocco	72	6.2
Slovenia	72	6.2
Turkey	72	6.2
Venezuela, Rep.	77	6.1
Tunisia	78	6.0
Bulgaria	79	5.9
Jamaica	79	5.9
China	81	5.8
Colombia	81	5.8
Sri Lanka	81	5.8
Tanzania	81	5.8
Barbados	85	5.7
Poland	85	5.7
Ghana	87	5.6
Cote d'Ivoire	88	5.5
Haiti	89	5.4
Nepal	89	5.4
Zimbabwe	89	5.4
Benin	92	5.3
India	92	5.3
Mali	92	5.3
Croatia	95	5.2
Brazil	96	5.1
Niger	97	5.0
Pakistan	97	5.0
Cameroon	99	4.9
Bangladesh	100	4.8
Senegal	100	4.8
Albania	102	4.7
Burundi	102	4.7
Chad	102	4.7
Iran	102	4.7
Ukraine	106	4.6
Congo, Rep. Of	107	4.5
Nigeria	107	4.5
Togo	107	4.5
C. African Rep.	110	4.4
Madagascar	110	4.4
Malawi	110	4.4
Rwanda	110	4.4
Gabon	114	4.3
Pap. New Guinea	114	4.3
Syria	114	4.3
Russia	117	3.9
Romania	118	3.8
Sierra Leone	119	3.5
Guinea-Bissau	120	3.3
Congo, Dem. R.	121	3.0
Algeria	122	2.6
Myanmar	123	1.9

Exhibit 1-3: Summary Ratings for 1990

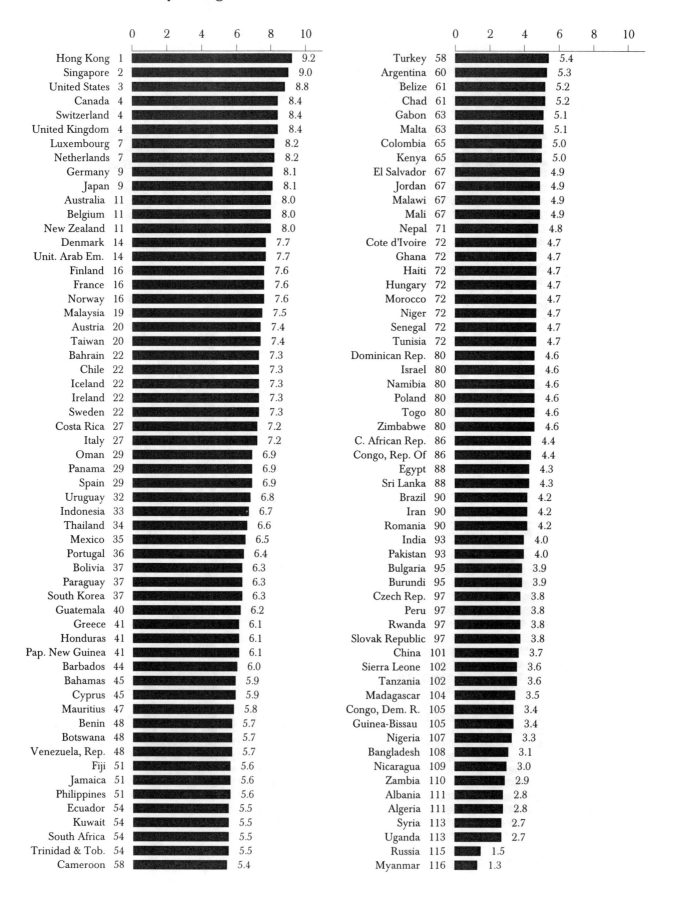

		Rating				Rating
Hong Kong	1	9.2	Turkey	58	5.4
Singapore	2	9.0	Argentina	60	5.3
United States	3	8.8	Belize	61	5.2
Canada	4	8.4	Chad	61	5.2
Switzerland	4	8.4	Gabon	63	5.1
United Kingdom	4	8.4	Malta	63	5.1
Luxembourg	7	8.2	Colombia	65	5.0
Netherlands	7	8.2	Kenya	65	5.0
Germany	9	8.1	El Salvador	67	4.9
Japan	9	8.1	Jordan	67	4.9
Australia	11	8.0	Malawi	67	4.9
Belgium	11	8.0	Mali	67	4.9
New Zealand	11	8.0	Nepal	71	4.8
Denmark	14	7.7	Cote d'Ivoire	72	4.7
Unit. Arab Em.	14	7.7	Ghana	72	4.7
Finland	16	7.6	Haiti	72	4.7
France	16	7.6	Hungary	72	4.7
Norway	16	7.6	Morocco	72	4.7
Malaysia	19	7.5	Niger	72	4.7
Austria	20	7.4	Senegal	72	4.7
Taiwan	20	7.4	Tunisia	72	4.7
Bahrain	22	7.3	Dominican Rep.	80	4.6
Chile	22	7.3	Israel	80	4.6
Iceland	22	7.3	Namibia	80	4.6
Ireland	22	7.3	Poland	80	4.6
Sweden	22	7.3	Togo	80	4.6
Costa Rica	27	7.2	Zimbabwe	80	4.6
Italy	27	7.2	C. African Rep.	86	4.4
Oman	29	6.9	Congo, Rep. Of	86	4.4
Panama	29	6.9	Egypt	88	4.3
Spain	29	6.9	Sri Lanka	88	4.3
Uruguay	32	6.8	Brazil	90	4.2
Indonesia	33	6.7	Iran	90	4.2
Thailand	34	6.6	Romania	90	4.2
Mexico	35	6.5	India	93	4.0
Portugal	36	6.4	Pakistan	93	4.0
Bolivia	37	6.3	Bulgaria	95	3.9
Paraguay	37	6.3	Burundi	95	3.9
South Korea	37	6.3	Czech Rep.	97	3.8
Guatemala	40	6.2	Peru	97	3.8
Greece	41	6.1	Rwanda	97	3.8
Honduras	41	6.1	Slovak Republic	97	3.8
Pap. New Guinea	41	6.1	China	101	3.7
Barbados	44	6.0	Sierra Leone	102	3.6
Bahamas	45	5.9	Tanzania	102	3.6
Cyprus	45	5.9	Madagascar	104	3.5
Mauritius	47	5.8	Congo, Dem. R.	105	3.4
Benin	48	5.7	Guinea-Bissau	105	3.4
Botswana	48	5.7	Nigeria	107	3.3
Venezuela, Rep.	48	5.7	Bangladesh	108	3.1
Fiji	51	5.6	Nicaragua	109	3.0
Jamaica	51	5.6	Zambia	110	2.9
Philippines	51	5.6	Albania	111	2.8
Ecuador	54	5.5	Algeria	111	2.8
Kuwait	54	5.5	Syria	113	2.7
South Africa	54	5.5	Uganda	113	2.7
Trinidad & Tob.	54	5.5	Russia	115	1.5
Cameroon	58	5.4	Myanmar	116	1.3

Exhibit 1-4: Economic Freedom and Income

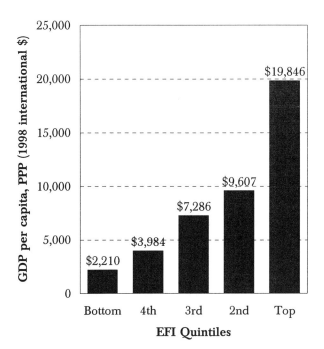

Exhibit 1-5: Economic Freedom and Growth

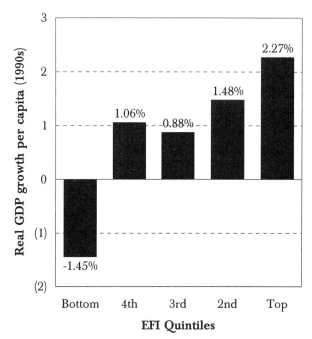

Perceptions Index (CPI) published annually by Transparency International.[6] Higher values for the CPI reflect less bribery and corruption. Exhibit 1-6 indicates that more economic freedom correlates with less corruption.

Exhibit 1-7 charts the economic freedom index against the United Nations Human Develop-

ment Index. The Human Development Index (HDI) "measures a country's achievements in three aspects of human development: longevity, knowledge, and a decent standard of living."[7] Exhibit 1-7 shows that countries with higher levels of economic freedom also score well on the United Nations Human Development Index.

Exhibit 1-6: Economic Freedom and Corruption

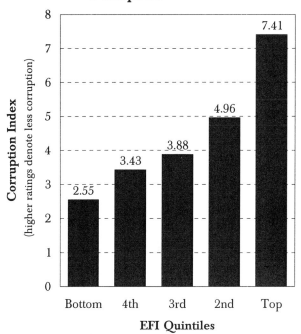

Exhibit 1-7: Economic Freedom and Human Development

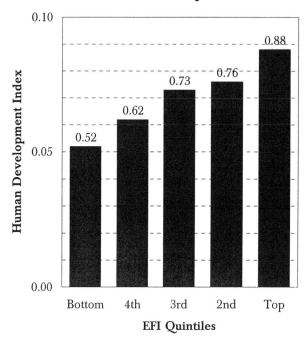

The United Nations also computes a Human Poverty Index for both developed (HPI-2) and developing countries (HPI-1). The two indexes are not comparable, however. Exhibit 1-8 looks at the relationship among the developing nations using HPI-1. According to the United Nations, the Human Poverty Index for developing nations (HPI-1) is similar to the HDI but "includes … social exclusion."[8] The HPI-1 is measured on a scale such that increasing values indicate more poverty. Economic freedom therefore is negatively correlated with poverty: more freedom, less poverty.

Exhibit 1-8: Economic Freedom and Human Poverty

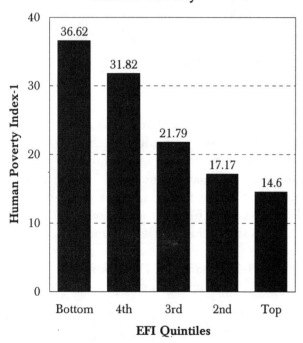

Exhibit 1-9 shows the relationship between the economic freedom quintiles and life expectancy. Not surprisingly, economic freedom corresponds with greater longevity.[9]

Exhibit 1-9: Economic Freedom and Life Expectancy

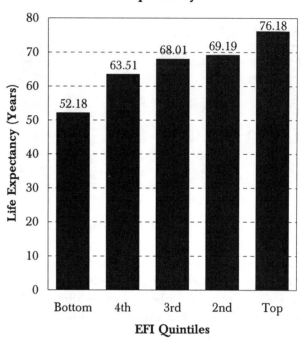

NOTES

(1) See Michael Walker, ed., *Freedom, Democracy, and Economic Welfare* (Vancouver: Fraser Institute, 1988); Walter Block, ed., *Economic Freedom: Toward a Theory of Measurement* (Vancouver: Fraser Institute, 1991); Stephen Easton and Michael Walker, eds., *Rating Global Economic Freedom* (Vancouver: Fraser Institute, 1992); James Gwartney, Robert Lawson and Walter Block, *Economic Freedom of the World: 1975-1995* (Vancouver: Fraser Institute, 1996); James Gwartney and Robert Lawson, *Economic Freedom of the World: 1997 Report* (Vancouver: Fraser Institute, 1997); James Gwartney and Robert Lawson, *Economic Freedom of the World: 1998/99 Interim Report* (Vancouver: Fraser Institute, 1998); James Gwartney and Robert Lawson with Dexter Samida, *Economic Freedom of the World: 2000 Report* (Vancouver, Fraser Institute, 1999).

(2) One of the important trade-offs associated with our decision to rely almost exclusively on regularly published international data is that we cannot rate more than about 120 to 125 countries. Many countries such as Cuba and North Korea that have poor records of maintaining economic freedom do not have the requisite data available and, hence, are not rated in our index.

(3) Component (V b), Viability of Contracts, was dropped. Consequently, Component (V c), Rule of Law, was designated (V b) in the new edition. Likewise, with the elimination of Component (VI b i), the previous Component (VI b ii), Actual Size of the Trade Sector Compared to the Expected Size, is now denoted (VI b).

(4) We have endeavored to use the most recent data available. In cases where data for 1999 were not available, data for 1998 or 1997 were used instead.

(5) Data on income and economic growth were obtained from the World Bank, *World Development Indicators 2000* (CD). For a more rigorous examination of the relationship between the economic freedom index and economic growth see, James Gwartney, Randall Holcombe and Robert Lawson, Economic Freedom and the Environment for Economic Growth, *Journal of Institutional and Theoretical Economics*, 155, 4 (December 1999): 1–21.

(6) Transparency International, *2000 Corruption Perceptions Index*, http://transparency.de/documents/cpi/2000/cpi2000.html (accessed 21 September 2000).

(7) United Nations Development Project, *Human Development Report 2000*, http://www.undp.org/hdr2000/ (accessed 26 November 2000).

(8) United Nations Development Project, *Human Development Report 2000*, http://www.undp.org/hdr2000/, HPI-1: deprivations in longevity are measured by the percentage of newborns not expected to survive to age 40. Deprivations in knowledge are measured by percentage of adults who are illiterate. Deprivations in a decent standard of living are measured by three variables: the percentage of people without access to safe water, the percentage of people without access to health services, and the percentage of moderately and severely underweight children below the age of five.

(9) Life expectancy data were obtained from the United Nations Development Project, *Human Development Report 2000*, http://www.undp.org/hdr2000/ (accessed 26 November 2000).

EXPLANATORY NOTES AND DATA SOURCES

Component

I a   The rating for this component is equal to: $(V_{max} - V_i) / (V_{max} - V_{min})$ multiplied by 10. The V_i is the country's actual government consumption as a proportion of total consumption, while the V_{max} and V_{min} were set at 40 and 6 respectively. Countries with a larger proportion of government expenditures received lower ratings. If the ratio of a country's government consumption to total consumption is close to the minimum value of this ratio during the 1990 base year, the country's rating will be close to 10. In contrast, if this ratio is close to the highest value during the base year, the rating will be close to 0.

Sources   World Bank, *World Development Indicators CD-ROM* (various editions) and International Monetary Fund, *International Financial Statistics* (various issues). The 1997 figures were primarily from the latter publication.

I b   The rating for this component is equal to: $(V_{max} - V_i) / (V_{max} - V_{min})$ multiplied by 10. The V_i is the country's ratio of transfers and subsidies to GDP, while the V_{max} and V_{min} represent the maximum and minimum values of this component during the 1990 base year. The formula will generate lower ratings for countries with larger transfer sectors. When the size of a country's transfer sector approaches that of the country with the largest transfer sector during the base year, the rating of the country will approach 0.

Sources   World Bank, *World Development Indicators CD-ROM* (various editions); International Monetary Fund, *International Financial Statistics* (various issues); International Monetary Fund, *Government Finance Statistics Yearbook* (various years); and Inter-American Development Bank, *Economic and Social Progress in Latin America, 1994.*

II a   Data on the number, composition, and share of output supplied by State-Operated Enterprises (SOEs) and government investment as a share of total investment were used to construct the 0-to-10 ratings. Countries with more government enterprise and government investment received lower ratings. When there were few SOEs and government investment was generally less than 15% of total investment, countries were given a rating of 10. When there were few SOEs other than those involved in industries where economies of scale reduce the effectiveness of competition (e.g., power generation) and government investment was between 15% and 20% of the total, countries received a rating of 8. When there were, again, few SOEs other than those involved in energy and other such industries and government investment was between about 20% and 25% of the total, countries were rated at 7. When SOEs were present in the energy, transportation, and communication sectors of the economy and government investment was between about 25% and 30% of the total, countries were assigned a rating of 6. When a substantial number of SOEs operated in many sectors, including manufacturing, and government investment was generally between 30% and 40% of the total, countries received a rating of 4. When numerous SOEs operated in many sectors, including retail sales, and government investment was between about 40% and 50% of the total, countries were rated at 2. A rating of 0 was assigned when the economy was dominated by SOEs and government investment exceeded 50% of the total.

Sources   World Bank Policy Research Report, *Bureaucrats in Business* (1995); Rexford A. Ahene and Bernard S. Katz, eds., *Privatization and Investment in Sub-Saharan Africa* (1992); Manuel Sanchez and Rossana Corona, eds., *Privatization in Latin America* (1993); Iliya Harik and Denis J. Sullivan, eds., *Privatization and Liberalization in the Middle East* (1992); OECD, *Economic Surveys* (various issues); and L. Bouten and M. Sumlinski, *Trends in Private Investment in Developing Countries: Statistics for 1970–1995* (1997).

II b   The more widespread the use of price controls, the lower the rating. The survey data of the International Institute for Management Development (IMD), *World Competitiveness Report*, various editions, were used to rate the 46 countries (mostly developed economies) covered by this report. For other countries, the Price Waterhouse series, *Doing Business in ...* and other sources were used to categorize countries. Countries were given a rating of 10 if no price controls or marketing boards were present. When price controls were limited to industries where economies of scale may reduce the effectiveness of competition (e.g., power generation), a country was given a rating of 8. When price controls were applied in only a few other industries, such as agriculture, a country was given a rating of 6. When price controls were levied on energy, agriculture, and many other staple products that are widely purchased by households, a rating of 4 was given. When price controls applied to a significant number of products in both agriculture and manufacturing, the rating was 2. A rating of 0 was given when there was widespread use of price controls throughout various sectors of the economy.

Sources   IMD, *World Competitiveness Report* (various issues); Price Waterhouse, *Doing Business in ...* publication series; World Bank, *Adjustment in Africa: Reforms, Results, and the Road Ahead* (1994); and US State Department, *Country Reports on Economic Policy and Trade Practices* (various years).

II c   Data on the top marginal tax rates and the income thresholds at which they take effect were used to construct a rating grid. Countries with higher marginal tax rates that take effect at lower income thresholds received lower ratings. The income threshold data were converted from local currency to 1982/1984 US dollars (using beginning-of-year exchange rates and the US Consumer Price Index). See *Economic Freedom of the World: 1997 Annual Report*, page 265, for the precise relationship between a country's rating and its top marginal tax and income threshold.

Source   Price Waterhouse, *Individual Taxes: A Worldwide Summary* (various issues).

II d   Data on the use and duration of military conscription were used to construct rating intervals. Countries with longer conscription periods received lower ratings. A rating of 10 was assigned to countries without military conscription. When length of conscription was six months or less, countries were given a rating of 5. When length of conscription was more than six months but not more than 12 months, countries were rated at 3. When length of conscription was more than 12 months but not more than 18 months, countries were assigned a rating of 1. When conscription periods exceeded 18 months, countries were rated 0.

Source   International Institute for Strategic Studies, *The Military Balance* (various issues).

III a   The M1 money supply figures were used to measure the growth rate of the money supply. The rating is equal to: $(V_{max} - V_i) / (V_{max} - V_{min})$ multiplied by 10. V_i represents the average annual growth rate of the money supply during the last five years adjusted for the growth of real GDP during the previous 10 years. The values for V_{min} and V_{max} were set at 0% and 50%, respectively. Therefore, if the adjusted growth rate of the money supply during the last five years was 0, indicating that money growth was equal to the long-term growth of real output, the formula generates a rating of 10. Ratings decline as the adjusted money supply growth differs from 0. When the adjusted annual money growth is equal to (or greater than) 50%, a rating of 0 results.

Sources   World Bank, *World Development Indicators CD-ROM* (various editions), with updates from International Monetary Fund, *International Financial Statistics* (various issues).

III b   The GDP deflator was used as the measure of inflation. When these data were unavailable, the Consumer Price Index was used. The following formula was used to determine the 0-to-10 scale rating for each country: $(V_{max} - V_i) / (V_{max} - V_{min})$ multiplied by 10. V_i represents the country's standard deviation of the annual rate of inflation during the last five years. The values for V_{min} and V_{max} were set at 0% and 25%, respectively. This procedure will allocate the highest ratings to the countries with least variation in the annual rate of inflation. A perfect 10 results when there is no variation in the rate of inflation over the five-year period. Ratings will decline toward 0 as the standard deviation of the inflation rate approaches 25% annually.

Sources   World Bank, *World Development Indicators CD-ROM* (various editions), with updates from International Monetary Fund, *International Financial Statistics* (various issues).

III c   The 0-to-10 country ratings were derived by the following formula: $(V_{max} - V_i) / (V_{max} - V_{min})$ multiplied by 10. V_i represents the rate of inflation during the most recent year. The values for V_{min} and V_{max} were set at 0% and 50%, respectively. The lower the rate of inflation, the higher the rating. Countries that achieve perfect price stability earn a rating of 10. As the inflation rate moves toward a 50% annual rate, the rating for this component moves toward 0. A 0 rating is assigned to all countries with an inflation rate of 50% or more.

Sources   World Bank, *World Development Indicators CD-ROM* (various editions), with updates from International Monetary Fund, *International Financial Statistics* (various issues).

IV a   When foreign currency bank accounts were permissible without restrictions both domestically and abroad, the rating was 10; when these accounts were restricted, the rating was 0. If foreign currency bank accounts were permissible domestically but not abroad (or vice versa), the rating was 5.

Sources   Currency Data and Intelligence, Inc., *World Currency Yearbook* (various issues) and International Monetary Fund, *Annual Report on Exchange Arrangements and Exchange Restrictions* (various issues).

IV b   The formula used to calculate the 0-to-10 ratings for this component was the following: $(V_{max} - V_i) / (V_{max} - V_{min})$ multiplied by 10. V_i is the country's black-market exchange rate premium. The values for V_{min} and V_{max} were set at 0% and 50%, respectively. This formula will allocate a rating of 10 to countries without a black-market exchange rate; *i.e.*, those with a domestic currency that is fully convertible without restrictions. When exchange rate controls are present and a black market exists, the ratings will decline toward 0 as the black market premium increases toward 50%. A 0 rating is given when the black market premium is equal to, or greater than, 50%.

Sources   World Bank, *World Development Report 2000*, Currency Data and Intelligence, Inc., *World Currency Yearbook* (various issues of the yearbook and the monthly report supplement) and International Monetary Fund, *International Financial Statistics* (various issues).

V a   Countries with more secure property rights received higher ratings. The data for 1999 are from the IMD, *World Competitiveness Report, 2000.* No reliable data were available for 1995. The data from 1980 to 1990 are from PRS Group, *International Country Risk Guide* (various issues). The 1970 and 1975 data are from Business Environment Risk Intelligence (BERI). The ICRG did not provide ratings for Barbados, Benin, Burundi, Central African Republic, Chad, Estonia, Latvia, Lithuania, Mauritius, Slovenia and Ukraine. We rated these countries based on the ratings for similar countries (in parentheses): for Barbados (Bahamas), Mauritius (Botwsana), Estonia, Latvia, and Lithuania (Poland and Russia), Slovenia (Czech Republic and Slovakia), Ukraine (Bulgaria and Russia), Benin, Burundi, Central African Republic, and Chad (Cameroon, Republic of Congo, Gabon, Mali, and Niger).

While the original rating scale for the ICRG data was 0-to-10, BERI data were on a one-to-four scale. We used regression analysis from the two sources during the initial overlapping year 1982 to merge the two data sets and place the 1970 and 1975 ratings on a scale comparable to that used for the other years. Likewise, regression analysis between the 1999 IMD data and the 1990 ICRG data was used to splice in the new data set.

Because of inconsistencies in the ICRG ratings over time, all ratings were adjusted using the maximum and minimum procedure used in other components in order to make the component consistent over time. The following formula was used to place the figures on a 0-to-10 scale: $(V_i - V_{min})/(V_{max} - V_{min})$ multiplied by 10. V_i is the country's actual value for the component. V_{max} and V_{min} were set at 10 and 2 standard deviations below the average, respectively.

Sources   IMD, *World Competitiveness Report, 2000*, PRS Group, *International Country Risk Guide* (various issues), and Business Environment Risk Intelligence.

V b   Countries with legal institutions that were more supportive of rule of law received higher ratings. The data from 1980 to 1999 on the rule of law are from PRS Group, *International Country Risk Guide* (various issues). In certain years, the ICRG did not provide ratings for Barbados, Benin, Burundi, Central African Republic, Chad, Estonia, Latvia, Lithuania, Mauritius, Slovenia and Ukraine. In those cases, we rated these countries based on the ratings for similar countries (in parentheses): Barbados (Bahamas), Mauritius (Botwsana), Estonia, Latvia, and Lithuania (Poland and Russia), Slovenia (Czech Republic and Slovakia), Ukraine (Bulgaria and Russia), Benin, Burundi, Central African Republic, and Chad (Cameroon, Republic of Congo, Gabon, Mali, and Niger).

Because of inconsistencies in the ICRG ratings over time, all ratings were adjusted each year using the maximum and minimum procedure used in other components in order to make the component more consistent over time. The following formula was used to place the figures on a 0-to-10 scale: $(V_i - V_{min})/(V_{max} - V_{min})$ multiplied by 10. V_i is the country's actual value for the component. V_{max} and V_{min} were set at 10 and 2 standard deviations below the average, respectively.

Source   PRS Group, *International Country Risk Guide* (various issues).

VI a i   The formula used to calculate the ratings for this component was: $(V_{max} - V_i) / (V_{max} - V_{min})$ multiplied by 10. V_i represents the revenue derived from taxes on international trade as a share of the trade sector. The values for V_{min} and V_{max} were set at 0% and 15%, respectively. This formula leads to lower ratings as the average tax rate on international trade increases. Countries with no specific taxes on international trade earn a perfect 10. As the revenues from these taxes rise toward 15% of international trade, ratings decline toward 0. (Note that except for two or three extreme observations, the revenues from taxes on international trade as a share of the trade sector are within the range of 0% to 15%.)

Sources   International Monetary Fund, *Government Finance Statistics Yearbook* (various issues), International Monetary Fund, *International Financial Statistics* (various issues), and Office of the United States Trade Representative, *Annual Report.*

VI a ii   The formula used to calculate the 0-to-10 rating for each country was: $(V_{max} - V_i) / (V_{max} - V_{min})$ multiplied by 10. V_i represents the country's mean tariff rate. The values for V_{min} and V_{max} were set at 0% and 50%, respectively. This formula will allocate a rating of 10 to countries that do not impose tariffs. As the mean tariff rate increases, countries are assigned lower ratings. The rating will decline toward 0 as the mean tariff rate approaches 50%. (Note that except for two or three extreme observations, all countries have mean tariff rates within the range of 0% to 50%.)

Sources   OECD, *Indicators of Tariff and Non-tariff Trade Barriers* (1996); World Bank, *World Development Report 2000;* J. Michael Finger, Merlinda D. Ingco, and Ulrich Reincke, *Statistics on Tariff Concessions Given and Received* (1996); Judith M. Dean, Seema Desai, and James Riedel, *Trade Policy Reform in Developing Countries since 1985: A Review of the Evidence* (1994); GATT, *The Tokyo Round of Multilateral Trade Negotiations, Vol. II: Supplementary Report* (1979); UNCTAD, *Revitalizing Development, Growth and International Trade: Assessment and Policy Options* (1987); R. Erzan and K. Kuwahara, The Profile of Protection in Developing Countries, *UNCTAD Review* 1, 1 (1989): 29–49; and Inter-American Development Bank (data supplied to the authors).

VI a iii   Compared to a uniform tariff, wide variation in tariff rates exerts a more restrictive impact on trade, and therefore on economic freedom. Thus, countries with greater variation in their tariff rates should be given lower ratings. The formula used to calculate the 0-to-10 ratings for this component was: $(V_{max} - V_i) / (V_{max} - V_{min})$ multiplied by 10. V_i represents the standard deviation of the country's tariff rates. The values for V_{min} and V_{max} were set at 0% and 25%, respectively. This formula will allocate a rating of 10 to countries that impose a uniform tariff. As the standard deviation of tariff rates increases toward 25%, ratings decline toward 0. (Note that except for a few very extreme observations, the standard deviations of the tariff rates for the countries in our study fall within the range of 0% to 25%.)

Sources   OECD, *Indicators of Tariff and Non-tariff Trade Barriers* (1996); World Bank, *1997 World Development Indicators CD-ROM;* Jang-Wha Lee and Phillip Swagel, *Trade Barriers and Trade Flows across Countries and Industries,* NBER Working Paper Series No. 4799 (1994); and Inter-American Development Bank (data supplied to the authors).

VI b   Regression analysis was used to derive an expected size of the trade sector based on various structural and geographic characteristics. A basic description of the methodology can be found in chapter 3. The actual size of the trade sector was then compared with the expected size for the country. If the actual size of the trade sector is greater than expected, this figure will be positive. If it is less than expected, the number will be negative. The percent change of the negative numbers was adjusted to make it symmetrical with the percent change of the positive numbers. The following formula was used to place the figures on a 0-to-10 scale: $(V_i - V_{min}) / (V_{max} - V_{min})$ multiplied by 10. V_i is the country's actual value for the component. V_{max} and V_{min} were set at 100% and minus 50%, respectively. (Note that minus 50% is symmetrical with positive 100%.) This procedure allocates higher ratings to countries with large trade sectors compared to what would be expected, given their population, geographic size, and location. On the other hand, countries with small trade sectors relative to the expected size receive lower ratings.

Sources   World Bank, *World Development Indicators CD-ROM* (various editions); International Monetary Fund, *International Financial Statistics* (various issues); and Central Intelligence Agency, *1997 World Factbook.*

VII a   Data on the percentage of bank deposits held in privately owned banks were used to construct rating intervals. Countries with larger shares of privately held deposits received higher ratings. When privately held deposits totaled between 95% and 100%, countries were given a rating of 10. When private deposits constituted between 75% and 95% of the total, a rating of 8 was assigned. When private deposits were between 40% and 75% of the total, the rating was 5. When private deposits totaled between 10% and 40%, countries received a rating of 2. A 0 rating was assigned when private deposits were 10% or less of the total.

Sources   Euromoney Publications, *The Telrate Bank Register* (various editions); World Bank, *Adjustment in Africa: Reforms, Results, and the Road Ahead* (1994); Price Waterhouse, *Doing Business in ...* publication series; H.T. Patrick and Y.C. Park, eds., *The Financial Development of Japan, Korea, and Taiwan: Growth, Repression, and Liberalization* (1994); D.C. Cole and B.F. Slade, *Building a Modern Financial System: The Indonesian Experience* (1996); and information supplied by member institutes of the Economic Freedom Network.

VII b   For this component, higher values are indicative of greater economic freedom. Thus, the formula used to derive the country ratings for this component was $(V_i - V_{min}) / (V_{max} - V_{min})$ multiplied by 10. V_i is the share of the country's total domestic credit allocated to the private sector. V_{max} is the maximum value and V_{min} the minimum value for the figure during the 1990 base year. Respectively, these figures were 99.9% and 0%. The formula allocates higher ratings as the share of credit extended to the private sector increases. A country's rating will be close to 10 when the private sector's share of domestic credit is near the base-year maximum (99.9%). A rating near 0 results when the private sector's share of credit is close to the base-year minimum (0%).

Sources   International Monetary Fund, *International Financial Statistics* (the 1997 yearbook and June 1998 monthly supplement) and *Statistical Yearbook of the Republic of China* (1996).

VII c   Data on credit-market controls and regulations were used to construct rating intervals. Countries with interest rates determined by the market, stable monetary policy, and positive real deposit and lending rates received higher ratings. When interest rates were determined primarily by market forces and the real rates were positive, countries were given a rating of 10. When interest rates were primarily determined by the market but the real rates were sometimes slightly negative (less than 5%) or the differential between the deposit and lending rates was large (8% or more), countries received a rating of 8. When the real deposit or lending rate was persistently negative by a single-digit amount or the differential between them was regulated by the government, countries were rated at 6. When the deposit and lending rates were fixed by the government and the real rates were often negative by single-digit amounts, countries were assigned a rating of 4. When the real deposit or lending rate was persistently negative by a double-digit amount, countries received a rating of 2. A rating of 0 was assigned when the deposit and lending rates were fixed by the government and real rates were persistently negative by double-digit amounts or hyperinflation had virtually eliminated the credit market.

Source   International Monetary Fund, *International Financial Statistics Yearbook* (various issues, as well as the monthly supplements).

VII d   Descriptive data on capital-market arrangements were used to place countries into rating categories. Countries with more restrictions on foreign capital transactions received lower ratings. When domestic investments by foreigners and foreign investments by citizens were unrestricted, countries were given a rating of 10. When these investments were restricted only in a few industries (e.g., banking, defence, and telecommunications), countries were assigned a rating of 8. When these investments were permitted but regulatory restrictions slowed the mobility of capital, countries were rated at 5. When either domestic investments by foreigners or foreign investments by citizens required approval from government authorities, countries received a rating of 2. A rating of 0 was assigned when both domestic investments by foreigners and foreign investments by citizens required government approval.

Sources   International Monetary Fund, *Annual Report on Exchange Arrangements and Exchange Restrictions* (various issues) and Price Waterhouse, *Doing Business in . . .* publication series.

CHAPTER 2: A MORE COMPREHENSIVE INDEX OF ECONOMIC FREEDOM FOR 58 COUNTRIES

by James Gwartney, Charles Skipton, and Robert Lawson

INTRODUCTION

More than a decade ago, we set out to develop an accurate measure of economic freedom. From the outset, we wanted the measure to be based to the fullest extent possible on objective quantifiable data and transparent procedures. We wanted an index that others, regardless of their political orientation, could replicate. We did not want our subjective views to influence the rating or ranking of any country.

Because of these standards, it was sometimes necessary to omit important dimensions of economic freedom. In some cases components were omitted because it was impossible to obtain the required data for a large number of countries. In other cases, potential variables were omitted because their nature virtually precluded objective measurement. It is particularly difficult to quantify the impact of regulation objectively. Nonetheless, restrictive regulations can exert an important influence on the degree of economic freedom present in a country.

To incorporate regulatory restraints into the index more fully, this chapter uses survey data to supplement the objective components of our current index and thereby develops a more comprehensive index of economic freedom. This broader index will integrate a number of factors that, until now, have either been omitted or poorly reflected in the index. Specifically, the broader index more accurately reflects cross-country differences in the freedom to contract and compete in business activities and labor markets. It also makes it easier to pinpoint the strengths and weaknesses of each country more accurately. Because of limitations of the data, at this time it is possible to construct the broader index for only 58 countries. We hope to expand coverage to more countries in the future.

BACKGROUND ON THE SURVEY DATA

The broad index uses the components of the economic freedom index for 2001 that was described in chapter 1. These data are supplemented with survey information from two other sources: the *Global Competitiveness Report 2000* (GCR) of the World Economic Forum and the *World Competitiveness Yearbook 2000* (WCY) of the International Institute for Management Development. The reports cover approximately 50 countries.[1]

The focus of the competitiveness reports differs decidedly from the emphasis of the Economic Freedom Index. The competitiveness reports seek to measure the attractiveness ("competitiveness") of a country for business activity. While they contain some information on policy and institutions, much of their focus is on the use of technology, quality of the physical infrastructure, and skill of the labor force. Variables like spending on research, number of telephones and internet hookups, miles of highways, cost of air travel, and the wages and educational levels of workers are included in these indexes. These indicators may be helpful to those making business and investment decisions but they have little to do with economic freedom.

The competitiveness reports, however, also contain information derived from annual surveys of business owners and managers operating in each of the countries. Some of the survey questions address the quality of the regulatory and institutional environment. This is particularly true for the *Global Competitiveness Report*. While we would prefer to have objective variables, the survey data do provide information on some of the elements of economic freedom that are elusive and difficult to measure. When available, these data can be used to improve our measurement of economic freedom.

AREAS OF THE MORE COMPREHENSIVE INDEX

To develop a broader index of economic freedom, we combined survey data from the competitiveness reports with components of the *Economic Freedom of the World* Index. The resulting, more comprehensive, index contains 45 components.[2] The components were categorized and used to rate each country in the seven major areas of the index. In turn, the seven area ratings were used to calculate a summary index. The areas of the more comprehensive index (which do not correspond exactly to the seven areas of the *Economic Freedom of the World* Index) are:

I   Size of Government

II   Legal Structure and Security of Property Rights

III Access to Sound Money

IV   Freedom to Trade with Foreigners

V   Regulation of Capital and Financial Markets

VI   Regulation of Labor Markets

VII Freedom to Operate and Compete in Business

While these seven areas are not the sum total of economic freedom, they clearly make up a major part of it.[3] The sections that follow will indicate the precise components used to measure the degree of economic freedom in each of the seven areas. We will also indicate the ratings and rankings of each country in the area. The concluding section presents the summary rating of this broader index for each of the 58 countries.

AREA I: SIZE OF GOVERNMENT

Box 1

a **Total government expenditures as a percentage of GDP.**

b Size of government consumption, transfers, and subsidies.

    i General government consumption expenditures as a percentage of total consumption.

    ii Transfers and subsidies as a percentage of GDP.

c Government enterprises and investment as a percentage of GDP.

d Price controls: extent to which businesses are free to set their own prices.

Note: **Bold-face type** indicates the variable is not in the current *Economic Freedom of the World* Index.

Box 1 indicates the five components that make up Area 1: Size of Government.[4] These components measure the extent to which countries rely on individual choice and markets rather than the political process to allocate resources, goods, and services. When government spending increases relative to spending by individuals, households, and businesses, government decision-making is substituted for personal choice and economic freedom is reduced. The first three components address this issue.

Total government expenditure as a share of GDP (Component I-a) is the most comprehensive indicator of government relative to private spending. As this ratio rises from 10% to 50%, the rating for this component falls from 10 to 0.[5] Economists often speak of the protective and productive functions of government. The protective function involves protecting citizens and their property against aggressors. It includes the provision of national defense, police protection, and a system of justice. The productive function involves the provision of a limited set of "public goods" like sound money, flood control, and environmental quality that are difficult to provide through markets. High-income countries currently spend only about 10% of GDP on these activities.[6] Thus, governments can spend sufficiently to perform their protective and productive functions and still earn the highest possible rating for this component.

The combined impact of government consumption as a share of total consumption and transfers and subsidies as a share of GDP is also in-

dicative of government size. When government consumption is a larger share of the total, political choice is substituted for private choice. Similarly, when governments tax some people in order to provide transfers to others, they reduce the freedom of individuals to keep what they earn. Thus, the greater the share of transfers and subsidies in an economy, the less economic freedom. The ratings for these two components are averaged and integrated into the index as an alternative measure for size of government.[7]

The fourth component measures the extent to which countries use private rather than government enterprises to produce goods and services. Government firms play by different rules than private enterprises. They are not dependent on consumers for their revenue or on investors for risk capital. They often operate in protected markets. Thus, economic freedom is reduced as government enterprises produce a larger share of total output. Governments may also undermine the operation of markets through the imposition of price controls. Thus, countries that rely more extensively on price controls receive a lower rating for the fifth component.

Taken together, the five components measure the degree of a country's reliance on personal choice and markets rather than government budgets and political decision-making. Therefore, countries with low levels of government spending as a share of the total, a smaller government enterprise sector, and few price controls earn the highest ratings in this area. Table 2-1 in the Appendix presents each country's component ratings and raw data on which they were based. The component ratings were averaged and used to derive the area rating.

Exhibit 2-1 indicates the size of government area rating for each country ranked from high to low. The five highest-ranked countries in this area are Hong Kong, El Salvador, Peru, Singapore, and Argentina. Mexico ranks sixth while Chile and the United States tied for seventh. The economies of these countries are characterized by small levels of government expenditures, few government enterprises, and few, if any, price controls. Thus, they rely extensively on voluntary exchange and market coordination to direct economic activities. In contrast, the economies of Israel, Ukraine, Slovakia, China, Jordan, and Poland are dominated by government. Therefore, these countries receive low ratings in this area.

As countries become richer, governments often engage more extensively in tax transfer activities. This increases both government spending and transfers as a share of GDP, pulling down the Area I rating. As a result, many high-income countries have a below-average rating in Area I. For example, the ratings of Germany, Finland, Luxembourg, Italy, Denmark, Norway, Sweden, Austria, France, and Belgium place them in the bottom half of the distribution. Countries such as China and Russia with extensive price controls and a sizable government enterprise sector are also rated low in this area.

AREA II: LEGAL STRUCTURE AND SECURITY OF PROPERTY RIGHTS

Box 2:

a Rule of law: legal institutions support the principles of the rule of law, and individuals have access to a nondiscriminatory judiciary.

b Legal security of private ownership: private property rights are clearly delineated and protected by law.

c **Protection of intellectual property (GCR-7.09).**

d **Judicial independence: the judiciary is independent and not subject to interference by the government or parties in disputes (GCR-4.05).**

e **Legal corruption: irregular payments to judges, court personnel, or other officials are rare (GCR-4.08).**

f **Impartial courts: a trusted legal framework exists for private businesses to challenge the legality of government actions or regulations (GCR-4.09).**

Note: **Bold-face type** indicates the variable is not in the current *Economic Freedom of the World* Index.

GCR = *Global Competitiveness Report.* The numbers indicate the specific component of the report.

Protection of persons and their rightfully acquired property is a central element of both economic freedom and a civil society. Indeed, it is the most important function of government. Thus, the legal system of an economically free country must provide for the security of property rights, enforcement of contracts, and the mutually agreeable settlement of disputes. Failure in this area will undermine the operation of a market exchange system. If individuals and businesses lack confidence that contracts will be enforced and the fruits of their productive efforts protected from aggressors, their incentive to engage in productive activity is eroded.

Area II focuses on how well this protective function of government is performed. Rule of law, protection of private property, an independent judiciary, and an impartial court system for the settlement of disputes are the key ingredients of a legal system consistent with economic freedom. As Box 2 indicates, the components in this area reflect these factors. Because development of an objective measure in this area is extremely difficult, the components are based on survey data. The "rule of law" component is from the *International Country Risk Guide* published by PRS Group; the other components are from the *Global Competitiveness Report*.

Table 2-2 of the appendix presents the component ratings for legal structure and security of property rights. The component ratings were averaged and used to derive the area rating. Exhibit 2-2 presents the country area rating for each of the 58 countries of our study. Luxembourg, Finland, Australia, Netherlands, Austria, Denmark, Germany, and the United Kingdom headed the list of countries with legal systems most consistent with economic freedom. Quite a num-

ber of countries had high ratings in this area: there were 12 countries with ratings of 9.0 or higher and another 10 with ratings above 8.0.

On the other hand, 13 countries received ratings of less than 5.0, indicating substantial problems with their legal systems. Peru, Indonesia, Ecuador, Venezuela, Ukraine, and Russia received the lowest ratings. Bolivia, Mexico, Colombia, El Salvador, Bulgaria, China, and the Philippines were also rated low. Poorly defined property rights not only reduce economic freedom, they also deter investment and retard economic growth. It is highly unlikely that countries with a low rating in this area will be able to sustain high rates of growth without substantially improving the quality of their legal system.

AREA III: ACCESS TO SOUND MONEY

Box 3

a   Average annual growth of the money supply in the last five years minus average annual growth of real GDP in the last ten years.

b   Standard deviation of annual inflation in the last five years.

c   Annual inflation in the most recent year.

d   Freedom of citizens to own foreign currency bank accounts domestically and abroad.

e   Difference between the official exchange rate and the black market rate.

Note: All the variables in this area are in the *Economic Freedom of the World* Index.

Money oils the wheels of exchange. An absence of sound money undermines gains from trade. As Milton Friedman informed us long ago, inflation is a monetary phenomenon. It is caused by "too much money chasing too few goods." High rates of monetary growth invariably lead to inflation. Similarly, when the rate of inflation increases, it also tends to become more volatile. High and volatile rates of inflation distort relative prices and make it virtually impossible for individuals and businesses to plan sensibly for the future.

It makes little difference who provides the sound money. The important thing is that individuals have access to it. Thus, in addition to a country's inflation rate, it is also important to consider how difficult it is to use alternative, more credible

currencies. Is it legal to conduct transactions in currencies other than the one issued by the government? Can the domestic currency be easily converted to other currencies? Can bankers offer saving and checking accounts in other currencies? If the answer to each of these questions is "yes," access to sound money is increased and economic freedom expanded.

As Box 3 shows, the area index contains five components. The first three are designed to measure the consistency of monetary policy (or institutions) with long-term price stability. Components (d) and (e) are designed to measure the ease with which other currencies can be used. In order to earn a high rating in this area, a country must follow policies and adopt institutions that lead to low (and stable) rates

Exhibit 2-1: Area I, Size of Government

Exhibit 2-2: Area II, Legal Structure

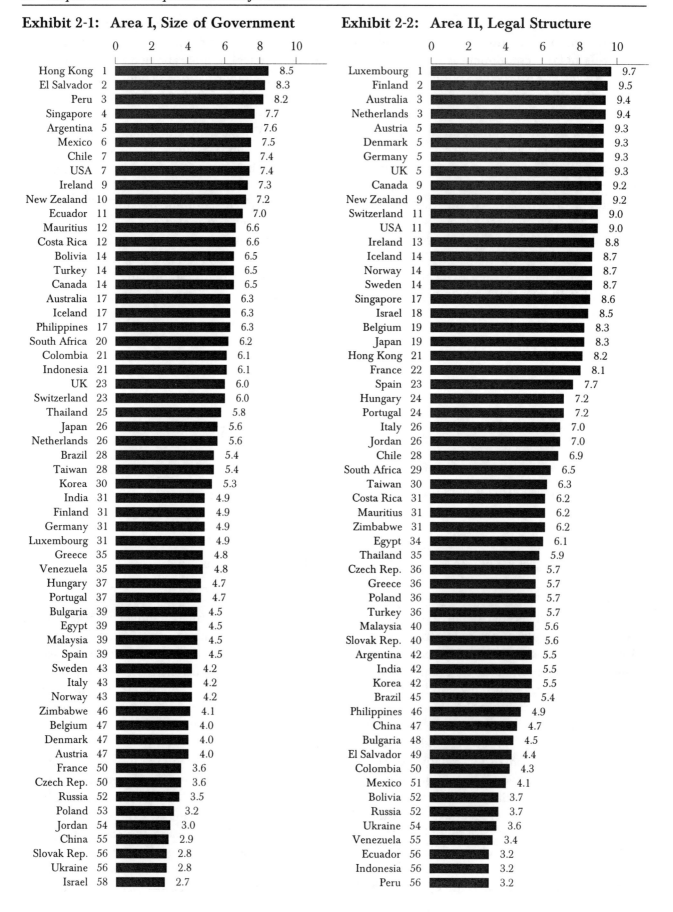

Rank	Country	Score
1	Hong Kong	8.5
2	El Salvador	8.3
3	Peru	8.2
4	Singapore	7.7
5	Argentina	7.6
6	Mexico	7.5
7	Chile	7.4
7	USA	7.4
9	Ireland	7.3
10	New Zealand	7.2
11	Ecuador	7.0
12	Mauritius	6.6
12	Costa Rica	6.6
14	Bolivia	6.5
14	Turkey	6.5
14	Canada	6.5
17	Australia	6.3
17	Iceland	6.3
17	Philippines	6.3
20	South Africa	6.2
21	Colombia	6.1
21	Indonesia	6.1
23	UK	6.0
23	Switzerland	6.0
25	Thailand	5.8
26	Japan	5.6
26	Netherlands	5.6
28	Brazil	5.4
28	Taiwan	5.4
30	Korea	5.3
31	India	4.9
31	Finland	4.9
31	Germany	4.9
31	Luxembourg	4.9
35	Greece	4.8
35	Venezuela	4.8
37	Hungary	4.7
37	Portugal	4.7
39	Bulgaria	4.5
39	Egypt	4.5
39	Malaysia	4.5
39	Spain	4.5
43	Sweden	4.2
43	Italy	4.2
43	Norway	4.2
46	Zimbabwe	4.1
47	Belgium	4.0
47	Denmark	4.0
47	Austria	4.0
50	France	3.6
50	Czech Rep.	3.6
52	Russia	3.5
53	Poland	3.2
54	Jordan	3.0
55	China	2.9
56	Slovak Rep.	2.8
56	Ukraine	2.8
58	Israel	2.7

Rank	Country	Score
1	Luxembourg	9.7
2	Finland	9.5
3	Australia	9.4
3	Netherlands	9.4
5	Austria	9.3
5	Denmark	9.3
5	Germany	9.3
5	UK	9.3
9	Canada	9.2
9	New Zealand	9.2
11	Switzerland	9.0
11	USA	9.0
13	Ireland	8.8
14	Iceland	8.7
14	Norway	8.7
14	Sweden	8.7
17	Singapore	8.6
18	Israel	8.5
19	Belgium	8.3
19	Japan	8.3
21	Hong Kong	8.2
22	France	8.1
23	Spain	7.7
24	Hungary	7.2
24	Portugal	7.2
26	Italy	7.0
26	Jordan	7.0
28	Chile	6.9
29	South Africa	6.5
30	Taiwan	6.3
31	Costa Rica	6.2
31	Mauritius	6.2
31	Zimbabwe	6.2
34	Egypt	6.1
35	Thailand	5.9
36	Czech Rep.	5.7
36	Greece	5.7
36	Poland	5.7
36	Turkey	5.7
40	Malaysia	5.6
40	Slovak Rep.	5.6
42	Argentina	5.5
42	India	5.5
42	Korea	5.5
45	Brazil	5.4
46	Philippines	4.9
47	China	4.7
48	Bulgaria	4.5
49	El Salvador	4.4
50	Colombia	4.3
51	Mexico	4.1
52	Bolivia	3.7
52	Russia	3.7
54	Ukraine	3.6
55	Venezuela	3.4
56	Ecuador	3.2
56	Indonesia	3.2
56	Peru	3.2

of inflation and avoid regulations that limit the use of alternative currencies should citizens want to use them. On the other hand, countries adopting policies that result in high and volatile rates of inflation, restrict the convertibility of the domestic currency, and place limitations on the use of alternative currencies are given a low rating.

Table 2-3 of the Appendix presents the component rating for the sound money area and Exhibit 2-3 presents the monetary area ratings. The ratings in the monetary area are exceedingly high: 27 of the 58 countries received a rating of 9.5 or higher and 34 had ratings of 9.0 or better. These high ratings reflect the fact that there has been a rather dramatic shift in monetary policy and insti-

tutions during the last two decades. In contrast with the 1970s, the focus of monetary policy in many, if not most, countries is now on the achievement of price stability.

During the last five years, only a few countries have followed the path of monetary expansion. Russia, Brazil, Ukraine, Turkey, Bulgaria, Venezuela, Zimbabwe, Ecuador and Colombia fall into this category. Even among this group, several countries have already adopted changes that promise to improve the situation in the future. For example, Bulgaria moved to a currency board in 1997 and Ecuador adopted the US dollar as its official currency in 2000. Perhaps future ratings in this area will be even higher.

AREA IV: FREEDOM TO TRADE WITH FOREIGNERS

Box 4: Area IV, Freedom to Trade with Foreigners

  a Taxes on international trade.

    i Revenue from taxes on international trade as a percentage of exports plus imports.

    ii Mean tariff rate.

    iii Standard deviation of tariff rates.

  b Non-tariff regulatory trade barriers.

    i Hidden import barriers: no barriers other than published tariffs and quotas (GCR-9.02).

    ii Customs administration: customs administration does not hinder the efficient transit of goods (WCY-3.33).

  c Costs of importing: the combined effect of import tariffs, licence fees, bank fees, and the time required for administrative red-tape raises costs of importing equipment by (10 = 10% or less; 0 = more than 50%) (GCR-9.01).

  d Actual size of trade sector compared to expected size.

  e Difference between official exchange rate and black market rate.

Note: **Bold-face type** indicates the variable is not in the current *Economic Freedom of the World* Index.
     GCR = *Global Competitiveness Report*; WCY = *World Competitiveness Yearbook*.

In our modern world of high technology and low communication and transportation costs, freedom of exchange across national boundaries is a key ingredient of economic freedom. The vast majority of our current goods and services are now either produced abroad or contain resources supplied from abroad. Of course, exchange is a

positive-sum activity. Both trading partners gain and the pursuit of the gain provides the motivation for the exchange. Thus, freedom to exchange with foreigners also contributes substantially to our modern living standards. Despite the overwhelming evidence that international exchange promotes economic progress, the freedom to trade with foreigners remains controversial. The protest demonstrations accompanying recent meetings of the World Trade Organization illustrate this point.

Responding to protectionist critics and special-interest politics, countries have adopted trade restrictions of various types. Tariffs and quotas are obvious examples of roadblocks that limit international trade. Because they reduce the convertibility of currencies, exchange-rate controls also retard international trade.[8] The volume of trade is also reduced by administrative factors that delay the passage of goods through customs. Sometimes these delays are the result of inefficiency while in other instances they reflect the actions of corrupt officials seeking to extract bribes.

As Box 4 shows, the index components in this area are designed to measure a wide variety of restraints, including tariffs, quotas, hidden administrative restraints, and exchange rate controls. In order to get a high rating in this area, a country must have low tariffs, a large trade sector, efficient administration of customs, and a freely convertible currency. Table 2-4 of the appendix presents the component ratings for each of the 58 countries. The component ratings are averaged and used to derive the area rating. Exhibit 2-4 presents the international trade rating for each of the 58 countries ranked from high to low.

By a substantial margin, Singapore and Hong Kong have the highest ratings in the international trade area. Ireland, Belgium, the Netherlands, Sweden, Finland, Luxembourg, Austria, and Malaysia round out the "top ten." The lowest ratings are earned by Russia, India, Ecuador, Colombia, Brazil, Argentina and Venezuela. Most OECD countries had relatively high ratings. Japan was an exception: there are only 10 countries with a lower rating than the 6.6 score of Japan.

AREA V: REGULATION OF CAPITAL AND FINANCIAL MARKETS

Box 5: Area V–Regulation of Capital and Financial Markets

a Ownership of banks: percentage of deposits held in privately owned banks.

b **Competition: domestic banks face competition from foreign banks (GCR-8.03).**

c Extension of credit: percentage of credit extended to private sector.

d Avoidance of interest rate controls and regulations that lead to negative real interest rates.

e **Interest rate gap: gap between interest rates for bank loans and interest rates for deposits compared to international norms (GCR-8.09).**

f **Interest rate controls: interest rate controls on bank deposits and/or loans are freely determined by the market (GCR-8.08).**

g Restrictions on the freedom of citizens to engage in capital transactions with foreigners.

h **Access to foreign capital markets: citizens are free to invest in stocks and bonds and to open bank accounts in other countries (GCR-9.08).**

i **Foreign access to capital markets: foreigners may invest in stocks and bonds (GCR-9.09).**

j **Index of capital controls: number of capital market restrictions among 13 IMF categories (0 = restrictions in all 13 categories; 10 = no restrictions in any of the 13 categories).**

Note: **Bold-face type** indicates the variable is not in the current *Economic Freedom of the World* Index.

The last three areas of the index focus on regulatory actions that reduce economic freedom. Because of the difficulties involved in developing objective measures of regulatory restraints, more of the components in these three areas are based on survey data. Area V focuses on banking, finance, and capital-market regulations that restrict the freedom to compete or reduce freedom of exchange.

Exhibit 2-3: Area III, Sound Money

Exhibit 2-4: Area IV, International Trade

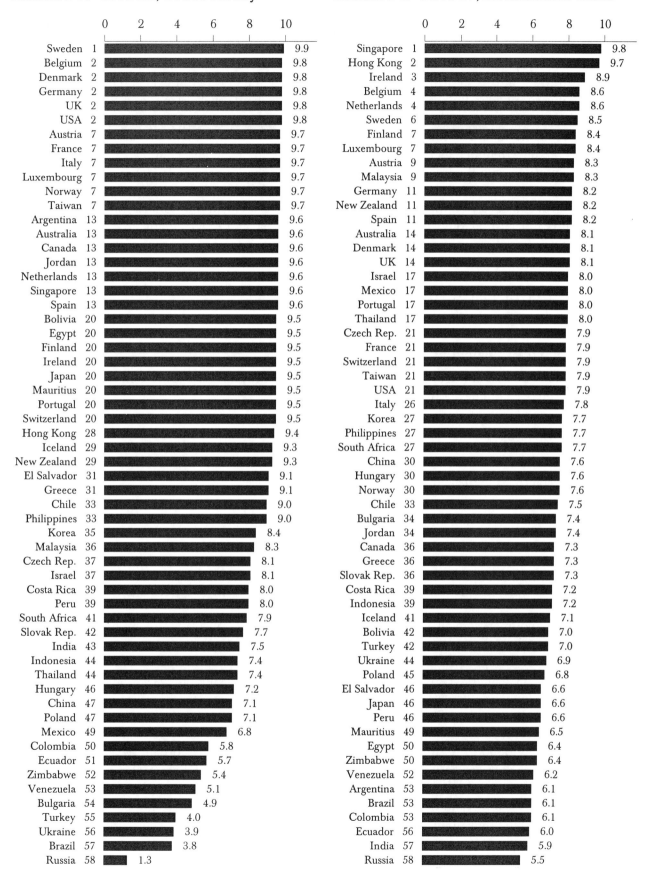

	Sound Money		International Trade
Sweden	1 — 9.9	Singapore 1	9.8
Belgium	2 — 9.8	Hong Kong 2	9.7
Denmark	2 — 9.8	Ireland 3	8.9
Germany	2 — 9.8	Belgium 4	8.6
UK	2 — 9.8	Netherlands 4	8.6
USA	2 — 9.8	Sweden 6	8.5
Austria	7 — 9.7	Finland 7	8.4
France	7 — 9.7	Luxembourg 7	8.4
Italy	7 — 9.7	Austria 9	8.3
Luxembourg	7 — 9.7	Malaysia 9	8.3
Norway	7 — 9.7	Germany 11	8.2
Taiwan	7 — 9.7	New Zealand 11	8.2
Argentina	13 — 9.6	Spain 11	8.2
Australia	13 — 9.6	Australia 14	8.1
Canada	13 — 9.6	Denmark 14	8.1
Jordan	13 — 9.6	UK 14	8.1
Netherlands	13 — 9.6	Israel 17	8.0
Singapore	13 — 9.6	Mexico 17	8.0
Spain	13 — 9.6	Portugal 17	8.0
Bolivia	20 — 9.5	Thailand 17	8.0
Egypt	20 — 9.5	Czech Rep. 21	7.9
Finland	20 — 9.5	France 21	7.9
Ireland	20 — 9.5	Switzerland 21	7.9
Japan	20 — 9.5	Taiwan 21	7.9
Mauritius	20 — 9.5	USA 21	7.9
Portugal	20 — 9.5	Italy 26	7.8
Switzerland	20 — 9.5	Korea 27	7.7
Hong Kong	28 — 9.4	Philippines 27	7.7
Iceland	29 — 9.3	South Africa 27	7.7
New Zealand	29 — 9.3	China 30	7.6
El Salvador	31 — 9.1	Hungary 30	7.6
Greece	31 — 9.1	Norway 30	7.6
Chile	33 — 9.0	Chile 33	7.5
Philippines	33 — 9.0	Bulgaria 34	7.4
Korea	35 — 8.4	Jordan 34	7.4
Malaysia	36 — 8.3	Canada 36	7.3
Czech Rep.	37 — 8.1	Greece 36	7.3
Israel	37 — 8.1	Slovak Rep. 36	7.3
Costa Rica	39 — 8.0	Costa Rica 39	7.2
Peru	39 — 8.0	Indonesia 39	7.2
South Africa	41 — 7.9	Iceland 41	7.1
Slovak Rep.	42 — 7.7	Bolivia 42	7.0
India	43 — 7.5	Turkey 42	7.0
Indonesia	44 — 7.4	Ukraine 44	6.9
Thailand	44 — 7.4	Poland 45	6.8
Hungary	46 — 7.2	El Salvador 46	6.6
China	47 — 7.1	Japan 46	6.6
Poland	47 — 7.1	Peru 46	6.6
Mexico	49 — 6.8	Mauritius 49	6.5
Colombia	50 — 5.8	Egypt 50	6.4
Ecuador	51 — 5.7	Zimbabwe 50	6.4
Zimbabwe	52 — 5.4	Venezuela 52	6.2
Venezuela	53 — 5.1	Argentina 53	6.1
Bulgaria	54 — 4.9	Brazil 53	6.1
Turkey	55 — 4.0	Colombia 53	6.1
Ukraine	56 — 3.9	Ecuador 56	6.0
Brazil	57 — 3.8	India 57	5.9
Russia	58 — 1.3	Russia 58	5.5

There are 10 components of the index in this area. The first two provide evidence on the extent to which the banking industry is dominated by private firms and whether foreign banks are permitted to compete in the market. Components (c), (d), (e), and (f) indicate the extent to which credit is supplied to the private sector and whether interest rate controls interfere with credit market operations. The four other components focus on the extent to which capital market regulations interfere with the freedom of citizens to engage in capital market transactions with foreigners. In order to receive a high rating in this area, a country must use a largely private banking system to allocate credit to private parties and refrain from the use of both interest rate and capital market controls.

The component ratings for Area V are presented in Table 2-5 of the Appendix; Exhibit 2-5 indicates the area ratings. Luxembourg, Netherlands, United Kingdom, Denmark, Hong Kong, New Zealand, Switzerland, and the United States head the list of countries receiving the highest ratings in the capital market area. Almost all of the world's high income countries had high ratings. Among the long-time OECD members, only Iceland and Greece had a rating below the median. Russia, India, Ukraine, China, Zimbabwe, Poland, Indonesia, and Brazil had the lowest ratings in this area among the 58 countries of the study.

AREA VI: REGULATION OF LABOR MARKETS

Box 6: Area VI, Regulation of Labor Markets

    a Impact of minimum wage: the minimum wage, set by law, has little impact on wages because it is too low or not obeyed (GCR-6.03).

    b Hiring and firing practices: hiring and firing practices of companies are determined by employers (GCR-6.06).

    c Share of labor force whose wages are set by centralized collective bargaining.

    d Top marginal tax rate (and income threshold at which it applies).

    e Unemployment insurance: the unemployment insurance program strikes a good balance between social protection and preserving the incentive to work (GCR-6.08).

    f Use of conscripts to obtain military personnel.

Note: **Bold-face type** indicates the variable is not in the current *Economic Freedom of the World* Index.

Many types of labor market regulations infringe on the economic freedom of employees and employers. Among the more prominent are minimum wages, dismissal regulations, centralized wage setting, extensions of union contracts to nonparticipating parties, unemployment benefits that undermine the incentive to accept employment, high marginal tax rates, and conscription.[9] As Box 6 shows, the components in this area are designed to measure the extent to which these restraints upon economic freedom are present across countries.[10]

To receive a high rating in this area, a country must allow market forces to determine wages and establish the conditions of dismissal, avoid high marginal tax rates and unemployment benefits that undermine incentives to work, and refrain from the use of conscription. Table 2-6 in the appendix presents the ratings for each of the components in this area.

Exhibit 2-6 shows the labor market area rating for each of the 58 countries, ranked from highest to lowest. Hong Kong, Jordan, Malaysia, Thailand, Costa Rica, Bolivia, United States, Philippines, New Zealand, and Singapore are the highest-rated countries. Western European countries with extensive labor market regulations, centralized wage setting structures, and lucrative unemployment compensation systems are heavily represented among those with the lowest ratings. Germany, France, Sweden, Finland, and Italy make up the bottom five. In fact, the 10 lowest rated countries are all Western European nations. Israel, China, and several of the former socialist countries of Eastern Europe also have heavily regulated labor markets.

While high marginal tax rates and conscription reduce economic freedom, their impact on the flexibility of labor markets is relatively minor. Minimum wages, dismissal regulations, centralized wage setting, and generous unemployment benefits exert a more direct impact on the flexibility of wages and operation of labor markets. Researchers interested only in labor market flexibility, might want to focus on these factors. Thus, we also calculated a cross-country labor market flexibility index that is based only on components (a), (b), (c), and (e) of Area VI. This rating is presented in the Appendix (Exhibit 2-10). While we do not believe this recalculated rating is a superior measure of economic freedom, it may well be a more reliable indicator of regulations that undermine the efficient operation of labor markets.

The labor market flexibility index indicates that Area VI overstates the labor market flexibility of several countries. The ratings of Argentina, Costa Rica, India, Luxembourg, and Mauritius are between 1.2 and 2.0 lower when based only on components (a), (b), (c), and (e). The rankings of these countries would also be affected substantially. If the labor rating were based on only the four labor market flexibility components, Argentina's ranking would fall from 13 to 32; Costa Rica's would plummet from 5 to 25; India's from 14 to 35; Luxembourg's from 37 to 48; and that of Mauritius from 14 to 41 (see Appendix, Exhibit 2-10). This indicates that the labor markets of these countries are not as flexible as the ratings of Area VI imply.

At the same time, Area VI understates the labor market flexibility of other countries. When only components (a), (b), (c), and (e) are included in the index, the ratings of Bulgaria, Chile, China, Egypt, Korea, Russia, and Ukraine were pushed upward by 1.2 or more. The rankings of these countries in the labor market flexibility index were at least 10 positions higher than for the entire Area VI index. These ratings and rankings indicate that the labor markets of these countries are more flexible than the ratings of Area VI imply.

AREA VII: FREEDOM TO OPERATE AND COMPETE IN BUSINESS

Box 7: Area VII–Freedom to Operate and Compete in Business

  a **Administrative conditions and new businesses: administrative procedures are not an important obstacle to starting a new business (GCR-10.07).**

  b **Time with government bureaucracy: senior management spends very little of its time dealing with government bureaucracy (GCR-4.02).**

  c **Starting a new business: starting a new business is generally easy (GCR-10.04).**

  d **Local competition: competition in local markets is intense and market shares fluctuate constantly (GCR-10.01).**

  e **Irregular payments: irregular, additional payments connected with import and export permits, business licenses, exchange controls, tax assessments, police protection, or loan applications are very rare (GCR-4.03).**

  f **Bank credit for business: extent to which credit flows from banks to business (WCY-4.04).**

Note: **Bold-face type** indicates the variable is not in the current *Economic Freedom of the World* Index.

The freedom to start and operate a business is an integral component of economic freedom and a vital source of prosperity. Like capital and labor market regulations, the regulation of business activities may inhibit economic freedom. Box 7 indicates the index components in this area. The

Exhibit 2-5:   Area V, Financial Markets   **Exhibit 2-6:   Area VI, Labor Markets**

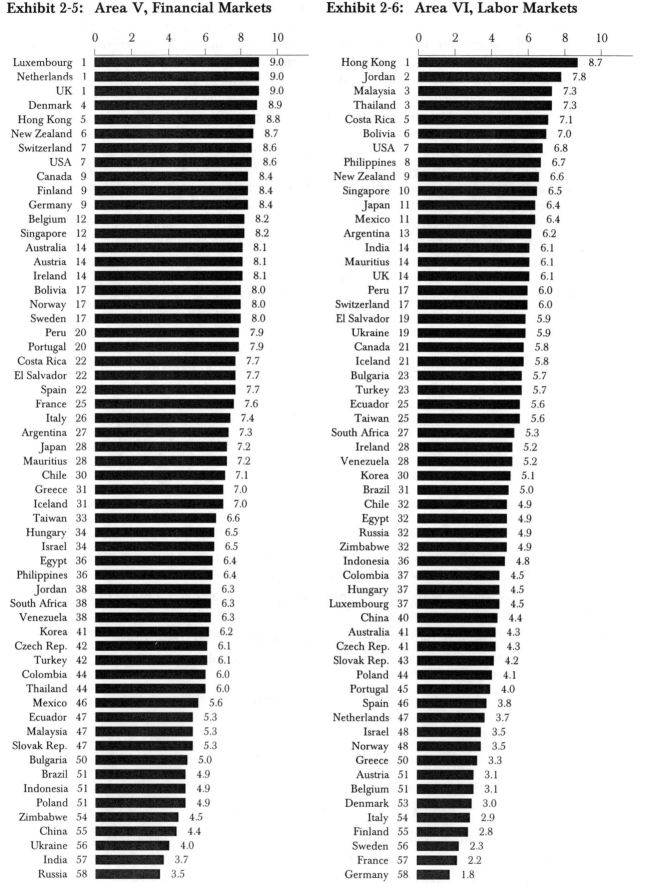

components are designed to identify the extent to which regulatory restraints and bureaucratic procedures limit competition and shift resources away from productive activities. In order to score high in this area, countries must refrain from regulatory activities that retard market entry and increase the cost of producing goods and services. They also must refrain from playing favorites–from using their power to extract financial payments and reward some businesses at the expense of others.

Table 2-7 of the Appendix provides the ratings for each component, while Exhibit 2-7 indicates the country rankings. Finland, Hong Kong, and the United States tied for the highest rating in this area. They were followed closely by Singapore, Iceland, Netherlands, Australia, Luxembourg, and the United Kingdom. At the other end of the scale,

Russia, Venezuela, Ukraine, Mexico, Ecuador, and Bulgaria registered the lowest scores. Bolivia, Indonesia, Argentina, and Colombia also received low ratings in this area.

Interestingly, the Northern European countries–particularly those in the Scandinavian region–scored substantially better than southern European countries. For example, the ratings of Finland, Netherlands, Iceland, United Kingdom, Denmark, Sweden, and Norway were all well above those of France, Greece, and Italy. Perhaps surprising to some, this implies that while the government spending of northern European countries is high, their regulatory climate is not particularly antagonistic toward private business and competitive markets.

THE SUMMARY RATINGS OF THE MORE COMPREHENSIVE INDEX

The ratings from the seven areas were averaged and used to derive a summary rating. Table 2-8 of the Appendix presents both the area and summary ratings for each of the 58 countries. Table 2-9 of the Appendix presents the area and summary rankings. Exhibit 2-8 presents the summary ratings for each of the countries ranked from high to low.

As in the regular *Economic Freedom of the World* Index, Hong Kong ranked first in this more comprehensive index. Hong Kong's 8.8 score was a half-point better than the 8.3 rating of Singapore. Hong Kong's rating was 8.2 or better in each of the seven areas. Among the 58 countries in this study, Hong Kong ranked in the "top five" in five of the seven areas covered by this index. The only blemishes on its record were rankings of 21 for its legal system (Area II) and 28 for access to sound money (Area III).

Singapore was the highest-rated country with regard to trade liberalization (Area IV). Its rankings were persistently high in each of the seven areas. In fact, Singapore's lowest ranking was its rank of 17 for legal system and security of property rights. Even though its 6.5 rating placed it at 10 in the labor regulation area, this was well below Hong Kong's score of 8.7. Basically, the gap in this area accounts for the difference between the ratings of Hong Kong and Singapore.

The United States ranked 3; its area rankings were consistently high. It ranked 11 or better in every area but one. Its ranking slipped to 21 in international trade (Area IV). The United States tied with Finland and Hong Kong for the highest rating in the freedom of business activity (Area VII). It tied for 2 in the sound money area (III) and placed at 7 in the size of government, financial market, and labor market areas.

New Zealand and the United Kingdom ranked at 4 and 5 respectively. Ireland placed at 6; Canada and Switzerland tied for 7, followed by Australia, Luxembourg, and the Netherlands (tied for 9). Interestingly, eight of the 11 highest ranked countries inherited their institutional framework from the British. This suggests that British common law and other English institutions are highly supportive of economic freedom.

At the other end of the spectrum, the 10 lowest-ranked countries were Russia, Ukraine, Venezuela, Brazil, Zimbabwe, China, Bulgaria, Ecuador, the Slovak Republic, Poland, and Colombia (the latter two were tied for 48). Six of the 11 lowest-rated countries were either socialist or former socialist countries. The ratings of the former socialist countries were generally low. Among this group, the rankings of Hungary (tied for 38) and the Czech Republic (44) were highest, while those of Bulgaria and

Exhibit 2-7: Area VII, Business Sector

Exhibit 2-8: Summary Index

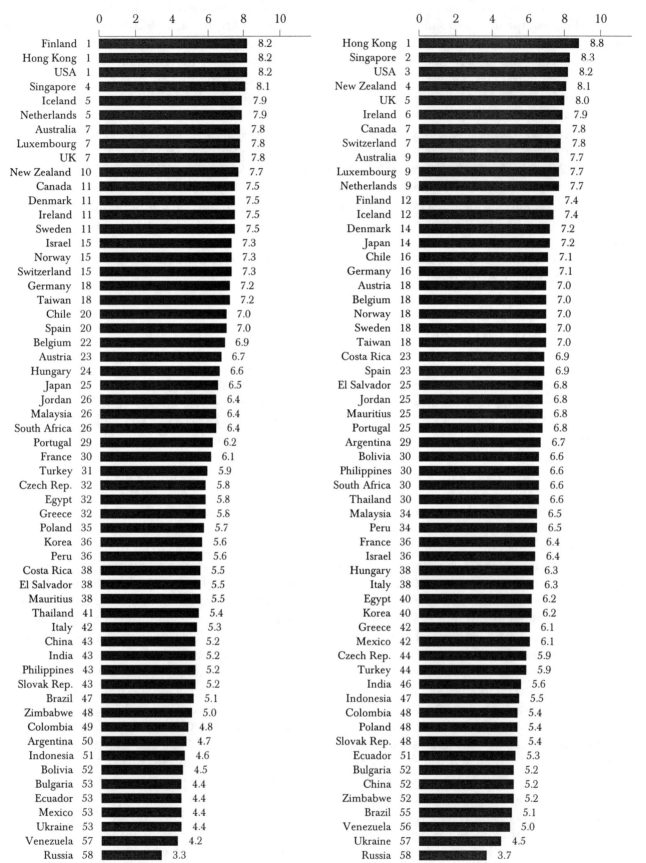

Country	Rank	Value
Finland	1	8.2
Hong Kong	1	8.2
USA	1	8.2
Singapore	4	8.1
Iceland	5	7.9
Netherlands	5	7.9
Australia	7	7.8
Luxembourg	7	7.8
UK	7	7.8
New Zealand	10	7.7
Canada	11	7.5
Denmark	11	7.5
Ireland	11	7.5
Sweden	11	7.5
Israel	15	7.3
Norway	15	7.3
Switzerland	15	7.3
Germany	18	7.2
Taiwan	18	7.2
Chile	20	7.0
Spain	20	7.0
Belgium	22	6.9
Austria	23	6.7
Hungary	24	6.6
Japan	25	6.5
Jordan	26	6.4
Malaysia	26	6.4
South Africa	26	6.4
Portugal	29	6.2
France	30	6.1
Turkey	31	5.9
Czech Rep.	32	5.8
Egypt	32	5.8
Greece	32	5.8
Poland	35	5.7
Korea	36	5.6
Peru	36	5.6
Costa Rica	38	5.5
El Salvador	38	5.5
Mauritius	38	5.5
Thailand	41	5.4
Italy	42	5.3
China	43	5.2
India	43	5.2
Philippines	43	5.2
Slovak Rep.	43	5.2
Brazil	47	5.1
Zimbabwe	48	5.0
Colombia	49	4.8
Argentina	50	4.7
Indonesia	51	4.6
Bolivia	52	4.5
Bulgaria	53	4.4
Ecuador	53	4.4
Mexico	53	4.4
Ukraine	53	4.4
Venezuela	57	4.2
Russia	58	3.3

Country	Rank	Value
Hong Kong	1	8.8
Singapore	2	8.3
USA	3	8.2
New Zealand	4	8.1
UK	5	8.0
Ireland	6	7.9
Canada	7	7.8
Switzerland	7	7.8
Australia	9	7.7
Luxembourg	9	7.7
Netherlands	9	7.7
Finland	12	7.4
Iceland	12	7.4
Denmark	14	7.2
Japan	14	7.2
Chile	16	7.1
Germany	16	7.1
Austria	18	7.0
Belgium	18	7.0
Norway	18	7.0
Sweden	18	7.0
Taiwan	18	7.0
Costa Rica	23	6.9
Spain	23	6.9
El Salvador	25	6.8
Jordan	25	6.8
Mauritius	25	6.8
Portugal	25	6.8
Argentina	29	6.7
Bolivia	30	6.6
Philippines	30	6.6
South Africa	30	6.6
Thailand	30	6.6
Malaysia	34	6.5
Peru	34	6.5
France	36	6.4
Israel	36	6.4
Hungary	38	6.3
Italy	38	6.3
Egypt	40	6.2
Korea	40	6.2
Greece	42	6.1
Mexico	42	6.1
Czech Rep.	44	5.9
Turkey	44	5.9
India	46	5.6
Indonesia	47	5.5
Colombia	48	5.4
Poland	48	5.4
Slovak Rep.	48	5.4
Ecuador	51	5.3
Bulgaria	52	5.2
China	52	5.2
Zimbabwe	52	5.2
Brazil	55	5.1
Venezuela	56	5.0
Ukraine	57	4.5
Russia	58	3.7

China (tied for 52), Ukraine (57), and Russia (58) were lowest. The development of economic freedom is an evolutionary process. The low scores of the former socialist countries illustrate that this evolutionary process is time-consuming and difficult.

Regional Rankings

It is interesting to consider the ratings of countries within regions. Among the Western European countries, the United Kingdom (5), Ireland (6),and Switzerland (tied for 7) were ranked highest; France (tied for 36), Italy (tied for 38) and Greece (tied for 42) were ranked lowest.

Of course, the rankings of Hong Kong and Singapore were the best in Asia. Japan (14) and Taiwan (18) were the next best in this region; India (46), Indonesia (47), and China (52) ranked lowest among the Asian nations.

In Central and South America, Chile (16), Costa Rica (23) and El Salvador (tied for 25) ranked highest, while Colombia (tied for 48), Ecuador (51), Brazil (55) and Venezuela (56) ranked lowest. Only three sub-Saharan African countries were included in the study. Mauritius tied with three other countries for 25; South Africa ranked

30 (tied with three other countries); and Zimbabwe tied with Bulgaria and China for 52.

Rating Patterns

Several interesting patterns emerge from analysis of the area ratings. The high-income industrial countries of Europe generally scored well in all categories except two: size of government (Area I) and regulation of labor markets (Area VI). Among the 58 countries of this study, Belgium, France, Austria, Sweden, Norway, Denmark, Italy, and Spain all ranked in the "bottom twenty" in the size of government area. Ireland and Iceland were the only Western European countries to make the "top twenty" in the size of government area.

The situation was similar in the labor market regulation area. Germany and France received the lowest scores in this area. The ratings of Sweden, Finland, and Italy were only slightly higher. Denmark, Belgium, Austria, Greece, and Norway also ranked in the "bottom 10" in the area of labor market regulation. The United Kingdom, Switzerland, Iceland, and Ireland were the only Western European countries with labor markets meriting an above-median rating.

COMPARING THE COMPREHENSIVE AND REGULAR INDEXES

Approximately half of the 45 component ratings of the more comprehensive index are based on survey data. As we discussed earlier, the survey data primarily concern differences in regulatory activities, particularly those that affect labor markets and business operation. They are also an indicator of the even-handedness of the judiciary and similar factors related to the operation of the legal system. These factors are captured in Areas II, VI, and VII of the more comprehensive index. As a result, most of the components in these three areas are included only in the more comprehensive index. In contrast, most of the components in the other four areas are from the regular *Economic Freedom of the World* Index. Put another way, the regular index can be expected to register cross-country differences with regard to size of government, sound money, international trade, and capital market operations accurately. As currently constituted, however, it does not reflect the impact of la-

bor and business regulation and the quality of the legal system adequately.

How do differences between the two indexes influence country ratings and rankings? Exhibit 2.9 arrays the countries on the basis of their ranking in the more comprehensive index and presents the parallel ratings and rankings from the two indexes. In this exhibit, the rankings from the regular index are based on the inclusion of only the 58 countries analyzed here.

Clearly, the two indexes are closely related. For example, the six highest-ranked countries in the two indexes are identical—Hong Kong, Singapore, United States, New Zealand, the United Kingdom, and Iceland—with only a slight variation in their order. Other top-ranking nations in both indexes include Australia, Luxembourg, Netherlands, and Switzerland.

The situation was much the same at the bottom end of the scale. Russia and Ukraine rank 58 and 57 respectively in both indexes. Both scales place Venezuela, Brazil, Zimbabwe, China, Bulgaria, Poland, and Colombia in positions between 48 and 56.

As column 5 of Exhibit 2-9 shows, there were only a few cases where a country's ranking in one index is more than eight positions different from its ranking in the other index. The comprehensive index ranked four countries–, Taiwan, Thailand, Jordan, and India–substantially higher than the regular index. Closer inspection reveals why these countries did better in the more comprehensive index. Taiwan rates high in the regulation of business area, indicating that regulation is relatively light. This boosted its position in the comprehensive index. Thailand, Jordan, and India had higher ratings and rankings in labor market regulation than was true for other areas. This pushed their ranking upward in the comprehensive index.

The comprehensive index suggests that the regular index ranks Argentina, Bolivia, Italy, and Greece too high. While Argentina and Bolivia tied for 11 in the regular index, they were 29 and 30 in the more comprehensive index. Bolivia and Argentina rate poorly in legal systems and regulation of business, two areas that are under-represented in the regular index. Argentina's labor market is highly regulated (see Appendix, Table 2-10). Thus its low ratings for the four labor market flexibility components of Area VI are also a drag on its rating in the broad index. The performance of Greece and of Italy is also extremely poor in labor-market regulation. This pushes their rankings downward in the comprehensive index.

Despite these outliers, statistical analysis indicates that the two indexes are highly correlated. The rank correlation coefficient between the two indexes is 0.935. The ratings correlation coefficient between the two indexes is even higher, 0.947. The size of these correlation coefficients indicates that while the regular index can be improved, it is nonetheless a reasonably good measure of cross-country differences in economic freedom.

CONCLUSION

The index developed here provides a more comprehensive measure of economic freedom than has heretofore been available. It will help both policy makers and social scientists pinpoint both the strengths and weaknesses of institutions and policies more accurately. It should also be of value to researchers seeking to enhance our knowledge of the factors underlying economic growth and the process of development. With time, it is our hope that it will contribute to changes that will improve the rate of economic progress.

Exhibit 2-9: Comparison of Comprehensive and 2001 EFW Rankings and Ratings

	Comprehensive Index		2001 EFW Index		Difference between comprehensive and 2001 EFW Indexes[b] (5)
	Rank (1)	Rating (2)	Rank (3)	Rating (4)	
Hong Kong	1	8.8	1	9.4	0
Singapore	2	8.3	2	9.3	0
United States	3	8.2	5	8.7	+2
New Zealand	4	8.1	3	8.9	−1
United Kingdom	5	8.0	4	8.8	−1
Ireland	6	7.9	6	8.5	0
Canada	7	7.8	13	8.2	+6
Switzerland	7	7.8	6	8.5	−1
Australia	9	7.7	6	8.5	−3
Luxembourg	9	7.7	9	8.4	0
Netherlands	9	7.7	9	8.4	0
Finland	12	7.4	14	8.1	+2
Iceland	12	7.4	15	8.0	+3
Denmark	14	7.2	15	8.0	+1
Japan	14	7.2	20	7.9	+6
Chile	16	7.1	15	8.0	−1
Germany	16	7.1	15	8.0	−1
Austria	18	7.0	15	8.0	−3
Belgium	18	7.0	20	7.9	+2
Norway	18	7.0	24	7.8	+6
Sweden	18	7.0	20	7.9	+2
Taiwan[d]	18	7.0	33	7.3	+15
Costa Rica	23	6.9	24	7.8	+1
Spain	23	6.9	28	7.6	+5
El Salvador	25	6.8	20	7.9	−5
Jordan[d]	25	6.8	38	6.8	+13
Mauritius	25	6.8	32	7.4	+7
Portugal	25	6.8	24	7.8	−1
Argentina[c]	29	6.7	11	8.3	−18
Bolivia[c]	30	6.6	11	8.3	−19
Philippines	30	6.6	28	7.6	−2

	Comprehensive Index		2001 EFW Index		Difference between comprehensive and 2001 EFW Indexes[b] (5)
	Rank (1)	Rating (2)	Rank (3)	Rating (4)	
South Africa	30	6.6	37	7.0	+7
Thailand[d]	30	6.6	38	6.8	+8
Malaysia	34	6.5	41	6.7	+7
Peru	34	6.5	28	7.6	−6
France	36	6.4	31	7.5	−5
Israel	36	6.4	41	6.7	+5
Hungary	38	6.3	35	7.1	−3
Italy[c]	38	6.3	24	7.8	−14
Egypt	40	6.2	38	6.8	−2
South Korea	40	6.2	35	7.1	−5
Greece[c]	42	6.1	33	7.3	−9
Mexico	42	6.1	44	6.5	+2
Czech Rep.	44	5.9	43	6.6	−1
Turkey	44	5.9	47	6.2	+3
India[d]	46	5.6	55	5.3	+9
Indonesia	47	5.5	47	6.2	0
Colombia	48	5.4	51	5.8	+3
Poland	48	5.4	53	5.7	+5
Slovak Republic	48	5.4	46	6.3	−2
Ecuador	51	5.3	45	6.4	−6
Bulgaria	52	5.2	50	5.9	−2
China	52	5.2	51	5.8	−1
Zimbabwe	52	5.2	54	5.4	+2
Brazil	55	5.1	56	5.1	+1
Venezuela, Rep.	56	5.0	49	6.1	−7
Ukraine	57	4.5	57	4.6	0
Russia	58	3.7	58	3.9	0

Note: The correlation coefficient between index ratings (columns 2 and 4) = 0.947; the rank correlation coefficient (columns 1 and 3) = 0.935.

(a) The mean value for the countries listed of the comprehensive index rating was 6.6 compared to 7.3 for the 2001 EFW index.

(b) 2001 EFW ranking minus comprehensive index ranking.

(c) Indicates that country's comprehensive index rank is at least 8 places higher than its 2001 EFW index rank.

(d) Indicates that country's comprehensive index rank is at least 8 places lower than its 2001 EFW index rank.

NOTES

(1) The ratings of the *Global Competitiveness Report* were based on a survey of more than 4,000 executives doing business in at least one of the 59 countries covered by the report. Of the 59 countries, all but Vietnam are also included in the *Economic Freedom of the World* Index. The original GCR ratings were scaled from 1 to 7. To make them comparable with other components, the following formula was used to convert them to a 0 to 10 scale: GCR rating minus 1, multiplied by 1.667. The *World Competitiveness Yearbook* contains information for 47 countries. The survey data are based on responses to a 110-item questionnaire by 3,263 top-level and mid-level executives representing both international and domestic companies. The original ratings of the yearbook are scaled from 0 to 10.

(2) Twenty-two of the 45 components are based on the survey data of the competitiveness reports. Because of its greater focus on institutional and regulatory issues, most (20 of the 22) of the survey variables are from the *Global Competitiveness Report.* Most of the other components of the index presented here are from the economic freedom index. The Appendix to Chapter 1 of this publication provides details on the derivation of the components used in *Economic Freedom of the World* and explains how the raw data were converted to a scale of 0 to 10.

(3) Freedom to own and lease housing and freedom to choose in the area of education are two major areas that are omitted. Eventually we hope to incorporate these two areas into a still more comprehensive index.

(4) The components of this area are like those of Areas I and II of our regular index.

(5) Total government expenditures include both on-budget and off-budget spending at all levels of government. Because this figure is unavailable for many countries, it was not included in the *Economic Freedom of the World* Index. However, we were able to obtain total government expenditures as a share of GDP (TGE) for most of the 58 countries here and integrate this component into the broader index. The following formula was used to convert the raw data to the scale of 0 to 10: 10 multiplied by (50 − TGE) / 40. The rating was restricted to values between 0 and 10. If total government spending was 10% or less of GDP, the rating would be 10. When government spending is equal to or greater than 50% of GDP, a rating of 0 is assigned.

(6) For evidence on this point, see James Gwartney, Robert Lawson, and Randall Holcombe, The Scope of Government and the Wealth of Nations, *Cato Journal*, 18, 2 (Fall 1998): 164–190.

(7) See the Appendix to Chapter 1 of this publication for details on precisely how the raw data for these two variables were converted to the rating scale from 0 to 10.

(8) Exchange-rate controls lead to black market exchange-rate premiums. A black market exchange-rate premium is both an obstacle to trade and an indicator of unsound money. Thus, it is included in both Areas III and IV.

(9) For information on how centralized wage setting, restrictive dismissal regulations, and lucrative unemployment benefits have reduced employment and increased unemployment among OECD countries, see Edward Bierhanzl and James Gwartney, Regulation, Unions, and Labor Markets, *Regulation* (Summer 1998): 40–53; and Horst Siebert, Labor Market Rigidities: At the Root of Unemployment in Europe, *Journal of Economic Perspectives* 11, 3 (1997): 37–54.

(10)   The centralized wage-setting component (VI-E) is a new categorical variable. The following system was used to rate each country. 10 = wages are set by agreements between employers and employees (or their representative); an employee cannot be required to join a union as a condition of employment, and fewer than 40% of employees have their wages set by collective bargaining. 8 = wages are set by agreements between employers and employees (or their representative); employees are sometimes required to join a union as a condition of employment but fewer than 40% of employees have their wages set by collective bargaining. 5 = 40% to 60% of employees have their wages set by collective bargaining. 2 = collective bargaining generally covers entire industries and occupations; wages of 60% to 80% of employees are set centrally. 0 = collective bargaining generally covers entire industries and occupations; wages of more than 80% of employees are set centrally.

APPENDIX: TABLES TO CHAPTER 2

TABLE 2-1 AREA I: SIZE OF GOVERNMENT

	I a Total government expenditures as a percentage of GDP		I b i General government consumption expenditures as a percentage of total consumption		I b ii Transfers & subsidies as a percentage of GDP		Composite Area 1 b	I c Government enterprises		I d Price controls	Total Area I
Argentina	4.9	(30.6)	8.1	(12.4)	7.2	(10.8)	7.7	10	(8.6)	8	7.6
Australia	4.4	(32.3)	4.8	(23.7)	7.1	(11.2)	5.9	8	(18.7)	7	6.3
Austria	0.0	(50.7)	4.1	(25.9)	3.5	(24.3)	3.8	4	( )	8	4.0
Belgium	0.5	(47.9)	3.5	(28.2)	3.2	(25.4)	3.3	6	( )	6	4.0
Bolivia	5.3	(29.0)	7.0	(16.1)	8.8	(4.8)	7.9	4	(40.3)	9	6.5
Brazil	3.3	(36.8)	5.3	(21.8)	N/A		5.3	6	(19.4)	7	5.4
Bulgaria	3.6	(35.7)	6.7	(17.1)	6.5	(13.3)	6.6	2	(54.1)	6	4.5
Canada	2.5	(40.2)	4.5	(24.6)	N/A		4.5	10	(11.5)	9	6.5
Chile	5.4	(28.3)	7.6	(14.3)	6.8	(12.1)	7.2	8	(19.2)	9	7.4
China	N/A		5.8	(20.4)	N/A		5.8	0	(54.1)	3	2.9
Colombia	8.4	(16.6)	6.0	(19.5)	N/A		6.0	4	(40.2)	6	6.1
Costa Rica	7.5	(20.0)	5.0	(22.9)	N/A		5.0	6	(23.2)	8	6.6
Czech Republic	1.0	(46.0)	3.8	(27.0)	2.8	(27.1)	3.3	6	( )	4	3.6
Denmark	0.0	(54.3)	1.8	(33.7)	N/A		1.8	7	( )	7	4.0
Ecuador	8.4	(16.3)	7.6	(14.2)	N/A		7.6	8	(18.1)	4	7.0
Egypt	3.5	(36.0)	8.3	(11.9)	8.9	(4.6)	8.6	2	(31.4)	4	4.5
El Salvador	9.0	(13.9)	8.7	(10.5)	9.5	(2.4)	9.1	7	(22.7)	8	8.3
Finland	0.7	(47.1)	3.0	(29.9)	4.8	(19.6)	3.9	6	( )	9	4.9
France	0.0	(52.2)	2.8	(30.4)	2.3	(28.8)	2.6	4	( )	8	3.6
Germany	1.1	(45.6)	4.5	(24.9)	4.5	(20.8)	4.5	6	( )	8	4.9

	I a — Total government expenditures as a percentage of GDP	I b i — General government consumption expenditures as a percentage of total consumption	I b ii — Transfers & subsidies as a percentage of GDP	Composite Area 1 b	I c — Government enterprises	I d — Price controls	Total Area I
Greece	1.6 (43.5)	6.6 (17.5)	N/A N/A	6.6	6 ( )	5	4.8
Hong Kong	7.2 (21.3)	7.8 (13.5)	N/A N/A	7.8	10 ( )	9	8.5
Hungary	0.8 (46.9)	7.5 (14.4)	4.7 (20.0)	6.1	4 ( )	8	4.7
Iceland	4.2 (33.4)	4.3 (25.4)	7.7 (9.0)	6.0	7 ( )	8	6.3
India	4.7 (31.1)	7.0 (16.2)	N/A N/A	7.0	4 (27.3)	4	4.9
Indonesia	N/A	9.4 (8.1)	9.1 (3.6)	9.3	7 (23.0)	2	6.1
Ireland	4.6 (31.5)	5.7 (20.6)	N/A N/A	5.7	10 (14.2)	9	7.3
Israel	0.4 (48.2)	2.1 (33.0)	4.4 (21.0)	3.2	2 ( )	5	2.7
Italy	0.4 (48.3)	4.8 (23.7)	4.1 (22.0)	4.5	6 ( )	6	4.2
Japan	3.0 (38.1)	7.6 (14.1)	N/A N/A	7.6	6 (26.5)	6	5.6
Jordan	3.6 (35.7)	3.6 (27.7)	9.4 (2.6)	6.5	0 ( )	2	3.0
Korea	6.1 (25.5)	7.0 (16.3)	9.1 (3.7)	8.1	6 ( )	1	5.3
Luxembourg	0.2 (49.3)	5.3 (21.9)	3.4 (24.8)	4.4	8 ( )	7	4.9
Malaysia	3.7 (35.1)	5.4 (21.5)	9.0 (4.1)	7.2	4 (27.2)	3	4.5
Mauritius	6.7 (23.4)	7.3 (15.3)	8.6 (5.7)	7.9	6 (26.5)	6	6.6
Mexico	7.1 (21.6)	8.0 (12.8)	7.6 (9.2)	7.8	8 (18.6)	7	7.5
Netherlands	1.7 (43.2)	2.5 (31.6)	2.8 (27.0)	2.6	10 ( )	8	5.6
New Zealand	2.3 (40.8)	6.2 (19.1)	6.5 (13.2)	6.4	10 (13.3)	10	7.2
Norway	1.0 (46.1)	2.8 (30.4)	4.7 (19.9)	3.8	4 ( )	8	4.2
Peru	7.9 (18.6)	8.5 (11.2)	9.2 (3.4)	8.8	8 (15.5)	8	8.2
Philippines	6.8 (23.0)	7.3 (15.2)	N/A N/A	7.3	7 (24.0)	4	6.3

	I a Total government expenditures as a percentage of GDP	I b i General government consumption expenditures as a percentage of total consumption	I b ii Transfers & subsidies as a percentage of GDP	Composite Area 1 b	I c Government enterprises	I d Price controls	Total Area I
Poland	1.4 (44.5)	7.1 (16.0)	3.7 (23.5)	5.4	2 (43.7)	4	3.2
Portugal	1.3 (44.7)	4.8 (23.6)	5.9 (15.4)	5.4	6 ( )	6	4.7
Russia	0.0 (55.0)	5.2 (22.4)	N/A	5.2	4 (35.0)	5	3.5
Singapore	6.0 (25.9)	5.8 (20.2)	9.8 (1.4)	7.8	8 ( )	9	7.7
Slovak Republic	2.0 (41.9)	2.9 (30.1)	3.6 (23.9)	3.3	2 ( )	4	2.8
South Africa	4.8 (30.7)	4.7 (24.0)	9.0 (4.2)	6.9	6 (27.3)	7	6.2
Spain	2.9 (38.6)	5.0 (23.1)	N/A	5.0	4 ( )	6	4.5
Sweden	0.0 (54.5)	1.5 (34.8)	2.4 (28.4)	2.0	6 ( )	9	4.2
Switzerland	3.3 (36.9)	6.0 (19.5)	5.5 (17.2)	5.7	8 ( )	7	6.0
Taiwan	6.0 (26.0)	6.5 (17.8)	8.5 (6.1)	7.5	2 ( )	6	5.4
Thailand	7.9 (18.3)	6.8 (16.8)	9.8 (1.3)	8.3	4 (33.7)	3	5.8
Turkey	4.9 (30.5)	7.2 (15.5)	9.3 (3.0)	8.3	7 (23.7)	6	6.5
Ukraine	N/A	2.5 (31.7)	N/A	2.5	0 ( )	6	2.8
United Kingdom	2.7 (39.3)	5.4 (21.8)	5.6 (16.5)	5.5	8 (14.5)	8	6.0
United States	5.0 (30.1)	6.5 (18.0)	6.5 (13.4)	6.5	10 (14.2)	8	7.4
Venezuela	5.7 (27.4)	9.0 (9.4)	7.7 (8.8)	8.4	0 (46.1)	5	4.8
Zimbabwe	4.0 (34.1)	6.3 (18.5)	N/A	6.3	2 ( )	4	4.1

Note: Area totals may not exactly equal the sum of their parts due to rounding.

TABLE 2-2 AREA II: LEGAL STRUCTURE AND SECURITY OF PROPERY RIGHTS

	II a Rule of law	II b Legal security of private ownership	II c Protection of intellectual property	II d Judicial independence	II e Legal corruption	II f Impartial courts	Total Area II
Argentina	10.0	5.8	4.0	3.2	5.0	5.2	5.5
Australia	10.0	9.0	8.2	9.5	9.9	9.7	9.4
Austria	10.0	9.4	8.9	9.0	9.5	9.0	9.3
Belgium	7.9	8.9	8.4	7.3	9.0	8.2	8.3
Bolivia	7.9	4.5	3.2	2.2	1.3	3.3	3.7
Brazil	1.7	7.0	5.8	5.5	6.2	6.2	5.4
Bulgaria	5.8	4.7	3.5	4.2	4.2	4.5	4.5
Canada	10.0	8.5	8.4	9.2	9.7	9.2	9.2
Chile	7.9	7.5	6.3	5.8	7.0	6.5	6.9
China	7.9	4.5	4.3	3.3	4.0	4.2	4.7
Colombia	1.7	6.0	4.0	3.5	5.0	5.8	4.3
Costa Rica	5.8	6.3	5.0	6.3	6.8	6.8	6.2
Czech Republic	7.9	4.7	5.0	6.0	6.2	4.5	5.7
Denmark	10.0	9.4	7.8	9.4	9.9	9.5	9.3
Ecuador	3.8	3.8	5.0	2.7	1.3	2.5	3.2
Egypt	5.8	5.5	5.0	6.8	7.5	5.7	6.1
El Salvador	3.8	5.5	4.8	4.3	3.7	4.2	4.4
Finland	10.0	9.7	8.7	9.7	10.0	8.9	9.5
France	7.9	8.5	8.5	6.3	9.0	8.0	8.1
Germany	10.0	9.2	8.5	9.4	9.7	9.2	9.3
Greece	3.8	6.7	5.2	6.3	6.8	5.7	5.7
Hong Kong	7.9	9.0	6.2	7.7	9.5	8.9	8.2
Hungary	10.0	7.2	5.8	6.5	7.5	6.3	7.2
Iceland	10.0	8.0	6.7	8.5	9.9	9.0	8.7
India	1.7	6.2	4.3	7.0	5.8	8.0	5.5
Indonesia	1.7	4.5	3.5	3.0	2.7	4.0	3.2
Ireland	10.0	8.7	6.7	8.7	9.5	9.2	8.8
Israel	7.9	8.7	6.5	9.2	9.4	9.4	8.5
Italy	10.0	7.0	7.2	4.8	7.0	5.7	7.0

	II a Rule of law	II b Legal security of private ownership	II c Protection of intellectual property	II d Judicial independence	II e Legal corruption	II f Impartial courts	Total Area II
Japan	10.0	8.0	7.3	8.0	9.2	7.0	8.3
Jordan	5.8	7.0	6.3	8.2	8.0	6.8	7.0
Korea	5.8	6.5	4.8	4.7	5.7	5.2	5.5
Luxembourg	10.0	9.7	9.0	9.7	10.0	9.7	9.7
Malaysia	3.8	7.0	5.3	4.5	6.7	6.0	5.6
Mauritius	4.1	7.2	5.0	6.2	7.8	7.0	6.2
Mexico	1.7	5.3	5.7	3.3	3.7	5.2	4.1
Netherlands	10.0	9.4	8.5	9.5	9.7	9.5	9.4
New Zealand	10.0	9.0	7.7	9.2	9.9	9.2	9.2
Norway	10.0	8.5	7.0	8.4	9.9	8.7	8.7
Peru	3.8	4.3	4.0	1.5	2.3	3.2	3.2
Philippines	5.8	5.3	4.7	4.5	3.5	5.5	4.9
Poland	7.9	4.7	4.5	5.3	6.0	5.8	5.7
Portugal	7.9	7.2	6.7	7.0	8.0	6.3	7.2
Russia	3.8	2.7	3.0	3.5	4.2	5.2	3.7
Singapore	10.0	8.9	8.2	7.3	9.7	7.7	8.6
Slovak Republic	7.9	5.2	5.5	5.0	4.5	5.2	5.6
South Africa	1.7	7.7	6.3	7.2	7.8	8.0	6.5
Spain	5.8	8.4	7.5	7.5	8.9	8.0	7.7
Sweden	10.0	8.2	7.2	8.7	9.7	8.4	8.7
Switzerland	10.0	8.9	8.7	8.7	9.5	8.5	9.0
Taiwan	5.8	7.7	6.7	5.3	6.5	5.7	6.3
Thailand	7.9	6.2	5.0	5.8	6.0	4.7	5.9
Turkey	3.8	6.5	5.5	5.3	6.8	6.5	5.7
Ukraine	5.8	2.8	2.5	3.2	3.7	3.5	3.6
United Kingdom	10.0	9.2	8.9	9.0	9.9	9.0	9.3
United States	10.0	9.0	8.9	8.0	9.2	9.0	9.0
Venezuela	5.8	3.8	2.7	1.7	2.8	3.7	3.4
Zimbabwe	5.8	4.8	5.3	6.2	7.7	7.3	6.2

Note: Area totals may not exactly equal the sum of their parts due to rounding.

TABLE 2-3   AREA III: ACCESS TO SOUND MONEY

	III a Average growth of money (last 5 years) minus growth of real GDP (last 10 years)	III b Standard deviation of annual inflation (last 5 years)	III c Annual inflation (most recent year)	III d Freedom of citizens to own foreign currency bank accounts domestically & abroad	III e Difference between official & black market exchange rates	Total Area III
Argentina	9.3 (3.6)	9.1 (2.3)	9.8 (−1.2)	10.0	10.0	9.6
Australia	8.6 (6.9)	9.5 (1.2)	9.7 (1.5)	10.0	10.0	9.6
Austria	8.8 (6.0)	9.8 (0.5)	9.9 (0.6)	10.0	10.0	9.7
Belgium	9.5 (2.7)	9.7 (0.7)	9.8 (1.1)	10.0	10.0	9.8
Bolivia	9.0 (5.0)	8.9 (2.8)	9.6 (2.2)	10.0	10.0	9.5
Brazil	0.0 (116.0)	0.0 (887.8)	9.0 (4.9)	0.0	10.0	3.8
Bulgaria	0.0 (127.2)	0.0 (35.8)	9.5 (2.6)	5.0	10.0	4.9
Canada	8.6 (7.0)	9.6 (1.0)	9.7 (1.7)	10.0	10.0	9.6
Chile	9.2 (3.9)	8.8 (3.0)	9.3 (3.3)	10.0	7.8	9.0
China	7.7 (11.5)	8.2 (4.4)	9.7 (−1.4)	0.0	10.0	7.1
Colombia	7.7 (11.3)	5.9 (10.2)	7.8 (11.2)	0.0	7.8	5.8
Costa Rica	5.1 (24.6)	6.7 (8.2)	8.0 (10.0)	10.0	10.0	8.0
Czech Republic	9.5 (−2.7)	6.4 (9.0)	9.6 (2.1)	5.0	10.0	8.1
Denmark	9.5 (2.6)	9.8 (0.4)	9.5 (2.5)	10.0	10.0	9.8
Ecuador	5.6 (22.2)	5.4 (11.5)	0.0 (52.2)	10.0	7.8	5.7
Egypt	8.6 (6.8)	9.4 (1.6)	9.4 (3.1)	10.0	10.0	9.5
El Salvador	9.5 (2.4)	8.5 (3.7)	9.9 (0.5)	10.0	7.8	9.1
Finland	8.4 (8.1)	9.3 (1.6)	9.8 (1.2)	10.0	10.0	9.5
France	8.6 (6.9)	9.7 (0.7)	9.9 (0.5)	10.0	10.0	9.7
Germany	9.1 (4.4)	9.8 (0.5)	9.9 (0.6)	10.0	10.0	9.8
Greece	7.2 (14.1)	8.6 (3.4)	9.5 (2.6)	10.0	10.0	9.1
Hong Kong	9.5 (−2.5)	8.3 (4.2)	9.2 (−4.0)	10.0	10.0	9.4
Hungary	6.9 (15.5)	6.0 (9.9)	7.9 (10.3)	5.0	10.0	7.2
Iceland	7.8 (11.1)	9.5 (1.4)	9.4 (3.2)	10.0	10.0	9.3
India	9.2 (−3.8)	9.3 (1.7)	9.1 (4.7)	0.0	10.0	7.5
Indonesia	6.9 (15.5)	6.6 (8.5)	5.9 (20.5)	10.0	7.8	7.4

	III a Average growth of money (last 5 years) minus growth of real GDP (last 10 years)		III b Standard deviation of annual inflation (last 5 years)		III c Annual inflation (most recent year)		III d Freedom of citizens to own foreign currency bank accounts domestically & abroad	III e Difference between official & black market exchange rates	Total Area III
Ireland	9.8	(1.2)	8.2	(4.5)	9.7	(1.6)	10.0	10.0	9.5
Israel	8.3	(8.3)	8.4	(3.9)	9.0	(5.2)	5.0	10.0	8.1
Italy	9.2	(3.9)	9.4	(1.6)	9.7	(1.6)	10.0	10.0	9.7
Japan	8.8	(6.0)	9.0	(2.6)	9.9	(−0.3)	10.0	10.0	9.5
Jordan	9.2	(−4.0)	9.7	(0.8)	9.1	(4.4)	10.0	10.0	9.6
Korea	8.8	(−5.8)	8.1	(4.7)	9.8	(0.8)	5.0	10.0	8.4
Luxembourg	9.3	(3.5)	9.3	(1.8)	9.8	(1.0)	10.0	10.0	9.7
Malaysia	9.4	(−2.9)	7.7	(5.8)	9.5	(2.7)	5.0	10.0	8.3
Mauritius	9.2	(4.0)	9.7	(0.8)	8.6	(6.9)	10.0	10.0	9.5
Mexico	7.4	(13.1)	4.9	(12.7)	6.7	(16.6)	5.0	10.0	6.8
Netherlands	8.8	(6.0)	9.7	(0.8)	9.6	(2.2)	10.0	10.0	9.6
New Zealand	6.8	(−15.8)	9.5	(1.2)	10.0	(−0.1)	10.0	10.0	9.3
Norway	9.6	(2.2)	9.3	(1.8)	9.5	(2.3)	10.0	10.0	9.7
Peru	3.5	(32.4)	7.3	(6.8)	9.3	(3.5)	10.0	10.0	8.0
Philippines	7.7	(11.7)	8.6	(3.5)	8.7	(6.7)	10.0	10.0	9.0
Poland	6.2	(19.2)	5.6	(11.0)	8.5	(7.3)	5.0	10.0	7.1
Portugal	8.2	(9.0)	9.6	(1.1)	9.5	(2.3)	10.0	10.0	9.5
Russia	0.0	(141.9)	0.0	(125.9)	0.0	(85.7)	5.0	1.4	1.3
Singapore	9.1	(−4.3)	9.0	(2.6)	9.9	(0.4)	10.0	10.0	9.6
Slovak Republic	9.1	(4.7)	8.7	(3.3)	7.9	(10.6)	5.0	7.8	7.7
South Africa	7.0	(15.0)	8.6	(3.6)	9.0	(5.2)	5.0	10.0	7.9
Spain	8.6	(6.8)	9.7	(0.8)	9.5	(2.3)	10.0	10.0	9.6
Sweden	9.7	(1.4)	9.7	(0.8)	9.9	(0.5)	10.0	10.0	9.9
Switzerland	8.2	(9.2)	9.7	(0.7)	9.8	(0.8)	10.0	10.0	9.5
Taiwan	9.2	(−4.0)	9.5	(1.2)	10.0	(0.2)	10.0	10.0	9.7
Thailand	9.4	(2.9)	7.6	(5.9)	9.9	(0.3)	0.0	10.0	7.4
Turkey	0.0	(76.6)	0.0	(45.2)	0.0	(64.9)	10.0	9.8	4.0
Ukraine	0.0	(106.5)	0.0	(378.2)	6.6	(17.2)	5.0	7.8	3.9

	III a Average growth of money (last 5 years) minus growth of real GDP (last 10 years)		III b Standard deviation of annual inflation (last 5 years)		III c Annual inflation (most recent year)		III d Freedom of citizens to own foreign currency bank accounts domestically & abroad	III e Difference between official & black market exchange rates	Total Area III
United Kingdom	9.6	(2.2)	9.8	(0.6)	9.7	(1.6)	10.0	10.0	9.8
United States	9.7	(−1.4)	9.5	(1.2)	9.6	(2.2)	10.0	10.0	9.8
Venezuela	0.0	(64.3)	0.0	(27.6)	5.3	(23.6)	10.0	10.0	5.1
Zimbabwe	3.9	(30.3)	7.0	(7.6)	3.6	(31.8)	5.0	7.2	5.4

Note: Area totals may not exactly equal the sum of their parts due to rounding.

TABLE 2-4 AREA IV: FREEDOM TO TRADE WITH FOREIGNERS

	IV a i Revenue from taxes on international trade (% of trade sector)	IV a ii Mean tariff rate	IV a iii Standard deviation of tariff rates	Composite Area IV a	IV b i Hidden import barriers	IV b ii Customs Administration	Composite Area IV b	IV c Costs of importing	IV d Actual versus expected size of trade sector	IV e Difference between official & black market exchange rates	Total Area IV
Argentina	7.1 (4.4)	7.3 (13.5)	7.2 (6.9)	7.2	5.7	3.6	4.7	6.7	2.0	10.0	6.1
Australia	9.0 (1.4)	9.0 (5.0)	7.3 (6.7)	8.5	8.2	6.0	7.1	9.5	5.3	10.0	8.1
Austria	9.9 (0.2)	8.9 (5.6)	7.6 (5.9)	8.8	8.9	7.0	7.9	9.5	5.4	10.0	8.3
Belgium	9.7 (0.4)	8.9 (5.6)	7.6 (5.9)	8.8	8.5	6.0	7.2	9.5	7.4	10.0	8.6
Bolivia	8.4 (2.4)	8.1 (9.7)	9.5 (1.2)	8.7	5.5	N/A	5.5	6.2	4.6	10.0	7.0
Brazil	N/A	7.1 (14.6)	7.1 (7.3)	7.1	5.2	3.3	4.3	6.7	2.5	10.0	6.1
Bulgaria	8.5 (2.2)	7.5 (12.6)	6.1 (9.1)	7.4	5.0	N/A	5.0	8.5	5.9	10.0	7.4
Canada	N/A	8.6 (7.1)	0.0 (25.7)	4.3	7.8	6.2	7.0	9.5	5.8	10.0	7.3
Chile	7.9 (3.1)	7.8 (11.0)	9.7 (0.7)	8.5	7.7	6.3	7.0	8.5	5.8	7.8	7.5
China	9.3 (1.0)	6.5 (17.5)	4.8 (13.0)	6.9	4.2	2.9	3.5	7.7	9.8	10.0	7.6
Colombia	7.8 (3.3)	7.7 (11.7)	7.5 (6.2)	7.6	5.2	3.3	4.2	7.3	3.7	7.8	6.1
Costa Rica	8.4 (2.4)	8.6 (7.2)	4.5 (13.8)	7.1	5.2	N/A	5.2	8.0	5.9	10.0	7.2
Czech Republic	9.6 (0.6)	8.6 (6.8)	5.6 (11.0)	7.9	6.7	4.7	5.7	8.5	7.4	10.0	7.9
Denmark	9.8 (0.3)	8.9 (5.6)	7.6 (5.9)	8.8	9.4	8.1	8.7	9.8	3.0	10.0	8.1
Ecuador	N/A	7.7 (11.3)	7.4 (6.4)	7.6	3.2	N/A	3.2	6.3	5.3	7.8	6.0
Egypt	5.1 (7.3)	6.1 (19.7)	N/A 5.6	5.2	N/A	N/A	5.2	6.7	4.7	10.0	6.4
El Salvador	8.5 (2.2)	8.9 (5.7)	6.8 (7.9)	8.1	6.2	N/A	6.2	8.5	2.7	7.8	6.6
Finland	9.7 (0.5)	8.9 (5.6)	7.6 (5.9)	8.7	9.2	8.1	8.6	9.8	4.6	10.0	8.4
France	9.8 (0.3)	8.9 (5.6)	7.6 (5.9)	8.8	8.0	5.9	7.0	9.2	4.8	10.0	7.9
Germany	9.7 (0.5)	8.9 (5.6)	7.6 (5.9)	8.7	8.2	6.6	7.4	9.3	5.6	10.0	8.2
Greece	9.7 (0.4)	8.9 (5.6)	7.6 (5.9)	8.8	8.2	5.7	6.9	9.5	1.4	10.0	7.3
Hong Kong	N/A	10.0 (0.0)	10.0 (0.0)	10.0	9.4	7.8	8.6	9.8	10.0	10.0	9.7
Hungary	9.2 (1.3)	7.1 (14.3)	3.2 (17.0)	6.5	7.3	5.1	6.2	8.8	6.5	10.0	7.6
Iceland	9.7 (0.5)	9.6 (1.9)	4.8 (13.0)	8.0	8.0	6.2	7.1	9.2	1.1	10.0	7.1

	IV a i Revenue from taxes on international trade (% of trade sector)	IV a ii Mean tariff rate	IV a iii Standard deviation of tariff rates	Composite Area IV a	IV b i Hidden import barriers	IV b ii Customs Administration	Composite Area IV b	IV c Costs of importing	IV d Actual versus expected size of trade sector	IV e Difference between official & black market exchange rates	Total Area IV
India	2.8 (10.8)	3.4 (32.9)	4.9 (12.7)	3.7	6.0	2.4	4.2	6.0	5.4	10.0	5.9
Indonesia	9.5 (0.7)	7.6 (11.9)	3.4 (16.6)	6.8	4.3	2.7	3.5	8.0	10.0	7.8	7.2
Ireland	9.7 (0.5)	8.6 (6.9)	7.6 (5.9)	8.6	8.5	7.7	8.1	9.7	8.2	10.0	8.9
Israel	9.8 (0.2)	9.6 (2.0)	N/A	9.7	7.7	6.1	6.9	9.3	4.0	10.0	8.0
Italy	9.8 (0.3)	8.6 (6.9)	7.6 (5.9)	8.7	8.2	5.3	6.7	9.3	4.5	10.0	7.8
Japan	9.0 (1.5)	8.7 (6.6)	6.3 (9.3)	8.0	6.0	5.4	5.7	9.3	0.0	10.0	6.6
Jordan	6.9 (4.7)	7.1 (14.4)	N/A	7.0	5.7	N/A	5.7	7.3	7.2	10.0	7.4
Korea	8.8 (1.8)	8.1 (9.4)	7.0 (7.6)	8.0	5.3	4.2	4.8	8.5	7.1	10.0	7.7
Luxembourg	9.9 (0.1)	8.9 (5.6)	7.6 (5.9)	8.8	9.7	6.9	8.3	10.0	4.8	10.0	8.4
Malaysia	8.9 (1.6)	8.2 (9.1)	2.2 (19.6)	6.4	6.7	5.0	5.8	9.2	10.0	10.0	8.3
Mauritius	6.7 (5.0)	4.2 (29.1)	0.0 (26.2)	3.6	6.7	N/A	6.7	7.0	5.0	10.0	6.5
Mexico	9.4 (0.9)	7.3 (13.3)	5.8 (10.6)	7.5	6.2	4.3	5.3	8.2	9.0	10.0	8.0
Netherlands	9.7 (0.5)	8.9 (5.6)	7.6 (5.9)	8.7	9.4	7.4	8.4	9.8	5.9	10.0	8.6
New Zealand	8.9 (1.6)	9.2 (3.8)	8.0 (5.1)	8.7	9.0	7.4	8.2	9.7	4.5	10.0	8.2
Norway	9.8 (0.3)	9.2 (4.1)	3.4 (16.5)	7.5	7.7	7.0	7.3	8.8	4.4	10.0	7.6
Peru	6.6 (5.2)	7.4 (13.2)	8.8 (2.9)	7.6	6.3	N/A	6.3	6.7	2.4	10.0	6.6
Philippines	7.6 (3.6)	8.0 (10.2)	6.1 (9.7)	7.2	4.5	2.3	3.4	7.8	10.0	10.0	7.7
Poland	8.2 (2.7)	6.5 (17.6)	0.0 (28.1)	4.9	5.8	4.4	5.1	8.7	5.5	10.0	6.8
Portugal	9.7 (0.5)	8.9 (5.6)	7.6 (5.9)	8.7	8.4	6.0	7.2	9.5	4.5	10.0	8.0
Russia	6.6 (5.1)	7.5 (12.6)	6.6 (8.4)	6.9	3.8	2.7	3.3	6.3	9.4	1.4	5.5
Singapore	9.9 (0.1)	9.9 (0.4)	9.9	9.0	8.7	8.8	10.0	10.0	10.0	9.8	
Slovak Republic	N/A	8.8 (6.0)	8.8	5.0	N/A	5.0	7.7	7.2	7.8	7.3	7.7
South Africa	9.9 (0.1)	8.6 (7.2)	6.0 (10.0)	8.2	6.7	4.4	5.6	8.5	6.4	10.0	7.7
Spain	9.7 (0.5)	8.9 (5.6)	7.6 (5.9)	8.7	8.2	5.9	7.0	9.8	5.5	10.0	8.2
Sweden	9.8 (0.3)	8.9 (5.6)	7.6 (5.9)	8.8	9.0	7.8	8.4	9.5	6.0	10.0	8.5
Switzerland	9.8 (0.3)	9.5 (2.4)	7.0 (7.4)	8.8	7.8	6.4	7.1	9.7	3.8	10.0	7.9

	IV a i Revenue from taxes on international trade (% of trade sector)	IV a ii Mean tariff rate	IV a iii Standard deviation of tariff rates	Composite Area IV a	IV b i Hidden import barriers	IV b ii Customs Admini-stration	Composite Area IV b	IV c Costs of importing	IV d Actual versus expected size of trade sector	IV e Difference between official & black market exchange rates	Total Area IV
Taiwan	9.1 (1.3)	8.1 (9.7)	5.6 (11.0)	7.6	7.7	5.2	6.4	9.3	6.3	10.0	7.9
Thailand	9.0 (1.5)	4.5 (27.6)	N/A	6.8	5.5	3.2	4.4	8.7	10.0	10.0	8.0
Turkey	9.4 (0.9)	7.3 (13.5)	0.0 (25.4)	5.6	6.5	4.7	5.6	8.3	5.9	9.8	7.0
Ukraine	N/A	8.0 (10.0)	5.6 (10.9)	6.8	4.5	N/A	4.5	7.0	8.4	7.8	6.9
United Kingdom	9.7 (0.5)	8.9 (5.6)	7.6 (5.9)	8.7	8.9	6.1	7.5	9.7	4.9	10.0	8.1
United States	9.4 (0.9)	9.0 (4.8)	5.4 (11.6)	7.9	7.7	6.0	6.8	9.5	5.0	10.0	7.9
Venezuela	6.7 (4.9)	7.6 (12.0)	7.6 (6.1)	7.3	4.3	2.1	3.2	6.5	4.1	10.0	6.2
Zimbabwe	5.1 (7.3)	5.6 (22.2)	2.9 (17.8)	4.5	5.2	N/A	5.2	6.5	8.6	7.2	6.4

Note: Area totals may not exactly equal the sum of their parts due to rounding.

TABLE 2-5   AREA V: REGULATION OF CAPITAL AND FINANCIAL MARKETS

	V a Ownership of banks	V b Competition in domestic banking	V c Extension of credit	V d Interest rate controls & regulations	V e Interest rate gap	V f Interest rate controls	V g Restrictions on citizens engaging in capital transactions with foreigners	V h Access to foreign capital markets	V i Foreign access to domestic capital markets	V j Index of capital controls	Total Area V
Argentina	5.0	8.9	6.9	10.0	1.7	8.7	10.0	9.0	9.5	3.8	7.3
Australia	10.0	7.7	9.3	10.0	4.8	7.5	8.0	9.4	9.4	5.4	8.1
Austria	8.0	7.7	7.7	10.0	5.5	7.8	8.0	9.5	9.5	6.9	8.1
Belgium	10.0	8.7	5.0	10.0	5.7	7.8	10.0	9.5	9.7	5.4	8.2
Bolivia	10.0	8.0	9.7	8.0	1.5	8.7	8.0	9.4	9.5	6.9	8.0
Brazil	5.0	7.7	6.3	8.0	1.5	5.0	0.0	6.5	8.7	0.8	4.9
Bulgaria	5.0	6.2	5.8	4.0	3.0	4.7	5.0	6.7	8.0	1.5	5.0
Canada	10.0	5.3	8.7	10.0	6.0	8.4	8.0	8.9	9.4	9.2	8.4
Chile	8.0	8.7	9.8	10.0	4.7	7.2	5.0	8.4	8.9	0.0	7.1
China	0.0	4.0	9.4	10.0	4.0	1.7	5.0	4.0	5.0	0.8	4.4
Colombia	8.0	7.2	8.5	8.0	1.8	5.7	5.0	7.2	8.0	0.8	6.0
Costa Rica	10.0	6.2	8.4	8.0	1.8	3.8	10.0	9.5	9.2	10.0	7.7
Czech Republic	2.0	7.2	8.2	8.0	3.5	6.5	8.0	4.8	8.2	4.6	6.1
Denmark	10.0	8.4	8.9	10.0	4.8	9.0	10.0	9.5	9.5	8.5	8.9
Ecuador	2.0	4.7	7.8	6.0	1.3	2.5	8.0	7.5	7.7	5.4	5.3
Egypt	5.0	5.2	7.3	10.0	4.3	4.2	5.0	9.2	8.7	5.4	6.4
El Salvador	N/A	5.5	9.7	10.0	2.8	6.7	8.0	9.0	8.7	9.2	7.7
Finland	8.0	9.2	8.7	10.0	5.8	8.9	8.0	9.9	9.9	6.2	8.4
France	10.0	7.2	7.1	10.0	5.5	6.3	5.0	8.5	9.0	6.9	7.6
Germany	5.0	8.0	7.4	10.0	6.0	9.0	10.0	9.7	9.7	9.2	8.4
Greece	5.0	7.5	5.6	10.0	2.0	5.2	8.0	8.4	9.5	8.5	7.0
Hong Kong	10.0	8.7	9.1	10.0	4.0	6.8	10.0	9.9	9.9	9.2	8.8
Hungary	8.0	7.8	6.9	10.0	2.5	7.0	5.0	7.0	8.9	1.5	6.5
Iceland	5.0	6.8	9.8	8.0	3.2	6.5	8.0	9.5	7.3	5.4	7.0
India	2.0	6.8	5.9	8.0	2.3	4.0	0.0	1.5	6.7	0.0	3.7

	V a Ownership of banks	V b Competition in domestic banking	V c Extension of credit	V d Interest rate controls & regulations	V e Interest rate gap	V f Interest rate controls	V g Restrictions on citizens engaging in capital transactions with foreigners	V h Access to foreign capital markets	V i Foreign access to domestic capital markets	V j Index of capital controls	Total Area V
Indonesia	5.0	7.0	3.8	8.0	1.8	4.0	0.0	8.7	8.9	1.5	4.9
Ireland	8.0	8.4	9.3	8.0	4.2	8.4	8.0	8.9	9.2	8.5	8.1
Israel	0.0	4.7	8.3	10.0	4.0	5.3	8.0	8.7	9.4	6.2	6.5
Italy	5.0	5.3	7.4	10.0	3.3	6.0	10.0	9.4	9.4	7.7	7.4
Japan	5.0	6.7	8.4	8.0	5.0	6.2	8.0	8.7	8.9	7.7	7.2
Jordan	5.0	5.7	8.6	10.0	2.8	4.3	2.0	9.2	8.9	6.9	6.3
Korea	5.0	6.7	9.4	10.0	3.2	4.0	8.0	6.0	8.0	1.5	6.2
Luxembourg	10.0	9.0	5.8	10.0	7.3	9.4	10.0	9.7	9.7	9.2	9.0
Malaysia	5.0	4.2	9.3	10.0	4.3	3.2	2.0	5.8	7.8	0.8	5.3
Mauritius	8.0	6.7	7.8	8.0	3.8	5.2	10.0	8.4	7.7	6.9	7.2
Mexico	8.0	7.0	3.7	4.0	2.2	6.7	5.0	8.5	8.9	2.3	5.6
Netherlands	10.0	8.9	8.0	10.0	6.2	8.4	10.0	9.9	9.7	9.2	9.0
New Zealand	10.0	9.4	9.4	10.0	4.5	8.5	8.0	9.5	9.4	8.5	8.7
Norway	8.0	7.3	9.2	10.0	4.5	7.3	8.0	9.2	9.2	6.9	8.0
Peru	8.0	7.7	8.9	8.0	1.3	8.2	10.0	9.0	9.0	8.5	7.9
Philippines	8.0	7.0	7.5	10.0	2.5	6.5	5.0	8.4	7.8	0.8	6.4
Poland	2.0	6.2	5.4	10.0	3.8	4.2	5.0	4.5	7.0	0.8	4.9
Portugal	5.0	8.0	9.3	10.0	5.0	8.4	8.0	9.4	9.4	6.9	7.9
Russia	2.0	4.0	4.6	2.0	3.5	4.8	2.0	4.7	7.0	0.0	3.5
Singapore	10.0	7.0	8.1	10.0	5.2	7.2	10.0	9.2	8.9	6.2	8.2
Slovak Republic	2.0	6.3	5.3	10.0	4.0	6.2	5.0	4.8	7.3	2.3	5.3
South Africa	10.0	7.3	9.1	10.0	3.3	6.3	2.0	5.0	9.0	0.8	6.3
Spain	8.0	8.2	7.6	10.0	5.2	7.5	8.0	9.2	9.5	3.8	7.7
Sweden	8.0	8.2	9.0	10.0	4.7	7.8	8.0	9.2	9.5	5.4	8.0
Switzerland	5.0	8.0	9.2	10.0	7.0	8.5	10.0	9.9	9.5	8.5	8.6
Taiwan	2.0	7.8	8.1	10.0	5.3	6.7	5.0	7.7	6.7	N/A	6.6
Thailand	8.0	7.3	9.3	10.0	2.2	6.3	2.0	4.8	8.0	2.3	6.0

	V a Ownership of banks	V b Competition in domestic banking	V c Extension of credit	V d Interest rate controls & regulations	V e Interest rate gap	V f Interest rate controls	V g Restrictions on citizens engaging in capital transactions with foreigners	V h Access to foreign capital markets	V i Foreign access to domestic capital markets	V j Index of capital controls	Total Area V
Turkey	8.0	7.3	5.3	8.0	2.7	7.2	2.0	9.0	9.2	2.3	6.1
Ukraine	0.0	4.3	7.7	6.0	2.0	5.3	2.0	4.5	7.5	0.8	4.0
United Kingdom	10.0	9.4	N/A	10.0	5.7	8.2	10.0	9.5	9.7	8.5	9.0
United States	10.0	8.2	9.2	10.0	6.3	8.5	8.0	9.5	9.5	6.9	8.6
Venezuela	8.0	7.3	8.3	2.0	1.0	5.8	5.0	9.2	9.2	6.9	6.3
Zimbabwe	5.0	5.8	7.3	6.0	1.3	5.5	2.0	2.5	8.0	1.5	4.5

Note: Area totals may not exactly equal the sum of their parts due to rounding.

TABLE 2-6 AREA VI: REGULATION OF LABOR MARKETS

	VI a Impact of minimum wage	VI b Hiring & firing practices	VI c Share of labor force with wages set by centralized collective bargaining	VI d Top marginal tax rate	VI e Unemployment insurance	VI f Use of conscripts	Total Area VI
Argentina	7.5	3.5	2.0	8 (35.0)	6.0	10	6.2
Australia	3.0	3.3	2.0	3 (47.0)	4.7	10	4.3
Austria	4.0	2.7	0.0	4 (50.0)	5.2	3	3.1
Belgium	3.0	1.8	0.0	1 (58–64)	2.7	10	3.1
Bolivia	8.4	5.0	10.0	10 (13.0)	5.5	3	7.0
Brazil	7.2	4.0	2.0	8 (27.5)	6.0	3	5.0
Bulgaria	8.0	5.8	N/A	5 (40.0)	6.8	3	5.7
Canada	3.5	5.5	8.0	3 (44–54)	4.8	10	5.8
Chile	6.0	3.2	10.0	4 (45.0)	6.5	0	4.9
China	7.0	4.0	5	4 (45.0)	6.2	0	4.4
Colombia	6.2	3.0	N/A	7 (35.0)	5.5	1	4.5
Costa Rica	5.5	4.3	N/A	9 (25.0)	6.5	10	7.1
Czech Republic	5.8	5.2	2.0	5 (40.0)	5.0	3	4.3
Denmark	2.5	5.7	2.0	1 (59–60)	4.0	3	3.0
Ecuador	7.7	3.8	N/A	10 (0.0)	3.7	3	5.6
Egypt	6.7	3.7	10.0	4 (42.0)	5.3	0	4.9
El Salvador	6.5	4.5	8.0	8 (30.0)	5.5	3	5.9
Finland	5.0	3.7	0.0	2 (54–60)	2.8	3	2.8
France	2.5	2.3	0.0	2 (54.4)	3.2	3	2.2
Germany	3.7	1.7	0.0	0 (66–68)	2.5	3	1.8
Greece	5.3	3.0	0.0	5 (45.0)	6.3	0	3.3
Hong Kong	7.5	7.2	10.0	10 (17.0)	7.7	10	8.7
Hungary	7.0	4.2	2	5 (40.0)	5.8	3	4.5
Iceland	7.2	6.8	0	4 (42.0)	7.0	10	5.8
India	6.0	2.3	5.0	8 (30.0)	5.3	10	6.1
Indonesia	5.8	4.2	N/A	8 (30.0)	5.8	0	4.8

	VI a Impact of minimum wage	VI b Hiring & firing practices	VI c Share of labor force with wages set by centralized collective bargaining	VI d Top marginal tax rate		VI e Unemployment insurance	VI f Use of conscripts	Total Area VI
Ireland	4.8	2.8	5.0	3	(46.0)	5.3	10	5.2
Israel	4.0	5.7	2.0	4	(50.0)	5.5	0	3.5
Italy	4.7	1.8	0.0	3	(50.3)	4.8	3	2.9
Japan	5.2	4.3	10.0	2	(65.0)	6.8	10	6.4
Jordan	7.2	5.2	10	N/A		6.5	10	7.8
Korea, South	6.3	5.0	8.0	5	(44.0)	6.0	0	5.1
Luxembourg	3.0	3.0	2.0	4	(48.5)	5.0	10	4.5
Malaysia	5.3	3.3	10.0	8	(30.0)	7.0	10	7.3
Mauritius	4.7	1.8	N/A	8	(30.0)	5.8	10	6.1
Mexico	7.7	4.3	8.0	7	(40.0)	6.5	5	6.4
Netherlands	2.8	3.0	0.0	2	(60.0)	4.5	10	3.7
New Zealand	4.3	3.3	10.0	7	(33.0)	4.8	10	6.6
Norway	3.8	2.5	2.0	5	(41.5)	4.8	3	3.5
Peru	8.0	4.7	10.0	8	(30.0)	5.5	0	6.0
Philippines	5.2	4.5	8	7	(33.0)	5.7	10	6.7
Poland	5.5	4.2	2.0	5	(40.0)	4.8	3	4.1
Portugal	5.5	2.8	2.0	5	(40.0)	5.5	3	4.0
Russia	9.0	6.7	8.0	0	(61.0)	5.5	0	4.9
Singapore	4.7	7.5	10.0	9	(28.0)	7.5	0	6.5
Slovak Republic	6.5	4.8	2	4	(54.6)	4.8	3	4.2
South Africa	4.7	2.0	5.0	4	(45.0)	6.2	10	5.3
Spain	5.8	2.8	2.0	4	(48.0)	5.0	3	3.8
Sweden	3.7	1.5	0.0	2	(56.0)	3.5	3	2.3
Switzerland	5.8	6.3	5.0	8	(31–40)	5.5	5	6.0
Taiwan	5.0	5.3	10.0	7	(40.0)	6.2	0	5.6
Thailand	5.0	5.3	10	7	(37.0)	6.5	10	7.3
Turkey	6.5	5.3	8	7	(40.0)	6.2	1	5.7

	VI a Impact of minimum wage	VI b Hiring & firing practices	VI c Share of labor force with wages set by centralized collective bargaining	VI d Top marginal tax rate	VI e Unemployment insurance	VI f Use of conscripts	Total Area VI
Ukraine	8.5	6.3	10	4	(42.5)	5.3	1	5.9
United Kingdom	5.0	4.0	5.0	6	(40.0)	6.5	10	6.1
United States	4.0	6.0	9.0	5	(42–49)	7.0	10	6.8
Venezuela	7.2	3.5	8	7	(34.0)	5.7	0	5.2
Zimbabwe	6.5	3.2	0	3	(50.0)	6.8	10	4.9

Note: Area totals may not exactly equal the sum of their parts due to rounding.

TABLE 2-7 AREA VII: FREEDOM TO OPERATE AND COMPETE IN BUSINESS

	VII a Administrative conditions & new businesses	VII b Time with government bureaucracy	VII c Starting a new business	VII d Local competition	VII e Irregular payments	VII f Bank credit for business	Total Area VII
Argentina	4.8	5.7	4.7	5.7	5.0	2.4	4.7
Australia	6.8	8.3	7.3	7.0	8.9	8.2	7.8
Austria	4.0	8.0	4.7	7.3	8.4	7.7	6.7
Belgium	5.2	8.3	6.3	7.2	7.2	7.3	6.9
Bolivia	5.5	5.7	4.0	4.5	3.0	N/A	4.5
Brazil	4.5	6.3	5.0	6.3	5.2	3.2	5.1
Bulgaria	3.5	6.0	2.7	5.0	4.7	N/A	4.4
Canada	6.5	8.3	7.0	7.3	8.7	7.2	7.5
Chile	5.2	8.3	5.8	7.7	8.7	6.2	7.0
China	5.5	5.3	5.3	7.8	4.8	2.5	5.2
Colombia	5.2	7.0	3.8	5.5	5.3	2.1	4.8
Costa Rica	4.8	6.7	4.3	6.5	5.2	N/A	5.5
Czech Republic	5.2	8.3	5.3	6.8	5.0	4.0	5.8
Denmark	5.2	8.7	6.5	7.3	9.2	8.0	7.5
Ecuador	3.3	7.7	3.3	4.0	3.5	N/A	4.4
Egypt	5.5	6.7	5.8	6.5	4.7	N/A	5.8
El Salvador	5.2	6.0	4.7	6.5	5.2	N/A	5.5
Finland	7.3	9.7	7.2	6.7	9.7	8.7	8.2
France	3.0	7.0	4.3	7.5	8.0	6.5	6.1
Germany	5.0	8.3	5.8	8.0	8.4	7.4	7.2
Greece	5.2	7.0	5.8	6.8	5.0	5.1	5.8
Hong Kong	8.7	8.3	8.9	7.5	9.0	6.8	8.2
Hungary	6.3	8.0	7.0	7.0	6.5	4.5	6.6
Iceland	7.7	8.7	8.4	6.5	8.7	7.6	7.9
India	4.8	6.3	5.0	7.0	3.3	4.6	5.2
Indonesia	4.2	5.3	6.5	5.7	3.8	2.3	4.6
Ireland	7.7	8.0	6.8	6.8	8.2	7.6	7.5
Israel	7.0	8.3	7.0	6.5	7.8	7.0	7.3
Italy	2.7	6.7	5.0	6.5	6.0	4.7	5.3

	VII a Administrative conditions & new businesses	VII b Time with government bureaucracy	VII c Starting a new business	VII d Local competition	VII e Irregular payments	VII f Bank credit for business	Total Area VII
Japan	5.0	9.0	5.3	7.3	8.4	4.0	6.5
Jordan	6.3	6.3	6.7	6.7	6.0	N/A	6.4
Korea	4.0	8.3	5.7	6.0	5.3	4.5	5.6
Luxembourg	7.3	9.3	8.0	5.3	9.7	7.3	7.8
Malaysia	5.8	8.3	6.7	6.0	6.0	5.8	6.4
Mauritius	4.3	7.0	5.7	5.7	4.8	N/A	5.5
Mexico	3.5	6.7	4.2	5.7	4.5	1.8	4.4
Netherlands	6.8	8.3	7.3	7.8	8.9	8.4	7.9
New Zealand	7.0	9.0	7.3	6.8	9.2	6.8	7.7
Norway	5.8	8.7	6.7	6.0	8.2	8.1	7.3
Peru	5.3	6.7	4.0	6.5	5.3	N/A	5.6
Philippines	4.7	7.3	5.8	6.2	2.8	4.2	5.2
Poland	5.0	6.3	5.7	6.5	4.8	5.5	5.7
Portugal	4.5	6.7	5.0	6.8	7.2	6.7	6.2
Russia	3.3	4.3	3.5	4.8	2.0	1.8	3.3
Singapore	8.2	8.7	8.2	6.5	9.0	7.9	8.1
Slovak Republic	5.7	5.7	5.0	5.3	4.2	N/A	5.2
South Africa	6.2	7.7	6.5	6.2	6.2	6.0	6.4
Spain	5.0	8.0	5.5	7.8	8.5	7.1	7.0
Sweden	5.8	8.7	7.0	6.2	8.9	8.2	7.5
Switzerland	6.7	9.0	6.3	7.0	8.7	6.2	7.3
Taiwan	7.0	7.7	7.5	7.0	7.5	6.5	7.2
Thailand	5.5	7.7	6.5	6.5	4.0	2.3	5.4
Turkey	6.0	6.3	7.2	6.8	5.3	3.9	5.9
Ukraine	4.2	6.0	3.7	4.8	3.3	N/A	4.4
United Kingdom	7.5	9.3	7.3	7.3	9.0	6.5	7.8
United States	7.5	8.3	8.2	8.2	8.5	8.4	8.2
Venezuela	4.2	6.3	3.5	3.8	4.2	3.3	4.2
Zimbabwe	4.8	6.3	5.0	4.5	4.2	N/A	5.0

Note: Area totals may not exactly equal the sum of their parts due to rounding.

TABLE 2-8 SUMMARY INDEX AND AREA COMPONENTS

	Area I	Area II	Area III	Area IV	Area V	Area VI	Area VII	Summary Index
Argentina	7.6	5.5	9.6	6.1	7.3	6.2	4.7	6.7
Australia	6.3	9.4	9.6	8.1	8.1	4.3	7.8	7.7
Austria	4.0	9.3	9.7	8.3	8.1	3.1	6.7	7.0
Belgium	4.0	8.3	9.8	8.6	8.2	3.1	6.9	7.0
Bolivia	6.5	3.7	9.5	7.0	8.0	7.0	4.5	6.6
Brazil	5.4	5.4	3.8	6.1	4.9	5.0	5.1	5.1
Bulgaria	4.5	4.5	4.9	7.4	5.0	5.7	4.4	5.2
Canada	6.5	9.2	9.6	7.3	8.4	5.8	7.5	7.8
Chile	7.4	6.9	9.0	7.5	7.1	4.9	7.0	7.1
China	2.9	4.7	7.1	7.6	4.4	4.4	5.2	5.2
Colombia	6.1	4.3	5.8	6.1	6.0	4.5	4.8	5.4
Costa Rica	6.6	6.2	8.0	7.2	7.7	7.1	5.5	6.9
Czech Republic	3.6	5.7	8.1	7.9	6.1	4.3	5.8	5.9
Denmark	4.0	9.3	9.8	8.1	8.9	3.0	7.5	7.2
Ecuador	7.0	3.2	5.7	6.0	5.3	5.6	4.4	5.3
Egypt	4.5	6.1	9.5	6.4	6.4	4.9	5.8	6.2
El Salvador	8.3	4.4	9.1	6.6	7.7	5.9	5.5	6.8
Finland	4.9	9.5	9.5	8.4	8.4	2.8	8.2	7.4
France	3.6	8.1	9.7	7.9	7.6	2.2	6.1	6.4
Germany	4.9	9.3	9.8	8.2	8.4	1.8	7.2	7.1
Greece	4.8	5.7	9.1	7.3	7.0	3.3	5.8	6.1
Hong Kong	8.5	8.2	9.4	9.7	8.8	8.7	8.2	8.8
Hungary	4.7	7.2	7.2	7.6	6.5	4.5	6.6	6.3
Iceland	6.3	8.7	9.3	7.1	7.0	5.8	7.9	7.4
India	4.9	5.5	7.5	5.9	3.7	6.1	5.2	5.6
Indonesia	6.1	3.2	7.4	7.2	4.9	4.8	4.6	5.5
Ireland	7.3	8.8	9.5	8.9	8.1	5.2	7.5	7.9
Israel	2.7	8.5	8.1	8.0	6.5	3.5	7.3	6.4
Italy	4.2	7.0	9.7	7.8	7.4	2.9	5.3	6.3
Japan	5.6	8.3	9.5	6.6	7.2	6.4	6.5	7.2

	Area I	Area II	Area III	Area IV	Area V	Area VI	Area VII	Summary Index
Jordan	3.0	7.0	9.6	7.4	6.3	7.8	6.4	6.8
Korea, South	5.3	5.5	8.4	7.7	6.2	5.1	5.6	6.2
Luxembourg	4.9	9.7	9.7	8.4	9.0	4.5	7.8	7.7
Malaysia	4.5	5.6	8.3	8.3	5.3	7.3	6.4	6.5
Mauritius	6.6	6.2	9.5	6.5	7.2	6.1	5.5	6.8
Mexico	7.5	4.1	6.8	8.0	5.6	6.4	4.4	6.1
Netherlands	5.6	9.4	9.6	8.6	9.0	3.7	7.9	7.7
New Zealand	7.2	9.2	9.3	8.2	8.7	6.6	7.7	8.1
Norway	4.2	8.7	9.7	7.6	8.0	3.5	7.3	7.0
Peru	8.2	3.2	8.0	6.6	7.9	6.0	5.6	6.5
Philippines	6.3	4.9	9.0	7.7	6.4	6.7	5.2	6.6
Poland	3.2	5.7	7.1	6.8	4.9	4.1	5.7	5.4
Portugal	4.7	7.2	9.5	8.0	7.9	4.0	6.2	6.8
Russia	3.5	3.7	1.3	5.5	3.5	4.9	3.3	3.7
Singapore	7.7	8.6	9.6	9.8	8.2	6.5	8.1	8.3
Slovak Republic	2.8	5.6	7.7	7.3	5.3	4.2	5.2	5.4
South Africa	6.2	6.5	7.9	7.7	6.3	5.3	6.4	6.6
Spain	4.5	7.7	9.6	8.2	7.7	3.8	7.0	6.9
Sweden	4.2	8.7	9.9	8.5	8.0	2.3	7.5	7.0
Switzerland	6.0	9.0	9.5	7.9	8.6	6.0	7.3	7.8
Taiwan	5.4	6.3	9.7	7.9	6.6	5.6	7.2	7.0
Thailand	5.8	5.9	7.4	8.0	6.0	7.3	5.4	6.6
Turkey	6.5	5.7	4.0	7.0	6.1	5.7	5.9	5.9
Ukraine	2.8	3.6	3.9	6.9	4.0	5.9	4.4	4.5
United Kingdom	6.0	9.3	9.8	8.1	9.0	6.1	7.8	8.0
United States	7.4	9.0	9.8	7.9	8.6	6.8	8.2	8.2
Venezuela	4.8	3.4	5.1	6.2	6.3	5.2	4.2	5.0
Zimbabwe	4.1	6.2	5.4	6.4	4.5	4.9	5.0	5.2

Note: Area totals may not exactly equal the sum of their parts due to rounding.

TABLE 2-9 SUMMARY INDEX AND AREA COMPONENT RANKINGS

	Area I	Area II	Area III	Area IV	Area V	Area VI	Area VII	Summary Index
Hong Kong	1	21	28	2	5	1	1	1
Singapore	4	17	13	1	12	10	4	2
United States	7	11	2	21	7	7	1	3
New Zealand	10	9	29	11	6	9	10	4
United Kingdom	23	5	2	14	1	14	7	5
Ireland	9	13	20	3	14	28	11	6
Canada	14	9	13	36	9	21	11	7
Switzerland	23	11	20	21	7	17	15	7
Luxembourg	31	1	7	7	1	37	7	9
Netherlands	26	3	13	4	1	47	5	9
Australia	17	3	13	14	14	41	7	9
Finland	31	2	20	7	9	55	1	12
Iceland	17	14	29	41	31	21	5	12
Denmark	47	5	2	14	4	53	11	14
Japan	26	19	20	46	28	11	25	14
Chile	7	28	33	33	30	32	20	16
Germany	31	5	2	11	9	58	18	16
Austria	47	5	7	9	14	51	23	18
Belgium	47	19	2	4	12	51	22	18
Norway	43	14	7	30	17	48	15	18
Sweden	43	14	1	6	17	56	11	18
Taiwan	28	30	7	21	33	25	18	18
Costa Rica	12	31	39	39	22	5	38	23
Spain	39	23	13	11	22	46	20	23
El Salvador	2	49	31	46	22	19	38	25
Jordan	53	26	13	34	38	2	26	25
Mauritius	12	31	20	49	28	14	38	25
Portugal	37	24	20	17	20	45	29	25
Argentina	5	42	13	53	27	13	50	29
Bolivia	14	52	20	42	17	6	52	30

	Area I	Area II	Area III	Area IV	Area V	Area VI	Area VII	Summary Index
Philippines	17	46	33	27	36	8	43	30
South Africa	20	29	41	27	38	27	26	30
Thailand	25	35	44	17	44	3	41	30
Malaysia	39	40	36	9	47	3	26	34
Peru	3	56	39	46	20	17	36	34
France	50	22	7	21	25	57	30	36
Israel	57	18	37	17	34	48	15	36
Hungary	37	24	46	30	34	37	24	38
Italy	43	26	7	7	26	54	42	38
Egypt	39	34	20	20	36	32	32	40
Korea	30	42	35	35	41	30	36	40
Greece	35	36	31	31	31	50	32	42
Mexico	6	51	49	49	46	11	53	42
Czech Republic	50	36	37	37	42	41	32	44
Turkey	14	36	55	55	42	23	31	44
India	31	42	43	43	57	14	43	46
Indonesia	21	56	44	44	51	36	51	47
Colombia	21	50	50	50	44	37	49	48
Poland	57	36	47	47	53	44	35	48
Slovak Republic	55	40	42	42	47	43	43	48
Ecuador	11	56	51	51	47	25	53	51
Bulgaria	39	48	54	54	50	23	53	52
China	54	47	47	47	55	40	43	52
Zimbabwe	46	31	52	52	54	32	48	52
Brazil	28	45	57	57	51	31	47	55
Venezuela	35	55	53	53	38	28	57	56
Ukraine	55	54	56	56	56	19	53	57
Russia	52	52	58	58	58	32	58	58

Note: Italics are used to denote a tied ranking.

TABLE 2-10 COMPARISON OF AREA VI AND LABOR MARKET FLEXIBILITY RANKINGS AND RATINGS

	Area VI Index		Labor Market flexibility index[1]		Rank difference[3]	Rating difference[4]
	Rank	Rating[2]	Rank	Rating[2]		
Argentina*	13	6.2	32	4.8	−19	+1.4
Australia	41	4.3	48	3.3	−7	+1.0
Austria	51	3.1	51	3.0	0	+0.1
Belgium	51	3.1	58	1.9	−7	+1.2
Bolivia	6	7.0	5	7.2	+1	−0.2
Brazil	31	5.0	32	4.8	−1	+0.2
Bulgaria*	23	5.7	8	6.9	+15	−1.2
Canada	21	5.8	25	5.5	−4	+0.3
Chile*	32	4.9	15	6.4	+17	−1.5
China*	40	4.4	23	5.6	+17	−1.2
Colombia	37	4.5	31	4.9	+6	−0.4
Costa Rica*	5.0	7.1	25	5.5	−20	+1.6
Czech Republic	41	4.3	36	4.5	+5	−0.2
Denmark	53	3.0	47	3.5	+6	−0.5
Ecuador	25	5.6	29	5.1	−4	+0.5
Egypt*	32	4.9	15	6.4	+17	−1.5
El Salvador	19	5.9	19	6.1	0	−0.2
Finland	55	2.8	52	2.9	+3	−0.1
France	57	2.2	56	2.0	+1	+0.2
Germany	58	1.8	56	2.0	+2	−0.2
Greece	50	3.3	46	3.7	+4	−0.4
Hong Kong	1	8.7	1	8.1	0	+0.6
Hungary	37	4.5	32	4.8	+5	−0.3
Iceland	21	5.8	27	5.3	−6	+0.5
India*	14	6.1	35	4.7	−21	+1.4
Indonesia	36	4.8	27	5.3	+9	−0.5
Ireland	28	5.2	36	4.5	−8	+0.7
Israel	48	3.5	40	4.3	+8	−0.8
Italy	54	2.9	53	2.8	+1	+0.1
Japan	11	6.4	10	6.6	+1	−0.2
Jordan	2	7.8	5	7.2	+3	+0.6

	Area VI Index		Labor Market flexibility index[1]		Rank difference[3]	Rating difference[4]
	Rank	Rating[2]	Rank	Rating[2]		
Korea*	30	5.1	18	6.3	+12	−1.2
Luxembourg*	37	4.5	48	3.3	−11	+1.2
Malaysia	3	7.3	15	6.4	−12	+0.9
Mauritius*	14	6.1	41	4.1	−27	+2.0
Mexico	11	6.4	10	6.6	+1	−0.2
Netherlands	47	3.7	54	2.6	−7	+1.1
New Zealand	9	6.6	23	5.6	−14	+1.0
Norway	48	3.5	48	3.3	0	+0.2
Peru*	17	6.0	7	7.1	+10	−1.1
Philippines	8	6.7	21	5.8	−13	+0.9
Poland	44	4.1	41	4.1	+3	0.0
Portugal	45	4.0	44	4.0	+1	0.0
Russia*	32	4.9	4	7.3	+28	−2.4
Singapore	10	6.5	3	7.4	+7	−0.9
Slovak Republic	43	4.2	36	4.5	+7	−0.3
South Africa	27	5.3	36	4.5	−9	+0.8
Spain	46	3.8	45	3.9	+1	−0.1
Sweden	56	2.3	55	2.2	+1	+0.1
Switzerland	17	6.0	22	5.7	−5	+0.3
Taiwan	25	5.6	10	6.6	+15	−1.0
Thailand	3	7.3	9	6.7	−6	+0.6
Turkey	23	5.7	13	6.5	+10	−0.8
United Kingdom	14	6.1	29	5.1	−15	+1.0
Ukraine*	19	5.9	2	7.6	+17	−1.7
United States	7	6.8	13	6.5	−6	+0.3
Venezuela	28	5.2	19	6.1	+9	−0.9
Zimbabwe	32	4.9	41	4.1	−9	+0.8

Note * Indicates either that a country's index rank differs (+ or −) by more than 10 positions and that its index rating differs (+ or −) by more than 1.0.
Note 1: Labor market flexibility index includes components a, b, c, and e of Area 6
Note 2: The mean value of both indices was 5.1
Note 3: Area 6 index ranking minus labor market flexibility index ranking
Note 4: Area 6 index rating minus labor market flexibility index rating.

CHAPTER 3: TRADE OPENNESS, INCOME LEVELS, AND ECONOMIC GROWTH, 1980–1998

by James Gwartney, Charles Skipton, and Robert Lawson[1]

Governments often restrict the freedom of their citizens to trade with foreigners. Tariffs, quotas, licenses, marketing restrictions, exchange rate controls, and regulations that limit the movement of capital are some of the policies that retard voluntary exchange across national boundaries. Such policies reduce economic freedom. This chapter develops a measure of cross-country differences in the freedom of individuals to engage in international exchange.

Economic theory indicates that with freedom of exchange individuals will be able to produce a larger output and achieve a higher income level than would otherwise be possible. Other things constant, one would expect that individuals will attain higher levels of income when they live in countries with greater freedom of international exchange. Freedom of international exchange also promotes entrepreneurial and innovative activities that are the engine of economic growth. This chapter will investigate the linkage between the openness of international trade on the one hand and income levels and growth rates on the other.

The chapter will also analyze the changes in openness during the last two decades. Have trade barriers been rising or falling? Which countries have reduced their trade barriers the most? Which have experienced the largest increases in trade as a share of the economy? The final section will provide answers to these questions.

CONSTRUCTION OF A TRADE OPENNESS INDEX (TOI)

The Trade Openness Index (TOI) is designed to measure the degree to which policies interfere with international exchange. The TOI has four general components: (a) tariff rates, (b) the black-market exchange rate premium, (c) restrictions on capital movements, and (d) the actual size of the trade sector compared to the expected size.

Tariff data were obtained for various years during the 1980 to 1998 period. Three factors were incorporated into the tariff rating: the level of taxes on international trade as a share of the trade sector, the mean tariff rate, and the standard deviation of tariff rates. Higher ratings were assigned to countries with smaller revenues from taxes on international trade as a share of the trade sector, lower mean tariff rates, and a smaller standard de-

viation of tariffs. The data for each of these three dimensions were transformed to a scale from 0 to 10 that reflects the actual data.[2]

When countries impose exchange rate controls and thereby restrict the convertibility of the domestic currency, a black market will emerge for foreign exchange. The size of the black-market exchange-rate premium is indicative of the restrictiveness of the exchange rate controls. Thus, countries with higher black-market premiums were assigned lower ratings.[3]

Capital market restrictions will also reduce the volume of international exchange. Descriptive information on capital markets supplied by the International Monetary Fund was used to place countries in various categories and assign ratings from 0 to 10. The greater the restrictions on capital movements into and out of the country, the lower the country's rating.[4]

Factors other than trade policy will influence the size of a country's trade sector. The larger a country in terms of population and geographic size, the greater the opportunity for realization of economies of scale within the domestic market. This suggests countries that are more populous and cover a larger geographic area are likely to have less international trade as a share of their economy. Countries with a lengthy coastline may have lower transport costs that will enhance their volume of international trade. Location relative to concentrations of world demand may also influence the size of a country's trade sector. In order to account for this factor, we developed a Distance Adjusted Demand Scalar (DADS) that measures the relative distance of each country from the distribution of world demand.[5]

The population, geographic size, miles of coastline, and DADS variables were incorporated into a regression equation and used to derive the expected size of the trade sector for the countries of the Economic Freedom Index. The regression was run across time periods and dummy variables were used to adjust for general changes in trade as a share of GDP through time. The country's actual trade sector was then compared with the expected size. A large actual size of the trade sector relative to the expected size would suggest that trade barriers are small. Thus, the larger the actual size relative to the expected, the higher the rating for this component.

The ratings for each of these four components–tariffs, black-market exchange premiums, capital market restrictions, and the actual size of the trade sector relative to the expected–were averaged and used to derive a Trade Openness Index (TOI) for various years during the period from 1980 to 1998. In order to achieve a high TOI rating a country must have low (and relatively uniform) tariffs, a convertible currency, few restrictions on the mobility of capital, and a large trade sector (given its size and location). Each of these factors imply greater freedom to trade with foreigners. Thus, higher TOI ratings are indicative of greater freedom of exchange across national boundaries.

THE TRADE OPENNESS INDEX (1998)

It was possible to derive the TOI for 109 countries in 1998. Exhibit 3-1 presents these ratings ranked from high to low. Table 3-1 of the appendix to this chapter presents the underlying data and ratings for each of the four components.

In 1998, the highest ranked countries were Hong Kong, Singapore, Estonia, Belgium, Ireland, Netherlands, Germany, Luxembourg, and United Kingdom. The TOI indicates that the trade policies of these countries were the most open in the world at that time. At the other end of the spectrum, the trade policies of Myanmar, Sierra Leone, Iran, Burundi, Algeria, Syria, Papua New Guinea, Bangladesh, Croatia, and Albania were the least open in 1998.

THE ECONOMICS OF LONG TERM OPENNESS

Current trade policy may be a misleading indicator of openness over a more lengthy period. The structure of trade policy over a long time period is vitally important. It takes time for markets to adjust to changes in the openness of an economy. It also takes time for a change in policy to acquire credibility. Initially, decision makers may be unsure whether a policy change is temporary or permanent. Until credibility is acquired, the response of traders, entrepreneurs, investors, and other decision makers will be limited.

As policies of openness are maintained over a lengthy time period, decision makers will eventually be convinced that the more liberal policies can be counted on to persist in the future. As this happens, trade will expand and the laws of economics will come into play. Resources will move toward the production of goods and services that

Exhibit 3-1: Trade Openness Index (1998)

Hong Kong	1	10.0
Singapore	1	10.0
Estonia	3	9.4
Belgium	4	9.0
Ireland	5	8.7
Netherlands	5	8.7
Germany	7	8.6
Luxembourg	8	8.4
UK	8	8.4
Costa Rica	10	8.3
Czech Rep.	10	8.3
Italy	10	8.3
Korea, South	10	8.3
Nicaragua	14	8.2
Sweden	14	8.2
Philippines	16	8.1
Spain	16	8.1
Switzerland	16	8.1
Austria	19	8.0
Lithuania	19	8.0
Panama	19	8.0
Australia	22	7.9
China	22	7.9
Denmark	22	7.9
Israel	22	7.9
Mexico	22	7.9
Bolivia	27	7.8
Finland	27	7.8
Paraguay	27	7.8
Portugal	27	7.8
USA	31	7.7
Canada	32	7.5
Norway	32	7.5
Peru	32	7.5
Honduras	35	7.4
Uruguay	35	7.4
Argentina	37	7.3
France	38	7.2
Slovak Rep.	38	7.2
Taiwan	38	7.2
Thailand	38	7.2
Botswana	42	7.1
Bulgaria	42	7.1
Ecuador	42	7.1
Latvia	42	7.1
Malaysia	42	7.1
Mauritius	42	7.1
Namibia	42	7.1
Zambia	42	7.1
Congo, Rep.	50	7.0
Greece	50	7.0
Guatemala	50	7.0
Hungary	50	7.0
Kenya	50	7.0
New Zealand	50	7.0
Dominican Rep.	56	6.9
Chile	57	6.8
Iceland	57	6.8
El Salvador	59	6.6
Oman	59	6.6
South Africa	59	6.6
Trinidad Tob.	59	6.6
Venezuela	59	6.6
Jamaica	64	6.5
Japan	64	6.5
Jordan	64	6.5
Poland	67	6.4
Bahrain	68	6.3
Egypt	68	6.3
Kuwait	68	6.3
Slovenia	68	6.3
Ukraine	68	6.3
Indonesia	73	6.2
Fiji	74	6.1
Colombia	75	6.0
Malta	75	6.0
Sri Lanka	75	6.0
Cote d'Ivoire	78	5.9
Turkey	79	5.8
Belize	80	5.7
Tunisia	81	5.6
Zimbabwe	81	5.6
Morocco	83	5.4
Cameroon	84	5.2
Mali	84	5.2
Cyprus	86	5.1
Madagascar	86	5.1
Malawi	86	5.1
Pakistan	89	4.9
Russian Fed.	89	4.9
India	91	4.8
Nepal	91	4.8
Senegal	91	4.8
Brazil	94	4.7
Barbados	95	4.6
Niger	95	4.6
Romania	97	4.5
Central Afr. Rep.	98	4.3
Tanzania	99	4.2
Albania	100	4.0
Croatia	101	3.9
Bangladesh	102	3.8
Pap. N. Guinea	103	3.5
Syria	104	3.3
Algeria	105	2.8
Burundi	106	2.3
Iran	107	1.7
Sierra Leone	108	1.3
Myanmar	109	0.0

can be supplied domestically at a low cost and away from those that can be supplied only at a high cost. If a good or service can be obtained more economically through trade, it makes sense to trade for it rather than to produce it domestically. When trading partners use more of their time and resources producing things they do best, they are able to produce a larger joint output and achieve a higher standard of living than would otherwise be possible. Economists refer to this as the *law of comparative advantage.*

In addition, open international markets encourage both innovation and efficient production. Increasingly, economic growth involves intellectual power, innovation, and the application of technology. Observation of, and interaction with, individuals employing different technologies often induces others to emulate successful approaches.

International competition also helps keep domestic producers on their toes and provides them with a strong incentive to improve the quality of their products.

Openness may also exert an indirect effect: it may encourage countries to adopt sound institutions and policies. If they do not, both labor and capital will move toward a more favorable environment. Neither domestic nor foreign investors will want to place their funds in countries characterized by hostility toward business, monetary instability, legal uncertainty, high taxes, and low-quality public services. When labor and capital are free to move elsewhere, it will be costly to adopt policies that penalize success and exploit factors of production. Thus, openness provides political decision makers with a strong incentive to avoid policies that undermine growth.

OPENNESS, INCOME, AND GROWTH (1980–1998)

Economic theory indicates that persistently open economies will be able to derive more output from their domestic resources, be more innovative and dynamic, and have a greater incentive to choose policies more consistent with investment and growth.[6] Therefore, economies that are open over lengthy time periods should achieve more rapid growth rates and higher levels of per-capita GDP than those that are persistently closed. In order to test this proposition, we constructed the Trade Openness Index for the period from 1980 to 1998.

Trade Openness (1980–1998)

The data were assembled and the TOI was derived for the periods, 1980–1982, 1985–1987, 1990–1992, and 1995–1997. The three-year time intervals of these estimates reduce the likelihood that an unusual change or temporary aberration during a single year will distort a country's rating. The ratings for these four periods were used, along with the 1998 figure, to estimate the average TOI during the period from 1980 to 1998.[7] Data were available to construct this average TOI for 91 countries. This average rating is an indicator of openness over the 19 year period.

Exhibit 3-2 presents the average TOI rating during the period from 1980 to 1998 for each of the 91 countries arrayed from high to low. Table 3-2 of the Appendix contains the country ratings for each of the five periods. The top-rated countries of Exhibit 3-2 had persistently high ratings throughout the period from 1980 to 1998, while those at the bottom had persistently low ratings. Hong Kong, Singapore, Belgium, Panama, Germany, United Kingdom, Netherlands, Luxembourg, and Switzerland head the list. The United States ranks 10, tied with Malaysia and Sweden. Ireland ranked 13 followed closely by Canada, New Zealand, Norway, and Italy. The TOI indicates that all of these economies were relatively open during the period.

At the other end of the spectrum, the TOI indicates that Myanmar, Bangladesh, Burundi, Iran, Sierra Leone, Syria and Algeria were the least open economies during the period from 1980 to 1998. Argentina, Brazil, India, Nepal, and Pakistan were also among the countries with low average ratings for this period.

Openness, Income, and Growth: Simple Comparisons

If trade makes a difference, the countries with persistently high openness ratings should have higher per-capita incomes and grow more rapidly than those with persistently low ratings. As Exhibit 3-3

Exhibit 3-2: Trade Openness Index (1980-1998)

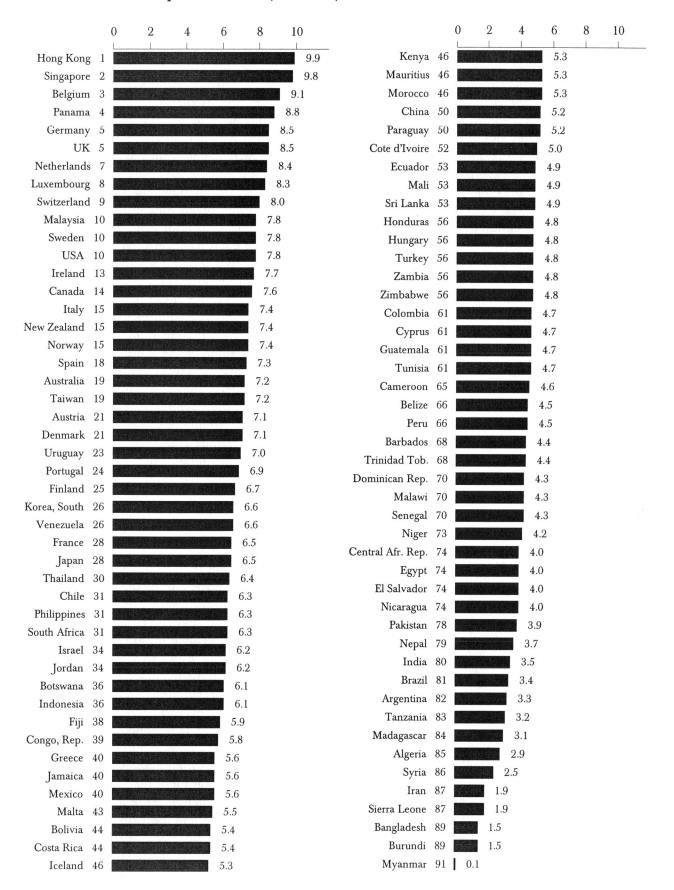

Hong Kong	1	9.9
Singapore	2	9.8
Belgium	3	9.1
Panama	4	8.8
Germany	5	8.5
UK	5	8.5
Netherlands	7	8.4
Luxembourg	8	8.3
Switzerland	9	8.0
Malaysia	10	7.8
Sweden	10	7.8
USA	10	7.8
Ireland	13	7.7
Canada	14	7.6
Italy	15	7.4
New Zealand	15	7.4
Norway	15	7.4
Spain	18	7.3
Australia	19	7.2
Taiwan	19	7.2
Austria	21	7.1
Denmark	21	7.1
Uruguay	23	7.0
Portugal	24	6.9
Finland	25	6.7
Korea, South	26	6.6
Venezuela	26	6.6
France	28	6.5
Japan	28	6.5
Thailand	30	6.4
Chile	31	6.3
Philippines	31	6.3
South Africa	31	6.3
Israel	34	6.2
Jordan	34	6.2
Botswana	36	6.1
Indonesia	36	6.1
Fiji	38	5.9
Congo, Rep.	39	5.8
Greece	40	5.6
Jamaica	40	5.6
Mexico	40	5.6
Malta	43	5.5
Bolivia	44	5.4
Costa Rica	44	5.4
Iceland	46	5.3

Kenya	46	5.3
Mauritius	46	5.3
Morocco	46	5.3
China	50	5.2
Paraguay	50	5.2
Cote d'Ivoire	52	5.0
Ecuador	53	4.9
Mali	53	4.9
Sri Lanka	53	4.9
Honduras	56	4.8
Hungary	56	4.8
Turkey	56	4.8
Zambia	56	4.8
Zimbabwe	56	4.8
Colombia	61	4.7
Cyprus	61	4.7
Guatemala	61	4.7
Tunisia	61	4.7
Cameroon	65	4.6
Belize	66	4.5
Peru	66	4.5
Barbados	68	4.4
Trinidad Tob.	68	4.4
Dominican Rep.	70	4.3
Malawi	70	4.3
Senegal	70	4.3
Niger	73	4.2
Central Afr. Rep.	74	4.0
Egypt	74	4.0
El Salvador	74	4.0
Nicaragua	74	4.0
Pakistan	78	3.9
Nepal	79	3.7
India	80	3.5
Brazil	81	3.4
Argentina	82	3.3
Tanzania	83	3.2
Madagascar	84	3.1
Algeria	85	2.9
Syria	86	2.5
Iran	87	1.9
Sierra Leone	87	1.9
Bangladesh	89	1.5
Burundi	89	1.5
Myanmar	91	0.1

shows, this was indeed the case. The $23,387 GDP per person of the 12 most open economies was more than seven times the comparable figure for the 12 least open economies.[8] The per-capita GDP of the 12 most open economies grew at an annual rate of 2.5% during the period from 1980 to 1998, compared to 0.3% per year for the 12 least open economies. All 12 of the open economies had positive growth rates and all but one grew at an annual rate of 1.2% or more. In contrast, four of the least open economies experienced reductions in per-capita GDP and only four of the 12 achieved a growth rate in excess of 1%. These striking differences suggest that openness exerts a major impact on growth and prosperity.

Exhibit 3-4 illustrates the linkage between openness and both the level and growth rate of per-capita GDP for the entire set of 90 countries (Germany was excluded due to unification) with TOI ratings for the period from 1980 to 1998. The countries were arrayed from highest to lowest based on their average TOI rating and the distribution was divided into quintiles. The top group was made up of the 18 countries with the highest TOI (1980–1998) ratings, the second group the 18 countries with the next highest ratings, and so on.

As Graph A of Exhibit 3-4 shows, the quintile with the highest TOI ratings had an average per-capita GDP of $22,306, 60% greater than the level of the second-highest quintile. In turn, the average per-capita income of the second quintile was more than twice that of the third. Similarly, the income level of the fourth and fifth quintile were lower than that of the quintile immediately above. Clearly, there was a strong relationship between openness over a lengthy time period and per-capita GDP.

Graph B of Exhibit 3-4 illustrates the relationship between the average TOI rating for the period from 1980 to 1998 and the annual growth rate of real per-capita GDP during the same period. The top quintile of countries with the highest TOI ratings achieved an average annual growth rate of 2.4% during the period from 1980 to 1998. The GDP growth of the next quintile of countries averaged 2.0%. The average growth rate of the third quintile fell to 1.3%, while the two lowest quintiles grew at an annual rate of only 0.5%. These figures suggest that more open economies are able to achieve higher rates of economic growth.

Openness, Income and Growth: Regression Analysis

Exhibits 3-3 and 3-4 show that there is a strong positive relationship between trade liberalization as measured by the TOI index and per-capita real GDP and its growth. However, this simplified analysis does not provide information on the statistical significance of the relationships. Neither does it reveal whether openness exerts an independent impact.[9] We now turn to an investigation of these issues.

Of course, factors other than trade openness influence income levels and growth rates. Both economic theory and prior research indicate that the stability of the price level and security of property rights are two key policy variables that influence economic performance. Measures of cross-country differences for these two variables were developed for the 90 countries with TOI ratings for the period from 1980 to 1998. The measure of price level variability is the standard deviation of the inflation rate for five-year periods from 1980 to 1998. The property rights variable is the rule-of-law rating from the *Country Risk Guide*. Using survey information supplied by experts familiar with conditions in various countries, this publication has provided rule-of-law ratings annually since 1982. We averaged the ratings for 1982, 1985, 1990, 1995, and 1998 to derive each country's rule-of-law rating for the period from 1980 to 1998. Both variables were converted to a scale from 0 to 10.[10]

Exhibit 3-5 uses regression analysis to investigate the linkage between trade openness, variability of inflation, and the security of property rights, on the one hand, and 1998 GDP per capita, on the other. The first two equations are for all 90 countries for which we were able to derive the TOI for the period from 1980 to 1998. As Equation 1 shows, the simple relationship between TOI and per-capita GDP is exceedingly strong. The R-squared indicates that TOI alone explains 55% of the cross-country variation in 1998 GDP per person. Equation 2 adds the inflation variability and property right variables into the model. All three of the variables are significant at the 90% level of confidence or higher and the R-squared indicates that the model explains 78% of the 1998 cross-country variation in GDP per person.

Exhibit 3-3: GDP per Person and the Growth of Nations with the Highest and Lowest
1980–1998 Trade Openness Indexes

	TOI (1980-98)	Real PPP GDP per capita 1998	Average annual growth rate of real GDP* per capita 1980–1998
Hong Kong	9.9	$24,120	4.1%
Singapore	9.8	$30,621	5.2%
Belgium	9.1	$24,415	1.8%
Panama	8.8	$7,705	1.5%
UK	8.5	$22,258	1.7%
Netherlands	8.4	$23,444	1.6%
Luxembourg	8.3	$37,795	2.5%
Switzerland	8.0	$28,493	0.9%
USA	7.8	$31,485	1.6%
Malaysia	7.8	$10,187	3.4%
Sweden	7.8	$20,852	1.2%
Ireland	7.7	$19,267	4.3%
Top 12:	8.5	$23,387	2.5%
India	3.5	$1,831	3.7%
Brazil	3.4	$6,560	0.4%
Argentina	3.3	$10,877	0.5%
Tanzania	3.2	$709	−0.1%
Madagascar	3.1	$978	−2.6%
Algeria	2.9	$5,033	0.1%
Syria	2.5	$3,258	1.3%
Sierra Leone	1.9	$530	−3.3%
Iran	1.9	$6,209	0.1%
Burundi	1.5	$527	−1.4%
Bangladesh	1.5	$1,155	1.8%
Myanmar	0.1	$1,333	3.3%
Bottom 12:	2.4	$3,250	0.3%

Notes: Germany is omitted from this analysis due to discontinuity in the income data resulting from unification.
   *Real GDP data are in 1998 US dollars and are calculated using the purchasing-power-parity method.

Some argue that high-income countries are in a better position to reduce their trade barriers than those with lower incomes. According to this view, the relationship illustrated by Equations 1 and 2 runs from high-income status to openness. In order to shed light on this view, the 21 countries (including Germany) that the World Bank classified as "high-income industrial" in 1980 were deleted from the data set. This left 70 countries that were classified as "less developed" in 1980. Equations 3 and 4 of Table 3-2 present these results. Even after the high-income countries are omitted, the TOI continues to explain a large share (42% in the simple model) of the cross-country variation in GDP per capita. In the three-variable model of Equation 4, both the TOI and rule-of-law variables are

Exhibit 3-4: Trade Openness, Income, and Growth

Graph A

Graph B

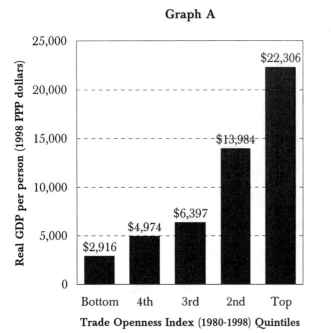
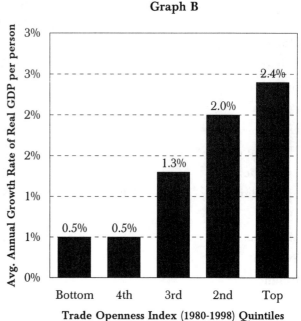

Exhibit 3-5: Trade Openness, Monetary Stability, Property Rights, and Income

Dependent variable: real GDP[a] per capita 1998
(*t*-statistic is in parentheses)

	Complete set[b]		Low- and middle-income countries[c]		Small population countries[d]	
	(1)	(2)	(3)	(4)	(5)	(6)
Trade Openness Index (1980-98)	3.63 (10.41)*	1.69 (5.30)*	2.15 (7.08)*	1.58 (5.42)*	4.03 (9.72)*	1.95 (4.98)*
Inflation variability rating		0.39 (1.82)***		0.19 (0.95)		0.36 (1.32)
Property rights rating 1980		2.21 (9.22)*		1.38 (5.07)*		2.18 (7.35)*
Intercept	–9.86	–15.67	–4.48	–9.98	–12.68	–17.27
n	90	90	70	70	66	66
Adj R-Squared	.55	.78	.42	.58	.59	.80

*   significant at 99% level;   ** significant at 95% level;   *** significant at 90% level

(a)   Real GDP numbers are derived using the purchasing power parity (PPP) method and are in 1998 US dollars.

(b)   The complete set (90 countries) includes the countries listed in Exhibit 3-2 except Germany, which was omitted because of discontinuity in income data resulting from unification.

(c)   There are 70 low-income and middle-income countries. Countries classified as high-income industrial by the World Bank in 1980 were omitted.

(d)   There are 66 small-population countries (fewer than 20 million people in 1980).

significant but the inflation variable is not. This indicates that some of the explanatory power of inflation variability observed in Equation 2 stems from its correlations with high-income status.

As we previously discussed, there is reason to believe that it is more important for small countries to maintain open economies than their larger counterparts. Equations 5 and 6 include only the 66 countries in our data base that have a population of less than 20 million. The R-squares for Equations 5 and 6 are larger than for the parallel equations for the other data sets. This is consistent with the view that openness is more important for smaller countries than for larger ones. The three-variable model of Equation 6 explains 80% of the variation in per-capita GDP across countries. Once again, the significance of both the openness and rule of law variables remains high, while the inflation variable continues to be insignificant at acceptable levels of confidence.

Exhibit 3-6 focuses on growth; the dependent variable for all equations is the average annual growth rate of per-capita real GDP during the period from 1980 to 1998.[11] In addition to openness, price stability and country size (both population and area) are included in the more comprehensive model. The rule-of-law variable is not included here because it was not significant in any of the equations. Population and area are incorporated primarily as control variables. A larger population may create greater opportunity for the realization of economies of scale within the domestic market. Thus, we expect the sign of this variable to be positive. The sign of the area variable is more ambiguous. The observed negative sign may indicate that transaction costs in the domestic market are higher when the population is spread over a larger geographic area.

Equation 1 of Exhibit 3-6 looks at the simple relationship between the TOI measure of openness and the growth rate of real per-capita GDP during the period from 1980 to 1998 for the entire data set of 90 countries. The t-ratio for the TOI is highly significant and the R-squared indicates that openness explains 12% of the cross-country variation in growth. When the inflation variability, population, and area variables are added to the model (Equation 2), all of the variables are significant at the 95% level or higher and the explanatory power increases to 0.35.

The coefficient of the openness variable (0.21) of Equation 2 indicates that a one unit change in TOI, if maintained over a lengthy period, would increase long-term growth by two-tenths of a percent. This is a sizeable amount. For example, it implies that a country like India, which had a TOI rating of 3.5 during the period from 1980 to 1998 could increase its long-term growth by about 1% annually if it were as open as Germany and the United Kingdom (countries with TOI ratings of 8.5 during the period from 1980 to 1998).

Some have argued that the relationship between openness and growth merely reflects the fact that high-income countries are more open and that they also grow more rapidly and that, thus, the relationship may be spurious. In order to see if this is the case, we omitted the high-income industrial economies and ran the model once again. The omission of the high-income countries exerted little impact on the simple relationship between openness and growth (Equation 3 versus Equation 1). As Equation 4 shows, all of the variables remain significant and have the expected sign. Both the t-ratio for TOI and the R-squared for the broader model increased when the high-income countries were omitted. Furthermore, the size of the openness coefficient increased from 0.21 in Equation 2 to 0.35 in Equation 4. This indicates that openness actually exerts a larger impact on the growth of developing countries than is true for high-income industrial nations.

Equations 5 and 6 of Exhibit 3-6 apply the growth model to small countries (population less than 20 million). The results are similar to those for developing countries (Equations 3 and 4). In the broad model, TOI remains significant at the 99% level. The TOI coefficient of 0.39 indicates that a one unit change in the openness measure is associated with approximately a four-tenths of a percent increase in the long-term growth of small countries. Just as we had anticipated, the difference in the size of the openness coefficient between Equations 2 and 6 indicates that trade openness is particularly important when countries are small. The R-squared of Equation 6 indicates that TOI and inflation variability, along with the size variables (population and area) explain slightly more than half (51%) of the variation in growth of per-capita GDP over the period from

Exhibit 3-6:   Trade Openness, Monetary Stability, Size, and Income Growth

	Complete set[b]		Low- and middle-income countries[c]		Small population countries[d]	
	Dependent variable: annual growth rate of real GDP[a] per capita *(t-statistic is in parentheses)*					
	(1)	(2)	(3)	(4)	(5)	(6)
Trade Openness Index (1980-98)	0.38 (3.69)*	0.21 (2.07)**	0.46 (3.26)*	0.35 (2.89)*	0.61 (5.08)*	0.39 (3.82)*
Inflation variability rating		0.30 (3.67)*		0.34 (3.71)*		0.31 (3.82)*
Log of population in 1980 (millions)		0.50 (3.45)*		0.69 (3.83)*		−0.01 (0.05)
Log of land area (thousands of square kilometers)		−0.29 (2.55)**		−0.33 (2.27)**		−0.19 (1.77)***
Intercept	−0.78	−1.47	−1.12	−2.90	−2.42	−1.73
n	90	90	70	70	66	66
Adj R-Squared	.12	.35	.12	.43	.33	.51

*   significant at 99% level;   ** significant at 95% level;   *** significant at 90% level

(a)   Real GDP numbers are derived using the purchasing power parity (PPP) method and are in 1998 US dollars.

(b)   The complete set (90 countries) includes the countries listed in Exhibit 3-2 except Germany, which was omitted because of discontinuity in income data resulting from unification.

(c)   There are 70 low-income and middle-income countries. Countries classified as high-income industrial by the World Bank in 1980 were omitted.

(d)   There are 66 small-population countries (fewer than 20 million people in 1980).

1980 to 1998. Except for population all of the variables were significant. The compression of the population measure for this data set undoubtedly contributed to its insignificance.

In summary, the results show that economies that are more open over lengthy periods of time grow faster and achieve higher per-capita income levels than economies that are more closed. Openness continues to exert a positive independent impact on economic performance even after the effects of inflation variability, rule of law (when significant), and the country size control variables are taken into account. Furthermore, the results are robust. The positive impact of openness is true for developing countries and small nations, as well as for the entire set of 90 countries. In fact, the positive effects are somewhat larger for developing economies and small countries than for the entire data set.

CHANGES IN OPENNESS (1980–1998)

Has there been a change in trade openness during the last two decades? Exhibit 3-7 illustrates the path of the mean Trade Openness Index (TOI) for the 91 countries for which data could be obtained throughout the period from 1980 to 1998. The mean TOI increased steadily, rising from 4.7 in 1980–1982 to 5.5 in 1990–1992 and 6.5 in 1998. Only 11 of the 91 countries had a lower TOI rating in 1998 than 1980 and six of these were countries with high initial ratings that experienced only a minimal decline (0.2 or less). Only one country, Venezuela, had a reduction of more than 1.0 on the 10-point rating scale. These findings indicate that trade openness has increased substantially during the last two decades.

The Trade Openness Index merely reflects the underlying trends with regard to tariff rates, non-tariff trade barriers, and the restrictiveness of

Exhibit 3-7: Change in Trade Openness, 1980 through 1998

	1980-1982	1990-1992	1998	Change between 1980 & 1998
TOI (period average)	4.7	5.5	6.5	+1.8
Subcomponents				
Tariff measures				
Tax revenues on trade as a % of Trade Sector*				
mean observation	6.1	5.0	4.3	−1.8
mean rating	6.0	6.8	7.3	+1.3
Mean tariff rate				
median observation	18.8	18.6	10.6	−8.2
mean rating	5.2	6.0	7.6	+2.4
Standard deviation of tariff rates				
median observation	**	11.3	7.9	-3.4
mean rating	**	4.5	6.2	+1.7
Composite tariff measure	5.6	5.8	6.8	+1.2
Black market exchange rate				
median observation	18.0	2.9	0.0	−18.0
mean rating	5.7	7.8	9.0	+3.3
Capital controls				
mean rating	2.6	3.3	5.2	+2.6
Trade Sector* (actual vs. expected)				
mean rating	5.1	5.0	5.2	+0.1

Notes: Medians are used when observations include extreme outliers that bias a mean representation of the average.

* "Trade sector" is defined as [(imports + exports) / GDP].

** The period change measure for the standard deviation of tariffs is based on the change between 1990/1992 and the 1998 data. Insufficient data were available to make comparisons with 1980/1982.

exchange rate and capital market controls. Exchange controls deter trade because they limit the ability of individuals to acquire currencies desired by trading partners in other nations. The black-market exchange-rate premium is indicative of the restrictiveness of these controls. As Exhibit 3-7 shows, the median black-market exchange rate declined sharply during the 1980s, and continued to fall during the 1990s. The mean rating for this subcomponent rose from 5.7 in 1980 to 7.8 in 1990-1992, and 9.0 in 1998.

Among the 91 countries in our study, 42 had average black-market exchange-rate premiums of 25% or more during the period 1980–1982. By 1990–1992, the number had fallen to 15, and by 1998 it declined to only 7. These figures illustrate

the dramatic reduction in the restrictiveness of exchange rate controls during the last two decades. The upward trend of the average country rating for this subcomponent is reflective of these changes.

The trend for tariffs is similar. As Exhibit 3-7 shows, revenues derived from taxes imposed on international trade fell from an average of 6.1% during 1980–1982 to 4.3% in 1998. The median observation of the mean tariff rate declined from 18.8% in 1980–1982 to 10.6% in 1998. The standard deviation of the tariff rate has also declined. This combination of factors–lower taxes on international trade and more uniform tariff structure–has led to a higher composite rating for the tariff component.

The capital market rating indicates the restrictiveness of regulations limiting the movement of direct investment and financial capital across national boundaries. The mean rating for the 91 countries for this component increased from 2.6 during 1980–1982 to 3.3 in 1990–1992 and 5.2 in 1998. This indicates that barriers limiting capital movements fell slightly during the 1980s and more sharply during the 1990s.

The size of the trade sector component is based on a comparison between the actual and expected size of the trade sector as a share of the economy. As we discussed previously, the expected size is influenced by population, area, miles of coastline, and location relative to world demand. Over time, the expected size is also adjusted for the growth of world trade. This means that the mean rating for this component will remain constant across time periods. Nonetheless, there is evidence that the trade sector of most countries has been increasing as a share the economy. Trade as a share of GDP grew between 1980–1982 and 1996–1998 in 59 of the 91 countries covered by this study. The mean increase between these two periods was 17.4%.

In summary, during the last two decades black-market exchange rates have fallen, tariffs have been reduced, capital controls liberalized, and the volume of international trade as a share of the economy has increased. All of these factors indicate that trade barriers are lower and most economies are more open today than was true in 1980. The upward trend in the Trade Openness Index is consistent with this view.

Countries with the Largest Increases in Trade Openness

Which countries have experienced the largest increases in openness? The changes in the TOI over time can be used to address this question. Exhibit 3-8 (top frame) indicates the 10 countries with the largest increases in TOI between 1980–1982 and 1995–1997. Mexico, Nicaragua, Argentina, Costa Rica, and Paraguay head this list. The TOI of these countries increased by 5 points or more during the period. The TOIs of Bolivia, China, Trinidad and Tobago, Honduras, and Ecuador also increased substantially. Some of these countries—Mexico and Costa Rica, for example—achieved steady increases throughout the period. In other instances—Nicaragua and Ar-

gentina—most of the increases have taken place during the last decade.

Interestingly, nine of the 10 countries with the largest increases in TOI are located in Latin America. The "import-substitution" view of trade dominated the region in the early 1980s. The low TOI ratings for 1980–1982 in this region merely confirm this point. However, many Latin American countries moved away from import-substitution and began liberalizing their trade sectors during the latter half of the 1980s and, particularly, during the 1990s. This change explains why the region is so dominant among the countries with large increases in TOI since 1980.

All 10 countries with the largest increases in the TOI had low ratings at the beginning of the period. This is not surprising since the low initial ratings provided ample opportunity for improvement. Exhibit 3-8 (bottom frame) also presents data on the increased openness of countries with at least an initial rating of 5.0. Even though these countries were relatively open in the early 1980s, they have nonetheless achieved substantial TOI increases during the last 15 years. This group is headed by the Philippines, Sweden, France, Portugal, and Australia.

In essence, the countries of Exhibit 3-8 deserve "gold stars" for their increases in openness. How did their more open policies affect trade? Exhibit 3-9 provides the answer. Many of them recorded huge increases in the size of the trade sector. For example, Mexico's international trade rose from 23.7% of GDP in 1980–1982 to 64.5% in 1998, an increase of 172%. The trade sector of Argentina doubled while that of China tripled as a share the economy during the 15-year period. The average increase in trade as a share of GDP for the 10 countries with the largest increases in openness was 75.2%, more than four times the average increase of the 90 countries covered by this study.

The countries with initial TOI ratings of 5.0 or more that opened their economies the most also registered impressive increases in trade. The trade sectors of every one of these countries rose relative to GDP. On average, their trade increased 34.8% as a share the economy during the 15-year period, twice the average of the entire group. Exhibit 3-9 illustrates clearly that there is a strong and consistent linkage between removal of trade barriers and increases in the volume of international trade.

Exhibit 3-8:   Countries with the Largest Increase in Trade Openness between 1980–1982 and 1995–1997

	TOI 1980-1982	TOI 1985–1987	TOI 1990–1992	TOI 1995–1997	Increase in TOI between 1980–1982 and 1995–1997
Mexico	1.8	4.8	7.0	7.5	5.7
Nicaragua	1.5	0.6	4.7	6.9	5.4
Argentina	1.5	1.0	2.0	6.9	5.3
Costa Rica	2.6	4.0	5.8	7.9	5.3
Paraguay	2.6	3.7	5.8	7.5	5.0
Bolivia	2.4	4.9	5.9	7.1	4.8
China	3.0	5.0	4.0	7.3	4.3
Trinidad & Tob.	2.8	3.0	3.4	7.1	4.2
Honduras	3.1	2.3	5.3	7.3	4.2
Ecuador	2.9	3.8	5.2	6.8	3.9

Countries with TOI (1980–1982) greater than or equal to 5

Philippines	5.2	5.6	6.0	7.4	2.2
Sweden	6.4	7.5	8.3	8.6	2.1
France	5.0	6.5	7.0	7.0	2.0
Portugal	5.9	6.3	7.0	7.8	1.9
Australia	6.1	7.0	7.4	7.8	1.7
Austria	6.4	6.5	7.0	7.9	1.5
Finland	6.4	6.3	5.7	7.8	1.4
Ireland	7.2	7.3	7.2	8.5	1.4
Spain	6.6	6.9	7.4	7.9	1.3
Congo, Rep.	5.5	5.3	5.2	6.7	1.2

Note: TOI 1998 is omitted in order to avoid bias that might result from a single non-smoothed data point.

Another way of viewing openness would be to focus on changes in the size of the trade sector directly. Exhibit 3-10 takes this approach. This exhibit shows the 10 countries with the largest increases in trade as a share of the economy between 1980–1982 and 1998. Four of these countries–China, Mexico, Philippines, and Argentina–were included among those with the largest increases in TOI. Turkey, Dominican Republic, Ne-pal, Thailand, Malaysia, and Zimbabwe are also included among the "top ten." This latter group of countries either had a high rating throughout the period (Malaysia) or a sizeable increase in TOI during the period from 1980 to 1998. This evidence, along with the huge increases in trade, indicate that these countries have also become more open in recent years.

Exhibit 3-9:   Increases in Trade Openness and Changes in the Size of the Trade Sector

	Increase in TOI between 1980–1982 and 1995–1997	Trade Share* 1980–1982	Trade Share* 1990–1992	Trade Share* 1998	Increase in relative size of Trade Share* between 1980–1982 and 1998
Mexico	5.7	23.7%	38.3%	64.5%	172.2%
Nicaragua	5.4	67.5%	71.4%	113.7%	68.5%
Argentina	5.3	11.5%	15.0%	23.3%	102.6%
Costa Rica	5.3	63.3%	76.0%	99.8%	57.7%
Paraguay	5.0	44.0%	72.7%	73.4%	66.8%
Bolivia	4.8	37.7%	47.0%	48.6%	28.9%
China	4.3	12.9%	26.8%	39.0%	202.3%
Trinidad Tob.	4.2	89.4%	70.9%	97.7%	9.3%
Honduras	4.2	80.3%	76.1%	97.9%	21.9%
Ecuador	3.9	50.6%	60.1%	61.5%	21.5%
				Average of this group of countries:	75.2%
				Average of the entire group of 90 TOI (80-98) countries**	17.4%

Countries with TOI (1980–1982) greater than or equal to 5

Philippines	2.2	52.0%	60.8%	115.6%	122.3%
Sweden	2.1	60.8%	59.5%	81.3%	33.7%
France	2.0	44.3%	45.1%	49.6%	12.0%
Portugal	1.9	63.0%	76.2%	67.5%	7.1%
Australia	1.7	33.9%	34.6%	41.4%	22.1%
Austria	1.5	74.0%	79.0%	90.3%	22.0%
Finland	1.4	67.1%	47.6%	69.8%	4.0%
Ireland	1.4	108.4%	111.3%	157.0%	44.8%
Spain	1.3	33.8%	37.5%	56.8%	68.0%
Congo, Rep.	1.2	120.1%	97.9%	134.9%	12.3%
				Average of this group of countries:	34.8%
				Average of the entire group of 90 TOI (80-98) countries:**	17.4%

Note: *Trade share is defined as ((imports + exports) / GDP).

** There are 90 countries because Germany is omitted due to discontinuity resulting from unification.

Exhibit 3-10: Increases in the Size of the Trade Sector and Trade Openness

	Increase in Relative Size of Trade Share 1980–1982 to 1998	Trade Share 1980–1982	Trade Share 1990–1992	Trade Share 1998	Increase in TOI 1980–1982 to 1995–1997
Turkey	209.9%	17.1%	30.9%	53.0%	+3.7
China	202.3%	12.9%	26.8%	39.0%	+4.3
Mexico	172.2%	23.7%	38.3%	64.5%	+5.7
Philippines	122.3%	52.0%	60.8%	115.6%	+2.2
Dominican Rep.	114.3%	48.1%	77.8%	103.1%	+3.6
Argentina	102.6%	11.5%	15.0%	23.3%	+5.4
Nepal	89.8%	30.3%	31.6%	57.5%	+1.3
Thailand	85.9%	54.5%	75.5%	101.3%	+1.0
Malaysia	83.7%	112.6%	150.6%	206.9%	+0.1
Zimbabwe	68.5%	55.6%	63.6%	93.7%	+1.7

Average of this group of countries:	+2.9
Average of the entire group of 90 TOI (80-98)** countries:	+1.6

Note: Trade share is defined as ((imports + exports) / GDP).

Note: Germany is omitted from the TOI 1980–1998 set due to discontinuity in income data, leaving 90 countries.

SUMMARY AND CONCLUSION

A Trade Openness Index (TOI) was constructed for both 1998 and the period from 1980 to 1998. The TOI measures the extent that a country has a fully convertible currency (no black-market exchange rate), low and relatively uniform tariffs, few restrictions on the movement of capital, and a large trade sector (given its size and location).

The index was used to analyze cross-country differences in openness and their impact on economic performance. The analysis of this chapter indicates that:

- Hong Kong, Singapore, Belgium, Panama, Germany, United Kingdom, and Netherlands were the most open economies during 1980-98. The United States ranked in position 10 (tied with Sweden and Malaysia). At the other end of the spectrum, Myanmar, Bangladesh, Burundi, Iran, Sierra Leone, Syria and Algeria were the most closed. (See Exhibit 3-2.)

- Economics indicates that more open economies will grow more rapidly and achieve higher living standards because openness stimulates (a) gains from specialization and trade, (b) innova-

tion and efficient production, and (c) adoption of sound policies. Our findings are consistent with this view: persistently open economies had higher levels of per-capita income and grew more rapidly than those that were more closed. (See Exhibits 3-3, 3-4, 3-5 and 3-6.)

- Our estimates indicate that a one-unit increase in the TOI over a lengthy time period increases growth by two-tenths of a percent. This indicates that, for example, if India were as open as the United Kingdom, its long-term growth rate would be increased by approximately 1%. (See Exhibit 3-6.)

- Openness is particularly important for developing economies and less populous nations.

- The average TOI rating rose substantially during period from 1980 to 1998, indicating that the world economy became more open. Mexico, China, Ireland, and the Philippines were among the countries registering both a sizable increase in TOI and a huge increase in trade as a share of GDP. (See Exhibits 3-7, 3-8, 3-9, and 3-10.)

NOTES

(1)   This chapter contains statistical analysis that was previously published in *Openness, Growth, and Trade Policy*, a staff report of the Joint Economic Committee of the United States Congress, December 2000. This report by Gwartney and Skipton is available at http://www.senate.gov~jec/.

(2)   In most cases, the taxes on international trade were less than 15% of the trade sector (imports plus exports). As this ratio rose from 0% to 15%, the assigned rating declined from 10 (indicating that no taxes were levied on international trade) to 0 (indicating that trade taxes were equal to, or greater than, 15% of the trade sector). The mean tariff rate generally ranged from 0% (no tariffs) to 50% (exceedingly high tariffs). As the mean tariff rate increased from 0% to 50% or greater, the assigned rating fell proportionally from 10 to 0. As the standard deviation of tariff rates increased from 0% (indicating that a flat tariff rate applies to all imports) to 25% (or more), the rating for this component declined proportionally from 10 to 0. See the Appendix to Chapter 1 of this publication for additional details.

(3)   As the black-market premium rose from 0% to 50% (and above), the assigned rating for this component fell proportionally from 10 (indicating full convertibility without restrictions) to 0. For additional details, see the Appendix to Chapter 1 of this publication.

(4)   If domestic investments by foreigners and foreign investments by citizens are unrestricted, the country is given a rating of 10. When these investments are restricted only in a few industries (for example, banking, defense, and telecommunications), countries are assigned a rating of 8. When investments are permitted, but regulatory restrictions slow the mobility of capital, a country is given a rating of 5. When either domestic investments by foreigners or foreign investments by citizens require approval from government authorities, a country receives a rating of 2. A rating of 0 is assigned when both domestic investments by foreigners and foreign investments by citizens require government approval. See Appendix to Chapter 1 of this publication for additional details.

(5)   The DADS variable for each country was derived by using the great-circle algorithm to adjust the real purchasing power parity GDP for distance from the potential trading partner. Countries that make up more than 99% of the world's GDP were used to derive the variable. The DADS provides an estimate for how close each country is to the mass of the world's GDP. This scalar will be large for countries that are located close to centers of world demand and small for those that are far from major GDP concentrations. The demand scalar analysis indicates that several European countries (Luxembourg, Belgium, Netherlands, etc.) are located most favorably relative to the distribution of the world's GDP. In contrast, New Zealand, Australia, Fiji, and Argentina are least favorably located relative to the concentrations of demand around the world. With time, increasing trade in services and lower transport and communications cost may significantly reduce the importance of distance as a determinant of trade. However, regression analysis indicates that distance as measured by the DADS variable continues to exert a statistically significant impact on the size of the trade sector in the 1990s.

(6)   International trade also enhances living standards by making it possible for consumers to choose among a more diverse bundle of goods. When trade is stifled, the domestic market will often be too small for firms to supply a broad set of goods at a low cost. Thus, trade barriers will mean more limited selection. This factor has been easily observable in countries like Mexico, Poland, Czech Republic, and China, that have become more open in recent years. Interestingly, GDP ignores the

welfare gains accompanying the availability of a broader selection of goods. Thus, GDP and its growth rate generally understate the benefits derived from increased trade and a more open economy. For an excellent discussion of this point, see Michael Cox and Richard Alm, *The Right Stuff: America's Move to Mass Customization: 1998 Annual Report* (Dallas, TX: Federal Reserve Bank of Dallas, 1998), http://www.dallasfed.org/htm/pubs/annual/arpt98.html.

(7) Because they cover a shorter period, the 1998 data were weighted only half as much as the data for each of the four other periods.

(8) Germany was excluded from this analysis because of the difficulties involved in comparing per capita GDP before and after unification.

(9) As we noted previously, countries that adopt more open trade policies may also be more likely to follow policies consistent with price stability, protection of property rights, and reliance on markets for the allocation of goods and resources. This makes it more difficult to determine the independent impact of openness.

(10) See the Appendix to Chapter 1 of this publication for details concerning how the original data were converted to a scale of 0 to 10.

(11) For an excellent analysis of the link between international trade and growth, see Jeffrey A. Frankel and David Romer, Does Trade Cause Growth? *American Economic Review* (June 1999): 379–99.

APPENDIX: TABLES TO CHAPTER 3

TABLE 3–1   TRADE OPENNESS INDEX (1998)

	Tariffs (i) Revenues from taxes on trade as a share of the trade sector	Tariffs (ii) Mean tariff rate	Tariffs (iii) Standard deviation of tariff rates	Composite tariff rating	Black Market Difference between the official and black market exchange rate	Capital Restrictions on citizens engaging in capital transactions with foreigners	Trade Actual relative to expected size of trade sector	TOI 1998
Albania	5.2 (7.2)	6.8 (15.9)	6.7 (8.3)	6.2	7.8 (11.1)	2	0.0 (−59.8%)	4.0
Algeria	3.9 (9.2)	5.2 (24.2)	3.3 (16.7)	4.1	0.0 (150.0)	2	5.1 (1.3%)	2.8
Argentina	7.1 (4.4)	7.3 (13.5)	7.2 (6.9)	7.2	10.0 (0.0)	10	2.0 (−37.1%)	7.3
Australia	9.0 (1.4)	9.0 (5.0)	7.3 (6.7)	8.5	10.0 (0.0)	8	5.3 (−6.4%)	7.9
Austria	9.9 (0.2)	8.9 (5.6)	7.6 (5.9)	8.8	10.0 (0.0)	8	5.4 (−7.5%)	8.0
Bahrain	9.1 (1.4)	N/A	N/A	9.1	10.0 (0.0)	2	4.0 (−17.3%)	6.3
Bangladesh	3.7 (9.5)	5.6 (22.1)	4.2 (14.6)	4.5	7.8 (11.1)	0	3.1 (−27.4%)	3.8
Barbados	N/A	6.2 (19.0)	N/A	6.2	9.8 (1.0)	0	2.2 (−35.6%)	4.6
Belgium	9.7 (0.4)	8.9 (5.6)	7.6 (5.9)	8.8	10.0 (0.0)	10	7.4 (48.9%)	9.0
Belize	5.6 (6.6)	N/A	N/A	5.6	9.2 (4.0)	5	2.8 (−30.3%)	5.7
Bolivia	8.4 (2.4)	8.1 (9.7)	9.5 (1.2)	8.7	10.0 (0.0)	8	4.6 (−7.9%)	7.8
Botswana	6.0 (6.1)	8.6 (7.2)	6.0 (10.0)	6.8	10.0 (0.0)	5	6.7 (33.5%)	7.1
Brazil	4.5 (8.3)	7.1 (14.6)	7.1 (7.3)	6.2	10.0 (0.0)	0	2.5 (−33.2%)	4.7
Bulgaria	8.5 (2.2)	7.5 (12.6)	6.1 (9.1)	7.4	10.0 (0.0)	5	5.9 (17.8%)	7.1
Burundi	4.1 (8.9)	N/A	N/A	4.1	5.0 (25.0)	0	0.0 (−72.7%)	2.3
Cameroon	N/A	6.3 (18.4)	N/A	6.3	9.6 (2.0)	0	4.8 (−4.2%)	5.2
Canada	9.8 (0.3)	8.6 (7.1)	0.0 (25.7)	6.1	10.0 (0.0)	8	5.8 (16.9%)	7.5
C. African Rep.	4.3 (8.6)	6.3 (18.6)	N/A	5.3	10.0 (0.0)	0	1.9 (−38.0)	4.3
Chile	7.9 (3.1)	7.8 (11.0)	9.7 (0.7)	8.5	7.8 (11.1)	5	5.8 (15.6%)	6.8
China	9.3 (1.0)	6.5 (17.5)	4.8 (13.0)	6.9	10.0 (0.0)	5	9.8 (95.2%)	7.9
Colombia	7.8 (3.3)	7.7 (11.7)	7.5 (6.2)	7.6	7.8 (11.1)	5	3.7 (−20.2%)	6.0

	Tariffs (i) Revenues from taxes on trade as a share of the trade sector		Tariffs (ii) Mean tariff rate		Tariffs (iii) Standard deviation of tariff rates		Composite tariff rating	Black Market Difference between the official and black market exchange rate		Capital Restrictions on citizens engaging in capital transactions with foreigners	Trade Actual relative to expected size of trade sector		TOI 1998
Rep. of Congo	8.8	(1.8)	N/A		N/A		8.8	9.6	(2.0)	0	9.5	(89.1%)	7.0
Costa Rica	8.4	(2.4)	8.6	(7.2)	4.5	(13.8)	7.1	10.0	(0.0)	10	5.9	(17.4%)	8.3
Côte d'Ivoire	1.2	(13.2)	9.0	(4.8)	9.6	(1.1)	6.6	9.6	(2.0)	0	7.4	(47.4%)	5.9
Croatia	7.7	(3.5)	N/A		N/A		7.7	1.4	(42.9)	2	4.5	(−8.6%)	3.9
Cyprus	8.5	(2.3)	6.7	(16.4)	N/A		7.6	10.0	(0.0)	0	2.7	(−31.5%)	5.1
Czech Rep.	9.6	(0.6)	8.6	(6.8)	5.6	(11.0)	7.9	10.0	(0.0)	8	7.4	(47.1%)	8.3
Denmark	9.8	(0.3)	8.9	(5.6)	7.6	(5.9)	8.8	10.0	(0.0)	10	3.0	(−28.9%)	7.9
Dominican Rep.	4.0	(9.0)	7.1	(14.5)	6.3	(9.2)	5.8	10.0	(0.0)	5	6.8	(36.9%)	6.9
Ecuador	6.5	(5.2)	7.7	(11.3)	7.4	(6.4)	7.2	7.8	(11.1)	8	5.3	(6.5%)	7.1
Egypt	5.1	(7.3)	6.1	(19.7)	N/A		5.6	10.0	(0.0)	5	4.7	(−5.4%)	6.3
El Salvador	8.5	(2.2)	8.9	(5.7)	6.8	(7.9)	8.1	7.8	(11.1)	8	2.7	(−31.5%)	6.6
Estonia	10.0	(0.0)	N/A		N/A		10.0	10.0	(0.0)	10	7.4	(48.6%)	9.4
Fiji	7.0	(4.5)	7.5	(12.4)	N/A		7.3	9.4	(3.0)	2	5.9	(18.1%)	6.1
Finland	9.7	(0.5)	8.9	(5.6)	7.6	(5.9)	8.7	10.0	(0.0)	8	4.6	(−7.2%)	7.8
France	9.8	(0.3)	8.9	(5.6)	7.6	(5.9)	8.8	10.0	(0.0)	5	4.8	(−3.2%)	7.2
Germany	9.7	(0.5)	8.9	(5.6)	7.6	(5.9)	8.7	10.0	(0.0)	10	5.6	(12.9%)	8.6
Greece	9.7	(0.4)	8.9	(5.6)	7.6	(5.9)	8.8	10.0	(0.0)	8	1.4	(−41.6%)	7.0
Guatemala	7.7	(3.4)	8.3	(8.4)	6.2	(9.5)	7.4	10.0	(0.0)	8	2.7	(−32.0%)	7.0
Honduras	8.1	(2.9)	8.4	(7.8)	6.8	(8.0)	7.8	10.0	(0.0)	5	6.7	(34.0%)	7.4
Hong Kong	9.8	(0.3)	10.0	(0.0)	10.0	(0.0)	9.9	10.0	(0.0)	10	10.0	(106.1%)	10.0
Hungary	9.2	(1.3)	7.1	(14.3)	3.2	(17.0)	6.5	10.0	(0.0)	5	6.5	(29.1%)	7.0
Iceland	9.7	(0.5)	9.6	(1.9)	4.8	(13.0)	8.0	10.0	(0.0)	8	1.1	(−43.8%)	6.8
India	2.8	(10.8)	3.4	(32.9)	4.9	(12.7)	3.7	10.0	(0.0)	0	5.4	(8.1%)	4.8

	Tariffs (i) Revenues from taxes on trade as a share of the trade sector	Tariffs (ii) Mean tariff rate	Tariffs (iii) Standard deviation of tariff rates	Composite tariff rating	Black Market Difference between the official and black market exchange rate	Capital Restrictions on citizens engaging in capital transactions with foreigners	Trade Actual relative to expected size of trade sector	TOI 1998
Indonesia	9.5 (0.7)	7.6 (11.9)	3.4 (16.6)	6.8	7.8 (11.1)	0	10.0 (114.7%)	6.2
Iran	3.9 (9.2)	N/A	N/A	3.9	0.0 (150.0)	0	2.8 (−30.2%)	1.7
Ireland	9.7 (0.5)	8.6 (6.9)	7.6 (5.9)	8.6	10.0 (0.0)	8	8.2 (63.7%)	8.7
Israel	9.8 (0.2)	9.6 (2.0)	N/A	9.7	10.0 (0.0)	8	4.0 (−17.2%)	7.9
Italy	9.8 (0.3)	8.6 (6.9)	7.6 (5.9)	8.7	10.0 (0.0)	10	4.5 (−9.9%)	8.3
Jamaica	3.6 (9.6)	6.2 (19.0)	5.6 (11.1)	5.1	7.8 (11.1)	8	5.3 (5.7%)	6.5
Japan	9.0 (1.5)	8.7 (6.6)	6.3 (9.3)	8.0	10.0 (0.0)	8	0.0 (−51.7%)	6.5
Jordan	6.9 (4.7)	7.1 (14.4)	N/A	7.0	10.0 (0.0)	2	7.2 (43.8%)	6.5
Kenya	6.2 (5.8)	5.9 (20.8)	N/A	6.0	7.8 (11.1)	8	6.1 (22.3%)	7.0
South Korea	8.8 (1.8)	8.1 (9.4)	7.0 (7.6)	8.0	10.0 (0.0)	8	7.1 (42.9%)	8.3
Kuwait	9.4 (1.0)	N/A	N/A	9.4	10.0 (0.0)	2	4.0 (−16.1%)	6.3
Latvia	9.7 (0.5)	8.8 (5.9)	5.7 (10.7)	8.1	10.0 (0.0)	5	5.4 (−8.1%)	7.1
Lithuania	9.6 (0.5)	9.1 (4.6)	6.3 (9.3)	8.3	10.0 (0.0)	8	5.7 (13.4%)	8.0
Luxembourg	9.9 (0.1)	8.9 (5.6)	7.6 (5.9)	8.8	10.0 (0.0)	10	4.8 (−3.3%)	8.4
Madagascar	3.4 (10.0)	N/A	N/A	3.4	10.0 (0.0)	2	4.9 (−1.5%)	5.1
Malawi	4.6 (8.1)	4.9 (25.3)	5.4 (11.6)	5.0	7.8 (11.1)	2	5.8 (16.1%)	5.1
Malaysia	8.9 (1.6)	8.2 (9.1)	2.2 (19.6)	6.4	10.0 (0.0)	2	10.0 (286.3%)	7.1
Mali	N/A	5.6 (22.1)	N/A	5.6	9.6 (2.0)	0	5.6 (11.3%)	5.2
Malta	9.5 (0.8)	8.5 (7.6)	7.7 (5.8)	8.5	9.4 (3.0)	2	4.0 (−17.2%)	6.0
Mauritius	6.7 (5.0)	4.2 (29.1)	0.0 (26.2)	3.6	10.0 (0.0)	10	5.0 (−1.0%)	7.1
Mexico	9.4 (0.9)	7.3 (13.3)	5.8 (10.6)	7.5	10.0 (0.0)	5	9.0 (79.0%)	7.9
Morocco	N/A	4.8 (26.0)	4.6 (13.5)	4.7	10.0 (0.0)	2	4.7 (−5.5%)	5.4
Myanmar	0.0 (35.9)	N/A	N/A	0.0	0.0 (2604.0)	0	0.0 (−96.7%)	0.0

	Tariffs (i) Revenues from taxes on trade as a share of the trade sector	Tariffs (ii) Mean tariff rate	Tariffs (iii) Standard deviation of tariff rates	Composite tariff rating	Black Market Difference between the official and black market exchange rate	Capital Restrictions on citizens engaging in capital transactions with foreigners	Trade Actual relative to expected size of trade sector	TOI 1998
Namibia	N/A	8.6 (7.2)	6.0 (10.0)	7.3	10.0 (0.0)	2	9.0 (80.9%)	7.1
Nepal	6.7 (5.0)	7.5 (12.4)	5.5 (11.3)	6.6	7.8 (11.1)	0	4.8 (−3.0%)	4.8
Netherlands	9.7 (0.5)	8.9 (5.6)	7.6 (5.9)	8.7	10.0 (0.0)	10	5.9 (17.6%)	8.7
New Zealand	8.9 (1.6)	9.2 (3.8)	8.0 (5.1)	8.7	10.0 (0.0)	8	4.5 (−9.7%)	7.8
Nicaragua	7.1 (4.3)	7.8 (10.9)	7.0 (7.5)	7.3	10.0 (0.0)	8	7.6 (51.6%)	8.2
Niger	N/A	5.6 (22.1)	3.4 (16.5)	5.6	9.6 (2.0)	0	3.4 (−24.7%)	4.6
Norway	9.8 (0.3)	9.2 (4.1)	N/A	7.5	10.0 (0.0)	8	4.4 (−10.3%)	7.5
Oman	9.4 (0.9)	N/A	N/A	9.4	10.0 (0.0)	2	4.8 (−3.4%)	6.6
Pakistan	5.0 (7.6)	N/A	N/A	5.0	7.8 (11.1)	2	4.8 (−4.7%)	4.9
Panama	7.3 (4.0)	8.2 (9.2)	7.6 (5.9)	7.7	10.0 (0.0)	10	4.4 (−10.0%)	8.0
Papua New Guinea	N/A	5.9 (20.7)	2.3 (19.2)	4.1	0.0 (66.7)	0	10.0 (118.0%)	3.5
Paraguay	7.1 (4.4)	8.1 (9.5)	7.4 (6.5)	7.5	7.8 (11.1)	10	5.9 (18.6%)	7.8
Peru	6.6 (5.2)	7.4 (13.2)	8.8 (2.9)	7.6	10.0 (0.0)	10	2.4 (−33.8%)	7.5
Philippines	7.6 (3.6)	8.0 (10.2)	6.1 (9.7)	7.2	10.0 (0.0)	5	10.0 (134.7%)	8.1
Poland	8.2 (2.7)	6.5 (17.6)	0.0 (28.1)	4.9	10.0 (0.0)	5	5.5 (10.9%)	6.4
Portugal	9.7 (0.5)	8.9 (5.6)	7.6 (5.9)	8.7	10.0 (0.0)	8	4.5 (−9.1%)	7.8
Romania	8.5 (2.3)	6.1 (19.4)	2.8 (18.1)	5.8	7.8 (11.1)	0	4.5 (−8.9%)	4.5
Russian Fed.	6.6 (5.1)	7.5 (12.6)	6.6 (8.4)	6.9	1.4 (42.9)	2	9.4 (87.3%)	4.9
Senegal	0.6 (14.1)	7.4 (12.8)	N/A	4.0	9.6 (2.0)	0	5.6 (11.8%)	4.8
Sierra Leone	0.0 (15.8)	N/A	N/A	0.0	5.0 (25.0)	0	0.0 (−68.4%)	1.3
Singapore	9.9 (0.1)	9.9 (0.4)	N/A	9.9	10.0 (0.0)	10	10.0 (115.2%)	10.0
Slovak Republic	N/A	8.8 (6.0)	N/A	8.8	7.8 (11.1)	5	7.2 (44.8%)	7.2
Slovenia	8.2 (2.7)	7.9 (10.6)	7.0 (7.4)	7.7	7.8 (11.1)	5	4.7 (−6.1%)	6.3

	Tariffs (i) Revenues from taxes on trade as a share of the trade sector	Tariffs (ii) Mean tariff rate	Tariffs (iii) Standard deviation of tariff rates	Composite tariff rating	Black Market Difference between the official and black market exchange rate	Capital Restrictions on citizens engaging in capital transactions with foreigners	Trade Actual relative to expected size of trade sector	TOI 1998
South Africa	9.9 (0.1)	8.6 (7.2)	6.0 (10.0)	8.2	10.0 (0.0)	2	6.4 (27.7%)	6.6
Spain	9.7 (0.5)	8.9 (5.6)	7.6 (5.9)	8.7	10.0 (0.0)	8	5.5 (11.0%)	8.1
Sri Lanka	7.6 (3.5)	6.0 (20.0)	3.8 (15.4)	5.8	10.0 (0.0)	2	6.2 (23.1%)	6.0
Sweden	9.8 (0.3)	8.9 (5.6)	7.6 (5.9)	8.8	10.0 (0.0)	8	6.0 (19.4%)	8.2
Switzerland	9.8 (0.3)	9.5 (2.4)	7.0 (7.4)	8.8	10.0 (0.0)	10	3.8 (−19.9%)	8.1
Syria	7.6 (3.7)	N/A	N/A	7.6	0.0 (400.0)	0	5.4 (9.0%)	3.3
Taiwan	9.1 (1.3)	8.1 (9.7)	5.6 (11.0)	7.6	10.0 (0.0)	5	6.3 (26.2%)	7.2
Tanzania	2.1 (11.9)	5.6 (22.1)	4.4 (13.9)	4.0	7.8 (11.1)	0	5.0 (−0.6)%	4.2
Thailand	9.0 (1.5)	4.5 (27.6)	N/A	6.8	10.0 (0.0)	2	10.0 (130.1%)	7.2
Trinidad & Tobago	3.2 (10.2)	6.1 (19.3)	5.4 (11.4)	4.9	10.0 (0.0)	8	3.7 (−21.0%)	6.6
Tunisia	4.1 (8.9)	4.0 (29.9)	4.9 (12.8)	4.3	10.0 (0.0)	2	6.0 (20.4%)	5.6
Turkey	9.4 (0.9)	7.3 (13.5)	0.0 (25.4)	5.6	9.8 (1.0)	2	5.9 (18.6%)	5.8
Ukraine	N/A	8.0 (10.0)	5.6 (10.9)	6.8	7.8 (11.1)	2	8.4 (68.6%)	6.3
United Kingdom	9.7 (0.5)	8.9 (5.6)	7.6 (5.9)	8.7	10.0 (0.0)	10	4.9 (−2.7%)	8.4
United States	9.4 (0.9)	9.0 (4.8)	5.4 (11.6)	7.9	10.0 (0.0)	8	5.0 (−0.2%)	7.7
Uruguay	8.2 (2.7)	7.6 (12.2)	6.8 (7.9)	7.5	10.0 (0.0)	10	1.9 (−38.5%)	7.4
Venezuela	6.7 (4.9)	7.6 (12.0)	7.6 (6.1)	7.3	10.0 (0.0)	5	4.1 (−15.2%)	6.6
Zambia	7.1 (4.3)	7.3 (13.6)	6.3 (9.3)	6.9	5.0 (25.0)	10	6.4 (27.2%)	7.1
Zimbabwe	5.1 (7.3)	5.6 (22.2)	2.9 (17.8)	4.5	7.2 (14.0)	2	8.6 (71.2%)	5.6

Notes: When ratings are transformations, actual data are presented in parentheses. Totals may not exactly equal the sum of their parts due to rounding.

TABLE 3–2   TRADE OPENNESS INDEX (1980–1998)

	TOI (1980–1982)	TOI (1985–1987)	TOI (1990–1992)	TOI (1995–1997)	TOI (1998)	TOI (1980–1998)*
Algeria	3.7	2.4	2.7	3.0	2.8	2.9
Argentina	1.5	1.0	2.0	6.9	7.3	3.3
Australia	6.1	7.0	7.4	7.8	7.9	7.2
Austria	6.4	6.5	7.0	7.9	8.0	7.1
Bangladesh	0.8	0.6	0.8	2.5	3.8	1.5
Barbados	4.8	4.5	3.7	4.4	4.6	4.4
Belgium	9.1	9.4	9.0	8.9	9.0	9.1
Belize	4.0	3.6	4.6	5.3	5.7	4.5
Bolivia	2.4	4.9	5.9	7.1	7.8	5.4
Botswana	5.5	5.5	6.4	6.5	7.1	6.1
Brazil	2.9	1.5	4.0	4.7	4.7	3.4
Burundi	1.0	1.9	1.6	1.3	2.3	1.5
Cameroon	3.3	5.3	4.7	4.7	5.2	4.6
Canada	7.5	7.7	7.5	7.9	7.5	7.6
Central African Republic	3.2	4.4	3.6	4.7	4.3	4.0
Chile	5.9	5.5	6.7	6.9	6.8	6.3
China	3.0	5.0	4.0	7.3	7.9	5.2
Colombia	3.4	3.9	4.4	6.2	6.0	4.7
Congo, Rep.	5.5	5.3	5.2	6.7	7.0	5.8
Costa Rica	2.6	4.0	5.8	7.9	8.3	5.4
Côte d'Ivoire	3.8	5.2	4.6	6.2	5.9	5.0
Cyprus	3.7	5.1	4.5	5.2	5.1	4.7
Denmark	7.0	7.0	6.7	7.3	7.9	7.1
Dominican Republic	2.0	4.6	3.5	5.6	6.9	4.3
Ecuador	2.9	3.8	5.2	6.8	7.1	4.9
Egypt	3.4	1.9	3.5	5.9	6.3	4.0
El Salvador	2.2	2.5	4.1	5.9	6.6	4.0
Fiji	6.0	5.7	5.9	5.9	6.1	5.9
Finland	6.4	6.3	5.7	7.8	7.8	6.7
France	5.0	6.5	7.0	7.0	7.2	6.5

	TOI (1980–1982)	TOI (1985–1987)	TOI (1990–1992)	TOI (1995–1997)	TOI (1998)	TOI (1980–1998)*
Germany	8.3	8.7	8.5	8.4	8.6	8.5
Greece	4.8	5.3	5.6	6.1	7.0	5.6
Guatemala	3.2	2.1	5.2	6.9	7.0	4.7
Honduras	3.1	2.3	5.3	7.3	7.4	4.8
Hong Kong	9.7	10.0	10.0	10.0	10.0	9.9
Hungary	3.1	4.1	4.3	6.6	7.0	4.8
Iceland	4.2	5.6	4.9	6.0	6.8	5.3
India	3.0	2.8	3.4	4.2	4.8	3.5
Indonesia	6.2	5.9	6.1	6.1	6.2	6.1
Iran	1.6	0.8	2.9	2.4	1.7	1.9
Ireland	7.2	7.3	7.2	8.5	8.7	7.7
Israel	5.7	5.9	6.1	6.2	7.9	6.2
Italy	7.2	7.2	6.7	7.8	8.3	7.4
Jamaica	3.8	5.6	5.5	7.1	6.5	5.6
Japan	6.2	6.6	6.7	6.5	6.5	6.5
Jordan	6.1	6.0	6.2	6.4	6.5	6.2
Kenya	4.2	4.5	3.9	7.5	7.0	5.3
South Korea	5.8	6.1	6.9	6.9	8.3	6.6
Luxembourg	8.3	8.6	8.3	8.1	8.4	8.3
Madagascar	1.9	2.7	3.3	3.4	5.1	3.1
Malawi	3.1	4.5	4.3	4.8	5.1	4.3
Malaysia	7.8	7.9	7.9	7.9	7.1	7.8
Mali	3.6	5.2	5.2	5.5	5.2	4.9
Malta	5.2	5.6	5.7	5.5	6.0	5.5
Mauritius	3.6	5.0	4.9	6.8	7.1	5.3
Mexico	1.8	4.8	7.0	7.5	7.9	5.6
Morocco	4.4	5.7	5.2	5.7	5.4	5.3
Myanmar	0.5	0.0	0.0	0.0	0.0	0.1
Nepal	3.1	3.9	3.1	4.4	4.8	3.7
Netherlands	8.4	8.5	8.2	8.6	8.7	8.4
New Zealand	7.0	7.0	7.7	8.1	7.8	7.5
Nicaragua	1.5	0.6	4.7	6.9	8.2	4.0

	TOI (1980–1982)	TOI (1985–1987)	TOI (1990–1992)	TOI (1995–1997)	TOI (1998)	TOI (1980–1998)*
Niger	3.8	4.6	4.0	4.2	4.6	4.2
Norway	6.7	7.4	7.8	7.5	7.5	7.4
Pakistan	2.1	4.0	4.0	4.8	4.9	3.9
Panama	9.0	8.6	8.4	9.5	8.0	8.8
Paraguay	2.6	3.7	5.8	7.5	7.8	5.2
Peru	4.0	2.0	3.7	7.0	7.5	4.5
Philippines	5.2	5.6	6.0	7.4	8.1	6.3
Portugal	5.9	6.3	7.0	7.8	7.8	6.9
Senegal	3.5	4.7	4.2	4.6	4.8	4.3
Sierra Leone	1.8	2.4	2.4	1.4	1.3	1.9
Singapore	9.5	10.0	9.9	9.9	10.0	9.8
South Africa	6.4	6.2	6.2	6.2	6.6	6.3
Spain	6.6	6.9	7.4	7.9	8.1	7.3
Sri Lanka	4.4	4.5	4.2	5.9	6.0	4.9
Sweden	6.4	7.5	8.3	8.6	8.2	7.8
Switzerland	8.2	8.3	7.8	7.8	8.1	8.0
Syria	1.9	2.1	2.4	3.2	3.3	2.5
Taiwan	6.8	7.0	7.6	7.5	7.2	7.2
Tanzania	2.2	2.2	2.6	5.2	4.2	3.2
Thailand	5.9	6.0	6.3	6.9	7.2	6.4
Trinidad & Tobago	2.8	3.0	3.4	7.1	6.6	4.4
Tunisia	3.4	4.4	5.1	5.5	5.6	4.7
Turkey	2.7	5.1	4.4	6.4	5.8	4.8
United Kingdom	8.5	8.7	8.3	8.5	8.4	8.5
United States	7.9	7.9	7.8	7.8	7.7	7.8
Uruguay	6.2	7.1	7.1	7.2	7.4	7.0
Venezuela	7.9	5.1	6.5	6.8	6.6	6.6
Zambia	4.5	3.8	3.9	6.0	7.1	4.8
Zimbabwe	4.0	3.6	5.5	5.7	5.6	4.8

Note: * TOI (1980–1998) is a weighted average giving full weight to all periods except 1998, which receives a 1/2 weight to compensate for its shorter period representation.

CHAPTER 4: INTELLECTUAL PROPERTY AND PATENT REGIMES

by Walter G. Park

Market economies function on the price system and on a system of well-defined property rights. In some regions, this includes the provision of property rights over intangible assets, such as knowledge capital. Through a system of intellectual property laws, individuals and organizations have the right and opportunity to engage in the production, consumption, trade, and exchange of ideas. The nature of intellectual property systems, however, varies across countries, as do legal systems governing real property. In recent years, as more and more of the wealth of nations is in the form of intellectual assets (and as these assets contribute importantly to productivity growth), a concept of property rights that applies only to physical assets is being seen as very limiting.

The purpose of this chapter is to discuss how to measure the strength of property rights protection over *ideas*. Such a measure could be used for academic research, policy evaluation, or comparisons of intellectual property regimes across countries and over time. This chapter focuses on quantifying the level of *patent rights* protection. Patent rights are one form of intellectual property protection (along with copyright protection, trademark rights, geographical indications, and others). Patent rights have received perhaps the most attention because of their close link to economic variables such as investment, technological progress, and productivity growth. However, a more complete picture of a nation's intellectual property regime would need to incorporate the other instruments of intellectual property protection. Though, in most cases, the strength of these individual instruments should be highly correlated, in some cases they may not; that is, in some nations, copyright laws might be strong but patent protection weak. In any event, the methodology presented here for measuring patent protection could be used to quantify the levels of other intellectual property rights. In some cases, intellectual property instruments might all share some common aspects; for example, the same enforcement or judicial mechanisms used to protect patent rights might be available to protect trademark rights.

This chapter is organized as follows: section 2 describes some of the institutional detail behind patent systems. The purpose is to define terms and provide some legal background. Section 3 describes the methodology for constructing an index of patent rights, discusses the possibility of gaps between measured protection and actual practice, and presents some estimates of patent rights for selected countries. Section 4 briefly explores the relationship between patent rights and economic freedom, and section 5 contains some concluding thoughts.

1: INSTITUTIONAL BACKGROUND

The patent is both a scientific and a legal document. It is a scientific document in that it contains a full description of the underlying technology, enabling those persons skilled in the art to make and use the invention. Insufficient technical disclosure is a ground for disqualifying a patent right. The patent document also acts as a legal title (or deed) to a piece of intellectual territory, within which others may not trespass and utilize without a license. Possession of this territory is temporary (usually 20 years at most), ownership rights must be renewed (through payment of renewal fees), and, like real estate, this intellectual territory can be sold or transferred. This territory of ideas must also be industrially applicable (not consisting of abstract ideas, such as scientific theories, mathematical knowledge, or organizational methods). The boundaries of the intellectual territory given to the patent holder are identified by the "claims" in the granted patent; each of these claims describes what the invention does or can do. The number and breadth of claims implicitly define the extent of the territory.[1]

The logic of why patent systems exist is discussed extensively in the literature.[2] It is therefore best here to clarify a few points. First, in the absence of a patent system, markets for ideas would be "missing" due to the nature of knowledge as a public good. A patent system therefore creates a market that would otherwise not exist. However, since the patent holder is granted *exclusive rights* to exploit the innovation, the market for that innovation is not one of perfect competition. Without the right to exclude, and price at a markup above the competitive price, the innovator might not be able to *recoup* her up-front research and development (R&D) costs over time. By enhancing the ability of the innovator to appropriate the returns to her R&D investments, the patent system generates incentives to innovate and thereby engenders a form of "competition" over time to create ideas. Thus, as the literature suggests, a trade-off exists between technology creation and diffusion: patent systems must provide, on the one hand, adequate incentives for technology creation and, on the other hand, opportunities for competitive diffusion.

This characterization of the patent system can create a few misconceptions. The first is that a patent makes a firm a monopolist in the traditional sense of a single firm in an industry. Rather, it gives the holder the right to exclude others from using the new idea commercially; it does not allow the holder to exclude other firms from entering the industry. A second misconception is that there is a trade-off between technology creation and knowledge diffusion; rather there is a trade-off between the former and the diffusion (or supply) of

output embodying the new knowledge. Patents do not restrict the diffusion of knowledge; on the contrary, they help diffuse it. The reason is that, in exchange for patent protection, inventors must (as pointed out earlier) disclose their new knowledge.

How do patent systems work? It is convenient to describe them in roughly the chronological order in which inventors apply for and enforce their patent rights. Table 4-1 presents an outline of the procedures from the *patent application* stage to the *patent enforcement* stage. It is precisely the institutional details governing these procedures that vary across countries and account for the differences in the strength of patent protection among countries.

Patent Application

The inventor must first decide whether to seek patent protection or keep the invention a *trade secret*. By choosing the latter course of action, the inventor risks being imitated and not being able to claim damages but some nations do provide some form of trade secrecy protection (which prohibits the obtaining of company secrets by illegal means). However, trade secret protection does not protect against another inventor independently developing the invention and patenting it, or against reverse engineering.

If the inventor decides to patent, another decision to make is whether to patent nationally only (i.e., in the domestic market only) or internationally (in more than one country). If the inventor decides to patent internationally, there are a number of "routes" in which to seek worldwide protection. One way is simply to file a patent in each country of interest. Obtaining a patent in one country does not automatically grant protection in other countries (unless there exists some specific agreement between countries, as in the case where one country "registers" patents obtained in another country).[3]

Filing patents in each country of interest may be efficient if the inventor is only interested in obtaining protection in a few countries; however, if the inventor is interested in a much broader geographic coverage, separate national filing is cumbersome. Hence an alternative way is to seek a regional patent. A European Patent Office (EPO) patent is one such regional patent. Through a single, centralized filing with the EPO, the applicant can try to obtain a patent in several EPO member

Table 4-1: Patent Application and Enforcement: An Outline of Procedures

(A) Patent Application

    1. Pre-Application Choice   Patenting vs. Trade Secrecy?

- If Choose to Patent,   National or International Patent?

- If International, which Route   Separate National Filings?
                                         PCT Filing?
                                         EPO Filing?
                                         EPO/PCT Filings?
                                         Some Combination of Filings?

    2. Pre-Grant Determinations:

- Priority Date of Application (depending on first-to-file versus first-to-invent, grace periods [if any])

- Publication of Application (18 months from date of application or upon patent grant [if at all])

- Patentable Matter (whether "subject matter" restricted: e.g. genetically engineered products, business methods, inventions against public order or morality, etc.)

- Patentability (search and examination for novelty, non-obviousness, and utility)

- Duration (length) and Scope (width) of Patent Protection

    3. Post-Grant Process:

- Oppositions (by third parties) against validity of patent grant (where laws allow)

- Conditions imposed on patent grant (e.g. working; compulsory licensing)

- Patent Renewal or Maintenance Fees (otherwise, patent rights expire); renewal schedules vary from country to country.

(B) Patent Enforcement

    1. Enforcement "Routes":

- Litigation

- Arbitration

- Settlement

    2. Statutory Provisions:

- Preliminary Injunctions

- Contributory Infringement

- Burden of Proof Reversals

- Doctrine of Equivalents

- Discovery

Note: PCT denotes Patent Cooperation Treaty of the World Intellectual Property Office (WIPO); EPO European Patent Office.

states. Another regional patent is the Patent Cooperation Treaty (or PCT) patent, administered by the World Intellectual Property Office (WIPO). An inventor can file a single PCT application and *designate* as many member states of WIPO as he chooses. Since EPO states are also member states of WIPO, if PCT applicants are also designating a number of EPO countries, the PCT patent has a provision whereby the patent applicant can designate the entire EPO as a block (treated as one member state unit), thus cutting down on those fees that vary with the number of states designated. In that case, the applicant is filing an EPO-PCT patent.[4]

Having decided upon the route for applying for a patent, the inventor goes through the appropriate review and examination. A crucial determination to be made early on is *priority*: who gets to apply for a patent for a particular invention? Is another application pending? In the United States, priority goes to the inventor who is the *first to invent*. In the rest of the world, it is generally the *first to file* an application who gets priority.[5] If someone else has priority, the inventor loses the right to seek a patent for that invention. For inventors filing patents internationally, the *Paris Convention Treaty* allows inventors (of signatory states) up to 12 months to file an application in other signatory countries after first filing in a signatory country. The inventor thus reserves that initial filing date, for 12 months, for purposes of establishing who was first to file. All relevant matters are referred to that filing date (or to the earliest date of priority) for official purposes.

Countries also vary in terms of when to disclose or *publish* information in the patent application. The United States keeps it secret until the patent is granted. If it is not granted, the information is not disclosed to the public. In the EPO and Japan, the application is made public after 18 months from the date of filing, even if the patent is not granted. In most of Africa, it is made public upon acceptance of a complete application. An advantage of early disclosure is that it enables other inventors to build on new and existing knowledge, avert infringement and costly litigation, and avoid duplicative research projects. A drawback is that the procedure may discourage inventors who are risk averse and not certain of successfully obtaining a grant.

Another important part of the patent application process is the determination of patentability. First, the laws generally indicate subject matters that are not patentable, perhaps because certain subjects are not novel, non-obvious, and industrially useful. For example, medical treatment is not considered patentable because it does not yield industrially applicable output. Or, subject matters may be declared unpatentable if they are considered contrary to public order, morality, health, and national security. One area of future controversy and of relevance to the future of the global biotechnology industry is the patentability of genetic innovations, which the United States permits to a limited degree.[6] Prior to 1995, several countries (Argentina, Austria, Denmark, and India) did not even provide pharmaceutical patent protection on national health grounds. Most now permit it.

During the determination of patentability, a crucial conclusion is arrived at concerning novelty. The invention must not be in the pool of existing (prior) knowledge. The inventor therefore disqualifies herself if she publicly discloses the invention before applying for a patent.[7] The United States, however, provides a 12-month grace period, allowing the invention to remain novel if the patent application is made within 12 months of public disclosure. The EPO and Japan permit grace periods of 6 months for certain types of public disclosure only (for example, public demonstrations).

Novelty, non-obviousness, and industrial applicability are determined after extensive search and examination by patent examiners. If, at the end of the process, a patent is granted, a determination of patent "scope" is also made. The scope of protection refers to the size of the protected intellectual territory (i.e., how many claims are accepted or how broadly they are written). If the scope of protection is very broad, competitors must develop inventions with an "inventive step" that is large enough to avoid infringing on the patent holder's rights. Economists have debated whether technological change is better served by a broad or narrow scope (see Merges and Nelson 1994). On the one hand, a broad scope gives more market power to an inventor and might be a strong inducement to invent; on the other hand, it makes it more difficult for competitors to develop new follow-on inventions.

Upon grant, inventors may face opposition from third parties. In the EPO, third-party oppositions occur for a limited time *after* a patent is grant. In Japan, oppositions take place *while* the patent application is being reviewed. In the United States, there are no formal oppositions during or after grant; instead patent validity challenges, if any, occur in court. An advantage of third-party oppositions might be that it helps spread the burden of fully determining patent validity to competitors. A disadvantage is that an expensive obstacle is placed in the path of a patent applicant. Rivals could especially try to delay, if not prevent, the applicant from getting a patent.

After a patent is granted, patent holders may also face conditions regarding working and licensing. Working requirements are essentially requirements that the patent holder practise or exploit the invention by a certain period of time, or else forfeit his patent right or face compulsory licensing. From the point of view of the patent holder, working requirements are restrictive. The patent holder may not be financially able to work the invention or the market may not yet be ready for it. On the other hand, some patent regimes operate on the premise that the purpose of a patent is not to profit inventors but to bring economic value to the community. For this reason, in some countries, if a patent is not worked within a certain time, the patentee is required to give a license to a third party willing and able to work the patent (in exchange for a "reasonable" royalty).

Compulsory licensing may also be imposed if inventions relate to food and medicine or if another patent is being blocked. Blocking patents are patents that contain enough overlapping or related subject matter that manufacturing one item would involve infringing the other. They usually arise when one patent is an improvement over the other. Without a patent, the improver would infringe on the core technology. But, even with a patent, the improver needs a license to use the core technology without which the improvement cannot work. The solution to this dilemma is to have improvers and pioneers approach each other with licensing agreements. Otherwise, if voluntary private bargaining cannot resolve the blocking problem, the authorities in some countries will impose compulsory cross-licensing. Blocking also

tends to arise in situations where the scope of protection is too narrow, allowing inventors to patent too closely to one another in "technology space." [8]

Finally, after grant, in order to keep the patent right in force the patent holder must pay renewal (or maintenance) fees. The dates and frequency of renewal vary across countries. In the United States, patent holders must renew three times: three and one-half years after grant, seven and one-half years after grant, and eleven and one-half years after grant. In Japan, patents are renewed annually from the date of application and, in European countries, they are typically renewed annually starting from the third year after the filing date. It should be noted that most patent rights are not held for the full duration that patent holders are entitled to. More than half of patents granted expire voluntarily within 10 years from the date of application. [9]

Patent Enforcement

During the duration of patent protection, the inventor may be required to defend or enforce her patent right. If infringement occurs, and the patent right has not expired, the patent rights holder must largely seek redress through the court system (not through the patent offices). Depending on what enforcement mechanisms are available, the patent rights holder can pursue litigation, arbitration, or outside settlement. (Litigation, however, is costly and lengthy. Combatants typically settle or defer to an arbitration board. Jury trials are relatively infrequent because of the high costs of getting expert testimony and acquiring documents, among other things.) How adequate enforcement mechanisms are, and how well they work, affect the inventor's *ex ante* incentive to innovate (and the imitator's incentive to imitate). Poor enforcement mechanisms have the effect of devaluing patent rights and discouraging patenting. New ideas are more apt to be kept trade secrets.

While litigation, arbitration, and settlement offer different enforcement routes should infringement occur, patent holders may also have recourse to a number of statutory provisions that can aid in enforcement: preliminary injunction, contributory infringement, burden of proof reversal, doctrine of equivalents, and discovery. Preliminary injunctions are pre-trial actions that require the accused infringer to cease the production or use of the patented product or process during the course of the trial. Preliminary injunctions are a means of protecting the patentee from infringement until a final decision is made in a trial. Contributory infringement refers to actions that do not in themselves infringe a patent right but cause or otherwise result in infringement by others. Examples include the supplying of materials or machinery parts that are essential to the use of a patented invention. Thus, contributory infringement permits third-parties also to be liable if they contribute negligently to the infringement. Burden of proof reversals, in patent process cases, put the onus on the accused to prove innocence (that is, to show that the process used is not the patented one). Under a burden-of-proof reversal, if a certain product is produced by another party, it is assumed that it was produced with the patented process. Given the difficulty patentees have of proving that others are infringing on their patented processes (since there are often several ways of producing the same product), the shift in

burden can be a powerful enforcement mechanism. The doctrine of equivalents would find the accused infringer liable if she uses the *essence* of the patented invention but does not *literally* infringe the patent. This is especially helpful if the imitator makes modest changes to an invention and claims by a technicality not to have infringed. According to the doctrine, if the modified invention operates in "substantially" the same way, it is "essentially" an equivalent invention and, therefore, infringes upon the original invention. Lastly, discovery permits the accuser to obtain evidence from the accused, such as documentation. Pre-trial discovery, by compelling parties to exchange information in their possession fully, helps to facilitate settlement as parties develop a more convergent assessment about the likely outcome of a trial.

This concludes a brief overview of what patents are and how patent systems work. The next section shows how to take some of the relevant institutional detail and develop a quantitative measure of the strength of patent systems.

2: MEASUREMENT OF PATENT RIGHTS

The following section is drawn from Ginarte and Park (1997), which developed an index measuring the strength of patent rights across countries and over time. The index scores a nation's patent system from 0 to 5. Higher values indicate stronger levels of protection. Two things should be noted at the outset. First, stronger levels of protection need not necessarily imply "better" (from a social-welfare point of view). It is possible that there exists some optimal level of protection, beyond which higher levels of protection may discourage follow-on innovations or reduce consumer choice.

Secondly, not every patent law or institutional feature can be incorporated into the patent rights index. Some features do not add much variability since almost every country provides them (or does not provide them). Thus a key criterion in designing the index was to select those institutional features that provide maximum variability across countries. Furthermore, in some cases, it is controversial (theoretically or empirically) whether a particular feature of the patent system contributes positively or negatively (or not at all) to the strength

of patent rights. For example, *discovery* is an important means of collecting evidence but it burdens both the defendant and plaintiff. *Broad scope* gives strong protection to the patent holder (*ex post*) but may weaken the right of rival inventors to obtain a patent (*ex ante*). In any case, "scope" cannot be measured well, since it is not statutorily addressed. Scope is determined at the examiner level. Third parties or observers (such as social scientists) could dispute whether too many claims (or too few) were granted for an invention. Likewise, the quality of litigation is determined at the trial level (not necessarily by statutes) and can only be assessed case by case. The outcome of a trial could be seen as too favorable (or unfavorable) for the patent rights holder. Thus, to incorporate scope or litigation quality or any other feature of this nature, one would need to obtain further data at the micro-level (e.g. at the examiner level or trial level).

Construction of the Index
Two points that come out of the previous paragraph are: (1) the index is based on "macro" legal features

(and not on micro-level data); (2) the index is "selective," incorporating a subset of legal features in existence. The information used to construct the index is obtained directly from national patent laws.[10]

The index contains five categories: (i) extent of coverage, (ii) membership in international patent agreements, (iii) provisions for loss of protection, (iv) enforcement mechanisms, and (v) duration of protection. Each of these categories (per country, per time period) is given a score ranging from 0 to 1, as discussed below. The unweighted sum of the scores from these categories yields the overall value of the patent rights index. The index, therefore, ranges in value from 0 to 5.

As for how each of these five categories is scored, each category (except duration) consists of several features. A country may have one or more of these features, or none at all. Thus the score in a category indicates the fraction of those features that are available in that country (for that time period). For example, if a country in 1995 has all three features required for strong enforcement, it scores 3 out of 3 and earns a value of 1 for enforcement for that year; if it has only 1 of the features, it receives a score of $^1/_3$ for enforcement for that year. The score for duration is simply the length of protection allowed by authorities as a fraction of 20 years from the date of application (or as a fraction of 17 years from the date of grant, for countries based on a grant-based system). Countries that provide this "standard" length of time or more receive a 1 for duration. Table 4-2 provides a summary of the categories and scoring mechanism.

In what follows, a brief description of the features in each category will be discussed.

Coverage
In this category, the strength of protection is measured by the patentability of the following seven items: pharmaceuticals, chemicals, food, plant and animal varieties, surgical products, microorganisms, and utility models.[11] The value of this category indicates the fraction of these seven elements that were specified as being patentable in the law or were not specifically declared unpatentable.

Membership in International Agreements
By participating in international intellectual property-rights treaties, signatories indicate a willingness

and capacity to provide national, nondiscriminatory treatment to foreigners. The three major agreements are: (a) the *Paris Convention* of 1883 (and subsequent revisions); (b) the *Patent Cooperation Treaty (PCT)* of 1970; and (c) the *International Convention for the Protection of New Varieties of Plants (UPOV)* of 1961. Countries that are signatories to all three receive a value of 1 in this category; those that are signatories to just one receive a value of $^1/_3$.

The Paris Convention provides for national treatment to foreign nationals in the provision of patent rights. The main objective of the PCT is to harmonize and simplify administrative procedures. The UPOV confers plant breeder's rights, a form of protection similar to a patent. Unlike the Paris Convention, this treaty requires signatories to adopt uniform standards as national law, helping to make application procedures and laws clear and non-discriminatory.[12]

Loss of Protection
Patent holders may lose their patent rights wholly or partially. This category indicates whether authorities refrain from: (a) working requirements; (b) compulsory licensing; and (c) revocation of patents. These actions have the effect of weakening (or eliminating) a patent right. A country that does not impose any of these measures receives a value of 1 in this category.

As indicated earlier, working requirements refer to the exploitation of inventions. Such requirements restrict the freedom of choice of the patentee. If a country does not require working at any point during the patent term, it receives a value of $^1/_3$. Compulsory licensing requires patentees to share exploitation of the invention with third-parties, and reduces the returns to the invention that the patentee can appropriate (especially if it is imposed within a short time after a patent is obtained). A country receives another $^1/_3$ score if it refrains from imposing compulsory licensing within 3 or 4 years from the date of patent grant or application (the time frame stipulated in the Paris Convention). Finally, countries that do not revoke patents for non-working receive another $^1/_3$ score.

Enforcement
In this category, the selected conditions are the availability of: (a) preliminary injunctions, (b)

Table 4-2: Index of Patent Rights–Categories and Scoring Method

The index of patent rights (IPR) consists of the following five categories and assigns the following values to each criteria:

(1) Coverage	Available	Not Available
Patentability of pharmaceuticals	$1/7$	0
Patentability of chemicals	$1/7$	0
Patentability of food	$1/7$	0
Patentability of plant and animal varieties	$1/7$	0
Patentability of surgical products	$1/7$	0
Patentability of microorganisms	$1/7$	0
Patentability of utility models	$1/7$	0
(2) Membership in International Treaties	**Available**	**Not Available**
Paris Convention and Revisions	$1/3$	0
Patent Cooperation Treaty	$1/3$	0
Protection of New Varieties (UPOV)	$1/3$	0
(3) Restrictions on Patent Rights	**Does Not Exist**	**Exists**
"Working" Requirements	$1/3$	0
Compulsory Licensing	$1/3$	0
Revocation of Patents	$1/3$	0
(4) Enforcement	**Available**	**Not Available**
Preliminary Injunctions	$1/3$	0
Contributory Infringement	$1/3$	0
Burden-of-Proof Reversal	$1/3$	0
(5) Duration of Protection*	**Full**	**Partial or No Protection**
	1	$0 < f < 1$

Note*: where *full* duration is 20 years from the date of application (or 17 years from the date of grant, for grant-based patent systems) and *f* equals the duration of protection as a *fraction* of the full duration.

Note: Each category (except for duration) consists of a number of legal criteria relevant to that category. Each category (including duration) is scored out of 1. Thus, the Index of Patent Rights overall varies from 0 to 5. All criteria (or patent law features) within a category are weighted equally so that the value of each criteria is simply equal to its "share" in the category. For example, if a country provides two out of the three enforcement features, it receives a score of $2/3$ for enforcement; if it permits patenting in all seven subject areas, it receives a score of $7/7$ (or 1) for coverage; if it is not a member of any international treaty and provides for working requirements, compulsory licensing, and revocation of rights, it receives 0 for the second and third categories above; finally, if it provides protection for 12 years from the date of application, it receives a score of $12/20$. Overall, this country's IPR value would be $= 2/3 + 1 + 0 + 0 + 12/20 = 68/30$ or 2.27.

contributory infringement pleadings, and (c) burden-of-proof reversals. A country that provides all three receives a value of 1 for this category. (These legal features were defined in the previous section.)

Duration of Protection

The length of the patent term is important for ensuring adequate returns to innovative activity. Due to cross-country variation in the definition of starting points of patent terms, two scales were established to measure the strength of protection. The scales differ according to whether the start of the patent term is set from the date of application or from the date of grant. For patent terms based on the date of application, the standard is 20 years of protection.[13] Countries that provide 20 years or more of protection receive a value of 1 for this category. Those that provide shorter terms receive a value equal to the fraction of the 20 years that are provided. For example, if a country provides 15 years of protection, it receives a value of 0.75 for this category. The same procedure is applied to patent terms established from the date of grant. The only difference is that the standard duration is 17 years.

Statutory versus Actual Protection

The focus thus far has been on the statutory provisions (that is, "the laws on the books"). In practice, there might be serious gaps between actual and perceived (statutory) protection. If so, the index described above would fail to capture the real strength of patent protection in practice. Determining whether laws are actually enforced is difficult to determine for any legal statute, let alone intellectual property laws. Nonetheless, some indirect evidence is worth considering. The concern is primarily with the measured indexes of the OECD countries rather than those of the less-developed, since the main concern about the latter is the absence of laws.[14] Hence if there is any overestimation of patent protection levels, it should be in the OECD's measures. It would be ideal to examine the execution of laws by studying court cases: the percentage of infringement cases that went to court; attitude of judges and enforcement officials; damages awarded (as to whether they were commensurate with the offense). Unfortunately, no such international database of court records exists.[15]

A second-best approach to studying the execution of laws is to examine *complaints* against the system (its courts, officials, and outcomes). The idea is that a number of complaints would be filed if the system is not working (relative to what the statutes provide). The nature of complaints would indicate whether there are any systematic problems with the execution of laws. Ginarte and Park (1997) have investigated the types of complaints filed by American firms to the *U.S. Trade Representative (USTR)* regarding their protection abroad. If American firms faced these difficulties, it is likely that other foreign agents faced similar treatment in those countries. The authors find, however, that the complaints were largely non-patent related (i.e. related to copyrights or trademarks). Furthermore, the complaints were primarily statutory (rather than enforcement-related)–that is, with the lack of laws in the case of less developed countries, and with procedural law differences in the case of developed nations (concerning coverage, exemptions, application procedures, etc.). Interestingly, there are few complaints about the enforcement of patent rights. Countries like Egypt, Pakistan, and Venezuela have received complaints about inadequate patent enforcement mechanisms while countries like Nigeria, Peru, and the Philippines have received criticisms for the weak execution of enforcement actions that are available under the law. However, no complaints about patent enforcement or execution have been levelled against OECD countries.

In summary, the main complaints are not about the carrying out of patent laws. Rather the subjects of complaints (statutory and institutional differences) are matters that the patent rights index already reflects. Hence, the evidence tends to support a narrow gap between the measured and actual levels of patent protection. This is not to say that there are no problems with the actual execution and administration of the laws, as difficulties do exist even in countries with strong patent systems (the United States, Japan, and the EPO). However, the availability of laws on the books acts as a strong signal to inventors of the strength of patent rights available. "Proof" that the index does help to capture the strength of patent rights in practice is "in the pudding." Numerous empirical studies (including Ph.D. dissertations) have been conducted with the Ginarte-Park index.[16] These studies find, for example, that the index has a statistically significant effect (as well as the hypothesized effect) on variables like innovation, research and development, patenting, trade, direct foreign investment, licensing, and productivity growth. This is indirect evidence that the index does what it is supposed to do: namely, help reflect the strength of national patent systems. If the index were pure noise, it would not have played any systematic role in explaining these economic phenomena.

Estimates

Tables 4-3A, 4-3B and 4-3C present a sample of the patent rights index for a select group of countries.[17] The countries are grouped according to their income level. The measure of country income used is the average per-capita Gross Domestic Product (GDP) in real 1990US dollars during the period from 1985 to 1995. Table 3 shows figures for the average of 1960–1975, the average of 1975–1990, and 1995.

In general, the high-income nations provide the strongest levels of patent protection and the low-income nations the lowest. Between 1960 and 1975 and 1975 and 1990, the gap in protection levels widened, as high-income nations worked to strengthen their patent systems further, while poor-income nations kept their systems relatively unchanged (or reduced the level of patent rights as in the case of Ecuador, Guatemala, India, and Peru). However, by 1995, a modest convergence in protection levels has taken place as countries began to adopt the provisions of the global TRIPS agreement (*Trade-Related Intellectual Property Agreement*). The agreement calls for the strengthening and harmonizing of intellectual property regimes among signatory states but the period of transition allowed is fairly long (up to 20 years for some countries) so that it will take some time before the agreement is fully implemented worldwide, if at all.[18]

Countries that have significantly strengthened their patent regimes include Korea and Singapore. Korea is now one of the top six patenting nations. Economic development has converted formerly imitating nations into innovating nations and leading proponents of global intellectual property re-

Exhibit 4-3A: Index of Patent Rights– High-income nations

	1960-1975	1975-1990	1995
Australia	2.90	3.26	3.86
Austria	3.43	3.95	4.24
Belgium	3.30	3.78	3.90
Canada	2.76	2.76	3.24
Denmark	2.65	3.76	3.71
France	3.08	3.90	4.04
Germany	2.79	3.76	3.86
Hong Kong	2.04	2.46	2.57
Japan	3.24	3.94	3.94
Netherlands	3.33	4.24	4.24
New Zealand	3.10	3.32	3.86
Singapore	2.37	2.57	3.91
Sweden	2.65	3.61	4.24
Switzerland	2.84	3.80	3.80
United Kingdom	2.95	3.57	3.57
United States	3.86	4.41	4.86

Note: Countries are sorted by income group, as measured by average per capita GDP (in 1990 U.S. dollars) during 1985–1995. Source of GDP data: World Bank (1998).

form. Hong Kong's level of patent rights is not as high as that of other newly industrialized countries and it has been a rather minor player in international patenting (at least until 1995). This may be due to its relative specialization in the financial rather than the technological sector. African countries score relatively high because of their patent registration systems: they have essentially adopted British laws and granted automatic patent protection to British patents. Their lack of enforcement mechanisms have worked to bring their scores below that of the United Kingdom. Among industrialized, OECD economies, Canada has not scored very high due to its previous use of compulsory licensing and non-recognition of pharmaceutical patents. Former socialist economies of Eastern Europe (e.g. Czech Republic, Hungary, Poland, Russia, etc.) have only recently reformed their patent systems along international standards.

Exhibit 4-3B: Index of Patent Rights– Medium-Income Nations

	1960-1975	1975-1990	1995
Argentina	2.10	2.26	3.20
Brazil	1.61	1.85	3.05
Bulgaria			2.57
Chile	2.19	2.41	2.74
Colombia	1.89	1.12	3.24
Czech Republic			3.19
Greece	2.46	2.42	2.32
Hungary			3.75
Ireland	2.69	2.99	2.99
Israel	3.39	3.57	3.57
Jordan	1.61	1.86	1.33
Korea	2.87	3.61	3.94
Mexico	1.85	1.48	2.52
Poland			3.23
Russia			3.04
South Africa	3.29	3.57	3.57
Thailand	1.51	1.85	2.24
Venezuela	1.35	1.35	2.75

Note: Countries are sorted by income group, as measured by average per capita GDP (in 1990 U.S. dollars) during 1985–1995. Source of GDP data: World Bank (1998).

Thus, no scores are available before 1995. The scores they do receive for 1995 are above average but it remains to be seen whether the actual execution of their laws is consistent with their statutory provisions.

Exhibit 4-3C: Index of Patent Rights– Low-Income Nations

	1960-1975	1975-1990	1995
Bangladesh	1.99	1.99	1.99
Botswana	1.70	1.90	1.90
Chad	2.30	2.71	2.71
Ecuador	1.80	1.54	2.71
Egypt	1.99	1.99	1.99
Ethiopia	0.00	0.00	0.00
Guatemala	1.51	0.97	1.08
Guyana	1.42	1.42	1.42
India	1.68	1.57	1.17
Indonesia	0.33	0.33	2.27
Kenya	2.37	2.57	2.91
Madagascar	1.37	1.86	2.28
Mozambique	0.00	0.00	0.00
Nicaragua	1.35	0.92	2.24
Pakistan	1.99	1.99	1.99
Peru	1.24	1.02	2.37
Romania			2.71
Senegal	2.08	2.46	2.57
Somalia	1.80	1.80	1.80
Sri Lanka	2.60	3.01	3.12
Togo	2.07	2.24	2.24
Tunisia	1.90	1.90	1.90
Zimbabwe	2.37	2.90	2.90

Note: Countries are sorted by income group, as measured by average per capita GDP (in 1990 U.S. dollars) during 1985–1995. Source of GDP data: World Bank (1998).

3: ECONOMIC FREEDOM AND PATENT RIGHTS

Now that the index of patent rights has been discussed, a question of interest is how patent rights relate to economic freedom, which is the subject of this book. Patent rights pose a quandary to some observers when it comes to economic freedom or competition. On the one hand, some argue that since patent protection restricts competition, an increase in patent rights should reduce economic freedom. On the other hand, in the absence of patent rights, markets for technology may not exist. Thus, patent rights solve a "missing market" problem and should enhance economic freedom. It would be a useful research topic to explore the extent to which intellectual property protection enhances or restricts economic freedom. For now, as the discussion below will point out, the two measures (patent rights and economic freedom) are positively correlated, indicating that in countries where patent rights are strong, economies tend to be freer. There must be some structural reason why this is the case. Certainly, there is no overlap between the two indexes; that is, there is no feature in one that is in the other that would be driving the correlation. This section provides a first look at the relationship between patent rights and economic freedom. Are there any causal links between the two? The purpose here is not to establish any sound conclusions but rather to stimulate further explorations of what the structural relationship might be.

The level of economic freedom could be interpreted as reflecting the strength of property rights *in general* while the level of patent rights could reflect that of intellectual property *in particular.* The results in this section suggest that from a causal or temporal point of view, economic freedom determines patent rights, not vice versa. An implication is that countries that have high levels of economic freedom are more likely to provide intellectual property protection. A general environment of property rights protection precedes particular kinds of property rights protection.

For this section, a sample of 94 countries was gathered, countries for which both patent rights data and economic freedom data are available for the period from 1980 to 1995.[19] Table 4-4, part A, shows the main sample statistics for these two indexes. "IPR" denotes the index of patent rights and "ECON," the index of economic freedom. The sample statistics indicate that both variables exhibit similar degrees of variability–that is, the coefficient of variation is roughly the same for both variables, although it is slightly higher for IPR. This suggests that the levels of patent rights around the world are slightly more diverse (showing greater extremes between high and low values) than the levels of economic freedom.

The sample statistics also show that the two variables are positively correlated. There are several reasons why this might be the case, one of which is that, if economic freedom represents property rights protection in general, then a high level of intellectual property protection in particu-

lar would contribute to a higher general state of property rights protection. Another reason has to do with the overall institutional, cultural, and policy climate. Countries that grant, protect, and enforce private property rights over physical assets such as land, reproducible capital, consumer goods, and so forth, are more likely to be open to the idea of protecting private intellectual assets or creations. Conversely, countries that tend not to protect private property rights (or protect them poorly) are likely to be less sympathetic to the notion of protecting intangible property. Thus, the overall institutional, cultural, and policy environment may play a role as a "third" factor in determining the levels of both economic freedom and patent rights and, hence, generate a correlation between them, even if there were no functional relationship between them.

Nonetheless, it would be of some interest to know if there is a relationship between the two variables in terms of which comes first or which influences which. Table 4-4, part B, presents the results of a simple causality test or test of precedence.[20] The basic idea behind the test is that some variable x causes another variable y if past values of x help to improve predictions for y. For example, consider the following equation for explaining y:

$$y = \alpha_0 + \alpha_1 y(-1) + \ldots + \alpha_n y(-n) + \beta_1 x(-1) + \ldots + \beta_n x(-n) + \varepsilon$$

where the $(-1), \ldots, (-n)$ refer to the variables lagged one period and n periods respectively, α's and β's to the parameters, and ε to the error term. If x does not cause y (in the *Granger* sense), the estimates of $\beta_1, \ldots, \beta_n$ should be zero.

The estimates of the parameters are obtained by statistically fitting the above equation to data from the 94 countries and four time periods (1980, 1985, 1990, and 1995). The first two columns of Table 4, part B represent the case where the lag length is just one period (where time periods are five years apart). That is, the causality test checks to see if data five years ago had an influence on current values. The next two columns represent the case where the maximum lag length is two periods. Longer lags (or data older than 10 years) were tried but found not to be statistically significant.

Table 4-4: Patent Rights and Economic Freedom

(A) Sample Statistics

	IPR	ECON
Mean	2.63	5.90
Standard Deviation	0.90	1.75
Coefficient of Variation	0.34	0.30
Correlation between IPR and MKT = 0.43		

(B) Regression Analysis:

	Dependent Variable			
	(1) IPR	(2) ECON	(3) IPR	(4) ECON
Constant	0.072	0.694	0.199	1.170
	(0.079)	(0.199)	(0.119)	(0.264)
IPR (−1)	0.918	−0.004	0.803	−0.529
	(0.034)	(0.063)	(0.128)	(0.347)
ECON(−1)	0.043	0.948	0.132	1.089
	(0.014)	(0.029)	(0.039)	(0.084)
IPR(−2)			0.077	0.501
			(0.138)	(0.361)
ECON(−2)			−0.093	−0.192
			(0.042)	(0.096)
Percentage of Data Explained	88.2%	79.1%	84.9%	78.5%
Number of Observations	282	282	188	188

Note 1: The sample statistics are computed for the period 1980–1995. The regression estimates are obtained for a panel of 94 countries sampled at 1995, 1990, 1985, and 1980.

Note 2: IPR denotes index of patent rights and ECON index of economic freedom. IPR(−1) and ECON(−1) refer to the variables lagged one period (i.e. by five years), and IPR(−2) and ECON(−2) to the variables lagged two periods (i.e. by 10 years).

Note 3: In the regression results, heteroskedastic-consistent standard errors are in parentheses.

The results indicate that it is indeed economic freedom that causes (or precedes) patent rights. The past value of economic freedom positively and significantly influences the current value of patent rights.[21] In other words, economies with a high degree of economic freedom tend to be behind strong patent regimes. In contrast, the past value of IPR does not significantly explain economic freedom. (However, both the past values of IPR and ECON are good predictors of their own current values–i.e., the past value of IPR is a strong determinant of the current level of IPR and likewise for ECON). The coefficient estimates of the variables' respective lagged variables are about 0.9. This shows a high degree of persistence or stability in the values of the indexes. The levels of economic freedom and patent rights are more likely to change gradually over time than abruptly.

Including more historical information (i.e., adding second period lags) does not alter the finding that the lag of ECON explains both ECON and IPR, but that the lag of IPR explains only IPR (and not ECON). Also, the second period lags–IPR(-2) and ECON(-2)–are insignificant in explaining present values of IPR and ECON, indicating that historical information about levels of economic freedom and patent rights beyond the first lagged period is not statistically important in predicting current levels of freedom and rights. All relevant historical information appears to be summarized in those first period lags.

Overall, the causality tests support the idea that countries with high levels of economic freedom are more likely to adopt and provide strong patent rights protection rather than vice versa. In other words, it is not plausible that strong patent regimes are the driving force for changes in economic freedom; rather, it appears to be the reverse. A policy implication may be that patent reform efforts should start with the strengthening of property rights institutions *in general*, which should help pave the way for *specialized* property protection in the areas of science, technology, and art. Countries that attempt to develop strong intellectual property regimes without developing an environment conducive to property rights protection in general may not succeed.

4: CONCLUSIONS

This chapter has discussed the measurement of patent rights across countries. The measure is country-specific, depending on national institutions, laws, and practices. It is also a measure of the strength of patent rights–not necessarily quality. The quality of patent systems is much harder to estimate. It would depend on what the nation's objectives are. Thus one criterion for measuring quality would be whether the patent system effectively achieves them. But a problem is that certain goals may not necessarily be shared by other nations or cultures. Another is that even if patent policy goals are roughly the same–i.e., to promote technological progress, economic efficiency, and enhance individual inventor liberty–countries differ on what weight they give (or what meaning they ascribe) to different aspects of such progress, efficiency, and liberty. For example, is technological progress identified more with the innovation or with technology diffusion?

In terms of improving the quality of the patent rights index to measure the strength of patent protection, there are a number of extensions that could be made in future work. The first is to incorporate the scope of patent protection. Since countries are granting about the same duration of patent protection (by international agreement), there is less variation in the statutory length of protection than in the breadth of protection. Secondly, as substantive laws converge (due to TRIPS), it would be useful to incorporate procedural law differences across countries, such as WIPO's Patent Law Treaty (PLT).[22] Thirdly, in the enforcement category, it would be useful to incorporate information about punishment for infringement (e.g. fines or sentences) and about the costs of enforcement (e.g. litigation). Fourthly, a limitation with the patent rights index is that it only varies by country, not say by industry. On the surface, this is justifiable. Except for the laws governing coverage (which state whether a particular technology field is patentable), the laws apply the *same* to all potential inventors, regardless of what line of business they are in. But in practice, there may be important interindustry differences in the perceived strength of patent protection. For example, national patent laws may be especially strong for the pharmaceutical industry but lax for the computer industry. Future work could explore the sources of these interindustry differences in the strength of patent rights. One source is *patent pendency* (the time it takes to grant a patent), which depends on the complexity of the innovation; another is scope, which should vary with the type of invention (whether the research field is new or crowded) and with the level of competition in an industry.

Finally, a few remarks about estimating patent rights and dealing with preconceptions. Some readers may find that the patent rights estimates for certain countries conflict with their *a priori* views about the patent systems in those countries. They may have also found that to be the case with the economic freedom index–that the estimates are higher or lower than they had anticipated. The question is whether to doubt the estimated index or to modify one's prior assumptions. The following are some general comments in defense of indexes.

(1) Utilizing *a priori* views about a regime defeats the purpose of constructing indexes. The approach adopted here is to let the chips fall where they may. Using *a priori* views might sway the collection of information. An independently constructed quantitative index is a valuable supplement to expert opinion and experience, and vice versa.

(2) Indexes help describe the characteristics of a regime, not the outcome or effects of that regime. For example, a common reason people doubt the value of an economic freedom index or a patent rights index is that the value is seen as too high (or too low) for that country's level of economic development. For example, as Table 3 showed, countries that have strong patent systems tend to be the industrialized economies. But there are exceptions: some poor economies have strong patent laws and some rich ones have weak laws. First, this is relatively easy to explain in that there are offsetting factors. The effects of a strong patent regime might be offset by poor fiscal policies; or those of a weak regime be offset by a good education system. Secondly, and most importantly, measures of economic freedom or patent rights are *not* measures of economic development. They help explain development or are determinants of development, but are not themselves indicators of it.

(3) Another source of confusion arises from not recognizing that indexes of economic freedom and patent rights are *flows*, not *stocks*. They reflect the value for a particular year or period and not the entire history of their respective institutions or experiences. This confusion leads some people to expect the more developed economies or countries with a longer history of strong and stable institutions to have higher index values than those with less economic or institutional development. But, it should be recognized that the indexes can change from time to time on a flow basis. As an extreme case, if the United Kingdom were to eliminate its patent system, its patent rights index would be 0 regardless of its past history.

The above remarks are general points. They do not preclude measurement error. In some situations, there might be strong reasons to doubt the validity of the estimates; for example, in the case of patent laws, a huge discrepancy might exist between what the laws state and how authorities behave. Of course, if this discrepancy had persisted, complaints about it would have been widely known (see discussion in section III) and could, therefore, have been incorporated as useful information into the index.

NOTES

(1)   Patent applicants who seek broader protection may often try to insert more claims. A kind of "negotiating" or compromising process may take place in which the patent examiner deletes certain patent claims (especially those that seem to extend beyond the scope of the invention or cross into the territory of prior patent holders). Applicants may risk rejection of a patent if their applications contain "too many" claims (especially if the claims are not part of a unifying "inventive" theme). They may be required to file separate patent applications instead.

(2)   See, for example, Kaufer (1989).

(3)   For example, certain African countries grant patent rights to inventors who obtained a patent in the United Kingdom.

(4)   Note, as a technical matter, that these regional patent filings (i.e. EPO or PCT) consist of two stages. In the first stage, the single, centralized filing takes place, which establishes a priority date (see below). Several months later, the applicant undergoes a second stage (known as the "validation" or national phase), where the applicant must eventually file the application in the separate national jurisdictions, meeting local legal requirements and paying local fees. The advantage of the regional patent is in establishing priority and obtaining some extension of time to improve upon the patent application and invention, assess market conditions, and, where applicable, translate the application into the different native languages of the countries designated in the regional patent application.

(5)   This difference in priority determination is a source of trade disputes between the United States and the rest of the world and is, thus, a heated subject of international negotiations.

(6)   For example, in 1988, Harvard University was issued a patent for an invention that produced a genetically altered mouse susceptible to cancer. Genetically altered animals was considered patentable because they are non-naturally occurring.

(7)   Even under a system where priority is based on "first to invent," the inventor must keep the invention undisclosed until an application is filed. This definition of novelty especially affects university researchers who tend to publish their results widely.

(8)   In the popular game *Monopoly*, a situation analogous to "blocking patents" can arise. If two or more players each own some of the same colored lots (e.g. blue), then none can build houses. One of them must have all two or three of the same colored lots. Thus, taking the colored lots as analogous to technologies, we can see that, if some product or process cannot be made unless all of its technological components are put to use and if different patent owners own different components, the entire product or process cannot be created unless the gridlock is broken by either private negotiation or compulsory sale. (How the latter is carried out varies by friends and family.)

(9)   See Cornelli and Schankerman (1999).

(10)   English translations of national patent laws are available at the Library of Congress, Washington, DC.

(11)   Utility models refer to relatively minor inventions–i.e., new arrangements or forms introduced or obtained in known objects. Protection is granted only to the new form or arrangement, provided that it results in an improved utilization of the object. The rationale for including utility models is that they help to distinguish the levels of patent protection among developing countries (or countries where innovative activity is relatively low).

(12) Further details about these international treaties can be found in WIPO (1998).

(13) This standard has been recommended by the Intellectual Property Task Force of the United States Chamber of Commerce. See Gadbaw and Richards (1988).

(14) Moreover, in African countries where the measured patent protection levels are relatively high (due to their adoption of British laws), there is as yet very little innovative activity going on. This is the case, despite strong patent laws, because of offsetting factors (e.g. political instability). Thus, with little innovation, there are few patents granted and, as a result, few instances of patent infringement and litigation activity. (There are also few instances of infringement because the imitative capacity of these countries is not very high.) Hence, due to the relative paucity of infringement and litigation activity, there have been few opportunities to "test" the laws and thereby determine whether the patent laws are actually carried out.

(15) As a future research project, it would be very useful to develop a micro-database of international patent cases.

(16) See, for example, Carlton (1996), Connolly (1998), Eaton et al. (1998), Maskus (2000), McCalman (1998), Oxley (1999), Nair (2000), Park and Ginarte (1997), Scalise (1997), Smith (1999), and Yang and Maskus (2000).

(17) The complete data for the period from 1960 to 1995 are available from the author upon request.

(18) If progress in implementation is made, however, the patent rights index will exhibit less and less variability (as national patent standards converge). In that case, to discriminate between regimes the index will have to incorporate: (a) other patent law treaties, for example WIPO's ongoing Patent Law Treaty (PLT), which seeks to reform patent law formalities and procedures; (b) new categories such as punishment, exhaustion (e.g. parallel importing), new subcategories such as the patentability of biotechnological innovations, internet tools, business models, etc., and micro-level features such as patent examination time, length of trial or arbitration, average scope, etc.; and (c) other forms of intellectual property protection such as copyright, trademark, trade secrecy, domain names, geographical indicators, etc.

(19) Data on economic freedom are from Gwartney and Lawson (2000).

(20) This test is referred to as the Granger-causality test. There is some controversy in the economics literature as to whether the Granger-causality test actually tests for causality in the "dictionary sense" of the term (that something is the reason or motive behind an effect or action). There appears to be more of a consensus that it tests for "precedence," that is, whether something precedes another in time (see Maddala 1992). Precedence may be necessary but not sufficient for a causal link between events.

(21) The statistical significance of a variable is judged by how large the ratio of its coefficient estimate is to its standard error. A variable is usually considered statistically important if the ratio exceeds 2 (in absolute value).

(22) Procedural laws govern matters such as notarization, signatures, and other legal formalities; patent filing procedures; renewal payments; and the use of local agent representation (i.e. patent attorneys or agents) for certain tasks.

REFERENCES

Carlton, Dennis W. (1996). A Critical Assessment of the Role of Imperfect Competition in Macroeconomics. *National Bureau of Economic Research*, Working Paper No. 5782.

Connolly, Michelle P. (1998). The Dual Nature of Trade: Measuring Its Impact on Imitation and Growth. Duke University, Department of Economics, Working Paper 97/33.

Cornelli, Francesca and Mark Schankerman (1999). Patent Renewal and R&D Incentives. *Rand Journal of Economics* 50, 2: 197–213.

Eaton, Jonathan, Eva Gutierrez, and Sam Kortum (1998). European Technology Policy: Research Efforts in Europe Matter. *Economic Policy* 27 (October): 403–30.

Gadbaw, R. Michael, and Timothy Richards (eds.) (1988). *Intellectual Property Rights: Global Consensus, Global Conflict.* Boulder, CO: Westview Press.

Ginarte, Juan Carlos, and Walter G. Park (1997). Determinants of Patent Rights: A Cross-National Study. *Research Policy* 26: 283–301.

Gwartney, James, and Robert Lawson (with Dexter Samida) (2000). *Economic Freedom of the World: 2000 Annual Report.* Vancouver, BC: The Fraser Institute:

Kaufer, Eric (1989). *The Economics of the Patent System.* New York: Harwood Academic Publishers.

Maddala, G. S. (1992). *Introduction to Econometrics, Second Edition.* New York: Macmillan.

Maskus, Keith E. (2000). *Intellectual Property Rights in the Global Economy.* Washington, DC: Institute for International Economics.

McCalman, Philip (1998). *Essays on the Multilateral Process.* Ph.D. dissertation, University of Wisconsin, Department of Economics.

Merges, Robert and Richard Nelson (1994). On Limiting or Encouraging Rivalry in Technical Progress: The Effect of Patent Scope Decisions. *Journal of Economic Behavior and Organization* 25: 1–24.

Nair, Usha (2000). Patent Regimes and the Internationalization of Economic Activities: Some Empirical Evidence from US Multinationals. Georgia Institute of Technology, Department of Economics, Working Paper.

Oxley, Joanne (1999). Institutional Environment and the Mechanisms of Governance: The Impact of Intellectual Property Protection on the Structure of Interfirm Alliances. *Journal of Economic Behavior and Organization* 38, 3: 283–309.

Park, Walter G., and Juan Carlos Ginarte (1997). Intellectual Property Rights and Economic Growth. *Contemporary Economic Policy* 15, 3: 51–61.

Scalise, Craig (1997). Natural Intellectual Property Protection Reform: Theory and Evidence, Ph.D. dissertation, University of Chicago, Graduate School of Business.

Smith, Pamela J. (1999). Are Weak Patent Rights a Barrier to US Exports. *Journal of International Economics* 48, 1: 151–77.

World Bank (1998). *World Development Indicators.* Washington, DC: World Bank.

World Intellectual Property Organization (1998). *Intellectual Property Reading Material.* Geneva: WIPO.

Yang, Lili, and Keith E. Maskus (2000). IPR and Licensing: An Econometric Investigation. University of Colorado, Department of Economics, Working Paper.

CHAPTER 5: COUNTRY DATA TABLES

This chapter presents detailed data on the component variables used in constructing the economic freedom index for the countries included in this study. For each country, we present the overall economic freedom index rating and the ranking of that country for the years 1970, 1975, 1980, 1985, 1990, 1995, and 1999 (or most recent year). Like all the scores in the index, these are values out of 10; 10 is the highest possible score and zero (0) is the lowest.

Under the column, Components of Economic Freedom, the titles in bold-face indicate the seven areas of economic freedom that are combined to generate an overall score. Each of the rows in

bold-face gives the scores (out of 10) for that particular area for each year.

Underneath each area title are the titles of the components that are combined to generate that particular area's score. In these rows are the scores (out of 10) for each year for which we have data. In parentheses beside some scores are the actual data used to derive that particular component rating.

A more complete description of each component, including the methodology used to calculate the ratings, can be found in the Chapter 1 Appendix: Explanatory Notes and Data Sources.

The full data-set is available on-line at the website: http://www.freetheworld.com/.

ALBANIA

Summary Ratings	1970	1975	1980	1985	1990	1995	1999
Summary Ratings					2.8	4.8	4.7
Rank					111	100	102

Components of Economic Freedom

	1970	1975	1980	1985	1990	1995	1999
I. Size of Government				**7.8**	**4.2**	**7.8**	**8.4**
(a) Government Consumption			7.7 (13.8)	7.8 (13.4)	4.9 (23.4)	7.8 (13.6)	9.0 (9.6)
(b) Transfers and Subsidies					3.5 (24.3)	7.8 (8.4)	7.8 (8.6)
II. Structure of the Economy and Use of Markets					**0.0**	**2.1**	**3.8**
(a) Government Enterprises		0.0		0.0	0.0	0.0	2.0
(b) Price Controls					0.0	4.0	4.0
(c) Top Marginal Tax Rate							10.0
(d) Conscription	0.0		0.0	0.0	0.0	3.0	10.0
III. Monetary Policy and Price Stability				**9.8**	**9.8**	**2.6**	**5.8**
(a) Annual Money Growth				9.6 (0.9)	9.6 (1.0)	0.0 (78.9)	3.4 (33.1)
(b) Inflation Variability						0.0 (86.9)	4.3 (14.3)
(c) Recent Inflation Rate				9.9 (0.4)	10.0 (0.0)	8.0 (9.8)	9.9 (0.4)
IV. Freedom to Use Alternative Currencies	0.0			0.0	0.0	**7.5**	**6.4**
(a) Ownership of Foreign Currency	0.0			0.0	0.0	5.0	5.0
(b) Black Market Exchange Rate	0.0 (1100.0)	0.0 (745.0)	0.0 (856.0)	0.0 (818.0)	0.0 (800.0)	10.0 (0.0)	7.8 (11.1)
V. Legal Structure and Property Rights				**5.7**	**5.6**	**7.0**	**1.7**
(a) Legal Security				4.8	4.6		
(b) Rule of Law				6.6	6.7	7.0	1.7
VI. International Exchange						**3.8**	**5.4**
(a) Taxes on International Trade							
i. Taxes as a Percentage of Exports and Imports						5.7 (6.5)	5.2 (7.2)
ii. Mean Tariff Rate							6.8 (15.9)
iii. Standard Deviation of Tariff Rates							6.7 (8.3)
(b) Size of Trade Sector			0.0 (-5.8)	0.0 (34.7)	0.0 (38.1)	0.0 (47.0)	0.0 (41.7)
VII. Freedom of Exchange in Financial Markets					**0.0**	**2.6**	**3.3**
(a) Private Ownership of Banks					0.0 (0)	2.0 (10-40)	2.0 (10-40)
(b) Extension of Credit to Private Sector						0.0 (7.0)	1.1 (10.9)
(c) Avoidance of Negative Interest Rates					0.0	6.0	8.0
(d) Capital Transactions with Foreigners	0.0		0.0		0.0	2.0	2.0

ALGERIA

Summary Ratings

	1970	1975	1980	1985	1990	1995	1999
Summary Ratings			4.4	4.0	2.8	3.4	2.6
Rank			75	90	111	119	122

Components of Economic Freedom

	1970	1975	1980	1985	1990	1995	1999
I. Size of Government	**5.5**	**5.8**	**4.6**	**4.5**	**5.2**	**6.6**	**4.8**
(a) Government Consumption	5.5 (21.2)	5.8 (20.3)	4.6 (24.2)	4.5 (24.7)	5.2 (22.3)	5.3 (22.0)	4.8 (23.6)
(b) Transfers and Subsidies						7.8 (8.4)	
II. Structure of the Economy and Use of Markets				**1.0**	**1.0**	**1.0**	**1.9**
(a) Government Enterprises	2.0 (23.8)		0.0 (34.6)	0.0 (55.8)	0.0 (57.6)	0.0	0.0
(b) Price Controls						2.0	4.0
(c) Top Marginal Tax Rate							
(d) Conscription	10.0		5.0	5.0	1.0	1.0	1.0
III. Monetary Policy and Price Stability	**8.5**	**6.1**	**6.5**	**8.2**	**6.1**	**5.2**	**7.2**
(a) Annual Money Growth	7.2 (14.0)	6.7 (16.4)	6.9 (15.5)	7.3 (13.4)	9.3 (3.4)	7.2 (13.9)	7.7 (11.3)
(b) Inflation Variability	9.4 (1.6)	2.6 (18.5)	7.7 (5.8)	8.3 (4.2)	5.5 (11.2)	4.1 (14.8)	5.0 (12.4)
(c) Recent Inflation Rate	8.9 (5.4)	8.9 (5.5)	4.9 (25.7)	9.1 (4.6)	3.1 (34.4)	4.3 (28.5)	8.7 (6.3)
IV. Freedom to Use Alternative Currencies	**0.0**			**0.0**	**0.0**	**0.0**	**0.0**
(a) Ownership of Foreign Currency	0.0			0.0	0.0	0.0	0.0
(b) Black Market Exchange Rate	0.0 (59.0)	0.0 (56.0)	0.0 (263.0)	0.0 (335.0)	0.0 (140.0)	0.0 (201.0)	0.0 (150.0)
V. Legal Structure and Property Rights	**3.6**	**3.0**	**3.6**	**3.3**	**3.3**	**7.0**	**1.7**
(a) Legal Security	3.6	3.0	4.0	3.5	3.2		
(b) Rule of Law			3.3	3.1	3.3	7.0	1.7
VI. International Exchange			**7.5**	**5.6**	**5.3**	**4.1**	**4.3**
(a) Taxes on International Trade							
i. Taxes as a Percentage of Exports and Imports						3.6 (9.6)	3.9 (9.2)
ii. Mean Tariff Rate			7.7 (11.7)	5.7 (21.7)	5.1 (24.6)	5.4 (22.9)	5.2 (24.2)
iii. Standard Deviation of Tariff Rates						2.2 (19.6)	3.3 (16.7)
(b) Size of Trade Sector	7.1 (51.0)	9.3 (76.5)	7.1 (64.7)	5.3 (43.9)	5.7 (48.4)	6.3 (58.6)	5.1 (46.7)
VII. Freedom of Exchange in Financial Markets				**0.0**	**0.5**	**0.8**	**0.8**
(a) Private Ownership of Banks	0.0 (0-10)			0.0 (0-10)	0.0 (0-10)	0.0 (0-10)	0.0 (0-10)
(b) Extension of Credit to Private Sector					1.7 (17.4)	1.4 (14.4)	1.1 (11.3)
(c) Avoidance of Negative Interest Rates						0.0	0.0
(d) Capital Transactions with Foreigners	0.0			0.0	0.0	2.0	2.0

ARGENTINA

Summary Ratings	1970	1975	1980	1985	1990	1995	1999
Summary Ratings	6.4	3.1	4.7	3.9	5.3	7.5	8.3
Rank	27	78	66	92	60	29	11

Components of Economic Freedom

Component	1970	1975	1980	1985	1990	1995	1999
I. Size of Government	**7.9**	**7.3**	**7.2**	**7.4**	**8.4**	**7.7**	**7.7**
(a) Government Consumption	7.9 (13.0)	6.5 (17.8)	6.9 (16.5)	7.9 (13.0)	8.5 (11.0)	8.1 (12.6)	8.1 (12.4)
(b) Transfers and Subsidies		8.0 (7.9)	7.5 (9.7)	6.9 (11.7)	8.2 (7.2)	7.3 (10.3)	7.2 (10.8)
II. Structure of the Economy and Use of Markets	**3.6**	**3.6**	**4.4**	**2.9**	**5.7**	**8.4**	**8.8**
(a) Government Enterprises	4.0 (33.6)	4.0 (33.6)	4.0 (39.5)	4.0 (38.3)	6.0 (30.0)	8.0 (8.5)	10.0 (8.6)
(b) Price Controls						8.0	8.0
(c) Top Marginal Tax Rate		4.0 (51)	6.0 (45)	2.0 (62)	7.0 (35)	9.0 (30)	8.0 (35)
(d) Conscription	0.0	1.0	1.0	1.0	1.0	10.0	10.0
III. Monetary Policy and Price Stability	**6.7**	**0.0**	**0.0**	**0.0**	**0.0**	**3.9**	**9.4**
(a) Annual Money Growth	5.0 (24.8)	0.0 (78.3)	0.0 (150.0)	0.0 (295.2)	0.0 (515.6)	2.5 (37.5)	9.3 (3.6)
(b) Inflation Variability	6.2 (9.5)	0.0 (61.9)	0.0 (119.8)	0.0 (208.3)	0.0 (1198.8)	0.0 (52.4)	9.1 (2.3)
(c) Recent Inflation Rate	8.8 (5.8)	0.0 (198.2)	0.0 (92.0)	0.0 (620.8)	0.0 (2064.2)	9.2 (3.9)	9.8 (-1.2)
IV. Freedom to Use Alternative Currencies	**10.0**	**5.0**	**9.9**	**6.0**	**10.0**	**10.0**	**10.0**
(a) Ownership of Foreign Currency	10.0	10.0	10.0	10.0	10.0	10.0	10.0
(b) Black Market Exchange Rate	10.0 (0.0)	0.0 (124.0)	9.8 (1.0)	2.0 (40.0)	10.0 (0.0)	10.0 (0.0)	10.0 (0.0)
V. Legal Structure and Property Rights	**3.6**	**0.6**	**4.2**	**4.7**	**6.8**	**7.0**	**8.6**
(a) Legal Security	3.6	0.6	5.2	1.2	5.3		7.1
(b) Rule of Law			3.3	8.2	8.3	7.0	10.0
VI. International Exchange		**0.6**	**3.3**	**2.7**	**2.8**	**6.4**	**6.5**
(a) Taxes on International Trade							
i. Taxes as a Percentage of Exports and Imports		1.4 (12.9)	3.7 (9.5)	1.5 (12.7)	3.4 (9.9)	7.5 (3.7)	7.1 (4.4)
ii. Mean Tariff Rate		0.0 (55.9)	4.4 (27.8)	4.6 (27.0)	5.9 (20.5)	7.9 (10.5)	7.3 (13.5)
iii. Standard Deviation of Tariff Rates					0.3 (24.3)	7.0 (7.6)	7.2 (6.9)
(b) Size of Trade Sector	0.0 (10.3)	0.0 (11.8)	0.0 (11.5)	1.2 (18.0)	0.0 (15.0)	0.0 (17.0)	2.1 (23.3)
VII. Freedom of Exchange in Financial Markets	**5.0**	**4.8**	**3.1**	**3.0**	**2.6**	**8.1**	**8.0**
(a) Private Ownership of Banks	5.0 (40-60)	5.0 (40-60)	5.0 (40-60)	5.0 (40-60)	5.0 (40-50)	5.0 (60)	5.0 (60)
(b) Extension of Credit to Private Sector	9.0 (89.5)	8.1 (81.0)	8.3 (33.3)	7.6 (76.0)	6.1 (60.8)	7.6 (76.0)	7.2 (71.6)
(c) Avoidance of Negative Interest Rates			0.0	0.0	0.0	10.0	10.0
(d) Capital Transactions with Foreigners	2.0	2.0	0.0	0.0	0.0	10.0	10.0

AUSTRALIA

Summary Ratings	1970	1975	1980	1985	1990	1995	1999
	8.0	6.5	7.4	7.8	8.0	8.4	8.5
Rank	7	17	12	10	11	7	6

Components of Economic Freedom

	1970	1975	1980	1985	1990	1995	1999
I. Size of Government	**6.2**	**6.4**	**6.2**	**5.8**	**6.2**	**5.9**	**5.9**
(a) Government Consumption	6.2 (19.0)	5.0 (22.9)	4.9 (23.2)	4.8 (23.8)	5.2 (22.3)	5.5 (21.4)	4.8 (23.7)
(b) Transfers and Subsidies		7.8 (8.5)	7.4 (10.1)	6.9 (11.9)	7.2 (10.7)	6.3 (14.2)	7.1 (11.2)
II. Structure of the Economy and Use of Markets		**5.0**	**5.0**	**5.0**	**5.6**	**6.5**	**6.6**
(a) Government Enterprises	6.0 (30.0)	6.0 (37.1)	6.0 (28.4)	6.0 (30.2)	6.0 (25.2)	7.0 (21.5)	8.0 (18.7)
(b) Price Controls				6.0	6.0	7.0	7.0
(c) Top Marginal Tax Rate		2.0 (64)	2.0 (62)	2.0 (60)	3.0 (49)	4.0 (47)	3.0 (47)
(d) Conscription	0.0	10.0	10.0	10.0	10.0	10.0	10.0
III. Monetary Policy and Price Stability	**9.4**	**7.9**	**8.6**	**9.1**	**8.7**	**9.1**	**9.3**
(a) Annual Money Growth	9.7 (1.6)	8.4 (7.8)	8.3 (8.6)	9.4 (3.2)	7.6 (12.0)	8.1 (9.3)	8.6 (6.9)
(b) Inflation Variability	9.6 (1.0)	8.3 (4.2)	9.4 (1.5)	9.1 (2.2)	9.2 (2.0)	9.7 (0.6)	9.5 (1.2)
(c) Recent Inflation Rate	8.9 (5.5)	7.0 (14.9)	8.0 (9.8)	8.8 (6.1)	9.3 (3.3)	9.4 (2.9)	9.7 (1.5)
IV. Freedom to Use Alternative Currencies	**10.0**	**9.9**	**9.9**	**10.0**	**10.0**	**10.0**	**10.0**
(a) Ownership of Foreign Currency	10.0	10.0	10.0	10.0	10.0	10.0	10.0
(b) Black Market Exchange Rate	10.0 (0.0)	9.8 (1.0)	9.8 (1.0)	10.0 (0.0)	10.0 (0.0)	10.0 (0.0)	10.0 (0.0)
V. Legal Structure and Property Rights	**9.6**	**5.5**	**8.5**	**9.4**	**9.3**	**10.0**	**9.8**
(a) Legal Security	9.6	5.5	7.0	8.7	8.6		9.6
(b) Rule of Law			10.0	10.0	10.0	10.0	10.0
VI. International Exchange	**6.9**	**6.4**	**6.9**	**7.2**	**6.3**	**7.4**	**8.0**
(a) Taxes on International Trade							
i. Taxes as a Percentage of Exports and Imports	7.5 (3.7)	7.1 (4.4)	7.6 (3.6)	7.9 (3.2)	7.9 (3.1)	8.8 (1.8)	9.0 (1.4)
ii. Mean Tariff Rate		6.6 (17.0)	7.1 (14.5)	7.3 (13.3)	7.2 (14.2)	8.4 (8.2)	9.0 (5.0)
iii. Standard Deviation of Tariff Rates					4.3 (14.3)	6.0 (10.1)	7.3 (6.7)
(b) Size of Trade Sector	5.6 (29.0)	4.7 (28.9)	4.9 (33.9)	5.4 (35.2)	5.0 (34.6)	5.4 (41.7)	5.3 (41.4)
VII. Freedom of Exchange in Financial Markets	**6.4**	**5.0**	**6.7**	**7.7**	**9.3**	**9.3**	**9.3**
(a) Private Ownership of Banks	8.0 (85-95)	8.0 (85-95)	8.0 (85-95)	8.0 (85-95)	10.0 (95-100)	10.0 (95-100)	10.0 (95-100)
(b) Extension of Credit to Private Sector	5.8 (57.6)	6.4 (63.6)	7.1 (71.3)	8.0 (79.9)	9.0 (90.2)	9.2 (91.8)	9.4 (94.0)
(c) Avoidance of Negative Interest Rates	10.0	4.0	10.0	10.0	10.0	10.0	10.0
(d) Capital Transactions with Foreigners	2.0	2.0	2.0	5.0	8.0	8.0	8.0

AUSTRIA

Summary Ratings	1970	1975	1980	1985	1990	1995	1999
Summary Ratings	7.1	6.0	6.7	6.7	7.4	7.6	8.0
Rank	18	28	17	21	20	28	15

Components of Economic Freedom

	1970	1975	1980	1985	1990	1995	1999
I. Size of Government	**5.8**	**4.8**	**4.3**	**4.1**	**4.2**	**3.6**	**3.8**
(a) Government Consumption	5.5 (21.5)	4.8 (23.8)	4.5 (24.8)	4.3 (25.2)	4.4 (25.0)	4.0 (26.4)	4.1 (25.9)
(b) Transfers and Subsidies	6.1 (14.9)	4.9 (19.4)	4.1 (22.1)	3.8 (23.1)	4.0 (22.4)	3.3 (25.2)	3.5 (24.3)
II. Structure of the Economy and Use of Markets		**3.1**	**2.4**	**2.4**	**3.8**	**4.6**	**5.3**
(a) Government Enterprises	2.0	2.0 (45.0)	2.0 (44.5)	2.0 (42.0)	2.0	2.0	4.0
(b) Price Controls					5.0	8.0	8.0
(c) Top Marginal Tax Rate	4.0 (62)	4.0 (54)	2.0 (62)	2.0 (62)	4.0 (50)	4.0 (50)	4.0 (50)
(d) Conscription	0.0	5.0	5.0	5.0	5.0	3.0	3.0
III. Monetary Policy and Price Stability	**9.5**	**8.9**	**9.5**	**9.5**	**9.4**	**9.3**	**9.5**
(a) Annual Money Growth	9.6 (1.8)	8.5 (7.7)	9.8 (1.0)	9.5 (2.3)	9.2 (4.0)	8.6 (6.8)	8.8 (6.0)
(b) Inflation Variability	9.7 (0.7)	9.5 (1.2)	9.6 (0.9)	9.5 (1.2)	9.7 (0.6)	9.7 (0.8)	9.8 (0.5)
(c) Recent Inflation Rate	9.1 (4.7)	8.7 (6.5)	9.0 (5.0)	9.4 (3.1)	9.3 (3.5)	9.6 (2.1)	9.9 (0.6)
IV. Freedom to Use Alternative Currencies	**7.5**	**7.5**	**7.5**	**7.5**	**10.0**	**10.0**	**10.0**
(a) Ownership of Foreign Currency	5.0	5.0	5.0	5.0	10.0	10.0	10.0
(b) Black Market Exchange Rate	10.0 (0.0)	10.0 (0.0)	10.0 (0.0)	10.0 (0.0)	10.0 (0.0)	10.0	10.0
V. Legal Structure and Property Rights			**9.6**	**9.4**	**10.0**	**10.0**	**9.9**
(a) Legal Security			9.2	8.7	10.0	10.0	9.9
(b) Rule of Law			10.0	10.0	10.0	10.0	10.0
VI. International Exchange	**7.7**	**7.2**	**7.8**	**8.1**	**7.5**	**8.1**	**8.3**
(a) Taxes on International Trade							
i. Taxes as a Percentage of Exports and Imports	8.3 (2.6)	8.9 (1.7)	9.5 (0.7)	9.6 (0.6)	9.5 (0.7)	9.9 (0.2)	9.9 (0.2)
ii. Mean Tariff Rate		6.9 (15.4)	7.7 (11.6)	8.0 (10.0)	8.3 (8.7)	8.7 (6.7)	8.9 (5.6)
iii. Standard Deviation of Tariff Rates					6.0 (10.1)	7.6 (5.9)	7.6 (5.9)
(b) Size of Trade Sector	6.5 (59.7)	4.3 (61.6)	4.6 (74.0)	5.4 (79.1)	5.1 (79.0)	4.6 (78.2)	5.4 (90.3)
VII. Freedom of Exchange in Financial Markets	**5.7**	**5.1**	**5.5**	**6.0**	**6.7**	**7.0**	**8.5**
(a) Private Ownership of Banks	5.0 (40-60)	5.0 (40-75)	5.0 (≤0-75)	5.0 (63)	5.0 (40-75)	5.0 (54)	8.0 (86-88)
(b) Extension of Credit to Private Sector	8.5 (84.6)	8.1 (80.6)	7.9 (78.7)	7.8 (77.7)	7.4 (73.8)	7.3 (72.8)	8.0 (79.5)
(c) Avoidance of Negative Interest Rates	8.0	6.0	8.0	10.0	10.0	8.0	10.0
(d) Capital Transactions with Foreigners	2.0	2.0	2.0	2.0	5.0	8.0	8.0

BAHAMAS

Summary Ratings

	1970	1975	1980	1985	1990	1995	1999
Summary Ratings	6.3	5.9	6.1	5.9	5.8	6.4	
Rank	18	34	34	45	72	64	

Components of Economic Freedom

	1970	1975	1980	1985	1990	1995	1999
I. Size of Government	**9.8**	**8.3**	**8.4**	**8.4**	**8.5**	**8.0**	
(a) Government Consumption		6.6 (17.6)	6.8 (16.9)	6.9 (16.5)	7.2 (15.6)	6.2 (18.9)	
(b) Transfers and Subsidies	9.8 (1.4)	10.0 (0.5)	10.0 (0.5)	10.0 (0.1)	9.9 (1.0)	9.9 (1.0)	
II. Structure of the Economy and Use of Markets		**8.0**	**7.1**	**6.1**	**5.4**	**6.7**	**6.7**
(a) Government Enterprises	6.0	6.0	4.0	2.0	2.0	6.0	6.0
(b) Price Controls					4.0	4.0	4.0
(c) Top Marginal Tax Rate	10.0 (0)	10.0 (0)	10.0 (0)	10.0 (0)	10.0 (0)	10.0 (0)	10.0 (0)
(d) Conscription	10.0	10.0	10.0	10.0	10.0	10.0	10.0
III. Monetary Policy and Price Stability	**9.0**	**8.7**	**8.2**	**8.6**	**9.1**	**9.3**	**9.2**
(a) Annual Money Growth		9.6 (-1.9)	7.9 (10.3)	9.6 (2.2)	8.7 (6.6)	9.1 (4.6)	9.0 (4.8)
(b) Inflation Variability	9.3 (1.8)	8.7 (3.3)	8.6 (3.5)	7.9 (5.3)	9.3 (1.7)	9.3 (1.6)	8.8 (2.9)
(c) Recent Inflation Rate	8.8 (6.2)	7.9 (10.7)	8.0 (10.0)	8.3 (8.5)	9.4 (3.2)	9.4 (2.8)	9.7 (1.3)
IV. Freedom to Use Alternative Currencies	**7.2**	**3.6**	**3.0**	**3.9**	**3.7**	**4.8**	**4.6**
(a) Ownership of Foreign Currency	0.0	0.0	0.0	0.0	0.0	0.0	0.0
(b) Black Market Exchange Rate	7.2 (14.0)	7.2 (14.0)	6.0 (20.0)	7.8 (11.0)	7.4 (13.0)	9.6 (2.0)	9.2 (4.0)
V. Legal Structure and Property Rights				**6.4**	**6.3**	**4.1**	**5.8**
(a) Legal Security				6.1	5.9		
(b) Rule of Law				6.6	6.7	4.1	5.8
VI. International Exchange	**4.7**	**4.7**	**4.3**	**3.8**	**3.6**	**3.1**	
(a) Taxes on International Trade							
i. Taxes as a Percentage of Exports and Imports	4.7 (7.9)	4.1 (8.8)	4.6 (8.1)	3.8 (9.3)	3.6 (9.6)	3.1 (10.3)	3.0 (35.0)
ii. Mean Tariff Rate			4.0 (29.8)	3.5 (32.3)			
iii. Standard Deviation of Tariff Rates							
(b) Size of Trade Sector	5.8	5.8 (151.9)	4.5 (133.3)	4.5 (124.1)	3.5 (108.7)	3.1 (114.0)	3.0
VII. Freedom of Exchange in Financial Markets	**6.3**	**6.4**	**6.3**	**6.9**	**6.8**	**6.9**	**6.9**
(a) Private Ownership of Banks	10.0 (95-100)	10.0 (95-100)	10.0 (95-100)	10.0 (95-100)	10.0 (95-100)	10.0 (95-100)	10.0 (95-100)
(b) Extension of Credit to Private Sector	9.5 (94.7)	8.0 (80.2)	7.9 (78.5)	8.1 (81.2)	7.9 (78.9)	8.2 (81.7)	8.3 (82.7)
(c) Avoidance of Negative Interest Rates		8.0	8.0	10.0	10.0	10.0	10.0
(d) Capital Transactions with Foreigners	0.0	0.0	0.0	0.0	0.0	0.0	0.0

BAHRAIN

Summary Ratings	1970	1975	1980	1985	1990	1995	1999
Summary Ratings			7.7	7.3	7.3	7.4	7.7
Rank			9	14	22	31	28

Components of Economic Freedom	1970	1975	1980	1985	1990	1995	1999
I. Size of Government			**6.5**	**5.0**	**4.8**	**5.4**	**6.4**
(a) Government Consumption			3.2 (29.0)	0.0 (43.5)	0.0 (43.8)	1.4 (35.2)	3.3 (28.8)
(b) Transfers and Subsidies			9.8 (1.2)	10.0 (0.0)	9.6 (1.8)	9.3 (3.1)	9.4 (2.5)
II. Structure of the Economy and Use of Markets		**6.1**	**7.1**	**7.1**	**6.0**	**6.0**	**6.0**
(a) Government Enterprises	0.0	2.0 (76.4)	4.0 (29.8)	4.0 (31.7)	4.0	4.0	4.0
(b) Price Controls					4.0	4.0	4.0
(c) Top Marginal Tax Rate		10.0 (0)	10.0 (0)	10.0 (0)	10.0 (0)	10.0 (0)	10.0 (0)
(d) Conscription		10.0	10.0	10.0	10.0	10.0	10.0
III. Monetary Policy and Price Stability	**9.0**	**7.0**	**7.4**	**8.1**	**8.4**	**9.4**	**9.8**
(a) Annual Money Growth	7.9 (10.5)	7.1 (14.4)	6.4 (18.1)	8.5 (7.7)	9.5 (2.7)	9.6 (-2.1)	9.9 (-0.5)
(b) Inflation Variability	9.4 (1.4)	7.1 (7.2)	6.8 (8.0)	6.3 (9.2)	6.9 (7.7)	8.7 (3.3)	9.6 (1.0)
(c) Recent Inflation Rate	9.7 (1.6)	6.8 (16.1)	9.2 (3.9)	9.6 (-1.8)	8.6 (6.8)	9.8 (1.0)	9.9 (-0.4)
IV. Freedom to Use Alternative Currencies	**10.0**	**10.0**	**10.0**	**10.0**	**10.0**	**10.0**	**10.0**
(a) Ownership of Foreign Currency	10.0	10.0	10.0	10.0	10.0	10.0	10.0
(b) Black Market Exchange Rate	10.0 (0.0)	10.0 (0.0)	10.0 (0.0)	10.0 (0.0)	10.0 (0.0)	10.0 (0.0)	10.0 (0.0)
V. Legal Structure and Property Rights				**6.4**	**6.3**	**7.0**	**7.9**
(a) Legal Security				6.1	5.9	7.0	7.9
(b) Rule of Law				6.6	6.7		
VI. International Exchange			**8.6**	**8.6**	**8.5**	**7.9**	**7.4**
(a) Taxes on International Trade							
i. Taxes as a Percentage of Exports and Imports			9.4 (0.9)	9.5 (0.7)	9.3 (1.1)	9.1 (1.4)	9.1 (1.4)
ii. Mean Tariff Rate				8.8 (6.0)			
iii. Standard Deviation of Tariff Rates							
(b) Size of Trade Sector		7.6 (241.2)	6.9 (239.3)	6.2 (191.6)	6.8 (221.7)	5.5 (195.4)	4.0 (146.2)
VII. Freedom of Exchange in Financial Markets	**6.4**	**6.4**	**6.2**	**6.0**	**6.8**	**6.5**	**6.9**
(a) Private Ownership of Banks		8.0 (80-90)	8.0 (30-90)	8.0 (80-90)	8.0 (90-95)	8.0 (90-95)	8.0 (90-95)
(b) Extension of Credit to Private Sector	10.0 (99.9)	9.9 (99.2)	9.4 (94.1)	8.7 (87.0)	7.5 (74.6)	8.7 (87.3)	8.1 (81.2)
(c) Avoidance of Negative Interest Rates					10.0		10.0
(d) Capital Transactions with Foreigners	2.0	2.0	2.0	2.0	2.0	2.0	2.0

BANGLADESH

Summary Ratings	1970	1975	1980	1985	1990	1995	1999
Summary Ratings	2.9	2.9	2.9	3.1	3.1	4.2	4.8
Rank		79	103	105	108	106	100

Components of Economic Freedom

	1970	1975	1980	1985	1990	1995	1999
I. Size of Government		**10.0**	**9.9**	**10.0**	**7.5**	**7.4**	**7.3**
(a) Government Consumption		10.0 (3.3)	9.9 (6.4)	10.0 (5.4)	7.5 (14.4)	7.4 (15.0)	7.3 (15.3)
(b) Transfers and Subsidies							
II. Structure of the Economy and Use of Markets			**2.7**	**2.7**	**2.0**	**2.9**	**2.9**
(a) Government Enterprises	2.0	2.0 (50.4)	2.0 (44.4)	2.0 (46.6)	2.0 (47.1)	4.0 (34.0)	4.0 (32.0)
(b) Price Controls					0.0	0.0	0.0
(c) Top Marginal Tax Rate			1.0 (60)	1.0 (60)			
(d) Conscription		10.0	10.0	10.0	10.0	10.0	10.0
III. Monetary Policy and Price Stability	**8.5**	**2.7**	**6.0**	**8.0**	**9.2**	**8.5**	**9.0**
(a) Annual Money Growth		7.8 (10.9)	6.4 (18.0)	7.4 (13.1)	9.5 (2.7)	7.7 (11.3)	8.5 (7.3)
(b) Inflation Variability	7.0 (7.5)	0.0 (29.1)	4.2 (14.4)	8.8 (3.1)	9.2 (2.1)	9.0 (2.4)	9.6 (1.0)
(c) Recent Inflation Rate	9.9 (0.5)	0.0 (74.5)	7.3 (13.4)	7.8 (11.1)	9.0 (4.9)	8.7 (6.7)	8.7 (6.3)
IV. Freedom to Use Alternative Currencies		**0.0**	**0.0**	**0.0**	**0.0**	**2.2**	**3.9**
(a) Ownership of Foreign Currency		0.0	0.0	0.0	0.0	0.0	0.0
(b) Black Market Exchange Rate		0.0 (51.0)	0.0 (111.0)	0.0 (168.0)	0.0 (165.0)	4.4 (28.0)	7.8 (11.1)
V. Legal Structure and Property Rights			**1.9**	**1.8**	**1.8**	**7.0**	**3.8**
(a) Legal Security			2.2	2.2	1.9		
(b) Rule of Law			1.7	1.4	1.7	7.0	3.8
VI. International Exchange		**3.2**	**0.7**	**0.5**	**0.9**	**0.8**	**4.3**
(a) Taxes on International Trade							
i. Taxes as a Percentage of Exports and Imports		4.7 (7.9)	1.1 (13.4)	0.0 (17.9)	1.9 (12.1)		3.7 (9.5)
ii. Mean Tariff Rate			0.0 (99.9)	0.0 (86.0)	0.0 (102.2)	0.0 (81.2)	5.6 (22.1)
iii. Standard Deviation of Tariff Rates					0.0 (50.4)	0.0 (26.1)	4.2 (14.6)
(b) Size of Trade Sector	1.9 (20.8)	0.0 (11.0)	1.7 (24.1)	2.8 (25.8)	2.7 (27.1)	3.9 (36.7)	3.1 (32.7)
VII. Freedom of Exchange in Financial Markets		**0.8**	**2.4**	**2.9**	**4.0**	**3.5**	**4.6**
(a) Private Ownership of Banks	0.0 (0-10)	0.0 (0-10)	0.0 (0-10)	0.0 (0-10)	0.0 (0-10)	0.0 (0-10)	2.0 (35)
(b) Extension of Credit to Private Sector		2.8 (27.8)	4.3 (43.1)	6.6 (65.5)	7.3 (72.7)	7.4 (73.6)	7.7 (77.2)
(c) Avoidance of Negative Interest Rates			6.0	6.0	10.0	8.0	10.0
(d) Capital Transactions with Foreigners	0.0	0.0	0.0	0.0	0.0	0.0	0.0

BARBADOS

Summary Ratings

	1970	1975	1980	1985	1990	1995	1999
Summary Ratings	5.4	5.4	5.6	6.1	6.0	6.0	5.7
Rank	40	40	40	34	44	63	85

Components of Economic Freedom

	1970	1975	1980	1985	1990	1995	1999
I. Size of Government	**8.2**	**8.2**	**8.0**	**7.3**	**7.3**	**7.5**	**4.5**
(a) Government Consumption	7.0 (16.2)	6.4 (18.3)	6.1 (-9.3)	4.5 (24.6)	4.7 (24.1)	5.1 (22.7)	4.5 (24.8)
(b) Transfers and Subsidies	9.3 (2.9)	10.0 (0.2)	10.0 (0.2)	10.0 (0.0)	10.0 (0.5)	10.0 (0.0)	
II. Structure of the Economy and Use of Markets	**4.7**	**4.7**	**4.7**	**4.7**	**5.9**	**6.1**	**6.1**
(a) Government Enterprises	8.0 (19.2)	6.0 (26.8)	6.0 (22.8)	6.0 (22.5)	6.0	6.0	6.0
(b) Price Controls					6.0	6.0	6.0
(c) Top Marginal Tax Rate		1.0 (65)	1.0 (60)	1.0 (60)	4.0 (50)	5.0 (40)	5.0 (40)
(d) Conscription	10.0	10.0	10.0	10.0	10.0	10.0	10.0
III. Monetary Policy and Price Stability	**8.8**	**7.4**	**6.7**	**8.9**	**8.7**	**9.4**	**9.0**
(a) Annual Money Growth		8.1 (9.5)	6.9 (15.3)	8.8 (5.8)	8.6 (7.1)	8.9 (-5.4)	8.2 (9.0)
(b) Inflation Variability	9.1 (2.3)	6.3 (9.2)	7.6 (6.0)	8.6 (3.5)	8.6 (3.4)	9.5 (1.3)	9.3 (1.8)
(c) Recent Inflation Rate	8.5 (7.3)	7.7 (11.7)	5.5 (22.6)	9.2 (4.1)	8.9 (5.5)	10.0 (0.3)	9.7 (1.6)
IV. Freedom to Use Alternative Currencies		**3.0**	**3.9**	**3.9**	**4.0**	**4.7**	**4.9**
(a) Ownership of Foreign Currency		0.0	0.0	0.0	0.0	0.0	0.0
(b) Black Market Exchange Rate		6.0 (20.0)	7.8 (11.0)	7.8 (11.0)	8.0 (10.0)	9.4 (3.0)	9.8 (1.0)
V. Legal Structure and Property Rights				**6.4**	**6.3**	**4.1**	**5.8**
(a) Legal Security				6.1	5.9		
(b) Rule of Law				6.6	6.7	4.1	5.8
VI. International Exchange	**5.7**	**5.6**	**6.2**	**6.4**	**5.1**	**5.8**	**4.9**
(a) Taxes on International Trade							
i. Taxes as a Percentage of Exports and Imports	6.6 (5.1)	7.1 (4.4)	7.5 (3.7)	7.7 (3.4)	7.6 (3.6)	7.8 (3.3)	6.2 (19.0)
ii. Mean Tariff Rate				6.6 (17.0)		7.2 (14.1)	
iii. Standard Deviation of Tariff Rates					4.5 (13.7)	4.8 (13.1)	
(b) Size of Trade Sector	3.9 (138.1)	2.7 (110.8)	3.6 (-42.2)	3.3 (127.8)	1.1 (100.8)	1.3 (115.8)	2.2 (130.4)
VII. Freedom of Exchange in Financial Markets	**5.2**	**5.2**	**5.3**	**6.1**	**6.1**	**6.0**	**5.7**
(a) Private Ownership of Banks	8.0	8.0 (75-90)	8.0 (75-90)	8.0 (75-90)	8.0 (75-90)	8.0 (75-90)	8.0 (75-90)
(b) Extension of Credit to Private Sector	9.5 (95.4)	8.1 (80.9)	7.6 (75.7)	7.1 (70.7)	6.7 (67.3)	6.6 (66.1)	7.4 (74.3)
(c) Avoidance of Negative Interest Rates		0.0	6.0	10.0	10.0	10.0	8.0
(d) Capital Transactions with Foreigners	0.0	0.0	0.0	0.0	0.0	0.0	0.0

BELGIUM

Summary Ratings

	1970	1975	1980	1985	1990	1995	1999
Summary Ratings	9.1	7.5	7.8	7.9	8.0	8.2	7.9
Rank	2	8	7	7	11	11	20

Components of Economic Freedom

	1970	1975	1980	1985	1990	1995	1999
I. Size of Government	**5.4**	**4.0**	**4.2**	**4.2**	**4.9**	**4.6**	**3.3**
(a) Government Consumption	6.4 (18.3)	5.6 (20.9)	5.4 (21.6)	5.8 (20.3)	6.4 (18.1)	6.2 (18.9)	3.5 (28.2)
(b) Transfers and Subsidies	4.5 (20.8)	2.4 (28.5)	3.1 (26.0)	2.6 (27.6)	3.3 (25.0)	3.0 (26.3)	3.2 (25.4)
II. Structure of the Economy and Use of Markets		**4.1**	**3.3**	**3.3**	**3.4**	**4.8**	**5.1**
(a) Government Enterprises	6.0	6.0 (25.0)	6.0 (26.8)	6.0 (25.3)	6.0 (27.0)	6.0	6.0
(b) Price Controls					2.0	5.0	6.0
(c) Top Marginal Tax Rate		2.0 (64)	0.0 (76)	0.0 (76)	2.0 (55-61)	1.0 (58-64)	1.0 (58-64)
(d) Conscription	1.0	3.0	3.0	3.0	3.0	10.0	10.0
III. Monetary Policy and Price Stability	**9.5**	**8.3**	**9.4**	**9.4**	**9.5**	**9.6**	**9.6**
(a) Annual Money Growth	9.7 (-1.3)	8.6 (6.9)	9.6 (1.9)	9.7 (1.6)	9.4 (2.9)	9.4 (3.0)	9.5 (2.7)
(b) Inflation Variability	9.7 (0.7)	8.8 (3.0)	9.4 (1.6)	9.8 (0.6)	9.6 (1.0)	9.6 (0.9)	9.7 (0.7)
(c) Recent Inflation Rate	9.1 (4.6)	7.5 (12.3)	9.2 (4.2)	8.8 (6.1)	9.4 (3.1)	9.7 (1.7)	9.8 (1.1)
IV. Freedom to Use Alternative Currencies	**10.0**	**10.0**	**10.0**	**10.0**	**10.0**	**10.0**	**10.0**
(a) Ownership of Foreign Currency	10.0	10.0	10.0	10.0	10.0	10.0	10.0
(b) Black Market Exchange Rate	10.0 (0.0)	10.0 (0.0)	10.0 (0.0)	10.0 (0.0)	10.0 (0.0)	10.0 (0.0)	10.0 (0.0)
V. Legal Structure and Property Rights	**10.0**	**8.6**	**9.3**	**9.4**	**10.0**	**10.0**	**8.7**
(a) Legal Security	10.0	8.6	8.6	8.7	10.0		9.5
(b) Rule of Law			10.0	10.0	10.0	10.0	7.9
VI. International Exchange	**9.5**	**8.5**	**8.6**	**9.0**	**8.4**	**8.4**	**8.6**
(a) Taxes on International Trade							
i. Taxes as a Percentage of Exports and Imports	9.7 (0.4)	10.0 (0.0)	9.8 (0.3)	9.8 (0.3)	9.7 (0.4)	9.7 (0.4)	9.7 (0.4)
ii. Mean Tariff Rate		8.1 (9.4)	8.2 (8.8)	8.5 (7.5)	8.5 (7.4)	8.7 (6.7)	8.9 (5.6)
iii. Standard Deviation of Tariff Rates					7.1 (7.2)	7.6 (5.9)	7.6 (5.9)
(b) Size of Trade Sector	9.0 (101.1)	6.3 (106.6)	6.7 (127.3)	8.6 (149.9)	7.9 (143.5)	7.0 (140.4)	7.4 (147.1)
VII. Freedom of Exchange in Financial Markets	**9.0**	**8.1**	**9.1**	**8.8**	**9.0**	**8.9**	**9.1**
(a) Private Ownership of Banks	10.0 (95-100)	10.0 (95-100)	10.0 (95-100)	10.0 (95-100)	10.0 (95-100)	10.0 (95-100)	10.0 (95-100)
(b) Extension of Credit to Private Sector	5.4 (53.7)	5.7 (57.0)	5.8 (57.9)	4.3 (43.3)	5.2 (52.0)	5.0 (49.5)	5.5 (55.3)
(c) Avoidance of Negative Interest Rates	10.0	6.0	10.0	10.0	10.0	10.0	10.0
(d) Capital Transactions with Foreigners	10.0	10.0	10.0	10.0	10.0	10.0	10.0

BELIZE

Summary Ratings	1970	1975	1980	1985	1990	1995	1999
Summary Ratings			5.5	4.9	5.2	6.2	6.3
Rank			43	68	61	57	68

Components of Economic Freedom	1970	1975	1980	1985	1990	1995	1999
I. Size of Government		**6.9**	**7.8**	**7.1**	**7.7**	**8.2**	**7.7**
(a) Government Consumption		6.9 (16.4)	6.1 (19.3)	5.0 (23.1)	5.6 (20.9)	6.6 (17.7)	5.7 (20.7)
(b) Transfers and Subsidies			9.4 (2.6)	9.2 (3.6)	9.8 (1.2)	9.8 (1.2)	9.7 (1.6)
II. Structure of the Economy and Use of Markets				**3.8**	**1.9**	**5.4**	**4.7**
(a) Government Enterprises		6.0 (34.4)	0.0 (51.0)	2.0 (49.9)	0.0 (55.5)	4.0 (38.3)	2.0 (47.7)
(b) Price Controls					0.0	6.0	6.0
(c) Top Marginal Tax Rate				4.0 (50)	4.0 (45)	5.0 (45)	
(d) Conscription			10.0	10.0	10.0	10.0	10.0
III. Monetary Policy and Price Stability	**8.7**	**6.6**	**8.3**	**8.8**	**9.1**	**9.5**	**9.7**
(a) Annual Money Growth			8.8 (6.2)	9.3 (3.3)	8.5 (7.6)	9.8 (1.0)	9.8 (1.1)
(b) Inflation Variability	9.0 (2.6)	6.7 (8.3)	8.5 (3.8)	7.5 (6.3)	8.8 (3.0)	9.6 (1.0)	9.7 (0.8)
(c) Recent Inflation Rate	8.5 (7.4)	6.6 (16.9)	7.7 (11.4)	9.6 (-1.9)	9.9 (0.3)	9.2 (3.9)	9.8 (-1.2)
IV. Freedom to Use Alternative Currencies		**3.6**	**1.6**	**0.0**	**2.5**	**4.7**	**4.6**
(a) Ownership of Foreign Currency			0.0	0.0	0.0	0.0	0.0
(b) Black Market Exchange Rate	3.6	3.6 (32.0)	3.2 (34.0)	0.0 (63.0)	5.0 (25.0)	9.4 (3.0)	9.2 (4.0)
V. Legal Structure and Property Rights							
(a) Legal Security							
(b) Rule of Law							
VI. International Exchange			**4.2**	**4.6**	**3.4**	**2.8**	**4.7**
(a) Taxes on International Trade							
i. Taxes as a Percentage of Exports and Imports			4.2 (8.7)	2.7 (10.9)	2.8 (10.8)	2.7 (10.9)	5.6 (6.6)
ii. Mean Tariff Rate				6.6 (17.0)			
iii. Standard Deviation of Tariff Rates							
(b) Size of Trade Sector		6.5 (165.1)	4.3 (124.0)	4.1 (109.8)	4.6 (125.4)	2.9 (103.2)	2.8 (102.0)
VII. Freedom of Exchange in Financial Markets			**6.9**	**6.8**	**8.3**	**8.4**	**8.0**
(a) Private Ownership of Banks					10.0 (95-100)	10.0 (95-100)	10.0 (95-100)
(b) Extension of Credit to Private Sector		9.1 (91.1)	8.2 (82.1)	7.7 (76.6)	8.2 (82.1)	8.7 (86.8)	9.2 (91.7)
(c) Avoidance of Negative Interest Rates			8.0	8.0	10.0	10.0	8.0
(d) Capital Transactions with Foreigners			5.0	5.0	5.0	5.0	5.0

BENIN

Summary Ratings	1970	1975	1980	1985	1990	1995	1999
Summary Ratings		5.1	5.3	5.0	5.7	4.9	5.3
Rank		46	49	63	48	96	92

Components of Economic Freedom	1970	1975	1980	1985	1990	1995	1999
I. Size of Government	**8.7**	**9.0**	**9.3**	**7.2**	**8.3**	**8.1**	**8.9**
(a) Government Consumption	8.7 (10.3)	9.0 (9.4)	9.3 (8.2)	7.2 (15.5)	8.3 (11.7)	8.1 (12.5)	8.9 (9.6)
(b) Transfers and Subsidies							
II. Structure of the Economy and Use of Markets						**1.0**	**2.8**
(a) Government Enterprises	2.0 (50.0)	2.0 (45.9)	0.0 (53.7)	0.0 (53.5)	0.0 (55.2)	0.0 (60.1)	4.0 (40.5)
(b) Price Controls						2.0	2.0
(c) Top Marginal Tax Rate							
(d) Conscription				1.0	1.0	1.0	1.0
III. Monetary Policy and Price Stability	**9.0**	**6.9**	**8.4**	**8.1**	**9.0**	**6.9**	**8.1**
(a) Annual Money Growth	8.6 (6.8)	5.8 (20.8)	8.4 (8.0)	8.0 (10.0)	9.9 (0.7)	8.7 (6.3)	8.6 (7.0)
(b) Inflation Variability	9.3 (1.8)	7.8 (5.4)	8.7 (3.2)	7.2 (6.9)	8.3 (4.2)	5.0 (12.5)	5.6 (11.0)
(c) Recent Inflation Rate	9.0 (5.1)	7.2 (14.3)	8.0 (10.2)	9.0 (-4.9)	8.8 (6.1)	6.9 (15.4)	9.9 (0.3)
IV. Freedom to Use Alternative Currencies	**4.8**	**4.8**	**4.8**	**4.9**	**4.6**	**4.9**	**4.8**
(a) Ownership of Foreign Currency	0.0	0.0	0.0	0.0	0.0	0.0	0.0
(b) Black Market Exchange Rate	9.6 (2.0)	9.6 (2.0)	9.6 (2.0)	9.8 (1.0)	9.2 (4.0)	9.8 (1.0)	9.6 (2.0)
V. Legal Structure and Property Rights		**4.2**	**4.9**	**4.3**	**4.5**	**5.2**	**3.8**
(a) Legal Security			4.0	3.8	3.8		
(b) Rule of Law			5.8	4.8	5.3	5.2	3.8
VI. International Exchange		**4.2**	**3.5**	**3.7**			
(a) Taxes on International Trade							
i. Taxes as a Percentage of Exports and Imports		3.9 (9.2)	2.9 (10.6)	2.5 (37.4)			
ii. Mean Tariff Rate							
iii. Standard Deviation of Tariff Rates							
(b) Size of Trade Sector	3.8 (50.4)	4.8 (59.9)	4.8 (66.3)	6.1 (76.9)	3.7 (52.3)	4.3 (62.9)	3.5 (55.4)
VII. Freedom of Exchange in Financial Markets	**2.7**	**2.8**	**3.6**	**4.0**	**4.4**	**4.6**	**5.5**
(a) Private Ownership of Banks	0.0 (0)	0.0 (0)	0.0 (0)	0.0 (0)	2.0 (10-40)	10.0 (100)	10.0 (100)
(b) Extension of Credit to Private Sector	9.8 (97.5)	9.9 (99.9)	9.9 (99.3)	9.8 (97.5)	8.8 (87.5)	6.6 (65.9)	8.6 (86.2)
(c) Avoidance of Negative Interest Rates		6.0	6.0	8.0	8.0	2.0	4.0
(d) Capital Transactions with Foreigners	0.0	0.0	0.0	0.0	0.0	0.0	0.0

BOLIVIA

Summary Ratings	1970	1975	1980	1985	1990	1995	1999
Summary Ratings			4.1	3.8	6.3	7.7	8.3
Rank			84	94	37	27	11

Components of Economic Freedom	1970	1975	1980	1985	1990	1995	1999
I. Size of Government	**9.9**	**8.6**	**8.2**	**8.9**	**8.6**	**8.4**	**7.9**
(a) Government Consumption		7.3 (15.1)	6.7 (17.1)	8.1 (12.5)	7.9 (13.3)	7.3 (15.2)	7.0 (16.1)
(b) Transfers and Subsidies	9.9 (1.0)	9.8 (1.3)	9.7 (1.6)	9.6 (1.8)	9.4 (2.8)	9.5 (2.5)	8.8 (4.8)
II. Structure of the Economy and Use of Markets			**2.5**	**4.4**	**4.8**	**6.1**	**7.1**
(a) Government Enterprises	2.0 (44.0)	4.0 (28.9)	2.0 (50.1)	2.0 (42.5)	0.0 (60.7)	2.0 (51.1)	4.0 (40.3)
(b) Price Controls				8.0	6.0	8.0	9.0
(c) Top Marginal Tax Rate			3.0 (48)	8.0 (30)	10.0 (10)	10.0 (13)	10.0 (13)
(d) Conscription	3.0	3.0	3.0	3.0	3.0	3.0	3.0
III. Monetary Policy and Price Stability	**9.2**	**5.1**	**3.6**	**0.0**	**3.0**	**6.8**	**9.1**
(a) Annual Money Growth	8.9 (5.6)	5.8 (20.9)	6.2 (19.1)	0.0 (566.0)	2.4 (38.0)	4.3 (28.3)	9.0 (5.0)
(b) Inflation Variability	9.4 (1.5)	1.0 (22.5)	3.8 (15.5)	0.0 (4769.2)	0.0 (85.9)	8.4 (4.0)	8.9 (2.8)
(c) Recent Inflation Rate	9.2 (3.8)	8.4 (7.8)	0.5 (47.3)	0.0 (12336.7)	6.7 (16.3)	7.7 (11.4)	9.6 (2.2)
IV. Freedom to Use Alternative Currencies	**6.1**	**9.5**	**7.8**	**4.1**	**9.7**	**9.9**	**10.0**
(a) Ownership of Foreign Currency	10.0	10.0	10.0	0.0	10.0	10.0	10.0
(b) Black Market Exchange Rate	2.2 (39.0)	9.0 (5.0)	5.6 (22.0)	8.2 (9.0)	9.4 (3.0)	9.8 (1.0)	10.0 (0.0)
V. Legal Structure and Property Rights			**1.6**	**0.7**	**2.8**	**7.0**	**7.0**
(a) Legal Security			1.6	0.0	3.9		6.1
(b) Rule of Law			1.7	1.4	1.7	7.0	7.9
VI. International Exchange	**3.8**	**4.9**	**4.3**	**5.1**	**7.0**	**8.2**	**8.1**
(a) Taxes on International Trade							
i. Taxes as a Percentage of Exports and Imports	2.6 (11.1)	4.1 (8.9)	4.8 (7.8)	5.3 (7.0)	8.5 (2.3)	8.6 (2.1)	8.4 (2.4)
ii. Mean Tariff Rate				6.0 (19.8)	6.7 (16.7)	8.1 (9.7)	8.1 (9.7)
iii. Standard Deviation of Tariff Rates						9.6 (1.1)	9.5 (1.2)
(b) Size of Trade Sector	6.1 (48.9)	6.5 (58.2)	3.4 (37.7)	2.4 (30.3)	4.9 (47.0)	4.7 (49.7)	4.6 (48.6)
VII. Freedom of Exchange in Financial Markets			**2.2**		**7.3**	**7.5**	**8.9**
(a) Private Ownership of Banks					10.0 (100)	8.0 (93)	10.0 (99)
(b) Extension of Credit to Private Sector	3.3 (33.4)	6.5 (65.1)	5.0 (49.7)		10.0 (99.9)	9.6 (96.4)	9.7 (96.8)
(c) Avoidance of Negative Interest Rates			0.0	0.0	8.0	8.0	8.0
(d) Capital Transactions with Foreigners	2.0		2.0	2.0	2.0	5.0	8.0

BOTSWANA

Summary Ratings

	1970	1975	1980	1985	1990	1995	1999
Summary Ratings		3.8	5.0	5.6	5.7	6.1	6.9
Rank		67	60	46	48	61	50

Components of Economic Freedom

	1970	1975	1980	1985	1990	1995	1999
I. Size of Government	**7.7**	**6.6**	**6.2**	**4.6**	**5.0**	**4.1**	**4.0**
(a) Government Consumption	5.6 (21.0)	4.5 (24.8)	3.7 (27.5)	1.0 (36.7)	1.6 (34.4)	0.0 (45.9)	0.0 (43.6)
(b) Transfers and Subsidies	9.7 (1.5)	8.6 (5.5)	8.8 (4.9)	8.1 (7.3)	8.3 (6.6)	8.2 (7.2)	8.0 (7.7)
II. Structure of the Economy and Use of Markets		**2.3**	**2.3**	**3.1**	**4.3**	**5.9**	**6.2**
(a) Government Enterprises	2.0 (34.6)	2.0 (46.3)	2.0 (44.9)	2.0 (53.2)	2.0	4.0	4.0
(b) Price Controls				6.0	6.0	6.0	6.0
(c) Top Marginal Tax Rate		0.0 (75)	0.0 (75)	2.0 (60)	3.0 (50)	7.0 (35)	8.0 (30)
(d) Conscription		10.0	10.0	10.0	10.0	10.0	10.0
III. Monetary Policy and Price Stability	**9.6**	**6.6**	**7.1**	**7.1**	**7.4**	**8.8**	**8.2**
(a) Annual Money Growth			8.6 (6.8)	9.2 (4.1)	6.9 (15.3)	10.0 (0.0)	7.9 (10.7)
(b) Inflation Variability	9.5 (1.3)	6.9 (7.7)	6.4 (8.9)	6.5 (8.9)	6.6 (8.6)	8.3 (4.3)	8.0 (4.9)
(c) Recent Inflation Rate	9.8 (1.1)	6.3 (18.8)	6.2 (19.1)	5.5 (22.7)	8.8 (6.0)	8.1 (9.3)	8.6 (7.1)
IV. Freedom to Use Alternative Currencies		**0.6**	**4.0**	**2.8**	**4.3**	**7.3**	**10.0**
(a) Ownership of Foreign Currency		0.0	0.0	0.0	0.0	5.0	10.0
(b) Black Market Exchange Rate		1.2 (44.0)	8.0 (10.0)	5.6 (22.0)	8.6 (7.0)	9.6 (2.0)	10.0 (0.0)
V. Legal Structure and Property Rights				**7.2**	**7.1**	**7.0**	**5.8**
(a) Legal Security				6.1	5.9	7.0	5.8
(b) Rule of Law				8.2	8.3		
VI. International Exchange		**4.4**	**5.3**	**7.2**	**6.6**	**4.4**	**6.8**
(a) Taxes on International Trade							
i. Taxes as a Percentage of Exports and Imports		3.1 (10.4)	1.5 (12.8)	5.3 (7.1)	5.6 (6.6)	5.2 (7.1)	6.0 (6.1)
ii. Mean Tariff Rate			8.1 (9.4)	8.8 (6.0)	7.8 (11.0)	6.1 (19.7)	8.6 (7.2)
iii. Standard Deviation of Tariff Rates					5.5 (11.3)	1.2 (21.9)	6.0 (10.0)
(b) Size of Trade Sector	5.9 (70.9)	7.2 (92.0)	7.0 (99.3)	7.7 (99.1)	8.1 (107.5)	5.6 (81.7)	6.7 (97.9)
VII. Freedom of Exchange in Financial Markets			**5.8**	**6.9**	**5.5**	**6.0**	**7.0**
(a) Private Ownership of Banks					5.0 (40-75)	5.0 (40-75)	5.0 (40-75)
(b) Extension of Credit to Private Sector		9.1 (91.1)	8.9 (89.4)	8.1 (81.3)	8.8 (87.5)	8.8 (87.6)	8.7 (87.0)
(c) Avoidance of Negative Interest Rates			4.0	8.0	4.0	6.0	10.0
(d) Capital Transactions with Foreigners			5.0	5.0	5.0	5.0	5.0

BRAZIL

Summary Ratings	1970	1975	1980	1985	1990	1995	1999
Summary Ratings	5.6	4.5	4.2	3.2	4.2	5.0	5.1
Rank	38	57	79	103	90	94	96

Components of Economic Freedom

	1970	1975	1980	1985	1990	1995	1999
I. Size of Government	**6.8**	**6.2**	**7.5**	**7.7**	**5.9**	**5.5**	**5.3**
(a) Government Consumption	7.6 (14.2)	7.7 (13.8)	8.3 (11.6)	7.9 (13.0)	4.5 (24.5)	4.5 (24.7)	5.3 (21.8)
(b) Transfers and Subsidies	5.9 (15.5)	4.7 (19.9)	6.8 (12.4)	7.4 (10.0)	7.2 (10.7)	6.5 (13.3)	
II. Structure of the Economy and Use of Markets	**4.6**	**4.2**	**2.9**	**2.7**	**4.5**	**6.2**	**6.6**
(a) Government Enterprises	4.0 (38.3)	4.0 (35.8)	2.0 (49.2)	4.0 (36.0)	6.0 (24.9)	6.0 (17.8)	6.0 (19.4)
(b) Price Controls					0.0	6.0	7.0
(c) Top Marginal Tax Rate	6.0 (45)	5.0 (50)	4.0 (55)	1.0 (60)	9.0 (25)	8.0 (35)	8.0 (27.5)
(d) Conscription	3.0	3.0	3.0	3.0	3.0	3.0	3.0
III. Monetary Policy and Price Stability	**6.2**	**4.8**	**1.7**	**0.0**	**0.0**	**0.0**	**2.9**
(a) Annual Money Growth	5.1 (24.3)	3.9 (30.6)	1.6 (41.8)	0.0 (137.8)	0.0 (648.7)	0.0 (708.0)	0.0 (116.0)
(b) Inflation Variability	6.9 (7.7)	7.3 (6.7)	3.4 (16.6)	0.0 (53.1)	0.0 (878.9)	0.0 (851.5)	0.0 (887.8)
(c) Recent Inflation Rate	6.6 (17.1)	3.2 (34.0)	0.0 (87.5)	0.0 (231.7)	0.0 (2509.5)	0.0 (77.6)	9.0 (4.9)
IV. Freedom to Use Alternative Currencies	**6.1**	**0.1**	**3.2**	**0.1**	**4.0**	**4.7**	**5.0**
(a) Ownership of Foreign Currency	5.0	0.0	0.0	0.0	0.0	0.0	0.0
(b) Black Market Exchange Rate	7.2 (14.0)	0.2 (49.0)	6.4 (18.0)	0.2 (49.0)	8.0 (10.0)	9.4 (3.0)	10.0 (0.0)
V. Legal Structure and Property Rights	**7.0**	**5.9**	**6.5**	**6.4**	**7.0**	**7.0**	**4.9**
(a) Legal Security	7.0	5.9	6.4	6.1	7.3		8.1
(b) Rule of Law			6.7	6.6	6.7	7.0	1.7
VI. International Exchange	**4.5**	**5.6**	**3.6**	**2.8**	**4.3**	**6.7**	**5.7**
(a) Taxes on International Trade							
i. Taxes as a Percentage of Exports and Imports	5.6 (6.6)	6.2 (5.7)	3.3 (10.0)	7.9 (3.2)	7.5 (3.7)	8.1 (2.8)	4.5 (8.3)
ii. Mean Tariff Rate				0.0 (55.6)	4.0 (30.0)	7.6 (12.0)	7.1 (14.6)
iii. Standard Deviation of Tariff Rates				0.0 (26.2)	3.0 (17.5)	7.2 (6.9)	7.1 (7.3)
(b) Size of Trade Sector	2.4 (14.5)	4.2 (19.0)	4.0 (20.4)	4.2 (19.3)	0.7 (12.7)	1.1 (14.7)	2.5 (17.5)
VII. Freedom of Exchange in Financial Markets	**4.6**	**4.6**	**3.8**	**2.5**	**2.8**	**3.1**	**4.7**
(a) Private Ownership of Banks	5.0 (40-75)	5.0 (40-75)	5.0 (40-75)	5.0 (40-75)	5.0 (54)	5.0 (61)	5.0 (57)
(b) Extension of Credit to Private Sector	8.3 (83.2)	8.4 (84.0)	6.8 (57.8)	5.3 (52.9)	6.8 (68.4)	8.2 (82.2)	6.6 (66.2)
(c) Avoidance of Negative Interest Rates	6.0	6.0	4.0	0.0	0.0	0.0	8.0
(d) Capital Transactions with Foreigners	0.0	0.0	0.0	0.0	0.0	0.0	0.0

BULGARIA

Summary Ratings	1970	1975	1980	1985	1990	1995	1999
Summary Ratings				6.0	3.9	5.1	5.9
Rank				37	95	91	79

Components of Economic Freedom	1970	1975	1980	1985	1990	1995	1999
I. Size of Government			**9.0**	**6.7**	**3.8**	**6.6**	**6.6**
(a) Government Consumption			9.0 (9.3)	8.1 (12.4)	4.9 (23.3)	6.5 (17.8)	6.7 (17.1)
(b) Transfers and Subsidies				5.4 (17.5)	2.7 (27.2)	6.6 (13.0)	6.5 (13.3)
II. Structure of the Economy and Use of Markets					**0.0**	**2.2**	**4.2**
(a) Government Enterprises		0.0		0.0	0.0 (96.4)	0.0 (55.6)	2.0 (54.1)
(b) Price Controls					0.0	4.0	6.0
(c) Top Marginal Tax Rate						3.0 (50)	5.0 (40)
(d) Conscription		0.0		0.0	0.0	1.0	3.0
III. Monetary Policy and Price Stability				**9.7**	**6.0**	**0.0**	**3.1**
(a) Annual Money Growth					7.4 (13.1)	0.0 (67.0)	0.0 (127.2)
(b) Inflation Variability				9.4 (1.4)	5.6 (10.9)	0.0 (66.4)	0.0 (35.8)
(c) Recent Inflation Rate				10.0 (0.2)	4.8 (26.2)	0.0 (62.9)	9.5 (2.6)
IV. Freedom to Use Alternative Currencies		0.0		0.0	0.0	7.0	7.5
(a) Ownership of Foreign Currency		0.0		0.0	0.0	5.0	5.0
(b) Black Market Exchange Rate		0.0 (175.0)	0.0 (161.0)	0.0 (435.0)	0.0 (100.0)	9.0 (5.0)	10.0 (0.0)
V. Legal Structure and Property Rights				**8.5**	**8.5**	**7.0**	**6.0**
(a) Legal Security				8.7	8.6		6.2
(b) Rule of Law				8.2	8.3	7.0	5.8
VI. International Exchange				**6.4**	**7.7**	**6.4**	**7.6**
(a) Taxes on International Trade							
i. Taxes as a Percentage of Exports and Imports				6.4 (5.4)	9.1 (1.3)	7.9 (3.2)	8.5 (2.2)
ii. Mean Tariff Rate					7.7 (11.4)	6.6 (17.2)	7.5 (12.6)
iii. Standard Deviation of Tariff Rates						4.7 (13.3)	
(b) Size of Trade Sector			4.7 (66.4)	6.5 (86.0)	5.0 (69.8)	6.6 (102.7)	5.9 (91.5)
VII. Freedom of Exchange in Financial Markets					**1.0**	**4.5**	**5.0**
(a) Private Ownership of Banks		0.0 (0)		0.0 (0)	0.0 (0-10)	2.0 (30)	5.0 (56)
(b) Extension of Credit to Private Sector					0.0 (10.0)	3.0 (29.8)	6.2 (62.2)
(c) Avoidance of Negative Interest Rates					4.0	8.0	4.0
(d) Capital Transactions with Foreigners		0.0		0.0	0.0	5.0	5.0

BURUNDI

Summary Ratings	1970	1975	1980	1985	1990	1995	1999
Rating		3.2	3.3	4.1	3.9	3.6	4.7
Rank		75	99	88	95	117	102

Components of Economic Freedom

	1970	1975	1980	1985	1990	1995	1999
I. Size of Government	**8.8**	**8.5**	**9.1**	**9.4**	**8.7**	**8.7**	**9.0**
(a) Government Consumption	8.8 (10.1)	8.5 (11.2)	9.1 (9.2)	9.4 (8.2)	8.7 (10.3)	8.1 (12.5)	8.5 (11.0)
(b) Transfers and Subsidies						9.3 (3.2)	9.4 (2.6)
II. Structure of the Economy and Use of Markets					**1.2**	**2.1**	**3.8**
(a) Government Enterprises	0.0 (72.5)		0.0 (67.7)	0.0 (82.4)	0.0 (82.5)	0.0	2.0
(b) Price Controls					0.0	2.0	4.0
(c) Top Marginal Tax Rate							
(d) Conscription		10.0	10.0	10.0	10.0	10.0	10.0
III. Monetary Policy and Price Stability	**8.9**	**7.3**	**6.5**	**8.2**	**8.7**	**7.5**	**8.1**
(a) Annual Money Growth	9.2 (4.1)	8.8 (6.1)	5.3 (23.3)	8.5 (7.3)	9.9 (0.8)	7.6 (12.0)	7.9 (10.4)
(b) Inflation Variability	8.4 (3.9)	7.2 (7.1)	7.6 (6.0)	7.1 (7.4)	7.2 (6.9)	8.1 (4.9)	7.0 (7.6)
(c) Recent Inflation Rate	9.0 (5.2)	5.8 (21.1)	6.7 (16.4)	9.0 (5.1)	8.8 (6.0)	7.0 (15.2)	9.3 (3.4)
IV. Freedom to Use Alternative Currencies	**5.4**	**0.4**	**0.5**	**2.5**	**4.4**	**0.6**	**5.0**
(a) Ownership of Foreign Currency		0.0	0.0	0.0	0.0	0.0	5.0
(b) Black Market Exchange Rate	5.4 (23.0)	0.8 (46.0)	1.0 (45.0)	5.0 (25.0)	8.8 (6.0)	1.2 (44.0)	5.0 (25.0)
V. Legal Structure and Property Rights			**4.9**	**4.3**	**4.5**	**5.2**	**3.8**
(a) Legal Security			4.0	3.8	3.8		
(b) Rule of Law			5.8	4.8	5.3	5.2	3.8
VI. International Exchange		**1.2**	**0.0**	**1.0**	**1.1**	**1.7**	**2.7**
(a) Taxes on International Trade							
i. Taxes as a Percentage of Exports and Imports		1.9 (12.2)	0.0 (18.1)	0.0 (17.0)	0.0 (22.9)	1.6 (12.6)	4.1 (8.9)
ii. Mean Tariff Rate				2.4 (37.9)	2.6 (37.0)	2.6 (36.9)	
iii. Standard Deviation of Tariff Rates							
(b) Size of Trade Sector	0.0 (28.9)	0.0 (27.3)	0.0 (32.1)	0.0 (31.7)	0.0 (35.6)	0.0 (32.7)	0.0 (21.7)
VII. Freedom of Exchange in Financial Markets	**1.9**	**1.9**	**2.1**	**2.8**	**2.2**	**2.6**	**3.2**
(a) Private Ownership of Banks	2.0 (10-40)	2.0 (10-40)	2.0 (10-40)	2.0 (10-40)	0.0 (0-10)	0.0 (0-10)	0.0 (0-10)
(b) Extension of Credit to Private Sector	4.3 (43.0)	4.3 (42.5)	4.8 (48.1)	3.9 (38.7)	5.8 (57.7)	7.8 (78.4)	8.3 (82.8)
(c) Avoidance of Negative Interest Rates		2.0	2.0	6.0	4.0	4.0	6.0
(d) Capital Transactions with Foreigners	0.0	0.0	0.0	0.0	0.0	0.0	0.0

CENTRAL AFRICAN REPUBLIC

Summary Ratings	1970	1975	1980	1985	1990	1995	1999
Summary Ratings			5.2	4.5	4.4	4.6	4.4
Rank			52	79	86	102	110

Components of Economic Freedom	1970	1975	1980	1985	1990	1995	1999
I. Size of Government	**5.3**	**7.0**	**7.7**	**7.2**	**7.4**	**7.7**	**8.2**
(a) Government Consumption	5.3 (21.9)	7.0 (16.3)	7.7 (13.9)	7.2 (15.7)	7.4 (14.8)	7.7 (14.0)	8.2 (12.2)
(b) Transfers and Subsidies							
II. Structure of the Economy and Use of Markets					**0.0**	**0.0**	**0.0**
(a) Government Enterprises	0.0 (68.3)	2.0 (39.0)	0.0 (65.7)	0.0 (67.0)	0.0 (51.8)	0.0 (54.8)	0.0
(b) Price Controls					0.0	0.0	0.0
(c) Top Marginal Tax Rate							
(d) Conscription	0.0	0.0	0.0	0.0	0.0	0.0	0.0
III. Monetary Policy and Price Stability	**8.4**	**7.5**	**6.5**	**5.9**	**9.5**	**6.8**	**8.2**
(a) Annual Money Growth	8.9 (5.6)	8.6 (7.0)	5.6 (22.1)	8.5 (7.3)	10.0 (-0.2)	7.0 (15.0)	8.6 (7.0)
(b) Inflation Variability	7.3 (6.8)	7.6 (6.1)	7.5 (6.2)	5.6 (10.9)	8.9 (2.9)	6.0 (9.9)	6.4 (9.1)
(c) Recent Inflation Rate	9.1 (4.5)	6.1 (19.3)	6.3 (18.3)	3.2 (34.2)	9.5 (2.3)	7.3 (13.4)	9.6 (-1.9)
IV. Freedom to Use Alternative Currencies	**4.8**	**4.8**	**4.8**	**4.9**	**4.6**	**4.9**	**5.0**
(a) Ownership of Foreign Currency	0.0	0.0	0.0	0.0	0.0	0.0	0.0
(b) Black Market Exchange Rate	9.6 (2.0)	9.6 (2.0)	9.6 (2.0)	9.8 (1.0)	9.2 (4.0)	9.8 (1.0)	10.0 (0.0)
V. Legal Structure and Property Rights			**4.9**	**4.3**	**4.5**	**5.2**	**3.8**
(a) Legal Security			4.0	3.8	3.8		
(b) Rule of Law			5.8	4.8	5.3	5.2	3.8
VI. International Trade			**3.7**	**4.0**	**3.0**	**5.6**	**4.6**
(a) Taxes on International Trade							
i. Taxes as a Percentage of Exports and Imports			2.9 (10.6)	3.6 (32.0)	2.3 (11.5)	6.3 (18.6)	4.3 (8.6)
ii. Mean Tariff Rate					3.6 (32.0)	6.2 (9.6)	6.3 (18.6)
iii. Standard Deviation of Tariff Rates							
(b) Size of Trade Sector	7.5 (73.5)	5.5 (61.1)	5.3 (66.3)	4.7 (54.3)	3.0 (43.1)	3.2 (48.5)	1.9 (40.9)
VII. Freedom of Exchange in Financial Markets			**0.0**	**2.5**	**4.5**	**3.4**	**3.3**
(a) Private Ownership of Banks	0.0 (0-10)	0.0 (0-10)	0.0 (0-10)	0.0 (0-10)	2.0 (10-40)	2.0 (10-40)	2.0 (10-40)
(b) Extension of Credit to Private Sector					6.9 (68.7)	6.6 (65.9)	6.1 (60.6)
(c) Avoidance of Negative Interest Rates				8.0	10.0	6.0	6.0
(d) Capital Transactions with Foreigners	0.0		0.0	0.0	0.0	0.0	0.0

CAMEROON

Summary Ratings	1970	1975	1980	1985	1990	1995	1999
Summary Ratings			5.1	5.4	5.4	5.3	4.9
Rank			56	50	58	83	99

Components of Economic Freedom	1970	1975	1980	1985	1990	1995	1999
I. Size of Government	**7.5**	**8.8**	**9.0**	**9.1**	**8.2**	**9.2**	**8.4**
(a) Government Consumption	7.5 (14.5)	7.9 (13.1)	8.2 (12.2)	8.2 (12.3)	7.0 (16.1)	8.6 (10.7)	8.4 (11.5)
(b) Transfers and Subsidies		9.8 (1.4)	9.9 (0.8)	10.0 (0.6)	9.4 (2.7)	9.7 (1.6)	
II. Structure of the Economy and Use of Markets			**3.5**	**3.1**	**2.4**	**2.2**	**2.2**
(a) Government Enterprises	2.0 (47.6)	2.0 (54.7)	4.0 (27.7)	2.0 (41.7)	4.0 (32.0)	4.0	4.0
(b) Price Controls					0.0	0.0	0.0
(c) Top Marginal Tax Rate				2.0 (60)	1.0 (60)	0.0 (66)	0.0 (68.8)
(d) Conscription	10.0	10.0	10.0	10.0	10.0	10.0	10.0
III. Monetary Policy and Price Stability	**7.6**	**8.6**	**7.2**	**8.5**	**9.4**	**7.8**	**8.5**
(a) Annual Money Growth	7.7 (11.6)	7.9 (10.4)	6.8 (15.8)	8.5 (7.7)	9.2 (-4.1)	9.4 (-3.2)	7.4 (12.9)
(b) Inflation Variability	6.8 (8.0)	9.0 (2.4)	7.6 (5.9)	9.3 (1.7)	9.4 (1.6)	7.3 (6.6)	8.1 (4.8)
(c) Recent Inflation Rate	8.4 (7.9)	8.8 (6.0)	7.2 (14.3)	7.8 (11.2)	9.7 (1.6)	6.6 (17.0)	10.0 (0.1)
IV. Freedom to Use Alternative Currencies	**4.8**	**4.8**	**4.8**	**4.9**	**4.6**	**4.9**	**4.8**
(a) Ownership of Foreign Currency	0.0	0.0	0.0	0.0	0.0	0.0	0.0
(b) Black Market Exchange Rate	9.6 (2.0)	9.6 (2.0)	9.6 (2.0)	9.8 (1.0)	9.2 (4.0)	9.8 (1.0)	9.6 (2.0)
V. Legal Structure and Property Rights			**6.4**	**6.5**	**6.4**	**7.0**	**3.8**
(a) Legal Security			4.6	4.8	4.6		
(b) Rule of Law			8.3	8.2	8.3	7.0	3.8
VI. International Exchange		**2.4**	**3.5**	**6.2**	**5.4**	**5.3**	**5.8**
(a) Taxes on International Trade							
i. Taxes as a Percentage of Exports and Imports		1.1 (13.4)	2.7 (11.0)	5.9 (6.1)	6.4 (5.4)	4.9 (7.7)	6.3 (18.4)
ii. Mean Tariff Rate						6.3 (18.7)	
iii. Standard Deviation of Tariff Rates						5.2 (12.0)	
(b) Size of Trade Sector	5.5 (50.9)	5.2 (48.2)	5.2 (54.2)	6.9 (65.0)	3.5 (37.7)	4.1 (45.6)	4.8 (51.5)
VII. Freedom of Exchange in Financial Markets		**1.9**	**1.9**	**1.9**	**3.6**	**2.8**	**3.5**
(a) Private Ownership of Banks	0.0 (0-10)	0.0 (0-10)	0.0 (0-10)	0.0 (0-10)	0.0 (0-10)	2.0 (10-40)	2.0 (10-40)
(b) Extension of Credit to Private Sector					7.7 (76.8)	5.1 (60.9)	6.8 (68.1)
(c) Avoidance of Negative Interest Rates	6.0	6.0	6.0	6.0	8.0	4.0	6.0
(d) Capital Transactions with Foreigners	0.0	0.0	0.0	0.0	0.0	0.0	0.0

CANADA

	1970	1975	1980	1985	1990	1995	1999
Summary Ratings	8.0	7.3	7.9	8.1	8.4	8.0	8.2
Rank	7	10	6	6	4	14	13

Components of Economic Freedom

	1970	1975	1980	1985	1990	1995	1999
I. Size of Government	**3.8**	**5.5**	**4.7**	**4.5**	**4.6**	**4.6**	**4.5**
(a) Government Consumption	3.8 (27.2)	3.3 (28.9)	3.3 (28.8)	3.3 (28.8)	3.3 (28.6)	3.7 (27.5)	4.5 (24.6)
(b) Transfers and Subsidies		7.7 (9.1)	6.2 (14.5)	5.7 (16.3)	5.9 (15.6)	5.5 (16.9)	
II. Structure of the Economy and Use of Markets	**5.3**	**6.0**	**6.0**	**6.0**	**7.5**	**6.8**	**7.9**
(a) Government Enterprises	8.0 (18.5)	8.0 (15.8)	8.0 (12.6)	8.0 (14.8)	8.0 (13.7)	8.0 (14.8)	10.0 (11.5)
(b) Price Controls		8.0	8.0		9.0	7.0	9.0
(c) Top Marginal Tax Rate	0.0 (82-91)	2.0 (59-67)	2.0 (60-68)	2.0 (50-63)	4.0 (44-54)	4.0 (44-54)	3.0 (44-54)
(d) Conscription	10.0	10.0	10.0	10.0	10.0	10.0	10.0
III. Monetary Policy and Price Stability	**9.1**	**8.4**	**8.9**	**8.6**	**9.4**	**9.4**	**9.3**
(a) Annual Money Growth	8.4 (7.8)	8.7 (6.5)	9.7 (1.7)	7.6 (11.9)	9.2 (3.9)	9.0 (5.1)	8.6 (7.0)
(b) Inflation Variability	9.8 (0.5)	8.5 (3.9)	9.3 (1.7)	8.7 (3.2)	9.6 (0.9)	9.7 (0.7)	9.6 (1.0)
(c) Recent Inflation Rate	9.0 (4.8)	8.0 (10.2)	7.8 (11.0)	9.5 (2.4)	9.4 (3.1)	9.5 (2.7)	9.7 (1.7)
IV. Freedom to Use Alternative Currencies	**10.0**	**10.0**	**10.0**	**10.0**	**10.0**	**10.0**	**10.0**
(a) Ownership of Foreign Currency	10.0	10.0	10.0	10.0	10.0	10.0	10.0
(b) Black Market Exchange Rate	10.0 (0.0)	10.0 (0.0)	10.0 (0.0)	10.0 (0.0)	10.0 (0.0)	10.0 (0.0)	10.0 (0.0)
V. Legal Structure and Property Rights	**10.0**	**6.5**	**8.4**	**9.4**	**10.0**	**10.0**	**9.6**
(a) Legal Security	10.0	6.5	6.7	8.7	10.0		9.2
(b) Rule of Law			10.0	10.0	10.0	10.0	10.0
VI. International Exchange	**8.2**	**6.8**	**7.3**	**7.6**	**7.4**	**5.9**	**6.1**
(a) Taxes on International Trade							
i. Taxes as a Percentage of Exports and Imports	8.4 (2.4)	7.5 (3.7)	8.4 (2.4)	8.9 (1.7)	9.2 (1.2)	9.5 (0.7)	9.8 (0.3)
ii. Mean Tariff Rate		7.4 (13.0)	7.8 (11.2)	7.9 (10.5)	8.1 (9.4)	8.0 (10.1)	8.6 (7.1)
iii. Standard Deviation of Tariff Rates					6.5 (8.8)	0.3 (24.2)	0.0 (25.7)
(b) Size of Trade Sector	7.7 (42.9)	3.9 (47.2)	4.2 (55.1)	4.5 (54.5)	3.9 (51.3)	5.3 (73.1)	5.8 (81.4)
VII. Freedom of Exchange in Financial Markets	**8.9**	**8.1**	**9.3**	**9.3**	**9.3**	**9.1**	**9.2**
(a) Private Ownership of Banks	10.0 (100)	10.0 (100)	10.0 (100)	10.0 (100)	10.0 (100)	10.0 (100)	10.0 (100)
(b) Extension of Credit to Private Sector	7.2 (71.9)	8.4 (83.9)	9.2 (91.5)	9.2 (92.4)	9.2 (92.0)	8.3 (83.0)	8.8 (88.1)
(c) Avoidance of Negative Interest Rates	10.0	6.0	10.0	10.0	10.0	10.0	10.0
(d) Capital Transactions with Foreigners	8.0	8.0	8.0	8.0	8.0	8.0	8.0

CHAD

Summary Ratings	1985	1990	1995	1999
Summary Ratings	5.2	5.2	5.3	4.7
Rank	57	61	83	102

Components of Economic Freedom	1970	1975	1980	1985	1990	1995	1999
I. Size of Government	**4.8**	**5.4**	**4.1**	**8.6**	**9.3**	**9.5**	**8.9**
(a) Government Consumption	4.8 (23.7)	5.4 (21.6)	4.1 (26.0)	8.6 (10.8)	8.7 (10.5)	9.1 (9.1)	8.9 (9.7)
(b) Transfers and Subsidies					9.9 (0.9)	9.9 (0.8)	
II. Structure of the Economy and Use of Markets					**1.8**	**1.8**	**3.5**
(a) Government Enterprises	0.0			0.0 (95.7)	0.0 (94.0)	0.0 (54.5)	4.0 (37.5)
(b) Price Controls					4.0	4.0	4.0
(c) Top Marginal Tax Rate							
(d) Conscription	10.0	10.0	10.0	0.0	0.0	0.0	0.0
III. Monetary Policy and Price Stability	**9.2**	**8.4**	**8.4**	**7.0**	**7.8**	**7.0**	**7.0**
(a) Annual Money Growth	9.1 (4.5)	7.7 (11.5)	7.3 (-3.5)	5.8 (20.9)	9.3 (-3.7)	9.7 (1.6)	7.5 (12.6)
(b) Inflation Variability	9.4 (1.5)	9.2 (1.9)	9.8 (0.6)	6.0 (10.0)	6.2 (9.5)	2.8 (17.9)	4.8 (12.9)
(c) Recent Inflation Rate	9.2 (3.9)	8.4 (8.2)	8.3 (8.7)	9.3 (3.8)	7.7 (11.4)	8.2 (8.9)	8.6 (-6.8)
IV. Freedom to Use Alternative Currencies	**4.8**	**4.8**	**4.8**	**4.9**	**4.6**	**4.9**	**4.8**
(a) Ownership of Foreign Currency	0.0	0.0	0.0	0.0	0.0	0.0	0.0
(b) Black Market Exchange Rate	9.6 (2.0)	9.6 (2.0)	9.6 (2.0)	9.8 (1.0)	9.2 (4.0)	9.8 (1.0)	9.6 (2.0)
V. Legal Structure and Property Rights			**4.9**	**4.3**	**4.5**	**5.2**	**3.8**
(a) Legal Security			4.0	3.8	3.8		
(b) Rule of Law			5.8	4.8	5.3	5.2	3.8
VI. International Exchange		**4.6**			**6.9**	**7.9**	
(a) Taxes on International Trade							
i. Taxes as a Percentage of Exports and Imports		3.9 (9.2)			7.4 (3.9)	8.5 (2.2)	
ii. Mean Tariff Rate							
iii. Standard Deviation of Tariff Rates							
(b) Size of Trade Sector	6.7 (54.4)	6.0 (57.2)	6.1 (65.1)	6.2 (61.4)	5.9 (60.3)	6.7 (75.9)	4.5 (51.0)
VII. Freedom of Exchange in Financial Markets				**3.2**	**3.3**	**2.3**	**2.4**
(a) Private Ownership of Banks		2.0 (10-40)	2.0 (10-40)	2.0 (10-40)	0.0 (0-10)	0.0 (0-10)	0.0 (0-10)
(b) Extension of Credit to Private Sector					6.3 (62.8)	6.4 (63.7)	6.7 (67.2)
(c) Avoidance of Negative Interest Rates				8.0	8.0	4.0	4.0
(d) Capital Transactions with Foreigners	0.0	0.0	0.0	0.0	0.0	0.0	0.0

CHILE

Summary Ratings

	1970	1975	1980	1985	1990	1995	1999
Summary Ratings	3.6	3.5	6.0	6.2	7.3	7.9	8.0
Rank	54	70	31	31	22	18	15

Components of Economic Freedom

	1970	1975	1980	1985	1990	1995	1999
I. Size of Government	**6.6**	**6.9**	**7.0**	**6.4**	**7.5**	**7.6**	**7.2**
(a) Government Consumption	7.2 (15.5)	6.6 (17.7)	7.4 (15.0)	6.9 (16.7)	7.8 (13.6)	7.8 (13.6)	7.6 (14.3)
(b) Transfers and Subsidies	5.9 (15.4)	7.3 (10.5)	6.6 (12.9)	6.0 (15.3)	7.3 (10.5)	7.4 (10.0)	6.8 (12.1)
II. Structure of the Economy and Use of Markets		**1.1**	**3.1**	**4.7**	**4.9**	**7.5**	**6.6**
(a) Government Enterprises	2.0 (42.1)	0.0 (77.0)	4.0 (32.2)	8.0 (16.1)	7.0 (20.5)	8.0 (16.6)	8.0 (19.2)
(b) Price Controls				10.0	10.0	10.0	9.0
(c) Top Marginal Tax Rate		2.0 (60)	2.0 (58)	2.0 (56)	4.0 (50)	6.0 (45)	4.0 (45)
(d) Conscription	3.0	3.0	3.0	0.0	0.0	0.0	0.0
III. Monetary Policy and Price Stability	**3.4**	**0.0**	**1.4**	**6.0**	**6.3**	**7.3**	**9.1**
(a) Annual Money Growth	1.0 (44.9)	0.0 (210.7)	0.0 (99.5)	7.9 (10.7)	4.8 (25.9)	5.4 (22.9)	9.2 (3.9)
(b) Inflation Variability	7.5 (6.2)	0.0 (233.7)	0.0 (80.6)	6.2 (9.6)	8.3 (4.2)	8.4 (4.0)	8.8 (3.0)
(c) Recent Inflation Rate	1.9 (40.7)	0.0 (334.7)	4.2 (28.8)	3.9 (30.7)	5.8 (21.2)	8.1 (9.3)	9.3 (3.3)
IV. Freedom to Use Alternative Currencies	**5.1**	**4.5**	**6.9**	**7.8**	**10.0**	**9.8**	**8.9**
(a) Ownership of Foreign Currency	10.0	0.0	5.0	10.0	10.0	10.0	10.0
(b) Black Market Exchange Rate	0.2 (49.0)	9.0 (5.0)	8.8 (6.0)	5.6 (22.0)	10.0 (0.0)	9.6 (2.0)	7.8 (11.1)
V. Legal Structure and Property Rights	**0.0**	**3.8**	**7.3**	**5.4**	**7.0**	**7.0**	**8.2**
(a) Legal Security	0.0	3.8	6.4	4.2	7.3		8.5
(b) Rule of Law			8.3	6.6	6.7	7.0	7.9
VI. International Exchange	**4.2**	**3.8**	**8.3**	**6.7**	**8.1**	**8.1**	**8.1**
(a) Taxes on International Trade							
i. Taxes as a Percentage of Exports and Imports	9.2 (1.2)	6.3 (5.6)	8.1 (2.8)	6.2 (5.7)	7.5 (3.7)	7.7 (3.5)	7.9 (3.1)
ii. Mean Tariff Rate	0.0 (105.0)	0.0 (55.0)	8.0 (10.0)	4.0 (30.0)	7.0 (15.0)	7.8 (11.0)	7.8 (11.0)
iii. Standard Deviation of Tariff Rates			10.0 (0.0)	10.0 (0.0)	10.0 (0.0)	10.0 (0.0)	9.7 (0.7)
(b) Size of Trade Sector	2.8 (28.6)	6.6 (52.8)	5.5 (49.8)	6.4 (53.9)	7.5 (65.5)	5.7 (55.4)	5.8 (56.4)
VII. Freedom of Exchange in Financial Markets		**3.5**	**5.9**	**6.5**	**6.6**	**8.1**	**8.1**
(a) Private Ownership of Banks		2.0 (10-40)	5.0 (40-75)	8.0 (75-85)	8.0 (75-85)	8.0 (84)	8.0 (86)
(b) Extension of Credit to Private Sector	7.5 (75.0)	7.5 (75.0)	9.6 (96.2)	8.6 (85.5)	9.3 (92.7)	9.9 (98.5)	9.8 (98.3)
(c) Avoidance of Negative Interest Rates			8.0	8.0	8.0	10.0	10.0
(d) Capital Transactions with Foreigners	2.0	2.0	2.0	2.0	2.0	5.0	5.0

CHINA

Summary Ratings	1970	1975	1980	1985	1990	1995	1999
Summary Ratings			3.2	4.3	3.7	5.1	5.8
Rank			101	82	101	91	81

Components of Economic Freedom	1970	1975	1980	1985	1990	1995	1999
I. Size of Government	**8.6**	**8.6**	**5.3**	**5.7**	**5.9**	**6.1**	**5.8**
(a) Government Consumption	8.6 (10.7)	8.6 (10.9)	5.3 (22.1)	5.7 (20.5)	5.9 (19.8)	6.1 (19.4)	5.8 (20.4)
(b) Transfers and Subsidies							
II. Structure of the Economy and Use of Markets				**2.3**	**1.9**	**2.8**	**2.0**
(a) Government Enterprises	0.0	0.0	0.0 (31.9)	0.0 (66.1)	0.0 (66.2)	0.0 (54.4)	0.0 (54.1)
(b) Price Controls				6.0	5.0	4.0	3.0
(c) Top Marginal Tax Rate				6.0 (45)	5.0 (45)	6.0 (45)	4.0 (45)
(d) Conscription	0.0	0.0	0.0	0.0	0.0	0.0	0.0
III. Monetary Policy and Price Stability	**8.7**	**9.8**	**8.2**	**8.0**	**8.6**	**7.1**	**8.5**
(a) Annual Money Growth			6.0 (20.0)	7.3 (13.3)	8.1 (9.3)	6.1 (19.7)	7.7 (11.5)
(b) Inflation Variability	8.4 (4.0)	9.7 (0.8)	9.5 (1.3)	8.6 (3.4)	8.9 (2.8)	8.1 (4.8)	8.2 (4.4)
(c) Recent Inflation Rate	9.1 (-4.7)	10.0 (-0.1)	9.2 (3.8)	8.0 (10.1)	8.9 (5.7)	7.4 (13.2)	9.7 (-1.4)
IV. Freedom to Use Alternative Currencies	**1.0**	**2.6**	**2.5**	**3.9**	**0.0**	**4.3**	**5.0**
(a) Ownership of Foreign Currency	0.0	0.0	0.0	0.0	0.0	0.0	0.0
(b) Black Market Exchange Rate	2.0 (40.0)	5.2 (24.0)	5.0 (25.0)	7.8 (11.0)	0.0 (159.0)	8.6 (7.0)	10.0 (0.0)
V. Legal Structure and Property Rights				**7.8**	**6.4**	**7.0**	**7.0**
(a) Legal Security				7.4	4.6		6.1
(b) Rule of Law				8.2	8.3	7.0	7.9
VI. International Exchange			**3.0**	**3.6**	**3.7**	**4.7**	**7.3**
(a) Taxes on International Trade							
i. Taxes as a Percentage of Exports and Imports			6.2 (5.7)	3.3 (10.0)	7.5 (3.7)	9.2 (1.2)	9.3 (1.0)
ii. Mean Tariff Rate			0.1 (49.5)	2.1 (39.5)	1.9 (40.3)	2.5 (37.5)	6.5 (17.5)
iii. Standard Deviation of Tariff Rates					0.0 (32.1)	0.0 (28.0)	4.8 (13.0)
(b) Size of Trade Sector	2.0 (5.2)	2.0 (10.2)	2.9 (12.9)	7.0 (24.0)	7.4 (26.8)	10.0 (40.4)	9.8 (39.0)
VII. Freedom of Exchange in Financial Markets			**0.0**	**0.7**	**1.7**	**4.4**	**5.8**
(a) Private Ownership of Banks	0.0 (0-10)	0.0 (0)	0.0 (0)	0.0 (0)	0.0 (0)	0.0 (0)	0.0 (0)
(b) Extension of Credit to Private Sector						9.8 (98.0)	9.4 (94.3)
(c) Avoidance of Negative Interest Rates	0.0	0.0	0.0	0.0	0.0	4.0	10.0
(d) Capital Transactions with Foreigners	0.0	0.0	0.0	2.0	5.0	5.0	5.0

COLOMBIA

	1970	1975	1980	1985	1990	1995	1999
Summary Ratings	4.9	4.6	4.5	5.0	5.0	5.3	5.8
Rank	43	55	71	63	65	83	81

Components of Economic Freedom

	1970	1975	1980	1985	1990	1995	1999
I. Size of Government	**8.4**	**8.9**	**8.7**	**8.4**	**8.5**	**7.7**	**6.0**
(a) Government Consumption	8.4 (11.3)	8.5 (11.0)	8.1 (12.6)	7.8 (13.4)	7.8 (13.6)	6.4 (18.3)	6.0 (19.5)
(b) Transfers and Subsidies		9.3 (3.0)	9.3 (2.9)	8.9 (4.4)	9.1 (3.7)	9.0 (4.1)	
II. Structure of the Economy and Use of Markets		**4.2**	**1.7**	**2.9**	**4.0**	**5.1**	**5.2**
(a) Government Enterprises	4.0 (31.7)	4.0 (32.8)	2.0 (41.5)	2.0 (53.9)	2.0 (43.9)	4.0 (34.1)	4.0 (40.2)
(b) Price Controls						5.0	6.0
(c) Top Marginal Tax Rate		6.0 (41)	2.0 (56)	5.0 (49)	8.0 (30)	8.0 (30)	7.0 (35)
(d) Conscription	3.0	0.0	0.0	0.0	0.0	1.0	1.0
III. Monetary Policy and Price Stability	**8.1**	**6.7**	**6.0**	**7.0**	**5.9**	**6.6**	**7.2**
(a) Annual Money Growth	7.4 (13.1)	6.9 (15.6)	5.3 (23.7)	6.6 (17.0)	4.4 (27.8)	4.8 (26.1)	7.7 (11.3)
(b) Inflation Variability	9.0 (2.6)	7.7 (5.6)	8.3 (4.2)	9.3 (1.7)	9.1 (2.3)	9.2 (2.1)	5.9 (10.2)
(c) Recent Inflation Rate	8.0 (9.9)	5.4 (22.9)	4.5 (27.6)	5.0 (24.9)	4.3 (28.6)	6.0 (19.8)	7.8 (11.2)
IV. Freedom to Use Alternative Currencies	**3.9**	**2.1**	**3.4**	**6.6**	**3.3**	**4.3**	**3.9**
(a) Ownership of Foreign Currency	0.0	0.0	0.0	5.0	0.0	0.0	0.0
(b) Black Market Exchange Rate	7.8 (11.0)	4.2 (29.0)	6.8 (16.0)	8.2 (9.0)	6.6 (17.0)	8.6 (7.0)	7.8 (11.1)
V. Legal Structure and Property Rights	**2.3**	**3.0**	**3.9**	**3.1**	**3.1**	**0.0**	**4.5**
(a) Legal Security	2.3	3.0	4.6	4.8	4.6		7.3
(b) Rule of Law			3.3	1.4	1.7	0.0	1.7
VI. International Exchange	**4.4**	**4.7**	**4.0**	**3.9**	**5.4**	**7.3**	**7.1**
(a) Taxes on International Trade							
i. Taxes as a Percentage of Exports and Imports	4.6 (8.1)	5.1 (7.4)	4.8 (7.8)	5.0 (7.5)	6.0 (6.0)	8.0 (2.9)	7.8 (3.3)
ii. Mean Tariff Rate			3.3 (33.5)	3.3 (33.6)	3.9 (30.4)	7.3 (13.3)	7.7 (11.7)
iii. Standard Deviation of Tariff Rates					6.7 (8.3)	8.0 (4.9)	7.5 (6.2)
(b) Size of Trade Sector	4.1 (30.1)	4.1 (29.9)	3.8 (31.8)	3.0 (26.3)	4.6 (35.4)	4.2 (36.3)	3.7 (33.5)
VII. Freedom of Exchange in Financial Markets			**5.3**	**5.3**	**6.0**	**7.2**	**7.3**
(a) Private Ownership of Banks		8.0 (75-90)	8.0 (75-90)	8.0 (75-90)	8.0 (75-95)	8.0 (75-95)	8.0 (75-95)
(b) Extension of Credit to Private Sector					8.6 (86.0)	8.1 (81.0)	8.6 (86.2)
(c) Avoidance of Negative Interest Rates			8.0	8.0	8.0	8.0	8.0
(d) Capital Transactions with Foreigners	0.0	0.0	0.0	0.0	0.0	5.0	5.0

CONGO, DEMOCRATIC REPUBLIC

Summary Ratings

	1970	1975	1980	1985	1990	1995	1999
Summary Ratings	4.6	3.2	2.9	3.9	3.4	3.9	3.0
Rank	45	75	103	92	105	112	121

Components of Economic Freedom

	1970	1975	1980	1985	1990	1995	1999
I. Size of Government	**7.2**	**8.8**	**9.5**	**9.1**	**9.0**	**10.0**	**9.0**
(a) Government Consumption	7.2 (15.5)	7.8 (13.4)	9.0 (9.3)	9.1 (9.0)	8.0 (12.7)	10.0 (5.7)	9.0 (9.3)
(b) Transfers and Subsidies		9.9 (1.0)	10.0 (0.6)		9.9 (0.8)	10.0 (0.5)	
II. Structure of the Economy and Use of Markets	**0.0**	**2.1**	**1.7**	**1.7**	**2.5**	**2.5**	**2.3**
(a) Government Enterprises	0.0 (56.8)	0.0 (58.8)	0.0 (60.2)	0.0 (45.5)	2.0 (31.1)	2.0	0.0
(b) Price Controls					2.0	2.0	2.0
(c) Top Marginal Tax Rate		2.0 (60)	1.0 (60)	1.0 (60)	1.0 (60)	1.0 (60)	3.0 (50)
(d) Conscription	10.0	10.0	10.0	10.0	10.0	10.0	10.0
III. Monetary Policy and Price Stability	**5.0**	**7.5**	**0.5**	**1.6**	**0.0**	**0.0**	**0.0**
(a) Annual Money Growth	5.7 (21.7)	6.7 (16.6)	1.6 (42.2)	0.0 (52.5)	0.0 (99.5)	0.0 (2294.3)	0.0 (2290.0)
(b) Inflation Variability	0.0 (26.2)	8.4 (3.9)	0.0 (25.5)	0.0 (25.3)	0.0 (30.2)	0.0 (9932.5)	0.0 (10660.2)
(c) Recent Inflation Rate	9.3 (-3.3)	7.5 (12.5)	0.0 (51.4)	4.8 (25.8)	0.0 (109.0)	0.0 (466.4)	0.0 (187.3)
IV. Freedom to Use Alternative Currencies	**8.1**	**0.0**	**0.0**	**4.4**	**3.0**	**4.6**	**7.0**
(a) Ownership of Foreign Currency	10.0	0.0	0.0	0.0	0.0	0.0	5.0
(b) Black Market Exchange Rate	6.2 (19.0)	0.0 (120.0)	0.0 (131.0)	8.8 (6.0)	6.0 (20.0)	9.2 (4.0)	9.0 (5.0)
V. Legal Structure and Property Rights	**1.7**		**1.7**	**1.8**	**1.8**	**0.0**	**0.0**
(a) Legal Security			1.7	2.2	1.9		
(b) Rule of Law			1.7	1.4	1.7	0.0	0.0
VI. International Exchange	**1.7**	**1.2**	**4.3**	**5.6**	**5.6**	**7.8**	
(a) Taxes on International Trade							
i. Taxes as a Percentage of Exports and Imports	0.0 (19.7)	0.0 (19.0)	3.1 (10.3)	4.4 (8.4)	3.9 (9.1)	7.8 (3.3)	7.9 (3.2)
ii. Mean Tariff Rate			5.3 (23.6)	5.5 (22.4)	5.9 (20.7)		
iii. Standard Deviation of Tariff Rates							
(b) Size of Trade Sector	5.2 (34.6)	3.5 (25.1)	4.5 (32.8)	8.1 (53.1)	8.6 (58.7)	7.9 (59.0)	
VII. Freedom of Exchange in Financial Markets	**2.6**	**2.9**	**3.2**	**3.4**	**2.4**	**2.5**	**0.7**
(a) Private Ownership of Banks	0.0 (0)	0.0 (0)	0.0 (0)	0.0 (0)	0.0 (0)	0.0 (0)	0.0 (0)
(b) Extension of Credit to Private Sector	6.9 (68.7)	7.8 (77.7)	8.7 (86.8)	9.5 (94.9)	8.6 (86.4)	9.3 (93.4)	
(c) Avoidance of Negative Interest Rates					0.0	0.0	0.0
(d) Capital Transactions with Foreigners	2.0	2.0	2.0	2.0	2.0	2.0	2.0

CONGO, REPUBLIC OF

Summary Ratings	1970	1975	1980	1985	1990	1995	1999
Rating			5.0	4.4	4.4	5.2	4.5
Rank			60	81	86	89	107

Components of Economic Freedom	1970	1975	1980	1985	1990	1995	1999
I. Size of Government	**8.2**	**5.8**	**3.7**	**4.7**	**6.4**	**8.3**	**7.1**
(a) Government Consumption	6.7 (17.2)	5.8 (20.3)	3.7 (27.3)	4.7 (23.9)	6.4 (18.2)	6.5 (17.9)	4.2 (25.8)
(b) Transfers and Subsidies	9.7 (1.4)					10.0 (0.0)	10.0 (0.0)
II. Structure of the Economy and Use of Markets					**1.9**	**1.6**	**1.6**
(a) Government Enterprises	4.0 (24.8)	0.0 (44.6)	0.0 (44.2)	0.0 (59.4)	0.0	0.0	0.0
(b) Price Controls					0.0	0.0	0.0
(c) Top Marginal Tax Rate					4.0 (50)	3.0 (50)	3.0 (50)
(d) Conscription		10.0	10.0	10.0	10.0	10.0	10.0
III. Monetary Policy and Price Stability	**8.7**	**8.8**	**7.1**	**8.1**	**7.8**	**7.7**	**7.3**
(a) Annual Money Growth	8.3 (8.7)	8.1 (9.3)	8.3 (8.6)	8.3 (8.4)	9.3 (-3.6)	9.6 (2.1)	8.6 (7.2)
(b) Inflation Variability	8.6 (3.6)	9.9 (0.3)	7.0 (7.4)	6.4 (9.0)	4.2 (14.5)	4.0 (14.9)	4.5 (13.8)
(c) Recent Inflation Rate	9.3 (3.7)	8.3 (8.3)	6.0 (20.1)	9.5 (2.5)	9.8 (-0.8)	9.3 (3.4)	8.9 (5.7)
IV. Freedom to Use Alternative Currencies	**4.8**	**4.8**	**4.8**	**4.9**	**4.6**	**4.9**	**4.8**
(a) Ownership of Foreign Currency	0.0	0.0	0.0	0.0	0.0	0.0	0.0
(b) Black Market Exchange Rate	9.6 (2.0)	9.6 (2.0)	9.6 (2.0)	9.8 (1.0)	9.2 (4.0)	9.8 (1.0)	9.6 (2.0)
V. Legal Structure and Property Rights			**4.9**	**2.7**	**2.6**	**7.0**	**0.0**
(a) Legal Security			4.0	2.2	1.9		
(b) Rule of Law			5.8	3.1	3.3	7.0	0.0
VI. International Exchange	**5.6**	**7.0**	**7.9**	**5.3**	**5.5**	**7.0**	**9.0**
(a) Taxes on International Trade							
i. Taxes as a Percentage of Exports and Imports	4.9 (7.7)	6.4 (5.4)	7.5 (3.8)		4.5 (8.2)	7.6 (3.6)	8.8 (1.8)
ii. Mean Tariff Rate				3.6 (32.0)		6.3 (18.6)	
iii. Standard Deviation of Tariff Rates						6.2 (9.5)	
(b) Size of Trade Sector	7.1 (92.5)	8.1 (99.6)	8.8 (120.1)	9.0 (112.8)	7.5 (97.9)	8.9 (127.6)	9.5 (134.9)
VII. Freedom of Exchange in Financial Markets	**0.0**		**1.9**	**2.5**	**3.8**	**1.9**	**3.2**
(a) Private Ownership of Banks	0.0 (0)		0.0 (0)	0.0 (0)	0.0 (0)	0.0 (0)	0.0 (0)
(b) Extension of Credit to Private Sector					6.4 (63.5)	6.6 (66.3)	8.2 (82.4)
(c) Avoidance of Negative Interest Rates	0.0		6.0	8.0	10.0	2.0	6.0
(d) Capital Transactions with Foreigners	0.0		0.0	0.0	0.0	0.0	0.0

COSTA RICA

Summary Ratings	1970	1975	1980	1985	1990	1995	1999
Summary Ratings	8.2	6.9	5.4	5.4	7.2	7.1	7.8
Rank	6	14	44	50	27	42	24

Components of Economic Freedom	1970	1975	1980	1985	1990	1995	1999
I. Size of Government	**8.6**	**7.8**	**6.9**	**6.9**	**6.9**	**6.6**	**6.6**
(a) Government Consumption	7.5 (14.6)	6.6 (17.5)	5.4 (21.8)	5.7 (20.8)	5.0 (22.9)	5.0 (22.9)	5.0 (22.9)
(b) Transfers and Subsidies	9.8 (1.2)	9.0 (4.1)	8.5 (6.0)	8.2 (7.2)	8.8 (5.0)	8.2 (7.0)	8.2 (7.0)
II. Structure of the Economy and Use of Markets		**6.2**	**5.2**	**4.4**	**7.1**	**6.4**	**7.8**
(a) Government Enterprises	6.0 (28.2)	6.0 (29.7)	4.0 (36.2)	4.0 (34.1)	6.0 (21.0)	4.0 (27.1)	6.0 (23.2)
(b) Price Controls				6.0	6.0	6.0	8.0
(c) Top Marginal Tax Rate	5.0 (50)	5.0 (50)	5.0 (50)	3.0 (50)	9.0 (25)	9.0 (25)	9.0 (25)
(d) Conscription	10.0	10.0	10.0	10.0	10.0	10.0	10.0
III. Monetary Policy and Price Stability	**8.9**	**6.1**	**7.1**	**3.2**	**7.5**	**6.9**	**6.6**
(a) Annual Money Growth	9.0 (4.9)	6.8 (16.0)	6.9 (15.6)	3.6 (32.1)	7.4 (13.0)	7.3 (13.4)	5.1 (24.6)
(b) Inflation Variability	9.1 (2.2)	6.5 (8.8)	8.2 (4.5)	0.2 (24.4)	8.7 (3.3)	7.6 (6.0)	6.7 (8.2)
(c) Recent Inflation Rate	8.5 (7.3)	5.1 (24.5)	6.2 (18.8)	5.9 (20.5)	6.3 (18.6)	5.7 (21.3)	8.0 (10.0)
IV. Freedom to Use Alternative Currencies	**10.0**	**9.2**	**5.0**	**7.6**	**10.0**	**10.0**	**10.0**
(a) Ownership of Foreign Currency	10.0	10.0	10.0	10.0	10.0	10.0	10.0
(b) Black Market Exchange Rate	10.0 (0.0)	8.4 (8.0)	0.0 (69.0)	5.2 (24.0)	10.0 (0.0)	10.0 (0.0)	10.0 (0.0)
V. Legal Structure and Property Rights		**5.6**		**5.7**	**6.0**	**4.1**	**6.7**
(a) Legal Security				4.8	5.3		7.5
(b) Rule of Law				6.6	6.7	4.1	5.8
VI. International Exchange	**6.2**	**5.6**	**3.3**	**2.1**	**5.5**	**7.0**	**7.0**
(a) Taxes on International Trade							
i. Taxes as a Percentage of Exports and Imports	7.3 (4.1)	6.1 (5.9)	6.5 (5.3)	5.4 (6.9)	5.3 (7.0)	6.9 (4.6)	8.4 (2.4)
ii. Mean Tariff Rate			0.0 (55.0)	0.0 (53.0)	6.7 (16.4)	8.0 (10.2)	8.6 (7.2)
iii. Standard Deviation of Tariff Rates				0.0 (61.8)	4.8 (12.9)	6.9 (7.7)	4.5 (13.8)
(b) Size of Trade Sector	4.2 (63.2)	4.7 (68.6)	3.6 (63.3)	4.1 (63.2)	4.9 (76.0)	5.0 (85.6)	5.9 (99.8)
VII. Freedom of Exchange in Financial Markets	**8.0**	**6.7**	**6.1**	**7.3**	**7.6**	**8.7**	**9.2**
(a) Private Ownership of Banks	10.0 (95-100)	10.0 (95-100)	10.0 (95-100)	10.0 (95-100)	10.0 (100)	10.0 (100)	10.0 (100)
(b) Extension of Credit to Private Sector	9.4 (93.5)	8.6 (86.3)	6.4 (63.6)	8.3 (82.7)	7.5 (75.0)	8.8 (87.8)	8.6 (85.7)
(c) Avoidance of Negative Interest Rates				6.0	8.0	8.0	8.0
(d) Capital Transactions with Foreigners	5.0	2.0	2.0	5.0	5.0	8.0	10.0

CÔTE D'IVOIRE

	1970	1975	1980	1985	1990	1995	1999
Summary Ratings			4.8	5.3	4.7	5.5	5.5
Rank			64	54	72	77	88

Components of Economic Freedom

	1970	1975	1980	1985	1990	1995	1999
I. Size of Government	**6.1**	**5.3**	**7.3**	**6.1**	**6.2**	**8.4**	**8.6**
(a) Government Consumption	6.1 (19.2)	5.3 (22.0)	5.5 (21.2)	6.1 (19.4)	6.2 (18.9)	7.4 (15.0)	7.6 (14.1)
(b) Transfers and Subsidies			9.0 (4.2)			9.4 (2.6)	9.6 (2.1)
II. Structure of the Economy and Use of Markets			**3.2**	**2.5**	**2.1**	**3.2**	**3.8**
(a) Government Enterprises	2.0 (39.6)	2.0 (39.7)	0.0 (52.4)	0.0 (66.7)	2.0 (42.1)	4.0 (32.8)	6.0 (29.8)
(b) Price Controls					0.0	2.0	2.0
(c) Top Marginal Tax Rate			5.0 (45)	5.0 (45)	4.0 (45)	3.0 (49)	3.0 (49)
(d) Conscription	0.0	10.0	10.0	5.0	5.0	5.0	5.0
III. Monetary Policy and Price Stability	**9.1**	**7.8**	**6.2**	**8.8**	**9.2**	**6.6**	**6.9**
(a) Annual Money Growth	8.8 (5.9)	8.3 (8.5)	7.2 (14.3)	9.0 (5.0)	9.2 (-3.9)	7.8 (10.9)	6.5 (17.3)
(b) Inflation Variability	9.2 (2.0)	6.0 (9.9)	6.2 (9.6)	7.6 (6.1)	9.3 (1.6)	3.6 (16.1)	4.4 (14.0)
(c) Recent Inflation Rate	9.4 (3.0)	9.1 (4.3)	5.2 (24.1)	9.9 (0.3)	9.1 (-4.5)	8.3 (8.5)	9.8 (0.8)
IV. Freedom to Use Alternative Currencies	**4.8**	**4.8**	**4.8**	**4.9**	**4.6**	**4.9**	**4.8**
(a) Ownership of Foreign Currency	0.0	0.0	0.0	0.0	0.0	0.0	0.0
(b) Black Market Exchange Rate	9.6 (2.0)	9.6 (2.0)	9.6 (2.0)	9.8 (1.0)	9.2 (4.0)	9.8 (1.0)	9.6 (2.0)
V. Legal Structure and Property Rights				**6.4**	**5.1**	**7.0**	**3.8**
(a) Legal Security				6.1	5.9		
(b) Rule of Law				6.6	4.2	7.0	3.8
VI. International Exchange			**3.8**	**4.6**	**3.6**	**4.6**	**6.7**
(a) Taxes on International Trade							
i. Taxes as a Percentage of Exports and Imports			1.5 (12.8)	2.1 (11.8)	2.7 (10.9)	0.0 (17.3)	1.2 (13.2)
ii. Mean Tariff Rate			4.5 (27.5)	5.3 (23.3)	3.4 (33.0)	3.4 (33.0)	9.0 (4.8)
iii. Standard Deviation of Tariff Rates						9.4 (1.5)	9.6 (1.1)
(b) Size of Trade Sector	6.5 (64.9)	7.4 (73.3)	7.0 (76.2)	8.0 (79.2)	5.8 (58.8)	6.9 (76.9)	7.4 (82.1)
VII. Freedom of Exchange in Financial Markets		**4.6**	**4.6**	**5.0**	**4.5**	**4.7**	**5.2**
(a) Private Ownership of Banks		2.0 (10-40)	2.0 (10-40)	2.0 (10-40)	2.0 (10-40)	8.0 (75-95)	8.0 (90-95)
(b) Extension of Credit to Private Sector			9.7 (96.6)	9.3 (93.4)	9.2 (91.6)	7.3 (72.8)	7.4 (73.9)
(c) Avoidance of Negative Interest Rates			8.0	10.0	8.0	4.0	6.0
(d) Capital Transactions with Foreigners	0.0	0.0	0.0	0.0	0.0	0.0	0.0

CROATIA

Summary Ratings	1970	1975	1980	1985	1990	1995	1999
Summary Ratings						4.1	5.2
Rank						109	95

Components of Economic Freedom	1970	1975	1980	1985	1990	1995	1999
I. Size of Government						**3.9**	**3.8**
(a) Government Consumption						1.9 (33.4)	2.8 (30.5)
(b) Transfers and Subsidies						5.9 (15.5)	4.8 (19.5)
II. Structure of the Economy and Use of Markets						**1.2**	**3.3**
(a) Government Enterprises						0.0	2.0
(b) Price Controls					0.0		4.0
(c) Top Marginal Tax Rate						2.0	4.0 (35-53)
(d) Conscription						3.0	3.0
III. Monetary Policy and Price Stability						**2.7**	**3.5**
(a) Annual Money Growth						0.0 (62.4)	1.4 (42.8)
(b) Inflation Variability						0.0 (573.3)	0.0 (34.7)
(c) Recent Inflation Rate					0.0 (500.0)	8.4 (8.0)	9.3 (3.7)
IV. Freedom to Use Alternative Currencies					**2.5**	**6.7**	**3.2**
(a) Ownership of Foreign Currency					5.0	5.0	5.0
(b) Black Market Exchange Rate					0.0 (106.0)	8.4 (8.0)	1.4 (42.9)
V. Legal Structure and Property Rights							**7.9**
(a) Legal Security							
(b) Rule of Law							7.9
VI. International Exchange						**6.2**	**6.6**
(a) Taxes on International Trade							
i. Taxes as a Percentage of Exports and Imports						7.0 (4.6)	7.7 (3.5)
ii. Mean Tariff Rate							
iii. Standard Deviation of Tariff Rates							
(b) Size of Trade Sector						4.8 (93.0)	4.5 (89.1)
VII. Freedom of Exchange in Financial Markets						**2.8**	**6.3**
(a) Private Ownership of Banks					0.0 (0-10)	0.0 (0-10)	10.0 (95-100)
(b) Extension of Credit to Private Sector						6.1 (61.0)	7.4 (73.6)
(c) Avoidance of Negative Interest Rates						4.0	6.0
(d) Capital Transactions with Foreigners					0.0	2.0	2.0

CYPRUS

	1970	1975	1980	1985	1990	1995	1999
Summary Ratings	6.2	5.7	5.7	5.9	6.3	6.4	
Rank	22	38	42	45	54	64	

Components of Economic Freedom	1970	1975	1980	1985	1990	1995	1999
I. Size of Government	**9.1**	**6.9**	**7.6**	**7.2**	**6.5**	**6.4**	**5.8**
(a) Government Consumption		6.6 (17.7)	6.8 (17.0)	6.5 (18.1)	5.2 (22.4)	5.5 (21.2)	4.8 (23.8)
(b) Transfers and Subsidies	9.1 (3.9)	7.3 (10.3)	8.3 (6.6)	7.9 (8.1)	7.9 (8.3)	7.3 (10.3)	6.9 (11.9)
II. Structure of the Economy and Use of Markets			**4.3**	**4.3**	**2.6**	**4.3**	**4.3**
(a) Government Enterprises	8.0 (11.1)	8.0 (12.3)	8.0 (18.1)	8.0 (17.4)	8.0	8.0	8.0
(b) Price Controls					0.0	2.0	2.0
(c) Top Marginal Tax Rate		3.0 (54)	1.0 (60)	1.0 (60)	0.0 (62)	4.0 (42)	4.0 (43)
(d) Conscription			0.0	0.0	0.0	0.0	0.0
III. Monetary Policy and Price Stability		**7.9**	**7.6**	**9.0**	**9.4**	**9.6**	**9.7**
(a) Annual Money Growth			6.4 (18.0)	9.1 (4.6)	9.5 (2.3)	9.8 (1.1)	9.8 (1.2)
(b) Inflation Variability		8.6 (3.6)	9.1 (2.4)	8.9 (2.8)	9.7 (0.7)	9.6 (0.9)	9.5 (1.2)
(c) Recent Inflation Rate	9.5 (2.4)	7.2 (14.2)	7.3 (13.5)	8.9 (5.7)	8.9 (5.3)	9.5 (2.6)	9.7 (1.6)
IV. Freedom to Use Alternative Currencies	**4.9**	**4.4**	**4.6**	**4.9**	**4.5**	**4.5**	**5.0**
(a) Ownership of Foreign Currency	0.0	0.0	0.0	0.0	0.0	0.0	0.0
(b) Black Market Exchange Rate	9.8 (1.0)	8.8 (6.0)	9.2 (4.0)	9.8 (1.0)	9.0 (5.0)	9.0 (5.0)	10.0 (0.0)
V. Legal Structure and Property Rights				**3.9**	**7.7**	**7.0**	**7.9**
(a) Legal Security				4.8	8.6		
(b) Rule of Law				3.1	6.7	7.0	7.9
VI. International Exchange	**5.4**	**6.4**	**6.4**	**6.3**	**5.3**	**6.8**	**6.6**
(a) Taxes on International Trade							
i. Taxes as a Percentage of Exports and Imports	6.2 (5.7)	7.7 (3.5)	7.3 (4.0)	7.1 (4.4)	7.2 (4.2)	8.3 (2.6)	8.5 (2.3)
ii. Mean Tariff Rate			6.6 (17.1)	6.5 (17.6)	6.7 (16.5)	7.2 (14.0)	6.7 (16.4)
iii. Standard Deviation of Tariff Rates					2.5 (18.7)		
(b) Size of Trade Sector	3.8 (85.4)	3.8 (92.2)	4.0 (108.3)	4.4 (107.6)	4.2 (109.0)	2.8 (96.8)	2.7 (95.7)
VII. Freedom of Exchange in Financial Markets	**5.3**	**6.1**	**5.1**	**6.0**	**6.4**	**6.5**	**6.4**
(a) Private Ownership of Banks		8.0 (75-95)	8.0 (75-95)	8.0 (75-95)	8.0 (75-95)	8.0 (75-95)	8.0 (75-95)
(b) Extension of Credit to Private Sector	9.1 (90.7)	9.2 (92.1)	9.3 (92.7)	8.9 (88.9)	8.5 (84.9)	8.7 (87.4)	8.4 (84.4)
(c) Avoidance of Negative Interest Rates	8.0	8.0	4.0	8.0	10.0	10.0	10.0
(d) Capital Transactions with Foreigners	0.0	0.0	0.0	0.0	0.0	0.0	0.0

Czech Rep.

Summary Ratings	1970	1975	1980	1985	1990	1995	1999
Summary Ratings					3.8	6.7	6.6
Rank					97	50	60

Components of Economic Freedom	1970	1975	1980	1985	1990	1995	1999
I. Size of Government		3.9	3.7	2.9	1.5	2.7	3.3
(a) Government Consumption		3.9 (26.6)	3.7 (27.3)	2.9 (30.1)	3.0 (29.9)	3.0 (29.7)	3.8 (27.0)
(b) Transfers and Subsidies					0.0 (37.2)	2.4 (28.4)	2.8 (27.1)
II. Structure of the Economy and Use of Markets					1.0	4.8	4.8
(a) Government Enterprises		0.0		0.0	0.0	4.0	6.0
(b) Price Controls					0.0	6.0	4.0
(c) Top Marginal Tax Rate		0.0		0.0	4.0 (55)	5.0 (43)	5.0 (40)
(d) Conscription		0.0		0.0	0.0	3.0	3.0
III. Monetary Policy and Price Stability				9.4	8.8	6.3	8.5
(a) Annual Money Growth				9.4 (3.0)	9.9 (0.4)	6.0 (20.0)	9.5 (-2.7)
(b) Inflation Variability				9.1 (2.2)	8.4 (4.0)	4.9 (12.8)	6.4 (9.0)
(c) Recent Inflation Rate		9.9 (0.7)	9.4 (2.9)	9.7 (1.7)	8.1 (9.5)	7.9 (10.4)	9.6 (2.1)
IV. Freedom to Use Alternative Currencies		0.0		0.0	0.0	7.5	7.5
(a) Ownership of Foreign Currency		0.0		0.0	0.0	5.0	5.0
(b) Black Market Exchange Rate	0.0 (525.0)	0.0 (359.0)	0.0 (387.0)	0.0 (423.0)	0.0 (61.0)	10.0 (0.0)	10.0 (0.0)
V. Legal Structure and Property Rights				7.8	8.5	10.0	7.1
(a) Legal Security				7.4	8.6		6.2
(b) Rule of Law				8.2	8.3	10.0	7.9
VI. International Exchange						8.3	7.9
(a) Taxes on International Trade							
i. Taxes as a Percentage of Exports and Imports					7.3 (4.0)	9.2 (1.1)	9.6 (0.6)
ii. Mean Tariff Rate						8.7 (6.7)	8.6 (6.8)
iii. Standard Deviation of Tariff Rates						7.4 (6.4)	5.6 (11.0)
(b) Size of Trade Sector						7.4 (123.1)	7.4 (121.4)
VII. Freedom of Exchange in Financial Markets		0.0		0.0	0.0	5.6	6.5
(a) Private Ownership of Banks		0.0 (0)		0.0 (0)	0.0 (0)	5.0 (40-75)	2.0 (10-20)
(b) Extension of Credit to Private Sector						6.5 (65.2)	8.4 (84.1)
(c) Avoidance of Negative Interest Rates						6.0	8.0
(d) Capital Transactions with Foreigners		0.0		0.0	0.0	5.0	8.0

DENMARK

	1970	1975	1980	1985	1990	1995	1999
Summary Ratings	7.2	6.3	6.5	6.7	7.7	8.0	8.0
Rank	16	18	21	21	14	14	15

Components of Economic Freedom

	1970	1975	1980	1985	1990	1995	1999
I. Size of Government	**3.7**	**3.8**	**3.1**	**3.3**	**2.8**	**2.4**	**1.8**
(a) Government Consumption	3.7 (27.3)	2.2 (32.4)	1.8 (34.0)	2.0 (33.2)	1.7 (34.3)	1.9 (33.6)	1.8 (33.7)
(b) Transfers and Subsidies		5.3 (17.8)	4.5 (20.8)	4.6 (20.4)	4.0 (22.6)	2.9 (26.5)	
II. Structure of the Economy and Use of Markets	**3.7**	**3.7**	**3.3**	**3.3**	**4.6**	**5.8**	**5.1**
(a) Government Enterprises	6.0	6.0 (27.3)	6.0 (25.0)	6.0 (26.0)	6.0 (20.3)	7.0 (24.9)	7.0
(b) Price Controls					7.0	9.0	7.0
(c) Top Marginal Tax Rate		1.0 (63)	0.0 (66)	0.0 (73)	0.0 (68)	1.0 (63.5)	1.0 (59-60)
(d) Conscription	3.0	3.0	3.0	3.0	3.0	3.0	3.0
III. Monetary Policy and Price Stability	**9.0**	**8.2**	**8.9**	**8.5**	**9.2**	**9.7**	**9.6**
(a) Annual Money Growth	8.9 (5.6)	8.0 (9.8)	8.6 (7.0)	7.5 (12.5)	8.5 (7.4)	9.6 (1.9)	9.5 (2.6)
(b) Inflation Variability	9.7 (0.7)	9.2 (2.0)	9.7 (0.8)	9.0 (2.4)	9.7 (0.7)	9.8 (0.6)	9.8 (0.4)
(c) Recent Inflation Rate	8.3 (8.3)	7.5 (12.4)	8.4 (8.2)	9.1 (4.3)	9.3 (3.4)	9.6 (2.1)	9.5 (2.5)
IV. Freedom to Use Alternative Currencies	**5.0**	**4.9**	**4.8**	**5.0**	**10.0**	**10.0**	**10.0**
(a) Ownership of Foreign Currency	0.0	0.0	0.0	0.0	10.0	10.0	10.0
(b) Black Market Exchange Rate	10.0 (0.0)	9.8 (1.0)	9.6 (2.0)	10.0 (0.0)	10.0 (0.0)	10.0 (0.0)	10.0 (0.0)
V. Legal Structure and Property Rights	**9.9**	**7.0**	**8.4**	**9.4**	**10.0**	**10.0**	**9.9**
(a) Legal Security	9.9	7.0	6.7	8.7	10.0		9.9
(b) Rule of Law			10.0	10.0	10.0	10.0	10.0
VI. International Exchange	**7.4**	**7.7**	**7.8**	**8.2**	**7.7**	**7.8**	**8.0**
(a) Taxes on International Trade							
i. Taxes as a Percentage of Exports and Imports	8.7 (1.9)	9.4 (0.9)	9.7 (0.5)	9.7 (0.4)	9.8 (0.3)	9.8 (0.3)	9.8 (0.3)
ii. Mean Tariff Rate		8.2 (9.0)	8.2 (8.8)	8.5 (7.5)	8.5 (7.4)	8.7 (6.7)	8.9 (5.6)
iii. Standard Deviation of Tariff Rates					7.1 (7.2)	7.6 (5.9)	7.6 (5.9)
(b) Size of Trade Sector	4.8 (58.8)	3.4 (61.1)	3.2 (66.5)	4.2 (73.0)	3.3 (65.6)	2.4 (64.2)	3.0 (68.7)
VII. Freedom of Exchange in Financial Markets	**7.7**	**8.0**	**8.3**	**8.1**	**8.2**	**9.1**	**9.8**
(a) Private Ownership of Banks	10.0 (100)	10.0 (100)	10.0 (100)	10.0 (100)	10.0 (100)	10.0 (100)	10.0 (100)
(b) Extension of Credit to Private Sector		9.3 (93.1)	8.2 (82.3)	7.2 (72.4)	8.0 (80.2)	8.2 (81.5)	9.0 (90.3)
(c) Avoidance of Negative Interest Rates	8.0	8.0	10.0	10.0	10.0	10.0	10.0
(d) Capital Transactions with Foreigners	5.0	5.0	5.0	5.0	5.0	8.0	10.0

DOMINICAN REPUBLIC

	1970	1975	1980	1985	1990	1995	1999
Summary Ratings	4.0	4.0	5.4	5.7	4.6	6.0	7.2
Rank	64	64	44	42	80	63	41

Components of Economic Freedom	1970	1975	1980	1985	1990	1995	1999
I. Size of Government	**8.7**	**9.4**	**9.4**	**9.4**	**9.9**	**9.8**	**8.9**
(a) Government Consumption	7.9 (13.1)	9.4 (7.9)	9.1 (9.0)	9.4 (8.2)	10.0 (6.0)	9.9 (6.4)	8.8 (10.1)
(b) Transfers and Subsidies	9.6 (2.0)	9.5 (2.5)	9.7 (1.6)	9.5 (2.5)	9.7 (1.5)	9.7 (1.7)	9.1 (3.9)
II. Structure of the Economy and Use of Markets		**2.4**	**3.3**	**4.3**	**4.2**	**7.1**	**7.1**
(a) Government Enterprises	6.0 (26.7)	4.0 (32.7)	4.0 (31.7)	6.0 (29.3)	6.0 (26.9)	6.0 (29.8)	6.0 (17.1)
(b) Price Controls					4.0	6.0	6.0
(c) Top Marginal Tax Rate		0.0 (73)	0.0 (73)	0.0 (73)	0.0 (73)	9.0 (25)	9.0 (25)
(d) Conscription	3.0	3.0	10.0	10.0	10.0	10.0	10.0
III. Monetary Policy and Price Stability	**9.6**	**7.4**	**8.2**	**3.5**	**2.1**	**5.7**	**8.4**
(a) Annual Money Growth	10.0 (-0.1)	8.3 (8.6)	9.3 (3.7)	7.3 (13.5)	2.7 (36.6)	7.5 (12.7)	7.5 (12.6)
(b) Inflation Variability	9.1 (2.2)	7.4 (6.6)	8.1 (4.6)	3.0 (17.5)	3.5 (16.3)	2.0 (20.0)	9.2 (2.0)
(c) Recent Inflation Rate	9.6 (2.1)	6.6 (17.0)	7.3 (13.7)	0.0 (50.5)	0.0 (51.1)	7.5 (12.6)	8.7 (6.5)
IV. Freedom to Use Alternative Currencies	**2.8**	**2.2**	**3.8**	**6.1**	**0.0**	**4.8**	**7.5**
(a) Ownership of Foreign Currency	0.0	0.0	5.0	5.0	0.0	0.0	5.0
(b) Black Market Exchange Rate	5.6 (22.0)	4.4 (28.0)	2.6 (37.0)	7.2 (14.0)	0.0 (66.0)	9.6 (2.0)	10.0 (0.0)
V. Legal Structure and Property Rights			**6.4**	**5.9**	**5.8**	**4.1**	**5.8**
(a) Legal Security			4.6	3.5	3.2		
(b) Rule of Law			8.3	8.2	8.3	4.1	5.8
VI. International Exchange	**0.9**	**1.5**	**3.2**	**5.2**	**5.2**	**4.8**	**6.0**
(a) Taxes on International Trade							
i. Taxes as a Percentage of Exports and Imports	0.0 (16.5)	0.0 (16.1)	3.5 (9.8)	5.7 (6.5)	5.8 (6.3)	4.0 (9.0)	4.0 (9.0)
ii. Mean Tariff Rate					4.4 (28.0)	6.0 (20.0)	7.1 (14.5)
iii. Standard Deviation of Tariff Rates							6.3 (9.2)
(b) Size of Trade Sector	2.6 (41.8)	4.5 (57.7)	2.6 (48.1)	4.3 (57.2)	5.7 (77.8)	4.0 (62.6)	6.8 (103.1)
VII. Freedom of Exchange in Financial Markets			**5.7**	**5.5**	**4.9**	**7.1**	**8.0**
(a) Private Ownership of Banks			8.0 (90-95)	8.0 (90-95)	10.0 (95-100)	10.0 (95-100)	10.0 (95-100)
(b) Extension of Credit to Private Sector	6.7 (67.2)	7.6 (75.9)	7.6 (75.7)	6.7 (66.7)	8.0 (79.6)	8.9 (88.9)	9.5 (94.6)
(c) Avoidance of Negative Interest Rates					0.0	8.0	8.0
(d) Capital Transactions with Foreigners	2.0	2.0	2.0	2.0	2.0	2.0	5.0

ECUADOR

Summary Ratings	1970	1975	1980	1985	1990	1995	1999
Summary Ratings	3.8	5.6	5.9	4.6	5.5	6.7	6.4
Rank	52	35	34	75	54	50	64

Components of Economic Freedom	1970	1975	1980	1985	1990	1995	1999
I. Size of Government	**8.0**	**6.4**	**7.4**	**8.2**	**9.0**	**8.4**	**7.6**
(a) Government Consumption	8.0 (12.8)	6.4 (18.2)	6.0 (19.6)	7.3 (15.1)	8.5 (11.2)	7.2 (15.7)	7.6 (14.2)
(b) Transfers and Subsidies			8.8 (4.9)	9.0 (4.0)	9.5 (2.3)	9.7 (1.5)	
II. Structure of the Economy and Use of Markets		**3.8**	**2.9**	**1.7**	**3.8**	**6.5**	**6.7**
(a) Government Enterprises	2.0 (40.1)	4.0 (37.5)	2.0 (40.2)	2.0 (41.3)	7.0 (21.7)	8.0 (18.3)	8.0 (18.1)
(b) Price Controls					0.0	4.0	4.0
(c) Top Marginal Tax Rate		5.0 (50)	5.0 (50)	2.0 (58)	5.0 (40)	9.0 (25)	10.0 (0)
(d) Conscription	0.0	0.0	0.0	0.0	3.0	3.0	3.0
III. Monetary Policy and Price Stability	**8.2**	**6.4**	**7.2**	**5.3**	**1.7**	**4.7**	**3.7**
(a) Annual Money Growth	7.4 (13.3)	6.7 (16.5)	7.3 (13.7)	6.0 (19.9)	1.9 (40.5)	3.1 (34.4)	5.6 (22.2)
(b) Inflation Variability	9.3 (1.8)	4.5 (13.7)	8.4 (4.1)	5.9 (10.4)	3.3 (16.8)	5.8 (10.5)	5.4 (11.5)
(c) Recent Inflation Rate	8.2 (9.1)	8.0 (10.0)	6.1 (19.5)	3.8 (30.9)	0.0 (54.0)	5.4 (23.2)	0.0 (52.2)
IV. Freedom to Use Alternative Currencies	**2.8**	**9.5**	**8.7**	**5.2**	**10.0**	**8.8**	**8.9**
(a) Ownership of Foreign Currency	0.0	10.0	10.0	10.0	10.0	10.0	10.0
(b) Black Market Exchange Rate	5.6 (22.0)	9.0 (5.0)	7.4 (13.0)	0.4 (48.0)	10.0 (0.0)	7.6 (12.0)	7.8 (11.1)
V. Legal Structure and Property Rights	**2.3**	**3.8**	**6.5**	**5.7**	**5.6**	**4.1**	**4.7**
(a) Legal Security	2.3	3.8	6.4	4.8	4.6		5.6
(b) Rule of Law			6.7	6.6	6.7	4.1	3.8
VI. International Exchange	**1.1**	**4.7**	**5.0**	**4.2**	**3.6**	**7.3**	**7.0**
(a) Taxes on International Trade							
i. Taxes as a Percentage of Exports and Imports	0.4 (14.4)	4.1 (8.9)	5.2 (7.2)	5.9 (6.2)	7.3 (4.0)	7.7 (3.5)	6.5 (5.2)
ii. Mean Tariff Rate				2.5 (37.7)	2.6 (37.1)	7.5 (12.3)	7.7 (11.3)
iii. Standard Deviation of Tariff Rates					0.0 (27.0)	7.8 (5.6)	7.4 (6.4)
(b) Size of Trade Sector	2.4 (32.6)	6.0 (58.9)	4.6 (50.6)	4.7 (47.6)	5.7 (60.1)	5.0 (58.3)	5.3 (61.5)
VII. Freedom of Exchange in Financial Markets			**4.4**	**3.2**	**4.7**	**7.0**	**5.9**
(a) Private Ownership of Banks			5.0 (47)	5.0 (74)	8.0 (87)	8.0 (91)	2.0 (30)
(b) Extension of Credit to Private Sector	5.3 (53.1)	5.7 (57.4)	7.3 (72.6)	6.2 (62.0)	9.4 (93.6)	9.3 (93.2)	8.0 (79.7)
(c) Avoidance of Negative Interest Rates			4.0	0.0	0.0	6.0	6.0
(d) Capital Transactions with Foreigners	2.0	2.0	2.0	2.0	2.0	5.0	8.0

EGYPT

Summary Ratings

	1970	1975	1980	1985	1990	1995
Summary Ratings	4.0	4.0	4.5	4.3	5.3	6.8
Rank	64	86	79	88	83	52

Components of Economic Freedom

Component	1970	1975	1980	1985	1990	1995	1999
I. Size of Government	**3.7**	**3.4**	**5.9**	**6.1**	**7.7**	**8.0**	**8.6**
(a) Government Consumption	3.7 (27.4)	3.4 (28.4)	6.3 (18.5)	5.8 (20.2)	7.8 (13.6)	8.1 (12.4)	8.3 (11.9)
(b) Transfers and Subsidies		3.3 (25.0)	5.4 (17.2)	6.3 (13.9)	7.7 (8.9)	7.8 (8.5)	8.9 (4.6)
II. Structure of the Economy and Use of Markets			**1.0**	**1.7**	**1.8**	**2.1**	**3.0**
(a) Government Enterprises	2.0 (47.0)	2.0 (43.8)	2.0 (39.7)	2.0 (30.7)	2.0 (37.8)	2.0 (34.0)	2.0 (31.4)
(b) Price Controls					2.0	2.0	4.0
(c) Top Marginal Tax Rate			0.0 (80)	2.0 (65)	2.0 (65)	3.0 (50)	4.0 (42)
(d) Conscription	0.0	0.0	0.0	0.0	0.0	0.0	0.0
III. Monetary Policy and Price Stability	**9.6**	**7.7**	**6.6**	**8.4**	**7.5**	**8.4**	**9.1**
(a) Annual Money Growth	9.6 (-1.8)	6.9 (15.5)	5.4 (22.9)	8.3 (8.5)	8.6 (6.8)	8.8 (5.9)	8.6 (6.8)
(b) Inflation Variability	9.5 (1.3)	8.3 (4.2)	8.1 (4.7)	8.6 (3.4)	7.4 (6.6)	8.2 (4.5)	9.4 (1.6)
(c) Recent Inflation Rate	9.6 (2.2)	7.9 (10.4)	6.4 (18.0)	8.2 (9.0)	6.3 (18.4)	8.1 (9.4)	9.4 (3.1)
IV. Freedom to Use Alternative Currencies	**0.0**	**4.9**	**9.1**	**5.0**	**5.0**	**7.2**	**10.0**
(a) Ownership of Foreign Currency	0.0	0.0	10.0	10.0	10.0	5.0	10.0
(b) Black Market Exchange Rate	0.0 (83.0)	9.8 (1.0)	8.2 (9.0)	0.0 (146.0)	0.0 (56.0)	9.4 (3.0)	10.0 (0.0)
V. Legal Structure and Property Rights	**0.0**	**3.0**	**2.2**	**5.9**	**3.3**	**4.1**	**6.4**
(a) Legal Security	0.0	3.0	2.8	3.5	3.2		6.9
(b) Rule of Law			1.7	8.2	3.3	4.1	5.8
VI. International Exchange	**2.8**		**2.5**	**2.7**	**3.6**	**3.5**	**5.4**
(a) Taxes on International Trade							
i. Taxes as a Percentage of Exports and Imports	0.0 (16.7)		1.3 (13.1)	1.9 (12.1)	6.1 (5.9)	4.8 (7.8)	5.1 (7.3)
ii. Mean Tariff Rate			0.5 (47.4)	1.4 (42.8)	3.3 (33.5)	4.3 (28.3)	6.1 (19.7)
iii. Standard Deviation of Tariff Rates					0.0 (425.8)	0.0 (28.9)	
(b) Size of Trade Sector	5.0 (32.9)	8.4 (61.5)	9.0 (73.4)	7.0 (52.0)	6.8 (52.8)	6.2 (53.0)	4.7 (40.2)
VII. Freedom of Exchange in Financial Markets			**2.9**	**3.8**	**3.8**	**6.2**	**6.8**
(a) Private Ownership of Banks		5.0 (40-60)	5.0 (40-60)	5.0 (40-60)	5.0 (40-60)	5.0 (40-45)	5.0 (40-50)
(b) Extension of Credit to Private Sector			2.8 (28.0)	4.6 (46.0)	4.3 (43.4)	4.7 (46.5)	7.6 (75.6)
(c) Avoidance of Negative Interest Rates			4.0	6.0	6.0	10.0	10.0
(d) Capital Transactions with Foreigners	0.0		0.0	0.0	0.0	5.0	5.0

EL SALVADOR

Summary Ratings	1970	1975	1980	1985	1990	1995	1999
Summary Ratings			3.7	4.2	4.9	7.9	7.9
Rank			90	85	67	18	20

Components of Economic Freedom

	1970	1975	1980	1985	1990	1995	1999
I. Size of Government	**8.1**	**8.6**	**8.2**	**8.3**	**9.3**	**9.2**	**9.1**
(a) Government Consumption	8.1 (12.4)	7.8 (13.5)	7.0 (16.3)	7.1 (16.0)	8.8 (10.0)	9.1 (9.0)	8.7 (10.5)
(b) Transfers and Subsidies		9.5 (2.5)	9.4 (2.7)	9.6 (2.0)	9.8 (1.4)	9.2 (3.3)	9.5 (2.4)
II. Structure of the Economy and Use of Markets		**4.5**	**4.5**	**4.1**	**4.5**	**6.6**	**7.2**
(a) Government Enterprises	8.0 (11.2)	8.0 (10.8)	6.0 (20.2)	6.0 (28.4)	8.0 (20.0)	8.0 (19.0)	7.0 (22.7)
(b) Price Controls					4.0	6.0	8.0
(c) Top Marginal Tax Rate		4.0 (55)	3.0 (60)	3.0 (48)	2.0 (60)	8.0 (30)	8.0 (30)
(d) Conscription	3.0		3.0	0.0	0.0	0.0	3.0
III. Monetary Policy and Price Stability	**9.3**	**7.9**	**7.0**	**7.3**	**6.7**	**8.2**	**9.3**
(a) Annual Money Growth	9.8 (-0.9)	7.5 (12.5)	7.0 (14.9)	7.8 (10.9)	7.5 (12.7)	7.4 (12.8)	9.5 (2.4)
(b) Inflation Variability	9.2 (2.1)	8.3 (4.4)	7.4 (6.5)	8.2 (4.4)	7.0 (7.5)	9.4 (1.5)	8.5 (3.7)
(c) Recent Inflation Rate	9.0 (4.8)	8.0 (9.9)	6.6 (17.0)	6.0 (20.2)	5.5 (22.5)	7.9 (10.4)	9.9 (0.5)
IV. Freedom to Use Alternative Currencies	**3.2**	**3.0**	**0.0**	**0.0**	**2.6**	**9.9**	**8.9**
(a) Ownership of Foreign Currency	0.0	0.0	0.0	0.0	0.0	10.0	10.0
(b) Black Market Exchange Rate	6.4 (18.0)	6.0 (20.0)	0.0 (100.0)	0.0 (195.0)	5.2 (24.0)	9.8 (1.0)	7.8 (11.1)
V. Legal Structure and Property Rights			**1.9**	**1.2**	**1.1**	**7.0**	**5.3**
(a) Legal Security			2.2	0.9	0.5		6.9
(b) Rule of Law			1.7	1.4	1.7	7.0	3.8
VI. International Exchange	**3.5**	**5.5**	**3.3**	**4.5**	**5.7**	**6.8**	**7.3**
(a) Taxes on International Trade							
i. Taxes as a Percentage of Exports and Imports	3.7 (9.4)	5.7 (6.4)	5.9 (6.2)	5.3 (7.1)	7.3 (4.1)	7.6 (3.6)	8.5 (2.2)
ii. Mean Tariff Rate			0.4 (48.0)		5.8 (21.1)	8.0 (10.2)	8.9 (5.7)
iii. Standard Deviation of Tariff Rates						7.0 (7.6)	6.8 (7.9)
(b) Size of Trade Sector	2.9 (49.4)	5.0 (71.3)	4.1 (67.4)	2.9 (52.2)	2.1 (49.8)	2.7 (59.3)	2.7 (58.8)
VII. Freedom of Exchange in Financial Markets				**6.2**	**6.1**	**8.0**	**9.2**
(a) Private Ownership of Banks							
(b) Extension of Credit to Private Sector	9.9 (98.8)	9.8 (98.4)	9.8 (98.4)	9.3 (93.1)	9.3 (92.9)	9.5 (94.7)	9.8 (97.6)
(c) Avoidance of Negative Interest Rates				8.0	8.0	10.0	10.0
(d) Capital Transactions with Foreigners	2.0	2.0	2.0	2.0	2.0	5.0	8.0

ESTONIA

Summary Ratings	1970	1975	1980	1985	1990	1995	1999
						5.9	7.4
Rank						68	36

Components of Economic Freedom	1985	1990	1995	1999
I. Size of Government		**5.7**	**4.8**	**4.9**
(a) Government Consumption		5.7 (20.5)	3.2 (29.1)	3.7 (27.5)
(b) Transfers and Subsidies			6.4 (13.6)	6.1 (15.0)
II. Structure of the Economy and Use of Markets			**4.9**	**6.2**
(a) Government Enterprises			2.0	6.0
(b) Price Controls		0.0	6.0	6.0
(c) Top Marginal Tax Rate			8.0 (26)	8.0 (26)
(d) Conscription		0.0	3.0	3.0
III. Monetary Policy and Price Stability	**8.8**	**4.2**	**1.4**	**6.4**
(a) Annual Money Growth			0.0 (74.6)	5.7 (21.7)
(b) Inflation Variability	8.7 (3.4)	5.2 (12.1)	0.0 (323.0)	4.2 (14.4)
(c) Recent Inflation Rate	8.9 (-5.6)	3.3 (33.7)	4.2 (29.0)	9.3 (3.3)
IV. Freedom to Use Alternative Currencies		**2.5**	**7.5**	**10.0**
(a) Ownership of Foreign Currency		5.0	5.0	10.0
(b) Black Market Exchange Rate		0.0 (1969.0)	10.0 (0.0)	10.0 (0.0)
V. Legal Structure and Property Rights				**5.8**
(a) Legal Security				
(b) Rule of Law				5.8
VI. International Exchange			**9.4**	**9.1**
(a) Taxes on International Trade		9.8 (0.3)		10.0 (0.0)
i. Taxes as a Percentage of Exports and Imports			9.9 (0.1)	
ii. Mean Tariff Rate			10.0 (0.1)	
iii. Standard Deviation of Tariff Rates			9.5 (1.2)	
(b) Size of Trade Sector			7.0 (159.7)	7.4 (169.2)
VII. Freedom of Exchange in Financial Markets			**5.2**	**8.4**
(a) Private Ownership of Banks		0.0 (0)	5.0 (50-75)	8.0 (80-90)
(b) Extension of Credit to Private Sector			7.9 (78.9)	9.5 (94.5)
(c) Avoidance of Negative Interest Rates			0.0	6.0
(d) Capital Transactions with Foreigners		0.0	8.0	10.0

Fiji

Summary Ratings	1970	1975	1980	1985	1990	1995	1999
Summary Ratings	5.0	5.2	5.3	5.6	6.0	6.2	
Rank	47	52	54	51	63	72	

Components of Economic Freedom	1970	1975	1980	1985	1990	1995	1999
I. Size of Government	**6.6**	**8.5**	**7.5**	**6.9**	**7.9**	**7.3**	**7.6**
(a) Government Consumption	6.6 (17.7)	7.4 (15.0)	5.6 (21.1)	5.0 (23.1)	5.9 (19.9)	5.5 (21.4)	5.9 (20.0)
(b) Transfers and Subsidies		9.6 (1.9)	9.5 (2.5)	8.9 (4.5)	9.9 (1.0)	9.2 (3.5)	9.3 (2.9)
II. Structure of the Economy and Use of Markets		**4.4**	**3.1**	**3.4**	**4.3**	**5.3**	**5.3**
(a) Government Enterprises	4.0 (29.8)	4.0 (30.0)	2.0 (45.0)	2.0 (37.0)	2.0 (62.0)	2.0	2.0
(b) Price Controls					6.0	6.0	6.0
(c) Top Marginal Tax Rate		3.0 (53)	2.0 (53)	3.0 (50)	3.0 (50)	7.0 (35)	7.0 (35)
(d) Conscription		10.0	10.0	10.0	10.0	10.0	10.0
III. Monetary Policy and Price Stability	**8.6**	**6.5**	**8.0**	**8.7**	**8.4**	**9.2**	**9.3**
(a) Annual Money Growth	8.7 (6.4)	7.8 (11.2)	9.8 (-1.3)	9.1 (4.5)	7.5 (12.3)	9.0 (4.9)	9.2 (3.8)
(b) Inflation Variability	8.5 (3.8)	6.4 (9.0)	7.7 (5.7)	8.4 (3.9)	9.2 (2.1)	9.1 (2.4)	9.0 (2.5)
(c) Recent Inflation Rate	8.6 (6.8)	5.1 (24.3)	6.5 (17.3)	8.5 (7.5)	8.6 (7.1)	9.7 (1.6)	9.6 (2.0)
IV. Freedom to Use Alternative Currencies	**4.8**	**3.3**	**3.2**	**4.2**	**4.6**	**4.9**	**4.7**
(a) Ownership of Foreign Currency		0.0	0.0	0.0	0.0	0.0	0.0
(b) Black Market Exchange Rate	4.8 (26.0)	6.6 (17.0)	6.4 (18.0)	8.4 (8.0)	9.2 (4.0)	9.8 (1.0)	9.4 (3.0)
V. Legal Structure and Property Rights							
(a) Legal Security							
(b) Rule of Law							
VI. International Exchange	**4.8**	**5.4**	**5.8**	**4.8**	**6.0**	**6.2**	**7.0**
(a) Taxes on International Trade							
i. Taxes as a Percentage of Exports and Imports	4.3 (8.6)	5.6 (6.6)	6.1 (5.8)	4.7 (7.9)	5.7 (6.4)	6.6 (5.1)	7.0 (4.5)
ii. Mean Tariff Rate							7.5 (12.4)
iii. Standard Deviation of Tariff Rates							
(b) Size of Trade Sector	5.9 (100.0)	4.9 (86.6)	5.1 (100.5)	4.9 (89.1)	6.7 (129.6)	5.3 (115.1)	5.9 (130.7)
VII. Freedom of Exchange in Financial Markets		**3.4**	**4.9**	**5.5**	**4.3**	**4.8**	**4.7**
(a) Private Ownership of Banks		2.0 (10-40)	2.0 (10-40)	2.0 (10-40)	2.0 (10-40)	2.0 (10-40)	2.0 (10-40)
(b) Extension of Credit to Private Sector	7.3 (72.6)	7.1 (70.8)	7.3 (72.6)	7.7 (77.2)	8.3 (83.3)	8.5 (84.6)	8.0 (79.6)
(c) Avoidance of Negative Interest Rates		0.0	6.0	8.0	6.0	8.0	8.0
(d) Capital Transactions with Foreigners	5.0	5.0	5.0	5.0	2.0	2.0	2.0

FINLAND

	1970	1975	1980	1985	1990	1995	1999
Summary Ratings	7.7	6.2	6.9	7.2	7.6	7.9	8.1
Rank	11	22	15	15	16	18	14

Components of Economic Freedom	1970	1975	1980	1985	1990	1995	1999
I. Size of Government	**5.8**	**5.6**	**5.3**	**4.8**	**4.6**	**3.6**	**3.9**
(a) Government Consumption	5.8 (20.3)	4.9 (23.4)	4.4 (24.9)	3.8 (27.0)	3.3 (28.7)	3.3 (28.7)	3.0 (29.9)
(b) Transfers and Subsidies		6.3 (14.1)	6.2 (14.3)	5.8 (15.8)	5.8 (16.0)	3.9 (22.8)	4.8 (19.6)
II. Structure of the Economy and Use of Markets	**4.6**	**4.6**	**4.2**	**4.2**	**4.2**	**5.7**	**5.7**
(a) Government Enterprises	7.0 (22.4)	7.0 (18.9)	7.0 (23.3)	7.0 (24.2)	6.0 (29.3)	6.0 (42.2)	6.0
(b) Price Controls					6.0	9.0	9.0
(c) Top Marginal Tax Rate		2.0 (61-68)	1.0 (65-71)	1.0 (64-70)	0.0 (63-69)	2.0 (55-61)	2.0 (54-60)
(d) Conscription	3.0	3.0	3.0	3.0	3.0	3.0	3.0
III. Monetary Policy and Price Stability	**8.9**	**7.1**	**8.7**	**8.7**	**9.0**	**7.6**	**9.1**
(a) Annual Money Growth	8.8 (5.8)	6.2 (18.8)	8.9 (5.5)	7.9 (10.3)	8.6 (6.8)	3.9 (30.3)	8.4 (8.1)
(b) Inflation Variability	8.8 (3.1)	7.9 (5.3)	9.3 (1.8)	9.3 (1.9)	9.6 (0.9)	9.7 (0.7)	9.4 (1.6)
(c) Recent Inflation Rate	9.2 (3.9)	7.3 (13.3)	8.1 (9.8)	8.9 (5.3)	8.8 (5.8)	9.5 (2.4)	9.8 (1.2)
IV. Freedom to Use Alternative Currencies	**7.5**	**7.4**	**7.4**	**7.5**	**10.0**	**10.0**	**10.0**
(a) Ownership of Foreign Currency	5.0	5.0	5.0	5.0	10.0	10.0	10.0
(b) Black Market Exchange Rate	10.0 (0.0)	9.8 (1.0)	9.8 (1.0)	10.0 (0.0)	10.0 (0.0)	10.0 (0.0)	10.0 (0.0)
V. Legal Structure and Property Rights	**8.3**	**5.3**	**7.9**	**9.4**	**10.0**	**10.0**	**10.0**
(a) Legal Security	8.3	5.3	5.8	8.7	10.0		10.0
(b) Rule of Law			10.0	10.0	10.0	10.0	10.0
VI. International Exchange	**7.7**	**7.4**	**7.9**	**8.2**	**7.3**	**8.1**	**8.2**
(a) Taxes on International Trade							
i. Taxes as a Percentage of Exports and Imports	9.0 (1.5)	8.9 (1.6)	9.5 (0.8)	9.7 (0.4)	9.6 (0.6)	9.9 (0.2)	9.7 (0.5)
ii. Mean Tariff Rate		7.4 (13.2)	7.9 (10.4)	8.6 (7.0)	8.5 (7.7)	8.7 (6.7)	8.9 (5.6)
iii. Standard Deviation of Tariff Rates					6.0 (10.1)	7.6 (5.9)	7.6 (5.9)
(b) Size of Trade Sector	5.1 (52.6)	4.2 (54.0)	4.8 (67.1)	4.4 (58.1)	2.8 (47.6)	4.5 (68.2)	4.6 (69.8)
VII. Freedom of Exchange in Financial Markets		**6.4**	**6.8**	**7.3**	**7.3**	**8.7**	**8.7**
(a) Private Ownership of Banks		8.0 (75-90)	8.0 (75-90)	8.0 (75-90)	8.0 (75-95)	8.0 (75-95)	8.0 (75-95)
(b) Extension of Credit to Private Sector	9.6 (96.1)	9.9 (99.0)	9.9 (98.8)	9.9 (99.0)	10.0 (99.6)	9.0 (90.3)	8.8 (88.3)
(c) Avoidance of Negative Interest Rates			8.0	10.0	10.0	10.0	10.0
(d) Capital Transactions with Foreigners	2.0	2.0	2.0	2.0	2.0	8.0	8.0

FRANCE

Summary Ratings	1970	1975	1980	1985	1990	1995	1999
Summary Ratings	7.2	6.0	6.3	6.3	7.6	7.9	7.5
Rank	16	28	25	27	16	18	34

Components of Economic Freedom

	1970	1975	1980	1985	1990	1995	1999
I. Size of Government	**5.4**	**4.4**	**3.9**	**3.8**	**4.1**	**2.7**	**2.6**
(a) Government Consumption	5.8 (20.2)	5.3 (22.0)	4.8 (23.5)	4.7 (24.1)	4.8 (23.5)	2.9 (30.3)	2.8 (30.4)
(b) Transfers and Subsidies	5.1 (18.5)	3.6 (24.0)	3.0 (26.1)	2.8 (26.8)	3.3 (25.2)	2.5 (27.9)	2.3 (28.8)
II. Structure of the Economy and Use of Markets		**4.2**	**3.5**	**2.7**	**4.3**	**5.3**	**4.7**
(a) Government Enterprises	4.0	4.0	4.0 (27.4)	4.0 (33.2)	4.0 (35.0)	4.0 (30.0)	4.0
(b) Price Controls					6.0	8.0	8.0
(c) Top Marginal Tax Rate		5.0 (48)	3.0 (60)	1.0 (65)	3.0 (53)	4.0 (51)	2.0 (54.4)
(d) Conscription	1.0	3.0	3.0	3.0	3.0	3.0	3.0
III. Monetary Policy and Price Stability	**9.4**	**8.2**	**8.4**	**8.8**	**9.5**	**9.8**	**9.4**
(a) Annual Money Growth	10.0 (0.2)	8.3 (8.4)	8.0 (10.2)	8.4 (8.1)	9.4 (2.8)	9.9 (-0.7)	8.6 (6.9)
(b) Inflation Variability	9.4 (1.4)	8.9 (2.6)	9.7 (0.8)	9.1 (2.3)	9.6 (0.9)	9.7 (0.7)	9.7 (0.7)
(c) Recent Inflation Rate	8.9 (5.6)	7.4 (13.0)	7.7 (11.4)	8.8 (5.8)	9.4 (3.1)	9.7 (1.6)	9.9 (0.5)
IV. Freedom to Use Alternative Currencies	**4.8**	**5.0**	**4.7**	**4.6**	**10.0**	**10.0**	**10.0**
(a) Ownership of Foreign Currency	0.0	0.0	0.0	0.0	10.0	10.0	10.0
(b) Black Market Exchange Rate	9.6 (2.0)	10.0 (0.0)	9.4 (3.0)	9.2 (4.0)	10.0 (0.0)	10.0 (0.0)	10.0 (0.0)
V. Legal Structure and Property Rights	**8.7**	**5.2**	**7.9**	**8.5**	**9.2**	**10.0**	**8.6**
(a) Legal Security	8.7	5.2	5.8	8.7	10.0		9.2
(b) Rule of Law			10.0	8.2	8.3	10.0	7.9
VI. International Exchange	**8.1**	**7.9**	**8.1**	**8.4**	**7.9**	**8.1**	**8.2**
(a) Taxes on International Trade							
i. Taxes as a Percentage of Exports and Imports	9.7 (0.4)	9.9 (0.1)	9.7 (0.5)	9.7 (0.4)	9.7 (0.4)	9.8 (0.3)	9.8 (0.3)
ii. Mean Tariff Rate		7.8 (11.0)	8.2 (8.8)	8.5 (7.5)	8.5 (7.4)	8.7 (6.7)	8.9 (5.6)
iii. Standard Deviation of Tariff Rates					7.1 (7.2)	7.6 (5.9)	7.6 (5.9)
(b) Size of Trade Sector	4.8 (31.1)	4.2 (36.9)	4.6 (44.3)	5.3 (47.2)	4.8 (45.1)	4.2 (44.6)	4.8 (49.6)
VII. Freedom of Exchange in Financial Markets	**6.7**	**7.2**	**7.1**	**7.0**	**7.9**	**8.3**	**8.1**
(a) Private Ownership of Banks	10.0 (95-100)	10.0 (95-100)	10.0 (95-100)	10.0 (95-100)	10.0 (95-100)	10.0 (95-100)	10.0 (95-100)
(b) Extension of Credit to Private Sector	9.4 (93.8)	8.7 (95.0)	8.7 (87.2)	8.5 (84.5)	9.0 (90.2)	8.4 (83.6)	7.4 (73.9)
(c) Avoidance of Negative Interest Rates	6.0	8.0	8.0	8.0	8.0	10.0	10.0
(d) Capital Transactions with Foreigners	2.0	2.0	2.0	2.0	5.0	5.0	5.0

GABON

Summary Ratings	1970	1975	1980	1985	1990	1995	1999
Summary Ratings			3.6	4.8	5.1	5.3	4.3
Rank			93	71	63	83	114

Components of Economic Freedom

	1970	1975	1980	1985	1990	1995	1999
I. Size of Government	**1.5**	**5.5**	**1.9**	**4.9**	**7.7**	**7.1**	**4.1**
(a) Government Consumption	1.5 (34.9)	1.7 (34.2)	1.9 (33.6)	0.4 (38.7)	5.5 (21.2)	4.3 (25.3)	4.1 (26.2)
(b) Transfers and Subsidies		9.3 (3.1)		9.4 (2.7)	9.8 (1.2)	9.8 (1.2)	
II. Structure of the Economy and Use of Markets					**2.4**	**3.1**	**2.9**
(a) Government Enterprises	2.0 (48.4)	2.0 (42.6)	2.0 (42.6)	4.0 (35.3)	4.0	4.0	4.0
(b) Price Controls					0.0	2.0	2.0
(c) Top Marginal Tax Rate					1.0 (60)	1.0 (60)	0.0 (90)
(d) Conscription	10.0	10.0	10.0	10.0	10.0	10.0	10.0
III. Monetary Policy and Price Stability	**9.6**	**4.7**	**6.0**	**8.2**	**7.3**	**7.2**	**6.8**
(a) Annual Money Growth	9.7 (1.4)	5.1 (24.5)	9.6 (2.2)	7.4 (13.0)	9.7 (-1.5)	9.6 (1.8)	7.7 (11.7)
(b) Inflation Variability	9.0 (2.5)	0.0 (26.3)	5.4 (11.4)	7.4 (6.5)	5.2 (12.1)	1.9 (20.3)	2.8 (17.9)
(c) Recent Inflation Rate	9.9 (-0.4)	9.1 (4.4)	2.6 (36.8)	9.7 (-1.3)	6.9 (15.4)	9.9 (-0.5)	10.0 (-0.1)
IV. Freedom to Use Alternative Currencies	**4.8**	**4.8**	**4.8**	**4.9**	**4.6**	**4.9**	**4.8**
(a) Ownership of Foreign Currency	0.0	0.0	0.0	0.0	0.0	0.0	0.0
(b) Black Market Exchange Rate	9.6 (2.0)	9.6 (2.0)	9.6 (2.0)	9.8 (1.0)	9.2 (4.0)	9.8 (1.0)	9.6 (2.0)
V. Legal Structure and Property Rights			**3.9**	**4.6**	**5.3**	**7.0**	**3.8**
(a) Legal Security			4.5	6.1	7.3		
(b) Rule of Law			3.3	3.1	3.3	7.0	3.8
VI. International Exchange	**4.4**	**5.2**	**3.7**	**5.2**	**6.2**	**5.7**	
(a) Taxes on International Trade							
i. Taxes as a Percentage of Exports and Imports	3.8 (9.3)	4.5 (8.2)	5.1 (7.3)	5.7 (6.4)	6.8 (4.8)	5.8 (6.3)	
ii. Mean Tariff Rate			1.3 (43.3)	4.1 (29.6)			
iii. Standard Deviation of Tariff Rates							
(b) Size of Trade Sector	5.6 (87.7)	6.5 (97.4)	5.9 (96.4)	6.6 (98.5)	4.9 (76.9)	5.4 (93.1)	5.4 (91.4)
VII. Freedom of Exchange in Financial Markets	**0.0**	**0.0**	**1.9**	**2.5**	**3.8**	**3.4**	**4.2**
(a) Private Ownership of Banks	0.0 (0-10)	0.0 (0-10)	0.0 (0-10)	0.0 (0-10)	2.0 (10-40)	5.0 (40-75)	5.0 (40-75)
(b) Extension of Credit to Private Sector					6.3 (62.9)	5.2 (51.9)	6.4 (64.1)
(c) Avoidance of Negative Interest Rates			6.0	8.0	8.0	4.0	6.0
(d) Capital Transactions with Foreigners	0.0	0.0	0.0	0.0	0.0	0.0	0.0

GERMANY

Summary Ratings	1970	1975	1980	1985	1990	1995	1999
Summary Ratings	8.0	7.3	7.7	7.7	8.1	8.0	8.0
Rank	7	10	9	11	9	14	15

Components of Economic Freedom

	1970	1975	1980	1985	1990	1995	1999
I. Size of Government	**5.6**	**4.7**	**4.7**	**4.5**	**4.8**	**4.2**	**4.5**
(a) Government Consumption	5.2 (22.4)	4.0 (26.5)	4.0 (26.3)	4.1 (26.1)	4.4 (25.2)	4.2 (25.8)	4.5 (24.9)
(b) Transfers and Subsidies	6.1 (14.8)	5.4 (17.4)	5.3 (17.6)	5.0 (19.0)	5.3 (17.9)	4.3 (21.6)	4.5 (20.8)
II. Structure of the Economy and Use of Markets	**4.3**	**4.3**	**4.3**	**3.9**	**5.6**	**5.5**	**4.9**
(a) Government Enterprises	7.0	7.0	7.0 (25.7)	7.0 (24.4)	6.0 (24.0)	6.0 (25.5)	6.0
(b) Price Controls					9.0	9.0	8.0
(c) Top Marginal Tax Rate	2.0 (62)	2.0 (65)	2.0 (65)	1.0 (65)	2.0 (65)	1.0 (66)	0.0 (66-68)
(d) Conscription	1.0	1.0	1.0	1.0	1.0	3.0	3.0
III. Monetary Policy and Price Stability	**9.3**	**9.1**	**9.2**	**9.5**	**9.0**	**9.4**	**9.6**
(a) Annual Money Growth	9.4 (2.9)	8.8 (6.2)	9.2 (4.1)	9.5 (2.6)	8.1 (9.7)	9.0 (5.0)	9.1 (4.4)
(b) Inflation Variability	9.2 (2.1)	9.7 (0.7)	9.6 (0.9)	9.5 (1.2)	9.5 (1.2)	9.5 (1.2)	9.8 (0.5)
(c) Recent Inflation Rate	9.3 (3.4)	8.8 (6.0)	8.9 (5.5)	9.6 (2.2)	9.5 (2.7)	9.6 (2.1)	9.9 (0.6)
IV. Freedom to Use Alternative Currencies	**10.0**	**10.0**	**10.0**	**10.0**	**10.0**	**10.0**	**10.0**
(a) Ownership of Foreign Currency	10.0	10.0	10.0	10.0	10.0	10.0	10.0
(b) Black Market Exchange Rate	10.0 (0.0)	10.0 (0.0)	10.0 (0.0)	10.0 (0.0)	10.0 (0.0)	10.0 (0.0)	10.0 (0.0)
V. Legal Structure and Property Rights	**10.0**	**7.6**	**9.1**	**8.8**	**10.0**	**10.0**	**9.9**
(a) Legal Security	10.0	7.6	8.2	9.4	10.0		9.8
(b) Rule of Law			10.0	8.2	10.0	10.0	10.0
VI. International Exchange	**8.2**	**8.2**	**8.3**	**8.6**	**8.1**	**8.1**	**8.3**
(a) Taxes on International Trade							
i. Taxes as a Percentage of Exports and Imports	9.7 (0.5)	9.7 (0.5)	9.7 (0.5)	9.7 (0.5)	9.7 (0.5)	9.7 (0.5)	9.7 (0.5)
ii. Mean Tariff Rate		8.1 (9.4)	8.2 (8.8)	8.5 (7.5)	8.5 (7.4)	8.7 (6.7)	8.9 (5.6)
iii. Standard Deviation of Tariff Rates					7.1 (7.2)	7.6 (5.9)	7.6 (5.9)
(b) Size of Trade Sector	5.4 (36.5)	5.6 (49.4)	5.6 (55.1)	6.9 (63.8)	6.3 (61.6)	4.6 (46.4)	5.6 (56.0)
VII. Freedom of Exchange in Financial Markets	**7.8**	**7.2**	**7.6**	**8.2**	**8.2**	**8.1**	**8.1**
(a) Private Ownership of Banks	5.0 (40-50)	5.0 (48-50)	5.0 (48-50)	5.0 (48-50)	5.0 (49)	5.0 (49)	5.0 (53.1)
(b) Extension of Credit to Private Sector	8.4 (84.0)	8.0 (79.8)	7.8 (78.2)	7.7 (77.3)	7.9 (79.3)	7.6 (76.4)	7.7 (76.5)
(c) Avoidance of Negative Interest Rates	10.0	8.0	10.0	10.0	10.0	10.0	10.0
(d) Capital Transactions with Foreigners	8.0	8.0	8.0	10.0	10.0	10.0	10.0

GHANA

	1970	1975	1980	1985	1990	1995	1999
Summary Ratings	3.3	2.6	1.9	2.4	4.7	6.0	5.6
Rank	56	81	107	108	72	63	87

Components of Economic Freedom

	1970	1975	1980	1985	1990	1995	1999
I. Size of Government	**8.5**	**8.3**	**8.9**	**9.3**	**9.1**	**8.5**	**8.3**
(a) Government Consumption	7.4 (14.7)	7.3 (15.1)	8.3 (11.7)	8.8 (10.1)	8.9 (9.9)	7.7 (13.8)	8.3 (11.9)
(b) Transfers and Subsidies	9.5 (2.4)	9.3 (3.1)	9.5 (2.4)	9.8 (1.3)	9.4 (2.6)	9.2 (3.3)	
II. Structure of the Economy and Use of Markets	**1.3**	**1.3**	**1.7**	**1.7**	**2.0**	**5.3**	**5.9**
(a) Government Enterprises	0.0 (45.8)	0.0 (34.1)	0.0 (35.4)	0.0	2.0 (25.0)	4.0	4.0
(b) Price Controls					0.0	4.0	6.0
(c) Top Marginal Tax Rate	0.0 (70)	0.0 (70)	1.0 (60)	1.0 (60)	2.0 (55)	7.0 (35)	7.0 (35)
(d) Conscription	10.0	10.0	10.0	10.0	10.0	10.0	10.0
III. Monetary Policy and Price Stability	**8.9**	**5.2**	**1.5**	**2.3**	**5.4**	**3.7**	**4.8**
(a) Annual Money Growth	9.6 (2.0)	4.9 (25.7)	1.4 (-2.9)	1.2 (44.2)	2.4 (37.9)	3.9 (30.4)	3.9 (30.7)
(b) Inflation Variability	7.6 (6.0)	6.7 (8.3)	3.2 (17.1)	0.0 (38.3)	8.0 (5.0)	5.6 (10.9)	3.5 (16.3)
(c) Recent Inflation Rate	9.4 (2.9)	4.1 (29.5)	0.0 (51.1)	5.9 (20.7)	5.9 (20.7)	1.4 (43.2)	7.1 (14.6)
IV. Freedom to Use Alternative Currencies	**0.0**	**0.0**	**0.0**	**0.0**	**4.3**	**7.3**	**7.5**
(a) Ownership of Foreign Currency	0.0	0.0	0.0	0.0	0.0	5.0	5.0
(b) Black Market Exchange Rate	0.0 (66.0)	0.0 (67.0)	0.0 (304.0)	0.0 (142.0)	8.6 (7.0)	9.6 (2.0)	10.0 (0.0)
V. Legal Structure and Property Rights			**2.2**	**2.2**	**6.4**	**7.0**	**3.8**
(a) Legal Security			2.8	2.9	4.6		
(b) Rule of Law			1.7	1.4	8.3	7.0	3.8
VI. International Exchange	**1.5**	**1.2**	**0.0**	**1.6**	**4.4**	**6.0**	
(a) Taxes on International Trade							
i. Taxes as a Percentage of Exports and Imports	0.0 (15.1)	0.0 (20.6)	0.0 (-7.3)	0.0 (21.7)	2.3 (11.6)	4.6 (8.1)	
ii. Mean Tariff Rate				4.0 (30.0)	6.5 (17.5)	7.0 (15.0)	
iii. Standard Deviation of Tariff Rates						6.7 (8.3)	
(b) Size of Trade Sector	4.6 (44.0)	3.7 (37.8)	0.0 (-7.6)	0.0 (23.3)	4.1 (42.7)	5.4 (59.8)	5.7 (63.1)
VII. Freedom of Exchange in Financial Markets		**2.0**	**1.2**	**1.7**	**2.7**	**4.2**	**4.3**
(a) Private Ownership of Banks		2.0 (10-40)	2.0 (10-40)	2.0 (10-40)	2.0 (10-40)	5.0 (40-75)	5.0 (40-75)
(b) Extension of Credit to Private Sector	6.1 (60.7)	4.6 (45.7)	3.3 (32.9)	5.4 (54.4)	7.8 (77.8)	9.0 (89.8)	4.7 (47.2)
(c) Avoidance of Negative Interest Rates			0.0	0.0	2.0	4.0	8.0
(d) Capital Transactions with Foreigners	0.0	0.0	0.0	0.0	0.0	0.0	0.0

GREECE

Summary Ratings	1970	1975	1980	1985	1990	1995	1999
Summary Ratings	6.3	5.8	5.7	5.2	6.1	7.2	7.3
Rank	31	32	38	57	41	37	38

Components of Economic Freedom	1970	1975	1980	1985	1990	1995	1999
I. Size of Government	**9.1**	**8.6**	**8.0**	**6.0**	**5.6**	**6.0**	**7.6**
(a) Government Consumption	8.5 (11.0)	7.9 (13.2)	7.4 (14.7)	6.6 (17.5)	6.7 (17.3)	6.9 (16.4)	6.6 (17.5)
(b) Transfers and Subsidies	9.6 (1.9)	9.3 (3.1)	8.6 (5.7)	5.3 (17.7)	4.6 (20.5)	5.0 (19.0)	8.6 (5.6)
II. Structure of the Economy and Use of Markets		**3.5**	**2.1**	**1.4**	**2.3**	**5.2**	**4.9**
(a) Government Enterprises	6.0 (28.4)	4.0 (29.0)	2.0 (32.0)	2.0 (41.0)	4.0 (37.5)	6.0 (35.8)	6.0
(b) Price Controls					0.0	6.0	5.0
(c) Top Marginal Tax Rate		4.0 (52)	3.0 (60)	1.0 (63)	4.0 (50)	5.0 (45)	5.0 (45)
(d) Conscription	0.0	0.0	0.0	0.0	0.0	0.0	0.0
III. Monetary Policy and Price Stability	**9.4**	**7.4**	**7.6**	**7.4**	**7.3**	**7.9**	**8.4**
(a) Annual Money Growth	9.3 (3.4)	7.4 (12.9)	7.2 (14.1)	6.7 (16.4)	6.3 (18.4)	7.2 (14.0)	7.2 (14.1)
(b) Inflation Variability	9.6 (1.1)	7.1 (7.2)	9.1 (2.4)	9.0 (2.5)	9.1 (2.4)	8.5 (3.8)	8.6 (3.4)
(c) Recent Inflation Rate	9.2 (3.9)	7.5 (12.3)	6.5 (17.7)	6.5 (17.7)	6.5 (17.7)	8.2 (8.9)	9.5 (2.6)
IV. Freedom to Use Alternative Currencies	**7.3**	**7.2**	**6.8**	**5.0**	**7.2**	**7.5**	**10.0**
(a) Ownership of Foreign Currency	5.0	5.0	5.0	5.0	5.0	5.0	10.0
(b) Black Market Exchange Rate	9.6 (2.0)	9.4 (3.0)	8.6 (7.0)	5.0 (25.0)	9.4 (3.0)	10.0 (0.0)	10.0 (0.0)
V. Legal Structure and Property Rights	**6.1**	**5.9**	**6.1**	**6.2**	**7.8**	**10.0**	**5.8**
(a) Legal Security	6.1	5.9	4.0	4.2	7.3		7.8
(b) Rule of Law			8.3	8.2	8.3	10.0	3.8
VI. International Exchange	**4.6**	**6.7**	**6.7**	**7.8**	**7.6**	**7.7**	**7.7**
(a) Taxes on International Trade							
i. Taxes as a Percentage of Exports and Imports	6.9 (4.7)	7.7 (3.5)	7.9 (3.2)	9.5 (0.7)	9.6 (0.6)	9.7 (0.4)	9.7 (0.4)
ii. Mean Tariff Rate		8.1 (9.4)	8.2 (8.8)	8.5 (7.5)	8.5 (7.4)	8.7 (6.7)	8.9 (5.6)
iii. Standard Deviation of Tariff Rates					7.1 (7.2)	7.6 (5.9)	7.6 (5.9)
(b) Size of Trade Sector	0.0 (23.5)	1.6 (36.0)	1.2 (38.6)	2.9 (44.4)	2.6 (44.9)	1.5 (43.4)	1.4 (43.1)
VII. Freedom of Exchange in Financial Markets	**4.1**	**3.1**	**3.6**	**3.5**	**4.7**	**5.7**	**7.3**
(a) Private Ownership of Banks	2.0 (10-40)	2.0 (10-40)	2.0 (10-40)	2.0 (10-40)	5.0 (40-60)	5.0 (40-60)	5.0 (40-60)
(b) Extension of Credit to Private Sector	4.7 (47.0)	4.6 (46.4)	4.7 (47.3)	4.4 (43.8)	3.9 (39.0)	4.9 (49.1)	6.0 (60.1)
(c) Avoidance of Negative Interest Rates	8.0	4.0	6.0	6.0	8.0	8.0	10.0
(d) Capital Transactions with Foreigners	2.0	2.0	2.0	2.0	2.0	5.0	8.0

GUATEMALA

Summary Ratings	1970	1975	1980	1985	1990	1995	1999
Summary Ratings	6.4	7.3	6.5	5.1	6.2	7.9	6.7
Rank	27	10	21	60	40	18	56

Components of Economic Freedom	1970	1975	1980	1985	1990	1995	1999
I. Size of Government	**9.5**	**9.7**	**9.4**	**9.6**	**9.6**	**10.0**	**9.9**
(a) Government Consumption	9.1 (9.2)	9.4 (8.0)	9.1 (9.2)	9.5 (7.8)	9.6 (7.3)	10.0 (6.0)	10.0 (6.0)
(b) Transfers and Subsidies	9.9 (0.7)	9.9 (0.8)	9.8 (1.2)	9.8 (1.3)	9.6 (1.8)	10.0 (0.5)	9.9 (1.0)
II. Structure of the Economy and Use of Markets		**8.6**	**8.3**	**5.8**	**6.4**	**6.6**	**7.0**
(a) Government Enterprises	8.0 (19.2)	8.0 (20.9)	8.0 (37.4)	8.0 (32.1)	8.0 (21.0)	8.0 (17.3)	8.0 (18.6)
(b) Price Controls					6.0	6.0	8.0
(c) Top Marginal Tax Rate		9.0 (34)	8.0 (40)	5.0 (48)	7.0 (34)	8.0 (30)	7.0 (35)
(d) Conscription	0.0	10.0	10.0	0.0	0.0	0.0	0.0
III. Monetary Policy and Price Stability	**9.4**	**7.5**	**8.1**	**7.4**	**5.5**	**7.2**	**8.0**
(a) Annual Money Growth	9.9 (-0.5)	8.1 (9.7)	7.9 (10.7)	8.0 (10.1)	6.3 (18.3)	6.9 (15.5)	6.4 (17.9)
(b) Inflation Variability	9.2 (2.0)	6.9 (7.8)	8.6 (3.6)	7.9 (5.3)	3.9 (15.2)	6.4 (9.1)	8.7 (3.2)
(c) Recent Inflation Rate	9.0 (5.0)	7.4 (13.1)	8.0 (10.0)	6.2 (18.8)	6.2 (18.8)	8.3 (8.7)	9.0 (4.9)
IV. Freedom to Use Alternative Currencies	**4.1**	**6.5**	**9.0**	**5.0**	**10.0**	**10.0**	**7.5**
(a) Ownership of Foreign Currency	0.0	5.0	10.0	10.0	10.0	10.0	5.0
(b) Black Market Exchange Rate	8.2 (9.0)	8.0 (10.0)	8.0 (10.0)	0.0 (89.0)	10.0 (0.0)	10.0 (0.0)	10.0 (0.0)
V. Legal Structure and Property Rights			**1.9**	**1.2**	**1.8**	**7.0**	**1.7**
(a) Legal Security			2.2	0.9	1.9		
(b) Rule of Law			1.7	1.4	1.7	7.0	1.7
VI. International Exchange	**4.7**	**5.4**	**3.3**	**2.0**	**4.2**	**6.7**	**6.8**
(a) Taxes on International Trade							
i. Taxes as a Percentage of Exports and Imports	5.9 (6.1)	6.3 (5.6)	6.8 (4.8)	5.0 (7.5)	7.6 (3.6)	7.1 (4.4)	7.7 (3.4)
ii. Mean Tariff Rate			0.0 (50.0)	0.0 (50.0)	5.4 (23.0)	8.0 (10.2)	8.3 (8.4)
iii. Standard Deviation of Tariff Rates			0.0 (26.7)		0.0 (26.7)	7.0 (7.4)	6.2 (9.5)
(b) Size of Trade Sector	2.3 (36.3)	3.7 (45.3)	3.2 (47.1)	0.0 (24.9)	3.0 (43.5)	2.6 (44.8)	2.7 (45.5)
VII. Freedom of Exchange in Financial Markets	**6.3**	**7.0**	**7.5**	**7.5**	**7.5**	**8.2**	**7.8**
(a) Private Ownership of Banks	8.0 (80-90)	8.0 (85)	8.0 (89)	8.0 (90)	8.0 (91)	8.0 (91)	8.0 (91)
(b) Extension of Credit to Private Sector	9.5 (95.1)	8.2 (82.1)	9.6 (95.7)	9.4 (93.7)	9.5 (94.7)	9.2 (91.5)	9.2 (91.7)
(c) Avoidance of Negative Interest Rates			8.0	8.0	8.0	8.0	6.0
(d) Capital Transactions with Foreigners	2.0	5.0	5.0	5.0	5.0	8.0	8.0

GUINEA-BISSAU

	1970	1975	1980	1985	1990	1995	1999
Summary Ratings				3.3	3.4	3.8	3.3
Rank				101	105	114	120
Components of Economic Freedom							
I. Size of Government	**5.7**	**5.4**		**7.5**	**8.6**	**9.9**	**9.3**
(a) Government Consumption	5.7 (20.6)	5.4 (21.7)		7.5 (14.6)	8.6 (10.6)	9.9 (6.3)	9.3 (8.6)
(b) Transfers and Subsidies							
II. Structure of the Economy and Use of Markets					**0.4**	**3.0**	**3.0**
(a) Government Enterprises	2.0	2.0	2.0	2.0	0.0 (71.9)	0.0 (68.0)	0.0 (72.0)
(b) Price Controls					0.0	6.0	6.0
(c) Top Marginal Tax Rate							
(d) Conscription				3.0	3.0	3.0	3.0
III. Monetary Policy and Price Stability		**8.7**	**8.1**	**2.9**	**1.1**	**1.8**	**3.0**
(a) Annual Money Growth		8.8 (3.0)	8.6 (3.5)		0.0 (65.1)	1.0 (45.2)	0.0 (59.3)
(b) Inflation Variability				2.3 (19.2)	0.0 (28.6)	3.6 (16.1)	0.4 (24.0)
(c) Recent Inflation Rate		8.6 (7.1)	7.7 (11.6)	3.5 (32.3)	3.5 (32.3)	1.1 (44.7)	8.7 (6.5)
IV. Freedom to Use Alternative Currencies		**0.0**	**0.0**	**2.1**	**4.1**	**4.8**	**1.8**
(a) Ownership of Foreign Currency		0.0	0.0	0.0	0.0	0.0	0.0
(b) Black Market Exchange Rate				4.2 (29.0)	8.2 (9.0)	9.6 (2.0)	3.6 (32.0)
V. Legal Structure and Property Rights				**1.2**	**2.5**	**0.0**	**0.0**
(a) Legal Security				0.9	3.2		
(b) Rule of Law				1.4	1.7	0.0	0.0
VI. International Exchange				**4.0**			
(a) Taxes on International Trade							
i. Taxes as a Percentage of Exports and Imports				4.8 (7.7)			
ii. Mean Tariff Rate							
iii. Standard Deviation of Tariff Rates							
(b) Size of Trade Sector	0.0 (34.2)	0.0 (31.1)	0.4 (52.3)	2.4 (61.5)	0.8 (53.2)	0.0 (46.8)	0.0 (50.0)
VII. Freedom of Exchange in Financial Markets					**4.1**	**4.4**	**4.3**
(a) Private Ownership of Banks							
(b) Extension of Credit to Private Sector					7.7 (77.4)	8.9 (89.1)	10.0 (99.8)
(c) Avoidance of Negative Interest Rates					0.0	0.0	2.0
(d) Capital Transactions with Foreigners	0.0	0.0	0.0	0.0	5.0	5.0	2.0

GUYANA

Summary Ratings

	1970	1975	1980	1985	1990	1995	1999
Summary Ratings			4.2	3.8		5.2	6.4
Rank			79	94		89	64

Components of Economic Freedom

	1970	1975	1980	1985	1990	1995	1999
I. Size of Government	**5.3**	**3.2**	**2.8**	**5.0**	**7.1**	**5.6**	**5.5**
(a) Government Consumption	5.3 (21.8)	3.2 (29.3)	2.8 (30.4)	5.0 (23.1)	7.1 (15.8)	5.6 (20.8)	5.5 (21.3)
(b) Transfers and Subsidies							
II. Structure of the Economy and Use of Markets							**4.9**
(a) Government Enterprises	0.0	0.0	0.0	0.0	0.0	0.0	2.0
(b) Price Controls							
(c) Top Marginal Tax Rate							7.0 (33.3)
(d) Conscription				10.0	10.0	10.0	10.0
III. Monetary Policy and Price Stability	**9.3**	**5.8**	**7.7**	**6.8**	**2.6**	**4.1**	**8.5**
(a) Annual Money Growth	9.4 (2.8)	5.5 (22.7)	8.4 (7.9)	5.8 (20.8)	0.9 (45.5)	4.5 (27.6)	8.8 (5.9)
(b) Inflation Variability	9.2 (2.0)	5.0 (12.4)	7.1 (7.3)	7.7 (5.9)	0.0 (53.1)	0.0 (48.3)	7.6 (5.9)
(c) Recent Inflation Rate	9.4 (3.0)	7.1 (14.7)	7.6 (11.8)	7.1 (14.5)	6.9 (15.5)	7.8 (11.2)	9.1 (4.6)
IV. Freedom to Use Alternative Currencies	**8.2**	**0.0**	**0.0**	**0.0**	**4.1**	**7.1**	**7.0**
(a) Ownership of Foreign Currency		0.0	0.0	0.0	0.0	5.0	5.0
(b) Black Market Exchange Rate	8.2 (9.0)		0.0 (267.0)	0.0 (743.0)	8.2 (9.0)	9.2 (4.0)	9.0 (5.0)
V. Legal Structure and Property Rights			**1.5**	**1.3**	**3.1**	**4.1**	**5.8**
(a) Legal Security			3.0	1.2	4.6		
(b) Rule of Law			0.0	1.4	1.7	4.1	5.8
VI. International Exchange	**6.3**	**3.3**	**9.2**	**7.0**			
(a) Taxes on International Trade							
i. Taxes as a Percentage of Exports and Imports	5.8 (6.3)	0.0 (15.3)	8.8 (1.8)	7.4 (3.9)			
ii. Mean Tariff Rate				6.6 (17.0)			
iii. Standard Deviation of Tariff Rates							
(b) Size of Trade Sector	7.4 (113.5)	10.0 (149.8)	10.0 (174.9)	7.0 (110.0)	8.6 (142.6)	8.9 (164.5)	10.0 (203.3)
VII. Freedom of Exchange in Financial Markets						**4.9**	**6.9**
(a) Private Ownership of Banks							
(b) Extension of Credit to Private Sector	6.8 (68.1)	3.6 (36.4)	3.0 (30.2)	2.4 (23.8)	4.6 (46.1)	5.8 (57.9)	8.0 (80.0)
(c) Avoidance of Negative Interest Rates						4.0	8.0
(d) Capital Transactions with Foreigners	0.0	0.0	0.0	0.0	5.0	5.0	5.0

HAITI

Summary Ratings

	1970	1975	1980	1985	1990	1995	1999
Summary Ratings			5.2	5.5	4.7	5.6	5.4
Rank			52	49	72	75	89

Components of Economic Freedom

	1970	1975	1980	1985	1990	1995	1999
I. Size of Government	**8.7**	**8.9**	**8.5**	**8.2**	**9.5**	**9.8**	**9.8**
(a) Government Consumption	8.7 (10.3)	8.9 (9.7)	8.5 (11.0)	8.3 (11.9)	9.5 (7.6)	9.8 (6.8)	9.8 (6.7)
(b) Transfers and Subsidies				8.1 (7.3)			
II. Structure of the Economy and Use of Markets					**5.8**	**3.8**	**4.7**
(a) Government Enterprises	8.0 (17.9)	6.0 (13.1)	6.0 (19.0)	6.0 (32.7)	6.0 (42.0)	6.0	6.0
(b) Price Controls					2.0	0.0	2.0
(c) Top Marginal Tax Rate					9.0 (30)		
(d) Conscription	10.0	10.0	10.0	10.0	10.0	10.0	10.0
III. Monetary Policy and Price Stability	**9.0**	**7.8**	**6.5**	**8.3**	**7.8**	**5.0**	**6.8**
(a) Annual Money Growth	8.6 (7.2)	7.1 (14.6)	7.1 (14.3)	8.3 (8.6)	8.4 (8.1)	4.9 (25.4)	8.0 (9.9)
(b) Inflation Variability	9.3 (1.7)	7.7 (5.9)	6.7 (8.3)	8.7 (3.1)	7.0 (7.5)	6.3 (9.2)	3.9 (15.2)
(c) Recent Inflation Rate	9.1 (4.7)	8.8 (5.8)	5.7 (21.4)	7.9 (10.4)	7.9 (10.4)	3.8 (31.0)	8.3 (8.7)
IV. Freedom to Use Alternative Currencies	**10.0**	**7.5**	**8.0**	**5.0**	**5.0**	**5.3**	**5.7**
(a) Ownership of Foreign Currency	10.0	5.0	10.0	10.0	10.0	10.0	10.0
(b) Black Market Exchange Rate	10.0 (0.0)	10.0 (0.0)	6.0 (20.0)	0.0 (60.0)	0.0 (151.0)	0.6 (47.0)	1.4 (42.9)
V. Legal Structure and Property Rights			**1.5**	**2.5**	**1.1**	**7.0**	**1.7**
(a) Legal Security			3.0	3.5	0.5		
(b) Rule of Law			0.0	1.4	1.7	7.0	1.7
VI. International Exchange		**2.8**	**3.7**	**5.4**	**4.3**		
(a) Taxes on International Trade							
i. Mean Tariff Rate		3.8 (9.3)	3.4 (9.9)	4.7 (8.0)	5.5 (6.7)		
ii. Standard Deviation of Tariff Rates			4.5 (27.7)	7.7 (11.6)			
(b) Size of Trade Sector	0.0 (31.5)	0.9 (37.5)	2.7 (52.1)	2.2 (45.2)	1.9 (45.2)	0.0 (36.3)	0.0 (40.6)
VII. Freedom of Exchange in Financial Markets					**2.9**	**3.6**	**5.6**
(a) Private Ownership of Banks							
(b) Extension of Credit to Private Sector	9.2 (92.2)	9.2 (92.4)	10.0 (99.9)	9.7 (97.0)	9.9 (99.3)	10.0 (99.8)	9.8 (98.4)
(c) Avoidance of Negative Interest Rates					0.0	0.0	6.0
(d) Capital Transactions with Foreigners	0.0	0.0	0.0	0.0	0.0	2.0	2.0

HONDURAS

	1970	1975	1980	1985	1990	1995	1999
Summary Ratings		8.1	5.4	5.4	6.1	7.2	6.6
Rank		3	44	50	41	37	60

Components of Economic Freedom

	1970	1975	1980	1985	1990	1995	1999
I. Size of Government	8.9	8.9	7.3	8.5	8.3	8.5	7.8
(a) Government Consumption	7.8 (13.5)	7.7 (13.7)	7.3 (15.3)	7.4 (14.8)	7.0 (16.2)	8.0 (12.8)	7.8 (13.4)
(b) Transfers and Subsidies	10.0 (0.6)	10.0 (0.5)		9.5 (2.3)	9.5 (2.2)	9.0 (4.0)	
II. Structure of the Economy and Use of Markets		7.7	7.3	4.8	4.6	5.9	6.2
(a) Government Enterprises	6.0 (35.1)	6.0 (31.1)	6.0 (37.4)	6.0 (62.6)	6.0 (32.0)	6.0 (37.2)	6.0
(b) Price Controls				4.0	4.0	4.0	4.0
(c) Top Marginal Tax Rate		9.0 (27)	8.0 (40)	5.0 (46)	5.0 (46)	7.0 (40)	8.0 (30)
(d) Conscription	10.0	10.0	10.0	0.0	0.0	10.0	10.0
III. Monetary Policy and Price Stability	9.3	8.4	7.9	9.4	7.7	6.1	6.1
(a) Annual Money Growth	9.2 (4.1)	8.7 (6.7)	7.5 (12.7)	9.7 (1.5)	6.9 (15.4)	6.6 (17.1)	5.3 (23.6)
(b) Inflation Variability	9.6 (1.0)	7.8 (5.6)	8.8 (3.0)	9.4 (1.5)	7.3 (6.6)	6.9 (7.8)	5.4 (11.5)
(c) Recent Inflation Rate	9.1 (4.5)	8.7 (6.4)	7.3 (13.3)	9.0 (5.3)	9.0 (5.3)	4.7 (26.3)	7.7 (11.6)
IV. Freedom to Use Alternative Currencies	7.0	10.0	8.0	5.0	10.0	9.9	10.0
(a) Ownership of Foreign Currency	10.0	10.0	10.0	10.0	10.0	10.0	10.0
(b) Black Market Exchange Rate	4.0 (30.0)	10.0 (0.0)	6.0 (20.0)	0.0 (65.0)	10.0 (0.0)	9.8 (1.0)	10.0 (0.0)
V. Legal Structure and Property Rights				2.7	3.3	7.0	1.7
(a) Legal Security				2.2	3.2		
(b) Rule of Law				3.1	3.3	7.0	1.7
VI. International Exchange	5.5	6.1	4.0		5.9	7.4	7.6
(a) Taxes on International Trade							
i. Taxes as a Percentage of Exports and Imports	5.7 (6.4)	6.5 (5.3)	5.5 (6.7)		6.0 (20.0)	8.0 (10.1)	8.1 (2.9)
ii. Mean Tariff Rate			1.8 (41.0)				8.4 (7.8)
iii. Standard Deviation of Tariff Rates						7.4 (6.5)	6.8 (8.0)
(b) Size of Trade Sector	4.9 (62.0)	5.5 (70.4)	5.7 (30.3)	4.1 (54.2)	5.7 (76.1)	6.3 (91.3)	6.7 (97.9)
VII. Freedom of Exchange in Financial Markets			3.7	4.9	4.9	5.7	7.5
(a) Private Ownership of Banks							
(b) Extension of Credit to Private Sector	9.0 (90.3)	8.7 (86.6)	8.2 (31.9)	7.4 (74.0)	7.5 (75.3)	8.6 (85.9)	10.0 (99.4)
(c) Avoidance of Negative Interest Rates		4.0	4.0	8.0	8.0	4.0	8.0
(d) Capital Transactions with Foreigners	2.0	2.0	0.0	0.0	0.0	5.0	5.0

HONG KONG

Summary Ratings	1970	1975	1980	1985	1990	1995	1999
Summary Ratings	9.5	9.4	9.7	9.3	9.2	9.7	9.4
Rank	1	1	1	1	1	1	1

Components of Economic Freedom	1970	1975	1980	1985	1990	1995	1999
I. Size of Government	**8.9**	**9.3**	**9.5**	**9.3**	**9.1**	**8.9**	**7.8**
(a) Government Consumption	8.9 (9.9)	8.8 (9.9)	9.0 (9.3)	8.7 (10.6)	8.4 (11.6)	8.0 (12.7)	7.8 (13.5)
(b) Transfers and Subsidies		9.8 (1.1)	10.0 (0.6)	9.9 (0.9)	9.9 (0.9)	9.8 (1.1)	
II. Structure of the Economy and Use of Markets	**10.0**	**10.0**	**10.0**	**9.6**	**9.7**	**9.7**	**9.7**
(a) Government Enterprises	10.0 (9.1)	10.0 (16.4)	10.0 (16.5)	10.0 (17.9)	10.0 (13.2)	10.0 (14.0)	10.0
(b) Price Controls					10.0	9.0	9.0
(c) Top Marginal Tax Rate	10.0 (15)	10.0 (15)	10.0 (15)	9.0 (25)	9.0 (25)	10.0 (20)	10.0
(d) Conscription	10.0	10.0	10.0	10.0	10.0	10.0	10.0
III. Monetary Policy and Price Stability	**8.3**	**8.9**	**8.0**	**9.1**	**8.7**	**9.1**	**9.0**
(a) Annual Money Growth		8.9 (5.5)	9.0 (4.8)	9.5 (2.6)	8.4 (8.2)	8.8 (6.1)	9.5 (-2.5)
(b) Inflation Variability	8.3 (4.4)	8.7 (3.3)	8.0 (5.0)	9.0 (2.6)	8.9 (2.9)	9.0 (2.6)	8.3 (4.2)
(c) Recent Inflation Rate	8.3 (8.6)	9.1 (4.6)	7.0 (15.0)	8.9 (5.7)	8.9 (5.7)	9.5 (2.6)	9.2 (-4.0)
IV. Freedom to Use Alternative Currencies	**10.0**	**10.0**	**10.0**	**10.0**	**10.0**	**10.0**	**10.0**
(a) Ownership of Foreign Currency	10.0	10.0	10.0	10.0	10.0	10.0	10.0
(b) Black Market Exchange Rate	10.0 (0.0)	10.0 (0.0)	10.0 (0.0)	10.0 (0.0)	10.0 (0.0)	10.0 (0.0)	10.0 (0.0)
V. Legal Structure and Property Rights	**9.1**	**7.6**	**9.7**	**7.2**	**6.7**	**10.0**	**8.8**
(a) Legal Security	9.1	7.6	9.4	6.1	6.6		9.6
(b) Rule of Law			10.0	8.2	6.7	10.0	7.9
VI. International Exchange	**9.9**	**9.6**	**9.6**	**9.8**	**9.9**	**9.9**	**9.9**
(a) Taxes on International Trade							
i. Taxes as a Percentage of Exports and Imports	10.0 (0.0)	9.5 (0.7)	9.7 (0.5)	9.6 (0.6)	9.7 (0.4)	9.8 (0.3)	9.8 (0.3)
ii. Mean Tariff Rate		10.0 (0.0)	10.0 (0.0)	10.0 (0.0)	10.0 (0.0)	10.0 (0.0)	10.0 (0.0)
iii. Standard Deviation of Tariff Rates					10.0 (0.0)	10.0 (0.0)	10.0 (0.0)
(b) Size of Trade Sector	9.8 (181.5)	8.9 (163.7)	8.8 (180.6)	10.0 (208.6)	10.0 (260.1)	10.0 (302.9)	10.0 (249.8)
VII. Freedom of Exchange in Financial Markets	**10.0**	**10.0**	**10.0**	**10.0**	**10.0**	**9.9**	**9.8**
(a) Private Ownership of Banks	10.0 (100)	10.0 (100)	10.0 (100)	10.0 (100)	10.0 (100)	10.0 (100)	10.0 (100)
(b) Extension of Credit to Private Sector					9.8 (98.1)	9.7 (96.7)	9.2 (92.2)
(c) Avoidance of Negative Interest Rates		10.0	10.0	10.0	10.0	10.0	10.0
(d) Capital Transactions with Foreigners	5.0	10.0	10.0	10.0	10.0	10.0	10.0

HUNGARY

Summary Ratings

	1970	1975	1980	1985	1990	1995	1999
Summary Ratings			4.5	4.8	4.7	6.9	7.1
Rank			71	71	72	46	43

Components of Economic Freedom

	1970	1975	1980	1985	1990	1995	1999
I. Size of Government	**7.3**	**7.4**	**7.5**	**4.4**	**4.9**	**5.5**	**6.1**
(a) Government Consumption	7.3 (15.1)	7.4 (15.0)	7.5 (14.4)	7.7 (13.9)	7.4 (14.7)	7.6 (14.2)	7.5 (14.4)
(b) Transfers and Subsidies				1.1 (33.3)	2.3 (28.7)	3.3 (25.0)	4.7 (20.0)
II. Structure of the Economy and Use of Markets					**1.3**	**5.3**	**5.5**
(a) Government Enterprises	0.0 (93.7)	0.0 (93.8)	0.0 (92.6)	0.0 (83.5)	0.0 (68.5)	4.0	4.0
(b) Price Controls						8.0	8.0
(c) Top Marginal Tax Rate					3.0 (50)	4.0 (44)	5.0 (40)
(d) Conscription	0.0	0.0	0.0	0.0	1.0	3.0	3.0
III. Monetary Policy and Price Stability	**9.2**	**9.1**	**8.6**	**9.1**	**7.5**	**6.4**	**7.0**
(a) Annual Money Growth			8.3	8.7 (6.7)	6.9 (15.5)	6.9 (15.7)	6.9 (15.5)
(b) Inflation Variability	9.3 (1.8)	9.0 (2.5)	8.9 (2.8)	9.8 (0.5)	6.9 (7.8)	7.6 (5.9)	6.0 (9.9)
(c) Recent Inflation Rate	9.0 (4.9)	9.1 (4.4)	8.8 (6.0)	8.8 (5.9)	8.8 (5.9)	4.7 (26.7)	7.9 (10.3)
IV. Freedom to Use Alternative Currencies	**0.0**	**0.0**	**0.0**	**0.0**	**2.8**	**7.5**	**7.5**
(a) Ownership of Foreign Currency	0.0	0.0	0.0	0.0	0.0	5.0	5.0
(b) Black Market Exchange Rate	0.0 (342.0)	0.0 (317.0)	0.0 (244.0)	0.0 (210.0)	5.6 (22.0)	10.0 (0.0)	10.0 (0.0)
V. Legal Structure and Property Rights				**7.0**	**8.5**	**10.0**	**9.1**
(a) Legal Security				7.4	8.6		8.2
(b) Rule of Law				8.2	8.3	10.0	10.0
VI. International Exchange			**6.3**	**7.0**	**5.7**	**6.4**	**6.5**
(a) Taxes on International Trade							
i. Taxes as a Percentage of Exports and Imports			6.7 (5.0)	7.5 (3.7)	6.6 (5.1)	6.1 (5.9)	9.2 (1.3)
ii. Mean Tariff Rate					5.6 (11.0)	7.8 (11.0)	7.1 (14.3)
iii. Standard Deviation of Tariff Rates						6.1 (9.7)	3.2 (17.0)
(b) Size of Trade Sector	7.3 (62.6)	7.0 (90.4)	5.5 (30.3)	6.1 (82.3)	4.0 (59.7)	4.8 (75.8)	6.5 (102.2)
VII. Freedom of Exchange in Financial Markets			**2.5**	**1.5**	**3.1**	**6.3**	**7.5**
(a) Private Ownership of Banks	0.0 (0-10)	0.0 (0-10)	0.0 (0-10)	0.0 (0-10)	2.0 (12)	8.0 (80)	8.0 (91)
(b) Extension of Credit to Private Sector			4.7 (46.8)	5.3 (53.2)	5.2 (52.0)	6.1 (61.0)	7.2 (72.0)
(c) Avoidance of Negative Interest Rates			6.0		6.0	6.0	10.0
(d) Capital Transactions with Foreigners	0.0	0.0	0.0	0.0	0.0	5.0	5.0

ICELAND

Summary Ratings	1970	1975	1980	1985	1990	1995	1999
Summary Ratings	6.0	3.8	5.3	5.7	7.3	7.9	8.0
Rank	35	67	49	42	22	18	15

Components of Economic Freedom

	1970	1975	1980	1985	1990	1995	1999
I. Size of Government	**6.7**	**6.4**	**6.2**	**6.2**	**6.1**	**5.9**	**6.0**
(a) Government Consumption	6.7 (17.3)	5.3 (21.9)	5.2 (22.2)	5.4 (21.5)	4.7 (23.9)	4.2 (25.6)	4.3 (25.4)
(b) Transfers and Subsidies		7.4 (9.9)	7.2 (10.6)	6.9 (11.7)	7.4 (10.1)	7.7 (9.1)	7.7 (9.0)
II. Structure of the Economy and Use of Markets			**5.3**	**5.6**	**6.6**	**6.2**	**6.8**
(a) Government Enterprises	8.0 (20.2)	8.0 (17.6)	8.0 (15.3)	8.0 (16.1)	7.0 (22.2)	7.0 (24.8)	7.0
(b) Price Controls				6.0	6.0	6.0	8.0
(c) Top Marginal Tax Rate			0.0 (63)	1.0 (56)	5.0 (40)	4.0 (47)	4.0 (42)
(d) Conscription	10.0	10.0	10.0	10.0	10.0	10.0	10.0
III. Monetary Policy and Price Stability	**7.6**	**4.1**	**3.2**	**2.7**	**5.7**	**9.0**	**8.8**
(a) Annual Money Growth	8.5 (7.4)	5.0 (24.8)	2.6 (37.1)	1.6 (41.8)	4.6 (26.9)	8.5 (7.3)	7.8 (11.1)
(b) Inflation Variability	7.6 (6.1)	5.5 (11.2)	6.9 (7.7)	2.8 (18.0)	8.8 (3.0)	9.2 (2.1)	9.4 (1.4)
(c) Recent Inflation Rate	6.7 (16.4)	1.6 (41.9)	0.0 (52.5)	3.7 (31.3)	3.7 (31.3)	9.5 (2.8)	9.4 (3.2)
IV. Freedom to Use Alternative Currencies	**4.5**	**0.0**	**4.1**	**3.4**	**10.0**	**10.0**	**10.0**
(a) Ownership of Foreign Currency	0.0	0.0	0.0	0.0	10.0	10.0	10.0
(b) Black Market Exchange Rate	9.0 (5.0)	0.0 (106.0)	8.2 (9.0)	6.8 (16.0)	10.0 (0.0)	10.0 (0.0)	10.0 (0.0)
V. Legal Structure and Property Rights	**8.3**	**5.3**	**7.9**	**9.4**	**10.0**	**10.0**	**9.4**
(a) Legal Security	8.3	5.3	5.8	8.7	10.0		8.8
(b) Rule of Law			10.0	10.0	10.0	10.0	10.0
VI. International Exchange	**3.9**	**4.0**	**5.8**	**6.9**	**6.9**	**7.5**	**7.1**
(a) Taxes on International Trade							
i. Taxes as a Percentage of Exports and Imports	3.3 (10.0)	4.6 (8.1)	5.7 (6.5)	6.9 (4.6)	7.3 (4.0)	9.6 (0.6)	9.7 (0.5)
ii. Mean Tariff Rate			8.1 (9.6)	8.7 (6.7)	9.2 (3.8)	9.3 (3.7)	9.6 (1.9)
iii. Standard Deviation of Tariff Rates					7.0 (7.5)	7.1 (7.3)	4.8 (13.0)
(b) Size of Trade Sector	5.1 (86.8)	2.7 (73.7)	1.3 (69.8)	3.0 (80.6)	1.1 (67.0)	0.3 (67.5)	1.1 (73.9)
VII. Freedom of Exchange in Financial Markets		**3.6**	**4.1**	**4.1**	**4.9**	**6.4**	**7.6**
(a) Private Ownership of Banks		2.0 (23)	2.0 (23)	2.0 (26)	2.0 (28)	2.0 (27)	5.0 (46)
(b) Extension of Credit to Private Sector	9.2 (92.0)	9.5 (94.8)	9.6 (96.0)	9.7 (96.8)	8.8 (88.2)	9.4 (94.1)	9.8 (98.4)
(c) Avoidance of Negative Interest Rates		2.0	4.0	4.0	8.0	10.0	8.0
(d) Capital Transactions with Foreigners	0.0	2.0	2.0	2.0	2.0	5.0	8.0

INDIA

	1970	1975	1980	1985	1990	1995	1999
Summary Ratings	4.1	3.4	4.4	4.0	4.0	4.5	5.3
Rank	51	71	75	90	93	103	92

Components of Economic Freedom

	1970	1975	1980	1985	1990	1995	1999
I. Size of Government	**8.7**	**8.8**	**8.5**	**8.0**	**7.8**	**8.0**	**7.7**
(a) Government Consumption	8.7 (10.5)	8.4 (11.4)	8.3 (11.7)	7.6 (14.1)	7.2 (15.7)	7.3 (15.2)	7.0 (16.2)
(b) Transfers and Subsidies		9.1 (3.8)	8.7 (5.4)	8.4 (6.5)	8.4 (6.5)	8.7 (5.2)	8.4 (6.4)
II. Structure of the Economy and Use of Markets	**2.3**	**1.3**	**1.7**	**1.3**	**2.4**	**4.1**	**5.5**
(a) Government Enterprises	2.0 (38.4)	0.0 (41.0)	0.0 (46.7)	0.0 (49.5)	0.0 (42.3)	2.0 (31.4)	4.0 (27.3)
(b) Price Controls				0.0	3.0	4.0	4.0
(c) Top Marginal Tax Rate	0.0 (85)	0.0 (77)	1.0 (60)	0.0 (62)	2.0 (53)	5.0 (40)	8.0 (30)
(d) Conscription	10.0	10.0	10.0	10.0	10.0	10.0	10.0
III. Monetary Policy and Price Stability	**8.9**	**8.3**	**8.1**	**8.6**	**8.6**	**8.4**	**9.2**
(a) Annual Money Growth	8.9 (5.4)	8.2 (8.9)	8.4 (7.9)	7.8 (10.8)	8.0 (9.8)	7.7 (11.4)	9.2 (-3.8)
(b) Inflation Variability	8.2 (4.6)	7.1 (7.2)	8.1 (4.8)	9.6 (1.1)	9.4 (1.5)	9.1 (2.3)	9.3 (1.7)
(c) Recent Inflation Rate	9.7 (1.7)	9.7 (-1.4)	7.7 (11.5)	8.5 (7.5)	8.5 (7.5)	8.4 (8.2)	9.1 (4.7)
IV. Freedom to Use Alternative Currencies	**0.0**	**4.1**	**4.5**	**3.6**	**4.0**	**4.2**	**5.0**
(a) Ownership of Foreign Currency	0.0	0.0	0.0	0.0	0.0	0.0	0.0
(b) Black Market Exchange Rate	0.0 (67.0)	8.2 (9.0)	9.0 (5.0)	7.2 (14.0)	8.0 (10.0)	8.4 (8.0)	10.0 (0.0)
V. Legal Structure and Property Rights	**4.1**	**1.7**	**6.4**	**5.2**	**4.5**	**4.1**	**4.5**
(a) Legal Security	4.1	1.7	4.6	7.4	7.3		7.4
(b) Rule of Law			8.3	3.1	1.7	4.1	1.7
VI. International Exchange		**1.0**	**0.7**	**0.7**	**0.6**	**1.6**	**4.0**
(a) Taxes on International Trade							
i. Taxes as a Percentage of Exports and Imports		0.1 (14.8)	0.0 (15.5)	0.0 (24.2)	0.0 (21.1)	2.2 (11.8)	2.8 (10.8)
ii. Mean Tariff Rate			0.0 (74.3)	0.0 (98.8)	0.0 (79.2)	0.0 (55.2)	3.4 (32.9)
iii. Standard Deviation of Tariff Rates					0.0 (45.2)	0.6 (23.6)	4.9 (12.7)
(b) Size of Trade Sector	0.0 (8.2)	2.6 (12.8)	3.7 (16.6)	3.5 (15.0)	4.4 (18.3)	6.1 (27.7)	5.4 (24.8)
VII. Freedom of Exchange in Financial Markets	**3.6**	**2.7**	**3.6**	**3.6**	**3.5**	**4.0**	**3.8**
(a) Private Ownership of Banks	0.0 (0-10)	0.0 (0-10)	0.0 (0-10)	0.0 (0-10)	0.0 (5-10)	2.0 (10-15)	2.0 (10-15)
(b) Extension of Credit to Private Sector	7.9 (79.1)	8.0 (79.7)	7.7 (76.6)	7.8 (78.3)	7.4 (73.9)	6.8 (67.8)	6.3 (63.0)
(c) Avoidance of Negative Interest Rates	8.0	4.0	8.0	8.0	8.0	8.0	8.0
(d) Capital Transactions with Foreigners	0.0	0.0	0.0	0.0	0.0	0.0	0.0

INDONESIA

Summary Ratings	1970	1975	1980	1985	1990	1995	1999
Rating	4.9	5.0	5.2	6.2	6.7	6.8	6.2
Rank	43	47	52	31	33	48	72

Components of Economic Freedom

	1970		1975		1980		1985		1990		1995		1999	
I. Size of Government	**9.2**		**9.0**		**8.0**		**8.2**		**8.8**		**9.2**		**9.3**	
(a) Government Consumption	9.0	(9.3)	8.2	(12.2)	6.8	(16.7)	7.0	(16.4)	7.9	(13.0)	8.4	(11.3)	9.4	(8.1)
(b) Transfers and Subsidies	9.4	(2.7)	9.7	(1.5)	9.2	(3.3)	9.5	(2.5)	9.6	(2.0)	9.9	(0.9)	9.1	(3.6)
II. Structure of the Economy and Use of Markets			**3.9**		**2.5**		**3.6**		**5.4**		**5.3**		**5.0**	
(a) Government Enterprises	4.0	(40.4)	4.0	(39.4)	2.0	(49.5)	2.0	(43.0)	4.0	(32.5)	7.0	(20.7)	7.0	(23.0)
(b) Price Controls									7.0		3.0		2.0	
(c) Top Marginal Tax Rate			4.0	(48)	3.0	(50)	7.0	(35)	7.0	(35)	8.0	(30)	8.0	(30)
(d) Conscription	3.0		3.0		3.0		0.0		0.0		0.0		0.0	
III. Monetary Policy and Price Stability	**2.4**		**4.9**		**5.0**		**8.7**		**8.2**		**8.7**		**6.5**	
(a) Annual Money Growth	0.0	(143.9)	3.6	(32.0)	5.2	(24.1)	8.3	(8.3)	7.5	(12.3)	8.6	(7.2)	6.9	(15.5)
(b) Inflation Variability	0.0	(449.9)	3.6	(16.1)	6.1	(9.8)	8.6	(3.5)	7.9	(5.4)	9.4	(1.5)	6.6	(8.5)
(c) Recent Inflation Rate	7.3	(13.6)	7.8	(11.2)	3.8	(31.0)	9.1	(4.3)	9.1	(4.3)	8.0	(9.9)	5.9	(20.5)
IV. Freedom to Use Alternative Currencies	**8.3**		**9.3**		**9.8**		**9.3**		**10.0**		**10.0**		**8.9**	
(a) Ownership of Foreign Currency	10.0		10.0		10.0		10.0		10.0		10.0		10.0	
(b) Black Market Exchange Rate	6.6	(17.0)	8.6	(7.0)	9.6	(2.0)	8.6	(7.0)	10.0	(0.0)	10.0	(0.0)	7.8	(11.1)
V. Legal Structure and Property Rights	**4.5**		**3.5**		**3.1**		**4.6**		**5.0**		**4.1**		**3.9**	
(a) Legal Security	4.5		3.5		4.6		6.1		6.6				6.1	
(b) Rule of Law					1.7		3.1		3.3		4.1		1.7	
VI. International Exchange	**5.5**		**5.5**		**6.6**		**7.6**		**6.2**		**6.6**		**7.3**	
(a) Taxes on International Trade														
i. Taxes as a Percentage of Exports and Imports	5.4	(6.9)	7.3	(4.0)	8.1	(2.9)	8.9	(1.6)	8.4	(2.4)	9.1	(1.3)	9.5	(0.7)
ii. Mean Tariff Rate			2.3	(38.5)	4.2	(29.0)	6.4	(18.1)	5.9	(20.3)	6.6	(17.0)	7.6	(11.9)
iii. Standard Deviation of Tariff Rates									3.3	(16.7)	3.6	(16.1)	3.4	(16.6)
(b) Size of Trade Sector	5.8	(28.4)	8.3	(45.0)	8.9	(54.4)	7.7	(43.5)	8.3	(49.9)	7.6	(51.7)	10.0	(73.3)
VII. Freedom of Exchange in Financial Markets	**0.6**		**0.6**		**2.1**		**3.1**		**5.0**		**5.8**		**4.3**	
(a) Private Ownership of Banks	0.0	(0-10)	0.0	(0-10)	0.0	(0-10)	2.0	(10-15)	2.0	(15-25)	5.0	(40-60)	5.0	(40-60)
(b) Extension of Credit to Private Sector					7.5	(75.2)	7.6	(75.7)	9.2	(92.4)	9.4	(93.9)	4.4	(44.2)
(c) Avoidance of Negative Interest Rates	2.0		2.0		2.0		4.0		10.0		10.0		8.0	
(d) Capital Transactions with Foreigners	0.0		0.0		0.0		0.0		0.0		0.0		0.0	

IRAN

Summary Ratings	1970	1975	1980	1985	1990	1995	1999
Summary Ratings	6.3	6.2	3.4	3.4	4.2	4.3	4.7
Rank	31	22	98	99	90	105	102

Components of Economic Freedom

	1970	1975	1980	1985	1990	1995	1999
I. Size of Government	**9.0**	**4.5**	**5.8**	**7.7**	**8.1**	**7.7**	**8.1**
(a) Government Consumption		1.2 (35.9)	3.4 (28.3)	6.0 (19.6)	7.3 (15.2)	6.1 (19.2)	6.7 (17.1)
(b) Transfers and Subsidies	9.0 (4.3)	7.7 (8.9)	8.2 (7.0)	9.3 (3.0)	8.9 (4.4)	9.3 (3.1)	9.4 (2.7)
II. Structure of the Economy and Use of Markets		**5.0**	**5.0**	**1.0**	**1.3**	**2.3**	**2.1**
(a) Government Enterprises	4.0	4.0	2.0 (47.6)	2.0 (40.0)	2.0 (42.2)	2.0 (44.1)	2.0 (44.5)
(b) Price Controls					2.0	2.0	2.0
(c) Top Marginal Tax Rate	8.0	8.0 (40)		0.0 (90)	0.0 (75)	4.0 (54)	3.0 (54)
(d) Conscription	0.0	0.0	3.0	0.0	0.0	0.0	0.0
III. Monetary Policy and Price Stability	**9.6**	**7.3**	**5.8**	**7.4**	**8.2**	**4.7**	**4.7**
(a) Annual Money Growth	9.6 (1.8)	4.7 (26.6)	4.6 (26.8)	5.9 (20.3)	6.9 (15.3)	4.7 (26.4)	5.0 (25.0)
(b) Inflation Variability	9.6 (1.1)	8.5 (3.8)	7.7 (5.9)	7.4 (6.5)	8.7 (3.2)	7.3 (6.7)	3.2 (16.9)
(c) Recent Inflation Rate	9.7 (1.7)	8.8 (5.8)	5.3 (23.4)	9.1 (4.7)	9.1 (4.7)	2.1 (39.5)	5.8 (21.0)
IV. Freedom to Use Alternative Currencies	**7.0**	**7.3**	**5.0**	**5.0**	**5.0**	**0.0**	**5.0**
(a) Ownership of Foreign Currency	5.0	5.0	10.0	10.0	10.0	0.0	10.0
(b) Black Market Exchange Rate	9.0 (5.0)	9.6 (2.0)	0.0 (-64.0)	0.0 (533.0)	0.0 (2197.0)	0.0 (115.0)	0.0 (150.0)
V. Legal Structure and Property Rights	**4.9**	**4.5**	**0.9**	**1.5**	**1.5**	**7.0**	**7.9**
(a) Legal Security	4.9	4.5	0.0	0.0	1.2		
(b) Rule of Law			1.7	3.1	1.7	7.0	7.9
VI. International Exchange	**3.7**	**8.4**	**3.1**	**2.6**	**6.2**	**6.7**	**3.5**
(a) Taxes on International Trade							
i. Taxes as a Percentage of Exports and Imports	2.4 (11.4)	7.6 (3.6)	0.0 (17.0)	0.5 (14.2)	6.4 (5.4)	8.7 (1.9)	3.9 (9.2)
ii. Mean Tariff Rate			5.9 (20.7)	5.9 (20.7)	5.9 (20.7)	5.9 (20.7)	
iii. Standard Deviation of Tariff Rates							
(b) Size of Trade Sector	6.2 (40.5)	10.0 (76.0)	3.6 (29.7)	0.0 (16.0)	6.3 (45.5)	4.5 (36.4)	2.8 (28.0)
VII. Freedom of Exchange in Financial Markets			**1.7**	**1.5**	**1.8**	**2.0**	**2.6**
(a) Private Ownership of Banks			0.0 (0-5)	0.0 (0-5)	0.0 (0)	0.0 (0-5)	0.0 (0-5)
(b) Extension of Credit to Private Sector	9.7 (97.2)	8.3 (83.3)	8.0 (80.2)	7.2 (71.8)	8.7 (86.6)	9.5 (94.7)	9.2 (92.0)
(c) Avoidance of Negative Interest Rates			0.0	0.0	0.0	0.0	0.0
(d) Capital Transactions with Foreigners	5.0	5.0	0.0	0.0	0.0	0.0	0.0

IRELAND

Summary Ratings	1970	1975	1980	1985	1990	1995	1999
Summary Ratings	6.8	6.1	6.6	6.7	7.3	8.6	8.5
Rank	23	27	19	21	22	6	6

Components of Economic Freedom

	1970	1975	1980	1985	1990	1995	1999
I. Size of Government	**6.7**	**5.3**	**5.3**	**5.0**	**5.6**	**5.3**	**5.4**
(a) Government Consumption	6.9 (16.5)	5.5 (21.3)	5.3 (22.0)	5.2 (22.5)	5.8 (20.3)	5.4 (21.5)	5.7 (20.6)
(b) Transfers and Subsidies	6.5 (13.2)	5.1 (18.3)	5.4 (17.5)	4.9 (19.3)	5.4 (17.3)	5.1 (18.5)	5.0 (18.8)
II. Structure of the Economy and Use of Markets		**4.3**	**5.1**	**4.8**	**6.7**	**7.9**	**7.9**
(a) Government Enterprises	6.0 (27.3)	6.0 (30.0)	7.0 (24.6)	7.0 (24.7)	10.0 (11.1)	10.0 (14.3)	10.0 (14.2)
(b) Price Controls					7.0	9.0	9.0
(c) Top Marginal Tax Rate		0.0 (80)	1.0 (60)	0.0 (65)	1.0 (58)	3.0 (48)	3.0 (46)
(d) Conscription		10.0	10.0	10.0	10.0	10.0	10.0
III. Monetary Policy and Price Stability	**8.8**	**7.5**	**7.7**	**8.8**	**9.0**	**9.5**	**9.2**
(a) Annual Money Growth	9.5 (2.6)	8.4 (7.8)	7.4 (12.9)	9.5 (2.8)	9.1 (4.3)	9.1 (4.6)	9.8 (1.2)
(b) Inflation Variability	8.9 (2.7)	8.1 (4.7)	8.6 (3.5)	8.1 (4.8)	9.0 (2.6)	9.5 (1.3)	8.2 (4.5)
(c) Recent Inflation Rate	8.1 (9.7)	6.0 (20.1)	7.1 (14.7)	9.0 (5.2)	9.0 (5.2)	9.9 (0.4)	9.7 (1.6)
IV. Freedom to Use Alternative Currencies	**5.0**	**5.0**	**5.0**	**4.7**	**4.9**	**10.0**	**10.0**
(a) Ownership of Foreign Currency	0.0	0.0	0.0	0.0	0.0	10.0	10.0
(b) Black Market Exchange Rate	10.0 (0.0)	10.0 (0.0)	10.0 (0.0)	9.4 (3.0)	9.8 (1.0)	10.0 (0.0)	10.0 (0.0)
V. Legal Structure and Property Rights	**10.0**	**7.3**	**8.2**	**7.6**	**9.2**	**10.0**	**9.7**
(a) Legal Security	10.0	7.3	8.2	8.7	10.0		9.4
(b) Rule of Law			8.3	6.6	8.3	10.0	10.0
VI. International Exchange	**5.6**	**7.1**	**7.6**	**8.0**	**7.7**	**8.2**	**8.6**
(a) Taxes on International Trade							
i. Taxes as a Percentage of Exports and Imports	5.4 (6.9)	6.8 (4.8)	7.7 (3.5)	8.0 (3.0)	8.0 (3.0)	8.8 (1.8)	9.7 (0.5)
ii. Mean Tariff Rate		8.1 (9.4)	8.2 (8.8)	8.5 (7.5)	8.5 (7.4)	8.7 (6.7)	8.6 (6.9)
iii. Standard Deviation of Tariff Rates					7.1 (7.2)	7.6 (5.9)	7.6 (5.9)
(b) Size of Trade Sector	6.1 (78.9)	5.5 (88.0)	6.0 (108.4)	6.9 (114.3)	6.4 (111.3)	6.9 (134.1)	8.2 (157.0)
VII. Freedom of Exchange in Financial Markets	**5.3**	**6.0**	**6.7**	**7.5**	**7.7**	**8.6**	**8.3**
(a) Private Ownership of Banks		8.0 (95)	8.0 (91)	8.0 (87)	8.0 (90)	8.0 (93)	8.0 (93)
(b) Extension of Credit to Private Sector	7.3 (73.1)	6.9 (69.1)	8.0 (80.3)	7.4 (73.6)	8.3 (83.1)	8.6 (86.3)	9.4 (93.5)
(c) Avoidance of Negative Interest Rates	4.0	4.0	6.0	10.0	10.0	10.0	8.0
(d) Capital Transactions with Foreigners	5.0	5.0	5.0	5.0	5.0	8.0	8.0

ISRAEL

Summary Ratings	1970	1975	1980	1985	1990	1995	1999
	4.5	4.1	3.6	4.3	4.6	5.9	6.7
Rank	46	62	93	82	80	68	56

Components of Economic Freedom

	1970	1975	1980	1985	1990	1995	1999
I. Size of Government	**4.0**	**2.7**	**2.2**	**2.6**	**3.8**	**3.7**	**3.2**
(a) Government Consumption	0.8 (37.3)	0.0 (42.3)	0.0 (43.2)	0.4 (38.5)	2.1 (32.9)	2.2 (32.4)	2.1 (33.0)
(b) Transfers and Subsidies	7.2 (10.8)	5.3 (17.7)	4.5 (20.8)	4.8 (19.7)	5.6 (16.7)	5.1 (18.6)	4.4 (21.0)
II. Structure of the Economy and Use of Markets			**1.4**	**2.1**	**2.5**	**3.3**	**3.3**
(a) Government Enterprises	2.0	2.0	2.0	2.0	2.0	2.0	2.0
(b) Price Controls						5.0	5.0
(c) Top Marginal Tax Rate			1.0 (66)	3.0 (60)	4.0 (51)	4.0 (50)	4.0 (50)
(d) Conscription	0.0	0.0	0.0	0.0	0.0	0.0	0.0
III. Monetary Policy and Price Stability	**8.5**	**5.1**	**0.7**	**0.0**	**2.3**	**8.1**	**8.6**
(a) Annual Money Growth	9.3 (3.4)	6.4 (18.0)	2.0 (40.0)	0.0 (169.3)	1.5 (42.6)	7.3 (13.5)	8.3 (8.3)
(b) Inflation Variability	8.1 (4.9)	5.9 (10.2)	0.0 (37.4)	0.0 (103.7)	5.3 (11.7)	8.6 (3.5)	8.4 (3.9)
(c) Recent Inflation Rate	8.1 (9.6)	3.0 (35.2)	0.0 (134.7)	0.0 (260.0)	0.0 (260.0)	8.3 (8.4)	9.0 (5.2)
IV. Freedom to Use Alternative Currencies	**2.0**	**2.5**	**7.4**	**6.8**	**7.1**	**7.5**	**7.5**
(a) Ownership of Foreign Currency	0.0	5.0	5.0	5.0	5.0	5.0	5.0
(b) Black Market Exchange Rate	4.0 (30.0)	0.0 (60.0)	9.8 (1.0)	8.6 (7.0)	9.2 (4.0)	10.0 (0.0)	10.0 (0.0)
V. Legal Structure and Property Rights	**7.4**	**7.0**	**4.0**	**7.8**	**4.5**	**7.0**	**8.6**
(a) Legal Security	7.4	7.0	6.4	7.4	7.3		9.4
(b) Rule of Law			1.7	8.2	1.7	7.0	7.9
VI. International Exchange	**4.3**	**4.7**	**6.1**	**7.2**	**7.6**	**7.3**	**8.6**
(a) Taxes on International Trade							
i. Taxes as a Percentage of Exports and Imports	4.1 (8.9)	4.7 (8.0)	6.6 (5.1)	8.1 (2.9)	9.4 (0.9)	9.8 (0.2)	9.8 (0.2)
ii. Mean Tariff Rate							9.6 (2.0)
iii. Standard Deviation of Tariff Rates						5.7 (10.8)	
(b) Size of Trade Sector	4.8 (70.0)	4.9 (76.5)	5.2 (90.8)	5.4 (86.3)	3.9 (69.1)	3.4 (69.1)	4.0 (75.0)
VII. Freedom of Exchange in Financial Markets	**2.4**	**2.4**	**1.7**	**1.3**	**3.2**	**4.2**	**6.4**
(a) Private Ownership of Banks	0.0 (0-5)	0.0 (0-5)	0.0 (0-5)	0.0 (0-10)	0.0 (0-10)	0.0 (0-10)	0.0 (0-10)
(b) Extension of Credit to Private Sector	5.9 (59.3)	5.8 (58.4)	5.2 (52.4)	3.4 (34.3)	5.4 (54.2)	8.1 (81.3)	8.5 (84.9)
(c) Avoidance of Negative Interest Rates				0.0	6.0	8.0	10.0
(d) Capital Transactions with Foreigners	2.0	2.0	2.0	2.0	2.0	2.0	8.0

ITALY

Summary Ratings	1970	1975	1980	1985	1990	1995	1999
Summary Ratings	6.8	5.4	5.6	5.9	7.2	7.2	7.8
Rank	23	40	40	40	27	37	24

Components of Economic Freedom

	1970	1975	1980	1985	1990	1995	1999
I. Size of Government	**6.1**	**5.8**	**5.2**	**3.9**	**4.2**	**4.0**	**4.5**
(a) Government Consumption	6.4 (18.3)	6.2 (18.8)	6.0 (19.7)	5.5 (21.4)	5.2 (22.3)	5.7 (20.7)	4.8 (23.7)
(b) Transfers and Subsidies	5.9 (15.6)	5.4 (17.5)	4.4 (20.9)	2.4 (28.5)	3.1 (25.8)	2.3 (28.7)	4.1 (22.0)
II. Structure of the Economy and Use of Markets		**3.8**	**2.1**	**2.1**	**3.5**	**4.5**	**5.0**
(a) Government Enterprises	4.0	4.0 (30.4)	4.0 (25.9)	4.0 (33.2)	4.0 (30.3)	6.0 (28.3)	6.0
(b) Price Controls					5.0	6.0	6.0
(c) Top Marginal Tax Rate		5.0 (48)	0.0 (72)	0.0 (81)	1.0 (66)	1.0 (67)	3.0 (50.25)
(d) Conscription	0.0	0.0	1.0	1.0	3.0	3.0	3.0
III. Monetary Policy and Price Stability	**8.4**	**7.3**	**7.1**	**8.3**	**8.9**	**9.3**	**9.4**
(a) Annual Money Growth	7.4 (12.8)	7.5 (12.7)	6.5 (17.7)	8.1 (9.7)	8.8 (6.3)	9.5 (2.5)	9.2 (3.9)
(b) Inflation Variability	9.3 (1.8)	7.8 (5.6)	9.0 (2.4)	8.5 (3.7)	9.7 (0.7)	9.4 (1.4)	9.4 (1.6)
(c) Recent Inflation Rate	8.6 (6.9)	6.8 (16.1)	5.8 (20.9)	8.2 (9.0)	8.2 (9.0)	9.0 (5.1)	9.7 (1.6)
IV. Freedom to Use Alternative Currencies	**4.8**	**4.1**	**5.0**	**5.0**	**10.0**	**10.0**	**10.0**
(a) Ownership of Foreign Currency	0.0	0.0	0.0	0.0	10.0	10.0	10.0
(b) Black Market Exchange Rate	9.6 (2.0)	8.2 (9.0)	10.0 (0.0)	10.0 (0.0)	10.0 (0.0)	10.0 (0.0)	10.0 (0.0)
V. Legal Structure and Property Rights	**7.0**	**3.8**	**6.3**	**7.8**	**9.2**	**7.0**	**9.0**
(a) Legal Security	7.0	3.8	4.3	7.4	10.0		8.1
(b) Rule of Law			8.3	8.2	8.3	7.0	10.0
VI. International Exchange	**8.2**	**8.0**	**8.2**	**8.4**	**7.9**	**8.2**	**8.1**
(a) Taxes on International Trade							
i. Taxes as a Percentage of Exports and Imports	9.9 (0.2)	9.8 (0.3)	9.7 (0.4)	9.8 (0.3)	9.8 (0.3)	9.8 (0.3)	9.8 (0.3)
ii. Mean Tariff Rate		7.8 (11.0)	8.2 (8.8)	8.5 (7.5)	8.5 (7.4)	8.7 (6.7)	8.6 (6.9)
iii. Standard Deviation of Tariff Rates					7.1 (7.2)	7.6 (5.9)	7.6 (5.9)
(b) Size of Trade Sector	4.8 (32.9)	4.9 (41.3)	5.0 (46.7)	5.3 (46.1)	4.2 (40.0)	5.0 (50.9)	4.5 (46.2)
VII. Freedom of Exchange in Financial Markets	**6.3**	**5.6**	**5.0**	**5.4**	**6.4**	**7.4**	**8.2**
(a) Private Ownership of Banks	5.0 (40-75)	5.0 (40-75)	5.0 (40-75)	5.0 (40-75)	5.0 (62)	5.0 (60-75)	5.0 (60-75)
(b) Extension of Credit to Private Sector	7.8 (77.9)	6.6 (66.0)	6.1 (60.5)	5.7 (57.2)	5.8 (57.9)	6.5 (65.3)	7.7 (76.9)
(c) Avoidance of Negative Interest Rates	8.0	6.0	4.0	6.0	10.0	10.0	10.0
(d) Capital Transactions with Foreigners	5.0	5.0	5.0	5.0	5.0	8.0	10.0

JAMAICA

Summary Ratings

	1970	1975	1980	1985	1990	1995	1999
Summary Ratings		4.9	3.9	4.8	5.6	7.0	5.9
Rank		49	88	71	51	43	79

Components of Economic Freedom

	1970	1975	1980	1985	1990	1995	1999
I. Size of Government	**7.0**	**6.8**	**4.7**	**8.3**	**8.0**	**7.7**	**5.6**
(a) Government Consumption	7.0 (16.1)	5.4 (21.7)	4.7 (24.1)	6.6 (17.4)	6.4 (18.4)	6.4 (18.3)	5.6 (21.1)
(b) Transfers and Subsidies		8.2 (7.0)		10.0 (0.5)	9.6 (2.0)	9.1 (3.9)	
II. Structure of the Economy and Use of Markets		**3.1**	**2.3**	**3.7**	**5.9**	**6.2**	**6.2**
(a) Government Enterprises	4.0 (34.4)	2.0 (45.6)	2.0 (26.5)	4.0 (13.4)	6.0 (21.3)	6.0	6.0
(b) Price Controls	0.0	2.0	0.0		4.0	4.0	4.0
(c) Top Marginal Tax Rate	0.0 (75)	2.0 (60)	0.0 (80)	1.0 (58)	7.0 (33)	8.0 (27)	8.0 (27)
(d) Conscription		10.0	10.0	10.0	10.0	10.0	10.0
III. Monetary Policy and Price Stability	**8.7**	**5.8**	**6.9**	**5.3**	**6.1**	**3.5**	**6.6**
(a) Annual Money Growth	8.0 (9.9)	6.6 (17.1)	6.4 (18.1)	6.4 (17.8)	6.2 (19.0)	0.8 (45.9)	6.9 (15.4)
(b) Inflation Variability	9.2 (1.9)	4.9 (12.8)	7.9 (5.3)	5.6 (11.0)	8.2 (4.5)	5.3 (11.7)	3.9 (15.2)
(c) Recent Inflation Rate	8.9 (5.6)	5.8 (20.8)	6.3 (8.3)	3.9 (30.7)	3.9 (30.7)	4.4 (27.9)	8.8 (6.0)
IV. Freedom to Use Alternative Currencies	**8.8**	**2.8**	**0.0**	**3.1**	**2.3**	**9.3**	**8.9**
(a) Ownership of Foreign Currency		0.0	0.0	0.0	0.0	10.0	10.0
(b) Black Market Exchange Rate	8.8 (6.0)	5.6 (22.0)	0.0 (61.0)	6.2 (19.0)	4.6 (27.0)	8.6 (7.0)	7.8 (11.1)
V. Legal Structure and Property Rights			**3.0**	**3.3**	**4.3**	**7.0**	**1.7**
(a) Legal Security			4.2	3.5	5.3		
(b) Rule of Law			1.7	3.1	3.3	7.0	1.7
VI. International Exchange		**6.5**	**7.5**	**7.5**	**6.3**	**6.2**	**5.2**
(a) Taxes on International Trade							
i. Taxes as a Percentage of Exports and Imports		7.3 (4.0)	9.4 (0.9)	8.9 (1.7)			3.6 (9.6)
ii. Mean Tariff Rate			6.7 (16.5)	6.6 (17.0)	6.6 (17.0)	7.2 (14.0)	6.2 (19.0)
iii. Standard Deviation of Tariff Rates						5.0 (12.5)	5.6 (11.1)
(b) Size of Trade Sector	4.0 (70.6)	4.7 (80.9)	5.3 (102.1)	6.8 (121.6)	5.7 (108.0)	6.5 (135.8)	5.3 (111.7)
VII. Freedom of Exchange in Financial Markets			**3.9**	**3.3**	**7.0**	**7.9**	**7.9**
(a) Private Ownership of Banks				2.0 (40)	10.0 (95-100)	10.0 (95-100)	10.0 (95-100)
(b) Extension of Credit to Private Sector	8.1 (81.4)	8.0 (80.2)	6.1 (61.2)	6.0 (59.8)	8.2 (81.6)	7.3 (72.8)	7.2 (71.6)
(c) Avoidance of Negative Interest Rates		4.0	4.0	4.0	8.0	6.0	6.0
(d) Capital Transactions with Foreigners	2.0	2.0	2.0	2.0	2.0	8.0	8.0

JAPAN

Summary Ratings	1970	1975	1980	1985	1990	1995	1999
Summary Ratings	7.3	6.9	7.5	7.6	8.1	8.1	7.9
Rank	15	14	11	12	9	13	20

Components of Economic Freedom

	1970	1975	1980	1985	1990	1995	1999
I. Size of Government	**8.9**	**7.8**	**7.6**	**7.4**	**7.4**	**7.2**	**7.6**
(a) Government Consumption	8.1 (12.5)	7.4 (14.9)	7.6 (14.3)	7.7 (14.0)	7.8 (13.5)	7.6 (14.0)	7.6 (14.1)
(b) Transfers and Subsidies	9.7 (1.6)	8.3 (6.7)	7.6 (9.2)	7.2 (10.9)	7.0 (11.5)	6.8 (12.2)	
II. Structure of the Economy and Use of Markets	**5.6**	**5.6**	**5.3**	**5.6**	**6.0**	**5.0**	**5.4**
(a) Government Enterprises	8.0 (12.7)	8.0 (15.6)	8.0 (19.6)	8.0 (17.9)	8.0 (20.4)	6.0 (28.5)	6.0 (26.5)
(b) Price Controls					6.0	5.0	6.0
(c) Top Marginal Tax Rate		1.0 (68)	0.0 (75)	1.0 (70)	2.0 (65)	2.0 (65)	2.0 (65)
(d) Conscription	10.0	10.0	10.0	10.0	10.0	10.0	10.0
III. Monetary Policy and Price Stability	**9.1**	**8.0**	**9.2**	**9.7**	**9.6**	**9.5**	**9.2**
(a) Annual Money Growth	8.9 (5.3)	7.9 (10.5)	9.5 (2.4)	9.8 (1.2)	9.6 (2.1)	9.1 (4.5)	8.8 (6.0)
(b) Inflation Variability	9.7 (0.7)	7.6 (5.9)	9.3 (1.8)	9.7 (0.9)	9.7 (0.8)	9.5 (1.2)	9.0 (2.6)
(c) Recent Inflation Rate	8.7 (6.5)	8.6 (7.2)	8.9 (5.4)	9.6 (2.1)	9.6 (2.1)	9.9 (-0.6)	9.9 (-0.3)
IV. Freedom to Use Alternative Currencies	**4.9**	**7.5**	**7.5**	**7.5**	**10.0**	**10.0**	**10.0**
(a) Ownership of Foreign Currency	0.0	5.0	5.0	5.0	10.0	10.0	10.0
(b) Black Market Exchange Rate	9.8 (1.0)	10.0 (0.0)	10.0 (0.0)	10.0 (0.0)	10.0 (0.0)	10.0 (0.0)	10.0 (0.0)
V. Legal Structure and Property Rights	**9.6**	**7.0**	**9.4**	**8.5**	**9.2**	**10.0**	**9.4**
(a) Legal Security	9.6	7.0	8.8	8.7	10.0		8.8
(b) Rule of Law			10.0	8.2	8.3	10.0	10.0
VI. International Exchange	**6.8**	**7.6**	**7.8**	**8.0**	**7.3**	**7.0**	**6.9**
(a) Taxes on International Trade							
i. Taxes as a Percentage of Exports and Imports	8.1 (2.8)	9.1 (1.3)	9.4 (0.9)	9.5 (0.8)	9.4 (0.9)	8.9 (1.6)	9.0 (1.5)
ii. Mean Tariff Rate		7.8 (11.0)	8.1 (9.5)	8.7 (6.7)	8.6 (6.9)	8.7 (6.3)	8.7 (6.6)
iii. Standard Deviation of Tariff Rates					6.7 (8.3)	6.6 (8.4)	6.3 (9.3)
(b) Size of Trade Sector	4.2 (20.3)	4.0 (25.6)	3.8 (28.3)	3.5 (25.5)	1.4 (20.6)	0.0 (17.3)	0.0 (20.2)
VII. Freedom of Exchange in Financial Markets	**5.7**	**5.6**	**6.2**	**7.0**	**7.9**	**7.9**	**7.3**
(a) Private Ownership of Banks	8.0 (82)	8.0 (77)	5.0 (71)	5.0 (69)	5.0 (74)	5.0 (66)	5.0 (60-70)
(b) Extension of Credit to Private Sector	9.5 (94.5)	9.2 (91.8)	8.4 (84.4)	8.6 (86.4)	8.9 (89.0)	8.9 (89.1)	8.6 (85.5)
(c) Avoidance of Negative Interest Rates	4.0	4.0	10.0	10.0	10.0	10.0	8.0
(d) Capital Transactions with Foreigners	2.0	2.0	2.0	5.0	8.0	8.0	8.0

JORDAN

Summary Ratings	1970	1975	1980	1985	1990	1995	1999
Summary Ratings		5.2	5.4	6.0	4.9	5.8	6.8
Rank		45	44	37	67	72	52

Components of Economic Freedom	1970	1975	1980	1985	1990	1995	1999
I. Size of Government		**3.1**	**6.2**	**6.9**	**6.7**	**6.6**	**6.5**
(a) Government Consumption		3.1 (29.6)	3.9 (26.8)	5.0 (22.9)	4.4 (25.1)	3.7 (27.4)	3.6 (27.7)
(b) Transfers and Subsidies			8.4 (5.3)	8.7 (5.1)	9.1 (3.7)	9.4 (2.7)	9.4 (2.6)
II. Structure of the Economy and Use of Markets					**2.8**	**2.1**	**2.1**
(a) Government Enterprises	0.0 (82.2)	0.0 (83.3)	0.0 (83.1)	0.0 (52.7)	0.0	0.0	0.0
(b) Price Controls					2.0	2.0	2.0
(c) Top Marginal Tax Rate					5.0 (45)		
(d) Conscription	0.0	10.0	10.0	10.0	10.0	10.0	10.0
III. Monetary Policy and Price Stability		**7.5**	**7.4**	**8.8**	**8.2**	**9.6**	**9.3**
(a) Annual Money Growth		7.0 (14.9)	5.9 (20.7)	9.5 (-2.5)	8.2 (9.0)	9.8 (1.0)	9.2 (-4.0)
(b) Inflation Variability		8.0 (4.9)	6.6 (8.4)	7.1 (7.3)	6.7 (8.1)	9.5 (1.2)	9.7 (0.8)
(c) Recent Inflation Rate	8.8 (5.9)	7.6 (12.2)	9.8 (1.1)	9.7 (-1.5)	9.7 (-1.5)	9.3 (3.4)	9.1 (4.4)
IV. Freedom to Use Alternative Currencies	**4.4**	**4.9**	**7.5**	**7.2**	**3.9**	**4.9**	**10.0**
(a) Ownership of Foreign Currency	0.0	0.0	5.0	5.0	0.0	0.0	10.0
(b) Black Market Exchange Rate	8.8 (6.0)	9.8 (1.0)	10.0 (0.0)	9.4 (3.0)	7.8 (11.0)	9.8 (1.0)	10.0 (0.0)
V. Legal Structure and Property Rights				**3.3**	**3.9**	**7.0**	**6.9**
(a) Legal Security				3.5	4.6	7.0	8.1
(b) Rule of Law				3.1	3.3		5.8
VI. International Exchange		**6.1**	**6.0**	**6.8**	**5.7**	**6.6**	**7.0**
(a) Taxes on International Trade							
i. Taxes as a Percentage of Exports and Imports		5.5 (6.8)	5.3 (7.1)	5.9 (6.1)	6.7 (5.0)	6.2 (5.7)	6.9 (4.7)
ii. Mean Tariff Rate				7.2 (13.8)			7.1 (14.4)
iii. Standard Deviation of Tariff Rates					2.6 (18.5)		
(b) Size of Trade Sector	2.0 (44.6)	7.3 (110.8)	7.4 (124.1)	7.5 (113.1)	9.9 (154.6)	7.5 (126.2)	7.2 (119.5)
VII. Freedom of Exchange in Financial Markets		**4.8**	**5.1**	**4.9**	**4.6**	**5.3**	**6.2**
(a) Private Ownership of Banks		5.0 (40-75)	5.0 (40-75)	5.0 (40-75)	5.0 (40-75)	5.0 (40-75)	5.0 (40-75)
(b) Extension of Credit to Private Sector	9.3 (93.0)	8.3 (82.5)	9.0 (90.1)	8.4 (83.9)	8.2 (81.5)	9.3 (93.0)	8.8 (87.5)
(c) Avoidance of Negative Interest Rates					4.0	6.0	10.0
(d) Capital Transactions with Foreigners	2.0	2.0	2.0	2.0	2.0	2.0	2.0

KENYA

Summary Ratings	1970	1975	1980	1985	1990	1995	1999
Summary Ratings	5.1	4.8	4.6	5.1	5.0	5.7	6.3
Rank	42	52	69	60	65	74	68

Components of Economic Freedom	1970	1975	1980	1985	1990	1995	1999
I. Size of Government	**7.6**	**7.5**	**7.1**	**6.9**	**7.2**	**7.9**	**7.7**
(a) Government Consumption	5.5 (21.3)	5.5 (21.2)	4.6 (24.2)	4.9 (23.3)	5.0 (23.1)	6.6 (17.6)	6.2 (18.9)
(b) Transfers and Subsidies	9.7 (1.6)	9.4 (2.7)	9.5 (2.3)	8.9 (4.7)	9.4 (2.8)	9.2 (3.4)	9.2 (3.4)
II. Structure of the Economy and Use of Markets	**3.3**	**2.3**	**1.7**	**2.3**	**2.3**	**3.6**	**5.9**
(a) Government Enterprises	4.0 (30.5)	2.0 (42.1)	0.0 (55.1)	2.0 (49.5)	0.0 (58.3)	2.0 (43.3)	4.0 (40.8)
(b) Price Controls					2.0	4.0	6.0
(c) Top Marginal Tax Rate	0.0 (70)	0.0 (70)	1.0 (65)	0.0 (65)	3.0 (50)	3.0 (50)	7.0 (32.5)
(d) Conscription	10.0	10.0	10.0	10.0	10.0	10.0	10.0
III. Monetary Policy and Price Stability	**7.9**	**7.7**	**8.1**	**9.0**	**8.4**	**7.2**	**8.5**
(a) Annual Money Growth	9.1 (4.8)	8.9 (5.5)	8.5 (7.3)	9.1 (4.5)	7.5 (12.3)	6.7 (16.7)	8.6 (7.2)
(b) Inflation Variability	7.7 (5.6)	6.4 (9.0)	7.5 (6.2)	9.5 (1.3)	9.4 (1.4)	7.3 (6.7)	7.6 (6.0)
(c) Recent Inflation Rate	6.9 (15.3)	7.6 (11.8)	8.1 (9.6)	8.4 (8.2)	8.4 (8.2)	7.7 (11.3)	9.5 (2.6)
IV. Freedom to Use Alternative Currencies	**1.9**	**4.2**	**4.0**	**4.8**	**4.4**	**7.3**	**8.9**
(a) Ownership of Foreign Currency	0.0	0.0	0.0	0.0	0.0	5.0	10.0
(b) Black Market Exchange Rate	3.8 (31.0)	8.4 (8.0)	8.0 (10.0)	9.6 (2.0)	8.8 (6.0)	9.6 (2.0)	7.8 (11.1)
V. Legal Structure and Property Rights	**4.9**	**3.5**	**4.2**	**5.7**	**5.8**	**4.1**	**1.7**
(a) Legal Security	4.9	3.5	5.2	4.8	3.2		
(b) Rule of Law			3.3	6.6	8.3	4.1	1.7
VI. International Exchange	**6.6**	**6.9**	**4.6**	**4.1**	**3.3**	**5.2**	**6.0**
(a) Taxes on International Trade							
i. Taxes as a Percentage of Exports and Imports	6.3 (5.6)	6.3 (5.5)	5.9 (6.1)	5.1 (7.4)	5.8 (6.3)	6.3 (5.6)	6.2 (5.8)
ii. Mean Tariff Rate			1.9 (40.3)	2.2 (39.2)	1.3 (43.7)	3.2 (34.0)	5.9 (20.8)
iii. Standard Deviation of Tariff Rates					1.4 (21.6)	4.7 (13.3)	
(b) Size of Trade Sector	7.4 (60.5)	7.9 (64.3)	7.5 (67.0)	6.3 (51.7)	6.8 (57.6)	8.0 (73.0)	6.1 (56.9)
VII. Freedom of Exchange in Financial Markets	**5.0**	**3.2**	**4.3**	**4.7**	**5.3**	**6.1**	**7.1**
(a) Private Ownership of Banks		2.0 (10-40)	2.0 (10-40)	2.0 (39)	5.0 (40-75)	5.0 (40-75)	5.0 (40-75)
(b) Extension of Credit to Private Sector	7.9 (79.1)	7.8 (77.9)	8.5 (85.1)	8.1 (80.5)	7.0 (69.8)	7.3 (73.2)	7.7 (76.9)
(c) Avoidance of Negative Interest Rates	8.0	4.0	8.0	10.0	10.0	4.0	8.0
(d) Capital Transactions with Foreigners	0.0	0.0	0.0	0.0	0.0	8.0	8.0

KUWAIT

Summary Ratings

	1970	1975	1980	1985	1990	1995	1999
Summary Ratings			4.7	6.9	5.5	6.7	7.2
Rank			66	19	54	50	41

Components of Economic Freedom

	1970	1975	1980	1985	1990	1995	1999
I. Size of Government	**4.1**	**1.9**	**3.9**	**2.4**	**3.7**	**3.8**	**4.2**
(a) Government Consumption	4.1 (26.0)	1.9 (33.7)	3.9 (26.5)	2.4 (31.9)	0.0 (40.6)	0.0 (44.4)	1.4 (35.2)
(b) Transfers and Subsidies					7.5 (9.8)	7.5 (9.7)	7.1 (11.2)
II. Structure of the Economy and Use of Markets						**4.4**	**5.8**
(a) Government Enterprises		2.0	2.0 (43.5)	0.0 (61.3)	2.0 (46.0)	4.0 (21.8)	4.0
(b) Price Controls						6.0	6.0
(c) Top Marginal Tax Rate							10.0 (0)
(d) Conscription		1.0	1.0	1.0	0.0	0.0	0.0
III. Monetary Policy and Price Stability	**9.8**	**5.1**	**3.2**	**8.1**	**7.1**	**8.8**	**9.3**
(a) Annual Money Growth		5.5 (22.3)	5.9 (20.5)	8.2 (9.0)	8.6 (7.0)	10.0 (-0.2)	9.4 (-2.8)
(b) Inflation Variability	9.7 (0.7)	0.0 (61.7)	2.1 (19.8)	7.0 (7.4)	4.6 (13.6)	7.5 (6.2)	8.4 (4.1)
(c) Recent Inflation Rate	9.9 (0.6)	9.9 (-0.6)	1.5 (42.6)	9.0 (4.9)	8.0 (9.8)	8.7 (6.3)	10.0 (0.2)
IV. Freedom to Use Alternative Currencies	**10.0**	**10.0**	**10.0**	**10.0**	**10.0**	**10.0**	**10.0**
(a) Ownership of Foreign Currency	10.0	10.0	10.0	10.0	10.0	10.0	10.0
(b) Black Market Exchange Rate	10.0 (0.0)	10.0 (0.0)	10.0 (0.0)	10.0 (0.0)	10.0 (0.0)	10.0 (0.0)	10.0 (0.0)
V. Legal Structure and Property Rights			**1.0**	**6.5**	**2.2**	**7.0**	**7.9**
(a) Legal Security			1.0	4.8	1.9		
(b) Rule of Law				8.2	2.5	7.0	7.9
VI. International Exchange				**7.9**	**8.0**	**7.8**	**7.6**
(a) Taxes on International Trade							
i. Taxes as a Percentage of Exports and Imports				9.2 (4.0)	9.2 (1.2)	9.4 (0.9)	9.4 (1.0)
ii. Mean Tariff Rate							
iii. Standard Deviation of Tariff Rates							
(b) Size of Trade Sector	4.3 (83.9)	5.6 (106.5)	5.5 (112.6)	5.2 (96.4)	5.4 (103.0)	4.6 (103.8)	4.0 (91.8)
VII. Freedom of Exchange in Financial Markets		**5.3**	**5.3**	**6.1**	**2.8**	**5.0**	**5.5**
(a) Private Ownership of Banks		5.0 (40-75)	5.0 (40-75)	5.0 (40-75)	5.0 (40-75)	5.0 (40-75)	5.0 (40-75)
(b) Extension of Credit to Private Sector	10.0 (99.9)	9.9 (98.8)	9.8 (93.2)	8.0 (79.7)	1.1 (10.9)	3.0 (29.7)	5.2 (51.8)
(c) Avoidance of Negative Interest Rates				10.0		10.0	10.0
(d) Capital Transactions with Foreigners	2.0	2.0	2.0	2.0	2.0	2.0	2.0

LATVIA

Summary Ratings	1970	1975	1980	1985	1990	1995	1999
						5.5	7.0
Rank						77	46

Components of Economic Freedom	1970	1975	1980	1985	1990	1995	1999
I. Size of Government					**7.6**	**4.6**	**5.1**
(a) Government Consumption					7.6 (14.0)	4.1 (26.2)	5.1 (22.5)
(b) Transfers and Subsidies						5.2 (18.2)	5.0 (18.8)
II. Structure of the Economy and Use of Markets						**3.8**	**5.8**
(a) Government Enterprises					0.0	0.0	4.0
(b) Price Controls						6.0	6.0
(c) Top Marginal Tax Rate						7.0 (35)	9.0 (25)
(d) Conscription					0.0	1.0	3.0
III. Monetary Policy and Price Stability					**7.1**	**2.2**	**6.9**
(a) Annual Money Growth					7.4 (6.4)	0.1 (49.5)	6.4 (17.9)
(b) Inflation Variability				8.9 (2.7)		0.0 (365.3)	4.8 (13.0)
(c) Recent Inflation Rate					6.9 (15.7)	6.8 (16.0)	9.5 (2.4)
IV. Freedom to Use Alternative Currencies					**2.5**	**7.3**	**10.0**
(a) Ownership of Foreign Currency					5.0	5.0	10.0
(b) Black Market Exchange Rate					0.0 (1969.0)	9.6 (2.0)	10.0 (0.0)
V. Legal Structure and Property Rights							**5.8**
(a) Legal Security							
(b) Rule of Law							5.8
VI. International Exchange						**7.9**	**7.7**
(a) Taxes on International Trade							
i. Taxes as a Percentage of Exports and Imports						9.5 (0.8)	9.7 (0.5)
ii. Mean Tariff Rate							8.8 (5.9)
iii. Standard Deviation of Tariff Rates							5.7 (10.7)
(b) Size of Trade Sector						4.8 (96.1)	5.4 (108.7)
VII. Freedom of Exchange in Financial Markets						**5.2**	**6.9**
(a) Private Ownership of Banks							
(b) Extension of Credit to Private Sector						5.4 (53.9)	7.9 (79.2)
(c) Avoidance of Negative Interest Rates						2.0	8.0
(d) Capital Transactions with Foreigners					0.0	8.0	5.0

LITHUANIA

Summary Ratings	1970	1975	1980	1985	1990	1995	1999
Rank						5.5	6.5
						77	62

Components of Economic Freedom	1970	1975	1980	1985	1990	1995	1999
I. Size of Government					**4.3**	**6.2**	**5.7**
(a) Government Consumption					4.3 (25.2)	5.1 (22.6)	4.2 (25.7)
(b) Transfers and Subsidies						7.3 (10.4)	7.2 (10.8)
II. Structure of the Economy and Use of Markets						**3.4**	**5.3**
(a) Government Enterprises						0.0	6.0
(b) Price Controls					0.0	4.0	4.0
(c) Top Marginal Tax Rate						7.0 (35)	7.0 (33)
(d) Conscription					0.0	3.0	3.0
III. Monetary Policy and Price Stability						**0.8**	**5.0**
(a) Annual Money Growth						0.0 (53.0)	4.3 (28.6)
(b) Inflation Variability						0.0 (329.2)	0.8 (22.9)
(c) Recent Inflation Rate					10.0 (-0.2)	2.4 (38.1)	9.8 (0.8)
IV. Freedom to Use Alternative Currencies					**2.5**	**7.5**	**7.5**
(a) Ownership of Foreign Currency					5.0	5.0	5.0
(b) Black Market Exchange Rate					0.0 (1969.0)	10.0 (0.0)	10.0 (0.0)
V. Legal Structure and Property Rights							**5.8**
(a) Legal Security							
(b) Rule of Law							5.8
VI. International Exchange						**8.1**	**8.0**
(a) Taxes on International Trade							
i. Taxes as a Percentage of Exports and Imports						9.6 (0.7)	9.6 (0.5)
ii. Mean Tariff Rate						9.1 (4.5)	9.1 (4.6)
iii. Standard Deviation of Tariff Rates						6.4 (9.0)	6.3 (9.3)
(b) Size of Trade Sector						6.3 (119.1)	5.7 (106.4)
VII. Freedom of Exchange in Financial Markets						**5.3**	**7.0**
(a) Private Ownership of Banks					0.0 (0)	5.0 (40-75)	5.0 (51.7)
(b) Extension of Credit to Private Sector						8.3 (83.1)	7.2 (72.3)
(c) Avoidance of Negative Interest Rates						0.0	8.0
(d) Capital Transactions with Foreigners					0.0	8.0	8.0

LUXEMBOURG

	1970	1975	1980	1985	1990	1995	1999
Summary Ratings	9.1	9.1	8.9	9.2	8.2	8.3	8.4
Rank	2	2	2	2	7	9	9

Components of Economic Freedom

	1970	1975	1980	1985	1990	1995	1999
I. Size of Government	**6.5**	**6.9**	**6.5**	**6.8**	**4.7**	**4.7**	**4.4**
(a) Government Consumption	7.8 (13.6)	6.9 (16.4)	6.5 (17.8)	6.8 (16.9)	6.5 (17.8)	6.1 (19.4)	5.3 (21.9)
(b) Transfers and Subsidies	5.3 (17.8)				2.9 (26.6)	3.3 (25.2)	3.4 (24.8)
II. Structure of the Economy and Use of Markets					**4.4**	**5.9**	**6.8**
(a) Government Enterprises	7.0	7.0	7.0 (22.0)	8.0 (18.2)	8.0 (19.2)	8.0	8.0
(b) Price Controls					2.0	5.0	7.0
(c) Top Marginal Tax Rate					1.0 (56)	3.0 (50)	4.0 (48.5)
(d) Conscription	10.0	10.0	10.0	10.0	10.0	10.0	10.0
III. Monetary Policy and Price Stability	**7.5**	**8.5**	**8.5**	**9.4**	**9.1**	**9.4**	**9.5**
(a) Annual Money Growth			8.6 (7.0)	9.8 (0.8)	8.4 (7.8)	9.1 (4.6)	9.3 (3.5)
(b) Inflation Variability	8.0 (4.9)	7.2 (7.1)	8.6 (3.6)	8.9 (2.7)	9.5 (1.2)	9.2 (1.9)	9.3 (1.8)
(c) Recent Inflation Rate	7.0 (15.1)	9.8 (-0.9)	8.4 (7.9)	9.4 (3.0)	9.3 (3.4)	9.9 (0.7)	9.8 (1.0)
IV. Freedom to Use Alternative Currencies	**10.0**	**10.0**	**10.0**	**10.0**	**10.0**	**10.0**	**10.0**
(a) Ownership of Foreign Currency	10.0	10.0	10.0	10.0	10.0	10.0	10.0
(b) Black Market Exchange Rate	10.0 (0.0)	10.0 (0.0)	10.0 (0.0)	10.0 (0.0)	10.0 (0.0)	10.0 (0.0)	10.0 (0.0)
V. Legal Structure and Property Rights	**10.0**	**10.0**	**9.3**	**10.0**	**10.0**	**10.0**	**10.0**
(a) Legal Security	10.0	10.0	8.6	10.0	10.0		
(b) Rule of Law			10.0	10.0	10.0	10.0	10.0
VI. International Exchange	**8.9**	**8.2**	**8.1**	**8.4**	**8.0**	**8.0**	**8.3**
(a) Taxes on International Trade							
i. Taxes as a Percentage of Exports and Imports	9.9 (0.2)	10.0 (0.0)	9.9 (0.0)	9.9 (0.1)	9.9 (0.1)	9.9 (0.1)	9.9 (0.1)
ii. Mean Tariff Rate		8.1 (9.4)	8.2 (8.8)	8.5 (7.5)	8.5 (7.4)	8.7 (6.7)	8.9 (5.6)
iii. Standard Deviation of Tariff Rates					7.1 (7.2)	7.6 (5.9)	7.6 (5.9)
(b) Size of Trade Sector	7.1 (162.0)	4.6 (177.7)	3.9 (174.9)	5.3 (208.6)	4.8 (194.3)	3.6 (172.3)	4.8 (208.8)
VII. Freedom of Exchange in Financial Markets	**10.0**	**10.0**	**10.0**	**10.0**	**10.0**	**9.2**	**9.2**
(a) Private Ownership of Banks	10.0 (95-100)	10.0 (95-100)	10.0 (95-100)	10.0 (95-100)	10.0 (95-100)	10.0 (95-100)	10.0 (95-100)
(b) Extension of Credit to Private Sector						6.3 (62.7)	6.2 (62.0)
(c) Avoidance of Negative Interest Rates	10.0	10.0	10.0	10.0	10.0	10.0	10.0
(d) Capital Transactions with Foreigners	10.0	10.0	10.0	10.0	10.0	10.0	10.0

MADAGASCAR

	1970	1975	1980	1985	1990	1995	1999
Summary Ratings	5.6	4.1	4.0	4.3	3.5	4.4	4.4
Rank	38	62	86	82	104	104	110

Components of Economic Freedom

	1970	1975	1980	1985	1990	1995	1999
I. Size of Government	**8.3**	**8.5**	**8.3**	**8.9**	**9.5**	**9.8**	**9.5**
(a) Government Consumption	7.6 (14.2)	8.5 (11.2)	8.3 (11.9)	8.9 (9.9)	9.3 (8.5)	9.7 (6.9)	9.3 (8.4)
(b) Transfers and Subsidies	9.0 (4.2)				9.8 (1.4)	9.8 (1.1)	9.8 (1.3)
II. Structure of the Economy and Use of Markets					**0.1**	**0.1**	**0.1**
(a) Government Enterprises	0.0 (70.3)	0.0 (59.2)	0.0 (65.4)	0.0 (79.9)	0.0 (53.5)	0.0 (54.8)	0.0 (58.7)
(b) Price Controls					0.0	0.0	0.0
(c) Top Marginal Tax Rate							
(d) Conscription	0.0	1.0	1.0	1.0	1.0	1.0	1.0
III. Monetary Policy and Price Stability	**8.8**	**8.3**	**7.6**	**7.6**	**7.3**	**3.4**	**5.2**
(a) Annual Money Growth	8.9 (5.4)	8.8 (5.8)	6.8 (15.9)	8.1 (9.7)	6.3 (18.7)	5.0 (25.1)	5.6 (22.1)
(b) Inflation Variability	9.0 (2.5)	7.0 (7.5)	8.9 (2.8)	6.9 (7.8)	8.1 (4.8)	4.0 (14.9)	2.1 (19.7)
(c) Recent Inflation Rate	8.6 (6.9)	9.1 (4.7)	7.0 (15.0)	7.9 (10.4)	7.7 (11.5)	1.0 (45.2)	8.0 (9.9)
IV. Freedom to Use Alternative Currencies	**9.6**	**2.7**	**0.0**	**4.1**	**4.3**	**4.8**	**5.0**
(a) Ownership of Foreign Currency		0.0	0.0	0.0	0.0	0.0	0.0
(b) Black Market Exchange Rate	9.6 (2.0)	5.4 (23.0)	0.0 (51.0)	8.2 (9.0)	8.6 (7.0)	9.6 (2.0)	10.0 (0.0)
V. Legal Structure and Property Rights				**4.4**	**2.7**	**7.0**	**3.8**
(a) Legal Security				2.2	1.9		
(b) Rule of Law				6.6	3.5	7.0	3.8
VI. International Exchange	**1.8**	**1.9**	**4.1**	**1.4**	**2.3**	**4.4**	**3.9**
(a) Taxes on International Trade							
i. Taxes as a Percentage of Exports and Imports	0.0 (15.1)	0.8 (13.8)	4.3 (8.5)		0.7 (14.0)	4.3 (8.5)	3.4 (10.0)
ii. Mean Tariff Rate			3.7 (31.5)	0.8 (46.0)	2.8 (36.0)	4.0 (30.0)	
iii. Standard Deviation of Tariff Rates							
(b) Size of Trade Sector	5.4 (40.7)	4.1 (36.7)	4.4 (43.1)	2.7 (30.6)	4.7 (43.6)	5.4 (54.8)	4.9 (50.4)
VII. Freedom of Exchange in Financial Markets	**2.7**	**2.5**	**2.6**	**2.7**	**2.0**	**2.4**	**4.8**
(a) Private Ownership of Banks	0.0 (0)	0.0 (0)	0.0 (0)	0.0 (0)	0.0 (0-10)	2.0 (10-40)	2.0 (10-40)
(b) Extension of Credit to Private Sector	9.5 (94.9)	8.7 (87.4)	9.3 (92.6)	9.7 (97.4)	9.3 (92.5)	9.0 (89.9)	8.1 (80.6)
(c) Avoidance of Negative Interest Rates				0.0	0.0	0.0	8.0
(d) Capital Transactions with Foreigners	0.0	0.0	0.0	0.0	0.0	0.0	2.0

MALAWI

Summary Ratings	1970	1975	1980	1985	1990	1995	1999
Summary Ratings		4.9	4.2	4.6	4.9	4.1	4.4
Rank		49	79	75	67	109	110

Components of Economic Freedom

	1970	1975	1980	1985	1990	1995	1999
I. Size of Government	**8.0**	**8.3**	**7.5**	**7.7**	**8.1**	**5.9**	**7.6**
(a) Government Consumption	6.4 (18.3)	6.8 (17.0)	5.4 (21.6)	5.8 (20.3)	6.7 (17.4)	5.9 (19.8)	7.6 (14.3)
(b) Transfers and Subsidies	9.6 (1.8)	9.9 (1.0)	9.6 (2.0)	9.5 (2.3)	9.5 (2.4)		
II. Structure of the Economy and Use of Markets	**2.3**	**2.3**	**2.8**	**2.5**	**1.6**	**4.0**	**3.5**
(a) Government Enterprises	6.0 (17.2)	2.0 (44.5)	0.0 (69.3)	0.0 (62.0)	0.0 (48.2)	0.0 (65.2)	0.0 (78.7)
(b) Price Controls					0.0	4.0	4.0
(c) Top Marginal Tax Rate	0.0	0.0 (69)	4.0 (45)	3.0 (50)	3.0 (50)	7.0 (35)	5.0 (38)
(d) Conscription	10.0	10.0	10.0	10.0	10.0	10.0	10.0
III. Monetary Policy and Price Stability	**8.4**	**7.9**	**8.2**	**8.5**	**6.9**	**1.2**	**1.5**
(a) Annual Money Growth	8.6 (6.8)	7.7 (11.5)	9.9 (-0.5)	8.4 (8.0)	5.7 (21.4)	3.4 (33.2)	3.3 (33.7)
(b) Inflation Variability	8.4 (4.0)	7.8 (5.5)	7.6 (5.9)	8.9 (2.7)	7.3 (6.6)	0.0 (28.5)	0.0 (32.9)
(c) Recent Inflation Rate	8.2 (8.8)	8.4 (8.2)	6.8 (15.8)	8.2 (8.9)	7.8 (10.9)	0.0 (90.4)	1.0 (44.9)
IV. Freedom to Use Alternative Currencies	**3.4**	**2.2**	**0.2**	**2.0**	**3.6**	**4.9**	**3.9**
(a) Ownership of Foreign Currency	0.0	0.0	0.0	0.0	0.0	0.0	0.0
(b) Black Market Exchange Rate	6.8 (16.0)	4.4 (28.0)	0.4 (48.0)	4.0 (30.0)	7.2 (14.0)	9.8 (1.0)	7.8 (11.1)
V. Legal Structure and Property Rights			**3.4**	**3.9**	**4.6**	**4.1**	**5.8**
(a) Legal Security			5.2	4.8	5.9		
(b) Rule of Law			1.7	3.1	3.3	4.1	5.8
VI. International Exchange	**6.3**	**7.2**	**5.5**	**5.3**	**6.3**	**4.7**	**5.1**
(a) Taxes on International Trade							
i. Taxes as a Percentage of Exports and Imports	6.6 (5.1)	7.5 (3.8)	5.6 (6.6)	4.1 (8.8)	6.2 (5.7)	6.2 (5.7)	4.6 (8.1)
ii. Mean Tariff Rate				6.7 (16.7)	7.0 (15.2)	3.8 (30.8)	4.9 (25.3)
iii. Standard Deviation of Tariff Rates						3.8 (15.5)	5.4 (11.6)
(b) Size of Trade Sector	5.6 (63.4)	6.8 (75.0)	5.2 (63.6)	4.8 (54.1)	5.0 (57.9)	5.7 (72.7)	5.8 (74.3)
VII. Freedom of Exchange in Financial Markets	**3.3**	**3.3**	**3.8**	**4.3**	**4.3**	**3.2**	**3.1**
(a) Private Ownership of Banks	2.0 (10-40)	2.0 (10-40)	2.0 (10-40)	2.0 (10-40)	2.0 (10-40)	2.0 (10-40)	2.0 (10-40)
(b) Extension of Credit to Private Sector	8.6 (85.5)	6.7 (67.2)	7.9 (79.4)	6.0 (59.5)	8.0 (80.4)	5.5 (54.6)	4.7 (47.2)
(c) Avoidance of Negative Interest Rates				8.0	6.0	4.0	4.0
(d) Capital Transactions with Foreigners	2.0	2.0	2.0	2.0	2.0	2.0	2.0

MALAYSIA

Summary Ratings	1970	1975	1980	1985	1990	1995	1999
Summary Ratings	6.5	6.3	7.0	7.0	7.5	7.4	6.7
Rank	26	18	13	17	19	31	56

Components of Economic Freedom

Component	1970		1975		1980		1985		1990		1995		1999	
I. Size of Government	**6.8**		**6.6**		**6.7**		**7.1**		**7.5**		**7.3**		**7.2**	
(a) Government Consumption	5.5	(21.4)	4.7	(23.9)	4.5	(24.6)	5.1	(22.7)	5.6	(21.0)	5.6	(20.9)	5.4	(21.5)
(b) Transfers and Subsidies	8.1	(7.3)	8.4	(6.4)	8.8	(4.8)	9.2	(3.6)	9.5	(2.4)	9.0	(4.0)	9.0	(4.1)
II. Structure of the Economy and Use of Markets	**4.8**		**4.8**		**4.0**		**4.6**		**5.4**		**5.3**		**5.2**	
(a) Government Enterprises	4.0	(32.3)	4.0	(37.6)	4.0	(37.3)	2.0	(46.8)	4.0	(35.5)	4.0	(29.2)	4.0	(27.2)
(b) Price Controls							5.0		5.0		4.0		3.0	
(c) Top Marginal Tax Rate			4.0	(50)	2.0	(60)	6.0	(45)	6.0	(45)	7.0	(32)	8.0	(30)
(d) Conscription	10.0		10.0		10.0		10.0		10.0		10.0		10.0	
III. Monetary Policy and Price Stability	**9.3**		**8.1**		**8.5**		**9.5**		**8.7**		**8.6**		**8.9**	
(a) Annual Money Growth	9.3	(-3.7)	8.1	(9.4)	8.1	(9.7)	9.8	(0.9)	8.7	(6.5)	7.5	(12.4)	9.4	(-2.9)
(b) Inflation Variability	8.8	(2.9)	6.7	(8.3)	8.8	(3.1)	8.9	(2.6)	7.9	(5.2)	9.4	(1.5)	7.7	(5.8)
(c) Recent Inflation Rate	9.9	(-0.4)	9.4	(-3.1)	8.6	(6.9)	9.7	(-1.5)	9.4	(3.0)	9.0	(5.0)	9.5	(2.7)
IV. Freedom to Use Alternative Currencies	**4.9**		**7.5**		**10.0**		**7.5**		**10.0**		**10.0**		**7.5**	
(a) Ownership of Foreign Currency	0.0		5.0		10.0		5.0		10.0		10.0		5.0	
(b) Black Market Exchange Rate	9.8	(1.0)	10.0	(0.0)	10.0	(0.0)	10.0	(0.0)	10.0	(0.0)	10.0	(0.0)	10.0	(0.0)
V. Legal Structure and Property Rights	**6.5**		**4.8**		**7.6**		**7.2**		**7.5**		**7.0**		**5.9**	
(a) Legal Security	6.5		4.8		8.4		6.1		6.6				8.1	
(b) Rule of Law					6.7		8.2		8.3		7.0		3.8	
VI. International Exchange	**6.1**		**7.2**		**7.1**		**7.4**		**7.2**		**7.4**		**6.9**	
(a) Taxes on International Trade														
i. Taxes as a Percentage of Exports and Imports	4.7	(8.0)	5.3	(7.0)	4.9	(7.7)	6.2	(5.7)	7.9	(3.2)	8.9	(1.6)	8.9	(1.6)
ii. Mean Tariff Rate			7.6	(12.0)	7.9	(10.6)	7.3	(13.6)	7.4	(13.0)	7.4	(12.8)	8.2	(9.1)
iii. Standard Deviation of Tariff Rates									5.0	(12.5)	4.4	(14.0)	2.2	(19.6)
(b) Size of Trade Sector	9.1	(79.9)	10.0	(86.8)	10.0	(-12.6)	10.0	(104.7)	10.0	(150.6)	10.0	(194.4)	10.0	(206.9)
VII. Freedom of Exchange in Financial Markets	**6.4**		**5.9**		**5.9**		**6.9**		**7.0**		**7.0**		**6.4**	
(a) Private Ownership of Banks	5.0	(40-75)	5.0	(40-75)	5.0	(40-75)	5.0	(40-75)	5.0	(40-75)	5.0	(40-75)	5.0	(40-75)
(b) Extension of Credit to Private Sector	9.9	(98.7)	8.2	(82.2)	7.9	(78.9)	8.0	(80.3)	8.4	(84.3)	8.7	(86.6)	9.4	(94.1)
(c) Avoidance of Negative Interest Rates					6.0		10.0		10.0		10.0		10.0	
(d) Capital Transactions with Foreigners	5.0		5.0		5.0		5.0		5.0		5.0		2.0	

MALI

	1970	1975	1980	1985	1990	1995	1999
Summary Ratings		4.7	5.4	5.2	4.9	5.4	5.3
Rank		53	44	57	67	80	92

Components of Economic Freedom	1970	1975	1980	1985	1990	1995	1999
I. Size of Government	**8.5**	**9.8**	**9.8**	**8.7**	**8.6**	**6.5**	**6.7**
(a) Government Consumption	8.5 (11.0)	10.0 (4.6)	10.0 (4.9)	7.9 (13.1)	7.3 (15.1)	6.5 (18.0)	6.7 (17.2)
(b) Transfers and Subsidies		9.5 (2.3)	9.5 (2.3)	9.5 (2.3)	10.0 (0.6)		
II. Structure of the Economy and Use of Markets					**1.7**	**3.5**	**3.5**
(a) Government Enterprises	6.0 (10.7)	6.0 (16.8)	4.0 (21.4)	4.0 (22.4)	4.0	4.0	4.0
(b) Price Controls					0.0	4.0	4.0
(c) Top Marginal Tax Rate							
(d) Conscription	10.0	10.0	10.0	0.0	0.0	0.0	0.0
III. Monetary Policy and Price Stability	**8.3**	**6.5**	**7.9**	**8.6**	**9.3**	**6.8**	**7.5**
(a) Annual Money Growth	9.1 (4.3)	7.0 (15.3)	8.1 (9.3)	7.7 (11.4)	9.0 (-5.0)	7.7 (11.6)	7.2 (13.9)
(b) Inflation Variability	6.9 (7.8)	7.2 (7.1)	8.8 (2.9)	8.3 (4.3)	9.4 (1.6)	5.2 (12.0)	5.6 (11.1)
(c) Recent Inflation Rate	8.8 (6.1)	5.4 (23.0)	6.7 (16.3)	9.7 (1.3)	9.5 (2.7)	7.5 (12.5)	9.8 (-1.2)
IV. Freedom to Use Alternative Currencies	**4.7**	**4.3**	**4.5**	**4.9**	**4.6**	**4.9**	**7.3**
(a) Ownership of Foreign Currency	0.0	0.0	0.0	0.0	0.0	0.0	5.0
(b) Black Market Exchange Rate	9.4 (3.0)	8.6 (7.0)	9.0 (5.0)	9.8 (1.0)	9.2 (4.0)	9.8 (1.0)	9.6 (2.0)
V. Legal Structure and Property Rights			**4.3**	**2.7**	**2.6**	**7.0**	**3.8**
(a) Legal Security			2.8	2.2	1.9		
(b) Rule of Law			5.8	3.1	3.3	7.0	3.8
VI. International Exchange		**1.9**	**5.1**	**5.2**	**5.8**	**6.2**	**5.6**
(a) Taxes on International Trade							
i. Taxes as a Percentage of Exports and Imports		0.6 (14.1)	7.5 (3.8)	6.7 (5.0)	6.9 (4.6)	6.8 (4.8)	5.6 (22.1)
ii. Mean Tariff Rate			3.0 (35.0)	3.0 (35.0)	5.0 (25.0)	3.0 (35.0)	
iii. Standard Deviation of Tariff Rates						9.0 (2.4)	
(b) Size of Trade Sector	4.2 (32.5)	4.5 (41.3)	4.9 (49.4)	7.0 (64.6)	5.2 (49.7)	5.7 (59.9)	5.6 (58.0)
VII. Freedom of Exchange in Financial Markets		**3.5**	**3.6**	**4.1**	**4.5**	**3.9**	**4.0**
(a) Private Ownership of Banks		2.0 (10-40)	2.0 (10-40)	2.0 (10-40)	2.0 (10-40)	2.0 (10-40)	2.0 (10-40)
(b) Extension of Credit to Private Sector	8.7 (87.0)	9.8 (97.7)	9.9 (98.7)	9.7 (96.9)	9.6 (95.6)	8.7 (87.0)	9.5 (95.3)
(c) Avoidance of Negative Interest Rates			4.0	6.0	8.0	6.0	6.0
(d) Capital Transactions with Foreigners	0.0			0.0	0.0	0.0	0.0

MALTA

Summary Ratings	1970	1975	1980	1985	1990	1995	1999
Summary Ratings	6.1	5.4	5.1	5.0	5.1	6.7	6.7
Rank	34	40	56	63	63	50	56

Components of Economic Freedom	1970	1975	1980	1985	1990	1995	1999
I. Size of Government	**6.2**	**5.9**	**6.3**	**5.8**	**5.6**	**5.4**	**5.0**
(a) Government Consumption	5.9 (19.9)	5.8 (20.4)	5.9 (20.0)	5.8 (20.2)	5.3 (21.9)	4.4 (25.1)	4.6 (24.3)
(b) Transfers and Subsidies	6.5 (13.3)	6.1 (14.7)	6.8 (12.2)	5.9 (15.7)	5.9 (15.6)	6.5 (13.4)	5.5 (17.2)
II. Structure of the Economy and Use of Markets			**3.3**	**4.3**	**2.8**	**5.3**	**5.3**
(a) Government Enterprises	4.0 (36.5)	2.0 (46.3)	4.0 (28.6)	6.0 (20.0)	6.0 (28.8)	6.0	6.0
(b) Price Controls				0.0	0.0	2.0	2.0
(c) Top Marginal Tax Rate			0.0 (55)	0.0 (65)	0.0 (65)	7.0 (35)	7.0 (35)
(d) Conscription			10.0	10.0	10.0	10.0	10.0
III. Monetary Policy and Price Stability	**9.1**	**8.9**	**8.4**	**9.4**	**9.7**	**9.5**	**9.6**
(a) Annual Money Growth	8.9 (5.7)	8.6 (7.1)	8.9 (5.5)	9.6 (-2.1)	10.0 (-0.2)	9.9 (-0.4)	9.8 (-1.0)
(b) Inflation Variability	8.9 (2.7)	9.1 (2.3)	8.8 (3.0)	8.8 (3.1)	9.7 (0.6)	9.6 (0.9)	9.5 (1.2)
(c) Recent Inflation Rate	9.5 (2.7)	8.9 (5.4)	7.5 (12.4)	9.9 (0.6)	9.4 (3.2)	8.9 (5.6)	9.6 (2.1)
IV. Freedom to Use Alternative Currencies	**9.4**	**4.5**	**3.8**	**4.3**	**4.8**	**4.6**	**4.7**
(a) Ownership of Foreign Currency	0.0	0.0	0.0	0.0	0.0	0.0	0.0
(b) Black Market Exchange Rate	9.4 (3.0)	9.0 (5.0)	7.6 (-2.0)	8.6 (7.0)	9.6 (2.0)	9.2 (4.0)	9.4 (3.0)
V. Legal Structure and Property Rights				**3.3**	**4.6**	**10.0**	**10.0**
(a) Legal Security				3.5	5.9		
(b) Rule of Law				3.1	3.3	10.0	10.0
VI. International Exchange	**4.6**	**6.3**	**6.0**	**6.0**	**6.0**	**7.8**	**7.9**
(a) Taxes on International Trade							
i. Taxes as a Percentage of Exports and Imports	4.9 (7.6)	6.9 (4.6)	6.7 (4.9)	7.0 (4.5)	6.7 (4.9)	9.5 (0.8)	9.5 (0.8)
ii. Mean Tariff Rate							8.5 (7.6)
iii. Standard Deviation of Tariff Rates							7.7 (5.8)
(b) Size of Trade Sector	3.9 (129.3)	4.9 (179.1)	4.6 (187.4)	4.1 (160.9)	4.5 (184.1)	4.5 (201.4)	4.0 (182.4)
VII. Freedom of Exchange in Financial Markets	**3.1**	**3.2**	**4.0**	**4.0**	**3.8**	**4.8**	**4.6**
(a) Private Ownership of Banks	0.0 (0-10)	0.0 (0-10)	0.0 (0-10)	0.0 (0)	0.0 (0)	0.0 (0-10)	0.0 (0-10)
(b) Extension of Credit to Private Sector	8.5 (84.8)	8.9 (89.4)	9.4 (94.4)	9.2 (91.6)	8.4 (84.2)	8.6 (86.4)	7.7 (76.8)
(c) Avoidance of Negative Interest Rates			6.0	6.0	6.0	10.0	10.0
(d) Capital Transactions with Foreigners	2.0	2.0	2.0	2.0	2.0	2.0	2.0

MAURITIUS

Summary Ratings / Rank

	1970	1975	1980	1985	1990	1995	1999
Summary Ratings		4.6	4.5	6.3	5.8	7.5	7.4
Rank		55	71	27	47	29	36

Components of Economic Freedom (rating, with underlying data in parentheses)

	1970	1975	1980	1985	1990	1995	1999
I. Size of Government	**8.3**	**7.8**	**7.8**	**8.1**	**8.1**	**8.0**	**7.9**
(a) Government Consumption	7.3 (15.2)	7.3 (15.2)	7.1 (15.7)	7.4 (14.7)	7.2 (15.4)	7.1 (15.7)	7.3 (15.3)
(b) Transfers and Subsidies	9.3 (3.2)	8.3 (6.6)	8.4 (6.5)	8.7 (5.2)	9.0 (4.2)	8.9 (4.4)	8.6 (5.7)
II. Structure of the Economy and Use of Markets			**4.4**	**5.9**	**5.3**	**5.5**	**6.9**
(a) Government Enterprises	4.0 (32.2)	6.0 (18.8)	4.0 (36.0)	4.0 (32.4)	4.0 (36.8)	4.0 (33.0)	6.0 (26.5)
(b) Price Controls					4.0	4.0	6.0
(c) Top Marginal Tax Rate			3.0 (50)	7.0 (35)	7.0 (35)	8.0 (30)	8.0 (30)
(d) Conscription	10.0	10.0	10.0	10.0	10.0	10.0	10.0
III. Monetary Policy and Price Stability	**9.6**	**4.9**	**6.5**	**9.2**	**8.0**	**9.2**	**9.2**
(a) Annual Money Growth	9.8 (1.1)	3.8 (30.9)	8.9 (5.7)	9.7 (-1.4)	6.7 (16.3)	9.0 (5.3)	9.2 (4.0)
(b) Inflation Variability	9.2 (2.0)	1.9 (20.2)	5.8 (10.5)	9.5 (1.1)	9.4 (1.6)	9.5 (1.4)	9.7 (0.8)
(c) Recent Inflation Rate	9.7 (1.6)	8.9 (5.3)	4.7 (26.6)	8.4 (8.2)	8.0 (10.1)	9.1 (4.7)	8.6 (6.9)
IV. Freedom to Use Alternative Currencies	**0.0**	**0.3**	**1.0**	**4.9**	**4.2**	**10.0**	**10.0**
(a) Ownership of Foreign Currency	0.0	0.0	0.0	0.0	0.0	10.0	10.0
(b) Black Market Exchange Rate	0.0 (55.0)	0.6 (47.0)	2.0 (40.0)	9.8 (1.0)	8.4 (8.0)	10.0 (0.0)	10.0 (0.0)
V. Legal Structure and Property Rights				**7.2**	**7.1**	**7.0**	**7.0**
(a) Legal Security				6.1	5.9		8.2
(b) Rule of Law				8.2	8.3	7.0	5.8
VI. International Exchange	**5.2**	**5.3**	**3.6**	**3.6**	**3.5**	**5.5**	**3.8**
(a) Taxes on International Trade							
i. Taxes as a Percentage of Exports and Imports	5.6 (6.6)	5.3 (7.1)	3.6 (9.6)	3.6 (9.6)	4.9 (7.6)	6.1 (5.9)	6.7 (5.0)
ii. Mean Tariff Rate			3.0 (34.9)	3.0 (34.9)	4.5 (27.6)	5.3 (23.4)	4.2 (29.1)
iii. Standard Deviation of Tariff Rates					0.0 (91.5)		0.0 (26.2)
(b) Size of Trade Sector	4.4 (85.1)	5.4 (112.3)	4.8 (112.6)	5.0 (108.9)	5.9 (137.7)	4.7 (121.9)	5.0 (129.8)
VII. Freedom of Exchange in Financial Markets		**5.3**	**5.4**	**6.7**	**6.0**	**8.3**	**8.5**
(a) Private Ownership of Banks	8.1 (80.7)	8.0 (75-90)	8.0 (75-90)	8.0 (75-90)	8.0 (90-100)	8.0 (90-100)	8.0 (90-100)
(b) Extension of Credit to Private Sector		5.9 (59.0)	6.6 (65.5)	7.4 (74.1)	6.4 (63.7)	6.9 (69.0)	8.0 (80.3)
(c) Avoidance of Negative Interest Rates				10.0	8.0	10.0	8.0
(d) Capital Transactions with Foreigners	2.0	2.0	2.0	2.0	2.0	8.0	10.0

MEXICO

Summary Ratings	1970	1975	1980	1985	1990	1995	1999
Summary Ratings	6.9	5.6	5.1	4.9	6.5	7.0	6.5
Rank	20	35	56	68	35	43	62

Components of Economic Freedom	1970	1975	1980	1985	1990	1995	1999
I. Size of Government	**9.4**	**8.7**	**8.4**	**8.4**	**8.9**	**7.9**	**7.8**
(a) Government Consumption	9.4 (8.2)	8.3 (11.7)	7.8 (13.4)	8.1 (12.5)	8.6 (10.8)	7.8 (13.5)	8.0 (12.8)
(b) Transfers and Subsidies	9.5 (2.2)	9.0 (4.1)	8.9 (4.4)	8.7 (5.4)	9.3 (3.2)	8.1 (7.5)	7.6 (9.2)
II. Structure of the Economy and Use of Markets	**3.5**	**3.5**	**3.1**	**3.1**	**3.5**	**5.8**	**7.2**
(a) Government Enterprises	4.0 (33.3)	2.0 (40.2)	2.0 (43.5)	2.0 (38.0)	4.0 (23.2)	6.0 (19.6)	8.0 (18.6)
(b) Price Controls					0.0	5.0	7.0
(c) Top Marginal Tax Rate		5.0 (47)	4.0 (55)	4.0 (55)	7.0 (40)	7.0 (35)	7.0 (40)
(d) Conscription	5.0	5.0	5.0	5.0	5.0	5.0	5.0
III. Monetary Policy and Price Stability	**8.8**	**7.5**	**6.5**	**1.0**	**1.4**	**4.4**	**6.4**
(a) Annual Money Growth	8.9 (5.5)	7.7 (11.5)	5.1 (24.7)	1.1 (44.3)	0.0 (67.4)	5.1 (24.4)	7.4 (13.1)
(b) Inflation Variability	9.2 (2.0)	8.2 (4.5)	9.1 (2.3)	1.9 (20.3)	0.0 (43.9)	5.6 (11.0)	4.9 (12.7)
(c) Recent Inflation Rate	8.2 (9.0)	6.4 (17.9)	5.4 (22.8)	0.0 (54.0)	4.4 (28.1)	2.4 (37.9)	6.7 (16.6)
IV. Freedom to Use Alternative Currencies	**10.0**	**10.0**	**5.0**	**7.5**	**10.0**	**7.5**	**7.5**
(a) Ownership of Foreign Currency	10.0	10.0	10.0	10.0	10.0	5.0	5.0
(b) Black Market Exchange Rate	10.0 (0.0)	10.0 (0.0)	0.0 (92.0)	5.0 (25.0)	10.0 (0.0)	10.0 (0.0)	10.0 (0.0)
V. Legal Structure and Property Rights	**4.9**	**4.1**	**7.1**	**5.9**	**7.8**	**7.0**	**4.2**
(a) Legal Security	4.9	4.1	7.6	3.5	7.3		6.8
(b) Rule of Law			6.7	8.2	8.3	7.0	1.7
VI. International Exchange	**3.4**	**3.2**	**2.1**	**5.7**	**7.6**	**8.2**	**7.7**
(a) Taxes on International Trade							
i. Taxes as a Percentage of Exports and Imports	4.8 (7.8)	4.7 (7.9)	0.0 (17.6)	8.3 (2.6)	8.7 (2.0)	9.3 (1.1)	9.4 (0.9)
ii. Mean Tariff Rate			3.8 (30.9)	4.0 (30.0)	7.8 (11.1)	7.5 (12.6)	7.3 (13.3)
iii. Standard Deviation of Tariff Rates					7.2 (7.0)	7.8 (5.4)	5.8 (10.6)
(b) Size of Trade Sector	0.7 (15.4)	0.0 (14.7)	2.9 (23.7)	4.0 (25.9)	5.9 (38.3)	8.2 (58.8)	9.0 (64.5)
VII. Freedom of Exchange in Financial Markets	**4.7**	**4.3**	**4.7**	**2.2**	**4.6**	**7.3**	**5.4**
(a) Private Ownership of Banks	8.0 (90)	8.0 (90)	8.0 (90)	0.0 (0)	0.0 (0)	8.0 (90)	8.0 (90)
(b) Extension of Credit to Private Sector	4.7 (47.2)	2.7 (26.7)	4.9 (48.7)	3.1 (30.8)	6.0 (59.5)	8.3 (83.2)	4.3 (43.3)
(c) Avoidance of Negative Interest Rates			4.0	4.0	8.0	8.0	4.0
(d) Capital Transactions with Foreigners	2.0	2.0	2.0	2.0	5.0	5.0	5.0

MOROCCO

Summary Ratings	1970	1975	1980	1985	1990	1995	1999
Summary Ratings	5.5	4.9	3.9	4.9	4.7	6.2	6.2
Rank	40	49	88	68	72	57	72

Components of Economic Freedom	1970	1975	1980	1985	1990	1995	1999
I. Size of Government	**7.6**	**7.3**	**7.3**	**7.5**	**7.8**	**7.5**	**5.5**
(a) Government Consumption	7.6 (14.1)	6.2 (19.0)	5.5 (21.3)	6.1 (19.4)	6.1 (19.2)	6.0 (19.6)	5.5 (21.3)
(b) Transfers and Subsidies		8.5 (6.0)	9.0 (4.1)	8.9 (4.6)	9.5 (2.3)	9.1 (3.9)	
II. Structure of the Economy and Use of Markets		**3.1**	**1.9**	**1.1**	**1.4**	**2.8**	**4.4**
(a) Government Enterprises	2.0 (40.3)	0.0 (60.5)	2.0 (46.8)	2.0 (47.5)	4.0 (31.7)	2.0 (41.7)	6.0 (29.2)
(b) Price Controls			2.0	0.0	0.0	4.0	4.0
(c) Top Marginal Tax Rate		8.0 (39)	2.0 (64)	0.0 (87)	0.0 (87)	3.0 (46)	4.0 (44)
(d) Conscription	1.0	1.0	1.0	1.0	1.0	1.0	1.0
III. Monetary Policy and Price Stability	**9.2**	**7.8**	**8.2**	**9.0**	**8.4**	**8.8**	**8.8**
(a) Annual Money Growth	9.4 (3.1)	7.2 (13.9)	8.2 (9.0)	9.0 (4.9)	7.2 (13.8)	8.8 (5.8)	8.7 (6.6)
(b) Inflation Variability	9.0 (2.4)	6.7 (8.4)	8.2 (4.5)	9.6 (0.9)	9.1 (2.4)	9.1 (2.2)	8.0 (5.0)
(c) Recent Inflation Rate	9.3 (3.5)	9.7 (1.5)	8.1 (9.5)	8.3 (8.4)	8.9 (5.7)	8.4 (8.0)	9.9 (0.7)
IV. Freedom to Use Alternative Currencies	**3.9**	**4.7**	**4.9**	**4.3**	**3.7**	**4.9**	**5.0**
(a) Ownership of Foreign Currency	0.0	0.0	0.0	0.0	0.0	0.0	0.0
(b) Black Market Exchange Rate	7.8 (11.0)	9.4 (3.0)	9.8 (1.0)	8.6 (7.0)	7.4 (13.0)	9.8 (1.0)	10.0 (0.0)
V. Legal Structure and Property Rights	**3.6**	**3.0**	**1.5**	**3.9**	**3.9**	**10.0**	**10.0**
(a) Legal Security	3.6	3.0	1.3	4.8	4.6	10.0	
(b) Rule of Law			1.7	3.1	3.3	10.0	10.0
VI. International Exchange	**5.4**	**5.4**	**2.0**	**5.7**	**5.0**	**5.3**	**4.7**
(a) Taxes on International Trade							
i. Taxes as a Percentage of Exports and Imports	5.7 (6.5)	5.0 (7.5)	2.9 (10.7)	5.7 (6.4)	4.3 (8.6)	5.5 (6.8)	
ii. Mean Tariff Rate			0.0 (54.0)	5.3 (23.5)	5.3 (23.5)	5.4 (22.8)	4.8 (26.0)
iii. Standard Deviation of Tariff Rates						4.7 (13.2)	4.6 (13.5)
(b) Size of Trade Sector	4.7 (39.2)	6.1 (55.8)	4.4 (45.3)	6.4 (59.7)	6.1 (59.0)	5.8 (61.3)	4.7 (50.1)
VII. Freedom of Exchange in Financial Markets			**4.3**	**4.6**	**5.0**	**5.2**	**5.6**
(a) Private Ownership of Banks	5.0 (40-75)	5.0 (40-75)	5.0 (40-75)	5.0 (40-75)	5.0 (40-75)	5.0 (40-75)	5.0 (40-75)
(b) Extension of Credit to Private Sector			6.4 (63.7)	5.7 (57.1)	5.3 (52.5)	6.2 (61.5)	8.0 (79.8)
(c) Avoidance of Negative Interest Rates				6.0	8.0	8.0	8.0
(d) Capital Transactions with Foreigners	0.0	2.0	2.0	2.0	2.0	2.0	2.0

MYANMAR

Summary Ratings

	1970	1975	1980	1985	1990	1995	1999
Summary Ratings			2.6	2.1	1.3	2.2	1.9
Rank			105	110	116	122	123

Components of Economic Freedom

	1970	1975	1980	1985	1990	1995	1999
I. Size of Government							
(a) Government Consumption							
(b) Transfers and Subsidies							
II. Structure of the Economy and Use of Markets					**1.2**	**2.0**	**2.8**
(a) Government Enterprises	0.0	0.0	0.0	0.0	0.0 (45.0)	2.0	2.0
(b) Price Controls					0.0	0.0	0.0
(c) Top Marginal Tax Rate							5.0 (40)
(d) Conscription	0.0	10.0	10.0	10.0	10.0	10.0	10.0
III. Monetary Policy and Price Stability	**8.8**	**4.9**	**9.1**	**9.6**	**5.2**	**5.8**	**6.0**
(a) Annual Money Growth	9.1 (-4.3)	6.4 (17.9)	8.9 (5.6)	9.5 (2.3)	6.0 (20.2)	3.8 (30.9)	4.8 (25.8)
(b) Inflation Variability	7.6 (6.0)	1.5 (21.2)	8.6 (3.5)	9.6 (1.0)	3.2 (17.1)	7.6 (6.0)	7.0 (7.4)
(c) Recent Inflation Rate	9.7 (-1.4)	6.7 (16.5)	9.8 (1.2)	9.7 (1.6)	6.3 (18.5)	6.1 (19.4)	6.3 (18.4)
IV. Freedom to Use Alternative Currencies	**0.0**	**0.0**	**0.0**	**0.0**	**0.0**	**0.0**	**0.0**
(a) Ownership of Foreign Currency	0.0	0.0	0.0	0.0	0.0	0.0	0.0
(b) Black Market Exchange Rate	0.0 (261.0)	0.0 (235.0)	0.0 (453.0)	0.0 (341.0)	0.0 (1134.0)	0.0 (1864.0)	0.0 (2604.0)
V. Legal Structure and Property Rights			**5.8**	**3.9**	**3.3**	**7.0**	**3.8**
(a) Legal Security			3.4	4.8	3.2		
(b) Rule of Law			8.3	3.1	3.3	7.0	3.8
VI. International Exchange	**1.6**	**0.0**	**0.7**	**0.0**	**0.0**	**0.0**	**0.0**
(a) Taxes on International Trade							
i. Taxes as a Percentage of Exports and Imports	2.4 (11.4)	0.0 (19.3)	0.5 (14.2)	0.0 (17.6)	0.0 (19.4)	0.0 (24.7)	0.0 (35.9)
ii. Mean Tariff Rate							
iii. Standard Deviation of Tariff Rates							
(b) Size of Trade Sector	0.0 (14.0)	0.0 (12.0)	0.9 (22.0)	0.0 (13.2)	0.0 (7.5)	0.0 (2.6)	0.0 (1.5)
VII. Freedom of Exchange in Financial Markets	**1.4**	**0.8**	**0.3**	**0.0**	**0.0**	**0.0**	**0.6**
(a) Private Ownership of Banks	0.0 (0-10)	0.0 (0-10)	0.0 (0-10)	0.0 (0-10)	0.0 (0-10)	0.0 (0-10)	0.0 (0-10)
(b) Extension of Credit to Private Sector	4.9 (49.4)	2.7 (27.1)	1.4 (14.0)	0.0 (6.1)			
(c) Avoidance of Negative Interest Rates	0.0		0.0	0.0	0.0	0.0	2.0
(d) Capital Transactions with Foreigners		0.0	0.0	0.0	0.0	0.0	0.0

NAMIBIA

Summary Ratings	1970	1975	1980	1985	1990	1995	1999
Summary Ratings					4.6	6.1	6.9
Rank					80	61	50

Components of Economic Freedom	1970	1975	1980	1985	1990	1995	1999
I. Size of Government				**1.3**	**5.4**	**5.2**	**2.5**
(a) Government Consumption			3.4 (28.4)	1.3 (35.6)	1.5 (34.9)	1.1 (36.3)	2.5 (31.4)
(b) Transfers and Subsidies					9.3 (3.2)	9.2 (3.4)	
II. Structure of the Economy and Use of Markets					**3.8**	**4.7**	**4.8**
(a) Government Enterprises			0.0 (57.9)	0.0 (64.5)	4.0 (38.3)	4.0 (35.1)	4.0 (37.8)
(b) Price Controls					2.0	4.0	4.0
(c) Top Marginal Tax Rate							5.0 (40)
(d) Conscription					10.0	10.0	10.0
III. Monetary Policy and Price Stability				**6.0**	**8.2**	**7.5**	**7.6**
(a) Annual Money Growth						5.8 (20.9)	6.6 (17.1)
(b) Inflation Variability				7.0 (7.6)	8.0 (5.0)	8.3 (4.2)	8.0 (5.0)
(c) Recent Inflation Rate				5.0 (24.8)	8.3 (8.3)	8.6 (7.2)	8.3 (8.3)
IV. Freedom to Use Alternative Currencies				**2.5**	**4.7**	**5.0**	**7.5**
(a) Ownership of Foreign Currency				0.0	0.0	0.0	5.0
(b) Black Market Exchange Rate				5.0 (25.0)	9.4 (3.0)	10.0 (0.0)	10.0 (0.0)
V. Legal Structure and Property Rights					**1.7**	**10.0**	**10.0**
(a) Legal Security					0.0		
(b) Rule of Law					3.3	10.0	10.0
VI. International Exchange						**4.4**	**7.6**
(a) Taxes on International Trade			8.1 (9.4)	8.8 (6.0)			
i. Taxes as a Percentage of Exports and Imports					5.1 (7.3)	4.3 (8.6)	
ii. Mean Tariff Rate					7.8 (11.0)	6.1 (19.7)	8.6 (7.2)
iii. Standard Deviation of Tariff Rates					5.5 (11.3)	1.2 (21.9)	6.0 (10.0)
(b) Size of Trade Sector						7.8 (109.1)	9.0 (126.3)
VII. Freedom of Exchange in Financial Markets					**5.5**	**6.1**	**6.6**
(a) Private Ownership of Banks							
(b) Extension of Credit to Private Sector					9.4 (93.6)	9.2 (91.8)	8.6 (86.4)
(c) Avoidance of Negative Interest Rates					6.0	8.0	10.0
(d) Capital Transactions with Foreigners					2.0	2.0	2.0

NEPAL

Summary Ratings	1970	1975	1980	1985	1990	1995	1999
Summary Ratings			5.3	5.1	4.8	5.0	5.4
Rank			49	60	71	94	89

Components of Economic Freedom

Component	1970	1975	1980	1985	1990	1995	1999
I. Size of Government		**9.3**	**9.5**	**8.6**	**9.0**	**8.7**	**8.6**
(a) Government Consumption		9.3 (8.4)	9.5 (7.5)	8.6 (10.8)	9.0 (9.4)	8.7 (10.6)	8.6 (10.9)
(b) Transfers and Subsidies							
II. Structure of the Economy and Use of Markets					**2.9**	**2.9**	**2.9**
(a) Government Enterprises	2.0 (49.0)	4.0 (32.5)	4.0 (37.3)	2.0 (45.8)	2.0 (43.2)	2.0	2.0
(b) Price Controls					2.0	2.0	2.0
(c) Top Marginal Tax Rate							
(d) Conscription	10.0	10.0	10.0	10.0	10.0	10.0	10.0
III. Monetary Policy and Price Stability	**8.3**	**5.9**	**7.8**	**8.2**	**8.0**	**8.0**	**8.7**
(a) Annual Money Growth	8.9 (5.3)	7.7 (11.6)	7.1 (14.4)	7.8 (10.8)	6.9 (15.7)	7.2 (13.9)	8.5 (7.7)
(b) Inflation Variability	7.2 (7.0)	5.5 (11.3)	7.9 (5.4)	9.1 (2.2)	9.5 (1.3)	8.2 (4.6)	9.3 (1.7)
(c) Recent Inflation Rate	8.6 (7.1)	4.5 (27.5)	8.5 (7.6)	7.7 (11.4)	7.9 (10.7)	8.7 (6.3)	8.4 (8.0)
IV. Freedom to Use Alternative Currencies	**0.0**	**1.0**	**5.0**	**3.9**	**3.4**	**3.1**	**3.9**
(a) Ownership of Foreign Currency	0.0	0.0	0.0	0.0	0.0	0.0	0.0
(b) Black Market Exchange Rate	0.0 (55.0)	2.0 (40.0)	10.0 (0.3)	7.8 (11.0)	6.8 (16.0)	6.2 (19.0)	7.8 (11.1)
V. Legal Structure and Property Rights							
(a) Legal Security							
(b) Rule of Law							
VI. International Exchange	**0.4**	**2.7**	**4.2**	**4.6**	**4.2**	**5.5**	**6.3**
(a) Taxes on International Trade	0.6 (14.1)	4.1 (8.9)	4.3 (8.6)	4.9 (7.7)	4.1 (8.8)	6.4 (5.4)	6.7 (5.0)
i. Taxes as a Percentage of Exports and Imports							
ii. Mean Tariff Rate			5.6 (22.1)	5.5 (22.6)	5.5 (22.6)	6.8 (16.1)	7.5 (12.4)
iii. Standard Deviation of Tariff Rates						3.6 (15.9)	5.5 (11.3)
(b) Size of Trade Sector	0.0 (13.2)	0.0 (22.3)	1.1 (30.3)	2.1 (31.5)	1.6 (31.6)	5.0 (58.8)	4.8 (57.5)
VII. Freedom of Exchange in Financial Markets			**2.7**	**2.6**	**3.9**	**3.8**	**4.2**
(a) Private Ownership of Banks	0.0 (0-10)	0.0 (0-10)	0.0 (0-10)	0.0 (0-10)	0.0 (0-10)	0.0 (0-10)	0.0 (0-10)
(b) Extension of Credit to Private Sector		6.0 (59.9)	6.0 (59.9)	5.5 (55.2)	6.7 (66.7)	8.5 (85.4)	8.1 (81.1)
(c) Avoidance of Negative Interest Rates		6.0	6.0	6.0	10.0	8.0	10.0
(d) Capital Transactions with Foreigners	0.0	0.0	0.0	0.0	0.0	0.0	0.0

NETHERLANDS

Summary Ratings	1970	1975	1980	1985	1990	1995	1999
Summary Ratings	8.5	7.1	7.8	7.9	8.2	8.4	8.4
Rank	5	13	7	7	7	7	9

Components of Economic Freedom

Component	1970	1975	1980	1985	1990	1995	1999
I. Size of Government	**5.4**	**4.2**	**3.7**	**3.6**	**4.1**	**4.1**	**2.6**
(a) Government Consumption	5.8 (20.3)	5.2 (22.2)	5.2 (22.2)	5.6 (21.0)	5.9 (19.9)	6.1 (19.3)	2.5 (31.6)
(b) Transfers and Subsidies	5.0 (18.7)	3.2 (25.6)	2.1 (29.4)	1.5 (31.6)	2.3 (28.7)	2.0 (29.7)	2.8 (27.0)
II. Structure of the Economy and Use of Markets		**3.8**	**4.1**	**4.1**	**5.7**	**6.4**	**7.3**
(a) Government Enterprises	4.0 (33.7)	4.0 (33.6)	8.0 (14.8)	8.0 (14.7)	10.0 (12.7)	10.0 (13.8)	10.0
(b) Price Controls		5.0	0.0	0.0	7.0	7.0	8.0
(c) Top Marginal Tax Rate		5.0 (46)	0.0 (72)	0.0 (72)	0.0 (72)	2.0 (60)	2.0 (60)
(d) Conscription	0.0	0.0	1.0	1.0	1.0	3.0	10.0
III. Monetary Policy and Price Stability	**9.2**	**8.7**	**9.2**	**9.3**	**9.4**	**9.5**	**9.3**
(a) Annual Money Growth	9.2 (3.8)	8.3 (8.5)	9.2 (3.9)	9.0 (4.8)	9.2 (4.2)	9.1 (4.3)	8.8 (6.0)
(b) Inflation Variability	9.6 (1.0)	9.7 (0.7)	9.3 (1.6)	9.3 (1.8)	9.6 (1.0)	9.9 (0.4)	9.7 (0.8)
(c) Recent Inflation Rate	8.8 (6.2)	8.0 (10.2)	8.9 (5.5)	9.6 (1.8)	9.5 (2.3)	9.7 (1.6)	9.6 (2.2)
IV. Freedom to Use Alternative Currencies	**10.0**	**10.0**	**10.0**	**10.0**	**10.0**	**10.0**	**10.0**
(a) Ownership of Foreign Currency	10.0	10.0	10.0	10.0	10.0	10.0	10.0
(b) Black Market Exchange Rate	10.0 (0.0)	10.0 (0.0)	10.0 (0.0)	10.0 (0.0)	10.0 (0.0)	10.0 (0.0)	10.0 (0.0)
V. Legal Structure and Property Rights	**10.0**	**7.3**	**8.8**	**10.0**	**10.0**	**10.0**	**9.9**
(a) Legal Security	10.0	7.3	7.6	10.0	10.0		9.9
(b) Rule of Law			10.0	10.0	10.0	10.0	10.0
VI. International Exchange	**8.7**	**8.1**	**8.4**	**8.8**	**8.1**	**8.2**	**8.3**
(a) Taxes on International Trade							
i. Taxes as a Percentage of Exports and Imports	8.9 (1.7)	9.1 (1.3)	9.7 (0.4)	9.7 (0.4)	9.7 (0.5)	9.7 (0.5)	9.7 (0.5)
ii. Mean Tariff Rate		8.1 (9.4)	8.2 (8.8)	8.5 (7.5)	8.5 (7.4)	8.7 (6.7)	8.9 (5.6)
iii. Standard Deviation of Tariff Rates					7.1 (7.2)	7.6 (5.9)	7.6 (5.9)
(b) Size of Trade Sector	8.5 (88.7)	6.1 (93.6)	6.1 (102.7)	7.5 (116.8)	6.4 (103.7)	5.6 (100.2)	5.9 (103.8)
VII. Freedom of Exchange in Financial Markets	**7.1**	**7.2**	**9.1**	**8.4**	**9.0**	**9.6**	**9.6**
(a) Private Ownership of Banks	10.0 (95-100)	10.0 (95-100)	10.0 (95-100)	8.0 (82)	10.0 (95-100)	10.0 (95-100)	10.0 (95-100)
(b) Extension of Credit to Private Sector	6.7 (67.2)	7.8 (77.6)	8.3 (83.2)	7.8 (77.6)	7.8 (77.7)	8.2 (82.4)	8.2 (81.8)
(c) Avoidance of Negative Interest Rates	10.0	6.0	10.0	10.0	10.0	10.0	10.0
(d) Capital Transactions with Foreigners	2.0	5.0	8.0	8.0	8.0	10.0	10.0

NEW ZEALAND

	1970	1975	1980	1985	1990	1995	1999
Summary Ratings	6.9	5.6	6.4	6.3	8.0	9.0	8.9
Rank	20	35	23	27	11	3	3
Components of Economic Freedom							
I. Size of Government	6.7	5.3	4.6	5.1	4.1	6.4	6.4
(a) Government Consumption	6.7 (17.1)	6.0 (19.6)	5.1 (22.6)	5.6 (20.9)	5.5 (21.2)	6.2 (18.9)	6.2 (19.1)
(b) Transfers and Subsidies		4.6 (20.2)	4.2 (21.9)	4.5 (20.6)	2.6 (27.5)	6.6 (12.8)	6.5 (13.2)
II. Structure of the Economy and Use of Markets	4.4	4.4	3.7	3.3	7.9	9.2	9.2
(a) Government Enterprises	4.0 (33.9)	4.0 (37.5)	4.0 (33.8)	4.0 (31.4)	7.0 (25.3)	10.0 (12.0)	10.0 (13.3)
(b) Price Controls				0.0	9.0	10.0	10.0
(c) Top Marginal Tax Rate		3.0 (60)	1.0 (61.5)	0.0 (66)	7.0 (33)	7.0 (33)	7.0 (33)
(d) Conscription	10.0	10.0	10.0	10.0	10.0	10.0	10.0
III. Monetary Policy and Price Stability	8.3	7.7	8.4	8.1	6.3	9.5	8.7
(a) Annual Money Growth	9.7 (-1.8)	7.6 (12.2)	8.9 (5.6)	8.3 (8.5)	1.8 (40.9)	9.1 (4.7)	6.8 (-15.8)
(b) Inflation Variability	7.8 (5.6)	8.5 (3.7)	9.2 (2.0)	8.7 (3.3)	7.8 (5.4)	9.9 (0.3)	9.5 (1.2)
(c) Recent Inflation Rate	7.3 (13.3)	7.2 (14.1)	6.9 (15.4)	7.2 (14.2)	9.5 (2.7)	9.5 (2.3)	10.0 (-0.1)
IV. Freedom to Use Alternative Currencies	3.9	4.5	5.0	4.6	10.0	10.0	10.0
(a) Ownership of Foreign Currency	0.0	0.0	0.0	0.0	10.0	10.0	10.0
(b) Black Market Exchange Rate	7.8 (11.0)	9.0 (5.0)	10.0 (0.0)	9.2 (4.0)	10.0 (0.0)	10.0 (0.0)	10.0 (0.0)
V. Legal Structure and Property Rights	9.6	5.5	9.6	9.4	10.0	10.0	9.8
(a) Legal Security	9.6	5.5	9.2	8.7	10.0		9.6
(b) Rule of Law			10.0	10.0	10.0	10.0	10.0
VI. International Exchange	7.2	6.9	7.3	7.3	6.3	7.3	8.1
(a) Taxes on International Trade							
i. Taxes as a Percentage of Exports and Imports	8.2 (2.7)	8.4 (2.4)	8.3 (2.5)	8.7 (2.0)	8.9 (1.7)	9.1 (1.4)	8.9 (1.6)
ii. Mean Tariff Rate		6.2 (18.9)	7.4 (3.0)	6.8 (16.0)	7.1 (14.5)	8.3 (8.5)	9.2 (3.8)
iii. Standard Deviation of Tariff Rates					3.7 (15.7)	5.8 (10.4)	8.0 (5.1)
(b) Size of Trade Sector	5.1 (48.3)	5.2 (54.9)	5.2 (62.1)	5.8 (64.6)	4.5 (54.7)	4.3 (58.7)	4.5 (60.7)
VII. Freedom of Exchange in Financial Markets	5.8	5.7	5.8	6.1	9.7	9.9	9.3
(a) Private Ownership of Banks	5.0 (40-75)	5.0 (40-75)	5.0 (40-75)	5.0 (40-75)	10.0 (95-100)	10.0 (95-100)	10.0 (95-100)
(b) Extension of Credit to Private Sector	8.0 (79.6)	7.4 (73.6)	7.5 (75.3)	6.9 (69.0)	8.8 (87.6)	9.6 (95.7)	9.5 (94.6)
(c) Avoidance of Negative Interest Rates			6.0	8.0	10.0	10.0	10.0
(d) Capital Transactions with Foreigners	5.0	5.0	5.0	5.0	10.0	10.0	8.0

NICARAGUA

Summary Ratings	1970	1975	1980	1985	1990	1995	1999
Summary Ratings	7.5	7.5	3.7	1.7	3.0	5.6	7.5
Rank	8	8	90	111	109	75	34

Components of Economic Freedom

	1970	1975	1980	1985	1990	1995	1999
I. Size of Government	**8.5**	**9.1**	**7.6**	**4.2**	**4.1**	**8.3**	**7.9**
(a) Government Consumption	8.5 (11.0)	8.7 (10.3)	6.1 (19.3)	0.0 (42.6)	0.0 (42.6)	8.0 (12.7)	7.9 (13.2)
(b) Transfers and Subsidies		9.5 (2.4)	9.0 (4.1)	8.4 (6.2)	8.3 (6.8)	8.5 (6.0)	
II. Structure of the Economy and Use of Markets		**7.4**	**2.5**	**1.9**	**0.9**	**4.2**	**5.5**
(a) Government Enterprises	4.0 (31.5)	6.0 (29.8)	0.0 (71.9)	0.0	2.0 (45.3)	0.0 (55.9)	4.0 (31.9)
(b) Price Controls					0.0	4.0	4.0
(c) Top Marginal Tax Rate		10.0 (21)	5.0 (50)	5.0 (50)		8.0 (30)	8.0 (30)
(d) Conscription	3.0	5.0	5.0	0.0	0.0	10.0	10.0
III. Monetary Policy and Price Stability	**9.2**	**7.9**	**4.0**	**0.0**	**0.0**	**2.6**	**7.4**
(a) Annual Money Growth	8.8 (5.9)	7.5 (12.3)	4.7 (26.7)	0.0 (69.6)	0.0 (2072.1)	0.0 (89.1)	5.5 (22.5)
(b) Inflation Variability	8.9 (2.7)	7.6 (6.0)	4.6 (13.6)	0.0 (60.1)	0.0 (4792.5)	0.0 (1852.1)	9.1 (2.3)
(c) Recent Inflation Rate	9.8 (-1.1)	8.7 (6.8)	2.7 (36.6)	0.0 (168.1)	0.0 (5012.7)	8.0 (9.8)	7.8 (11.2)
IV. Freedom to Use Alternative Currencies	**8.1**	**7.9**	**5.0**	**0.0**	**4.0**	**6.7**	**10.0**
(a) Ownership of Foreign Currency	10.0	10.0	10.0	0.0	0.0	5.0	10.0
(b) Black Market Exchange Rate	6.2 (19.0)	5.8 (21.0)	0.0 (91.0)	0.0 (382.0)	8.0 (10.0)	8.4 (8.0)	10.0 (0.0)
V. Legal Structure and Property Rights			**2.0**	**2.0**	**3.9**	**4.1**	**5.8**
(a) Legal Security			2.3	0.9	4.6		
(b) Rule of Law			1.7	3.1	3.3	4.1	5.8
VI. International Exchange	**6.0**	**6.2**	**2.6**	**2.2**	**5.9**	**5.7**	**7.4**
(a) Taxes on International Trade							
i. Taxes as a Percentage of Exports and Imports	7.0 (4.5)	6.7 (4.9)	4.2 (8.7)	5.1 (7.4)	7.1 (4.3)	6.1 (5.9)	7.1 (4.3)
ii. Mean Tariff Rate			0.0 (54.0)	0.0 (54.0)	5.0 (24.8)	7.9 (10.7)	7.8 (10.9)
iii. Standard Deviation of Tariff Rates						2.9 (17.8)	7.0 (7.5)
(b) Size of Trade Sector	4.1 (55.3)	5.0 (65.7)	4.6 (67.5)	0.9 (36.6)	5.2 (71.4)	6.0 (90.9)	7.6 (113.7)
VII. Freedom of Exchange in Financial Markets				**1.3**	**1.0**	**6.8**	**8.3**
(a) Private Ownership of Banks							
(b) Extension of Credit to Private Sector				4.4 (44.0)	3.5 (35.4)	10.0 (99.8)	9.1 (90.8)
(c) Avoidance of Negative Interest Rates	5.0	5.0	0.0	0.0	0.0	6.0	8.0
(d) Capital Transactions with Foreigners			0.0	0.0	0.0	5.0	8.0

NIGER

Summary Ratings

	1970	1975	1980	1985	1990	1995	1999
Summary Ratings		5.4	5.1	5.3	4.7	4.0	5.0
Rank		40	56	54	72	111	97

Components of Economic Freedom

	1970	1975	1980	1985	1990	1995	1999
I. Size of Government	**9.1**	**8.5**	**8.8**	**8.6**	**7.6**	**7.6**	**7.9**
(a) Government Consumption	9.1 (8.9)	8.5 (11.1)	8.2 (12.1)	8.6 (10.9)	7.6 (14.1)	7.6 (14.1)	7.9 (13.2)
(b) Transfers and Subsidies			9.5 (2.5)				
II. Structure of the Economy and Use of Markets					**0.0**	**3.5**	**3.5**
(a) Government Enterprises	4.0 (36.8)	4.0	4.0 (35.5)	4.0 (29.4)	0.0 (76.5)	4.0	4.0
(b) Price Controls					0.0	4.0	4.0
(c) Top Marginal Tax Rate							
(d) Conscription		10.0	0.0	0.0	0.0	0.0	0.0
III. Monetary Policy and Price Stability	**8.6**	**6.3**	**6.2**	**8.5**	**9.5**	**7.7**	**7.9**
(a) Annual Money Growth	9.4 (2.8)	6.1 (19.5)	5.0 (25.0)	9.3 (3.3)	9.9 (-0.6)	9.3 (3.5)	8.5 (-7.5)
(b) Inflation Variability	7.8 (5.6)	4.2 (14.6)	7.9 (5.4)	7.4 (6.6)	8.9 (2.9)	4.6 (13.4)	5.5 (11.2)
(c) Recent Inflation Rate	8.6 (7.1)	8.7 (-6.4)	5.8 (20.8)	8.8 (-5.9)	9.7 (-1.6)	8.9 (5.4)	9.5 (-2.3)
IV. Freedom to Use Alternative Currencies	**4.8**	**4.8**	**4.8**	**4.9**	**4.6**	**4.9**	**7.3**
(a) Ownership of Foreign Currency	0.0	0.0	0.0	0.0	0.0	0.0	5.0
(b) Black Market Exchange Rate	9.6 (2.0)	9.6 (2.0)	9.6 (2.0)	9.8 (1.0)	9.2 (4.0)	9.8 (1.0)	9.6 (2.0)
V. Legal Structure and Property Rights			**4.9**	**5.1**	**5.8**	**0.0**	**1.7**
(a) Legal Security			4.0	3.5	3.2		
(b) Rule of Law			5.8	6.6	8.3	0.0	1.7
VI. International Exchange		**5.5**	**4.9**	**4.2**	**3.5**	**3.0**	**4.9**
(a) Taxes on International Trade							
i. Taxes as a Percentage of Exports and Imports							
ii. Mean Tariff Rate		5.5 (6.7)	4.4 (8.4)	3.7 (9.5)	3.5 (9.8)	2.8 (10.8)	5.6 (22.1)
iii. Standard Deviation of Tariff Rates							
(b) Size of Trade Sector	2.9 (28.9)	5.3 (50.2)	6.1 (52.9)	5.4 (51.1)	3.6 (38.0)	3.3 (39.7)	3.4 (39.7)
VII. Freedom of Exchange in Financial Markets		**3.2**	**2.9**	**3.0**	**4.3**	**4.5**	**4.0**
(a) Private Ownership of Banks	9.6 (95.5)	2.0 (10-40)	2.0 (10-40)	2.0 (10-40)	2.0 (10-40)	5.0 (40-75)	5.0 (40-75)
(b) Extension of Credit to Private Sector		9.0 (89.7)	8.9 (89.0)	8.2 (82.3)	8.4 (83.7)	7.7 (77.2)	8.0 (79.8)
(c) Avoidance of Negative Interest Rates		2.0	2.0		8.0	6.0	4.0
(d) Capital Transactions with Foreigners	0.0	0.0	0.0	0.0	0.0	0.0	0.0

NIGERIA

Summary Ratings	1970	1975	1980	1985	1990	1995	1999
Summary Ratings	3.8	3.7	3.1	3.5	3.3	3.4	4.5
Rank	52	69	102	98	107	119	107

Components of Economic Freedom

	1970	1975	1980	1985	1990	1995	1999
I. Size of Government	**9.5**	**8.2**	**6.6**	**8.5**	**5.5**	**7.8**	**7.9**
(a) Government Consumption	9.0 (9.3)	7.1 (15.9)	6.6 (17.6)	7.2 (15.5)	5.5 (21.4)	7.8 (13.6)	7.9 (13.0)
(b) Transfers and Subsidies	9.9 (0.8)	9.4 (2.8)		9.8 (1.3)			
II. Structure of the Economy and Use of Markets	**3.3**		**1.7**	**2.5**	**1.4**	**2.6**	**4.5**
(a) Government Enterprises	8.0 (14.6)	4.0 (30.7)	0.0 (50.9)	0.0 (49.8)	0.0 (88.1)	0.0	0.0
(b) Price Controls					0.0	0.0	4.0
(c) Top Marginal Tax Rate			1.0 (70)	3.0 (55)	2.0 (55)	7.0 (35)	9.0 (25)
(d) Conscription	10.0	10.0	10.0	10.0	10.0	10.0	10.0
III. Monetary Policy and Price Stability	**3.5**	**4.5**	**7.2**	**8.4**	**5.5**	**1.1**	**5.6**
(a) Annual Money Growth	8.0 (10.0)	4.8 (25.9)	4.9 (25.5)	8.6 (7.1)	6.0 (20.1)	2.2 (38.9)	6.4 (18.2)
(b) Inflation Variability	2.1 (19.8)	3.5 (16.3)	9.4 (1.4)	7.4 (6.5)	1.9 (20.2)	1.1 (22.4)	1.6 (21.0)
(c) Recent Inflation Rate	0.0 (51.3)	5.3 (23.5)	7.5 (12.4)	9.3 (3.7)	8.6 (7.2)	0.0 (55.8)	8.7 (6.6)
IV. Freedom to Use Alternative Currencies	**0.0**	**0.7**	**0.0**	**0.0**	**2.7**	**0.0**	**2.5**
(a) Ownership of Foreign Currency	0.0	0.0	0.0	0.0	0.0	0.0	5.0
(b) Black Market Exchange Rate	0.0 (62.0)	1.4 (43.0)	0.0 (72.0)	0.0 (270.0)	5.4 (23.0)	0.0 (286.0)	0.0 (400.0)
V. Legal Structure and Property Rights	**2.8**	**3.5**	**2.7**	**1.8**	**2.5**	**7.0**	**3.8**
(a) Legal Security	2.8	3.5	3.6	2.2	3.2		
(b) Rule of Law			1.7	1.4	1.7	7.0	3.8
VI. International Exchange	**4.5**	**5.9**	**4.5**	**4.5**	**4.4**	**2.2**	
(a) Taxes on International Trade							
i. Taxes as a Percentage of Exports and Imports	5.6 (6.6)	5.6 (6.6)	4.3 (8.5)	6.6 (5.1)	7.3 (4.0)		
ii. Mean Tariff Rate			3.5 (32.6)	2.6 (37.0)	3.1 (34.3)	3.4 (32.8)	
iii. Standard Deviation of Tariff Rates					0.0 (30.8)	0.0 (25.0)	
(b) Size of Trade Sector	2.2 (19.6)	6.6 (41.2)	7.0 (48.6)	4.4 (28.5)	10.0 (72.2)	4.0 (30.1)	7.7 (55.2)
VII. Freedom of Exchange in Financial Markets	**1.3**	**1.3**	**1.3**	**1.9**	**2.4**	**3.2**	**4.3**
(a) Private Ownership of Banks	2.0 (10-40)	2.0 (10-20)	2.0 (10-40)	2.0 (10-40)	2.0 (10-40)	5.0 (40-75)	5.0 (40-75)
(b) Extension of Credit to Private Sector					8.7 (86.8)	8.7 (87.0)	6.6 (66.2)
(c) Avoidance of Negative Interest Rates	2.0	2.0	2.0	4.0	0.0	0.0	4.0
(d) Capital Transactions with Foreigners	0.0	0.0	0.0	0.0	0.0	0.0	2.0

NORWAY

	1970	1975	1980	1985	1990	1995	1999
Summary Ratings	6.9	5.7	6.0	6.7	7.6	7.9	7.8
Rank	20	33	31	21	16	18	24

Components of Economic Freedom	1970	1975	1980	1985	1990	1995	1999
I. Size of Government	**4.6**	**4.1**	**3.7**	**4.0**	**2.9**	**3.6**	**3.8**
(a) Government Consumption	4.7 (24.0)	3.8 (27.1)	3.4 (23.6)	3.7 (27.5)	3.1 (29.6)	3.0 (29.8)	2.8 (30.4)
(b) Transfers and Subsidies	4.5 (20.6)	4.4 (21.0)	4.1 (22.1)	4.3 (21.4)	2.7 (27.3)	4.2 (21.8)	4.7 (19.9)
II. Structure of the Economy and Use of Markets		**2.1**	**2.1**	**2.5**	**4.2**	**5.2**	**5.5**
(a) Government Enterprises	4.0 (31.7)	4.0 (30.5)	4.0 (35.9)	4.0 (34.2)	4.0 (37.4)	4.0 (43.1)	4.0
(b) Price Controls					6.0	7.0	8.0
(c) Top Marginal Tax Rate		0.0 (74)	0.0 (75)	1.0 (64)	3.0 (54)	5.0 (42)	5.0 (41.5)
(d) Conscription	1.0	1.0	1.0	1.0	1.0	3.0	3.0
III. Monetary Policy and Price Stability	**8.3**	**8.4**	**8.7**	**8.4**	**8.2**	**9.2**	**9.5**
(a) Annual Money Growth	8.8 (6.0)	8.0 (10.2)	9.7 (1.5)	7.5 (12.7)	6.6 (16.8)	8.8 (5.9)	9.6 (2.2)
(b) Inflation Variability	8.6 (3.6)	9.2 (2.1)	8.9 (2.6)	8.9 (2.8)	8.9 (2.7)	9.4 (1.4)	9.3 (1.8)
(c) Recent Inflation Rate	7.4 (12.8)	8.0 (10.0)	7.4 (13.1)	9.0 (5.2)	9.2 (3.9)	9.4 (3.1)	9.5 (2.3)
IV. Freedom to Use Alternative Currencies	**5.0**	**4.9**	**4.7**	**5.0**	**10.0**	**10.0**	**10.0**
(a) Ownership of Foreign Currency	0.0	0.0	0.0	0.0	10.0	10.0	10.0
(b) Black Market Exchange Rate	10.0 (0.0)	9.8 (1.0)	9.4 (3.0)	10.0 (0.0)	10.0 (0.0)	10.0 (0.0)	10.0 (0.0)
V. Legal Structure and Property Rights	**9.1**	**5.9**	**8.2**	**9.7**	**10.0**	**10.0**	**9.6**
(a) Legal Security	9.1	5.9	6.4	9.4	10.0		9.2
(b) Rule of Law			10.0	10.0	10.0	10.0	10.0
VI. International Exchange	**8.3**	**8.3**	**8.5**	**8.6**	**8.1**	**7.5**	**7.0**
(a) Taxes on International Trade							
i. Taxes as a Percentage of Exports and Imports	8.9 (1.6)	9.7 (0.5)	9.8 (0.3)	9.8 (0.3)	9.8 (0.3)	9.7 (0.4)	9.8 (0.3)
ii. Mean Tariff Rate	8.3	8.3 (8.5)	8.8 (6.2)	8.9 (5.7)	8.9 (5.7)	8.8 (5.9)	9.2 (4.1)
iii. Standard Deviation of Tariff Rates					7.2 (6.9)	5.7 (10.7)	3.4 (16.5)
(b) Size of Trade Sector	7.0 (74.1)	5.8 (78.8)	5.2 (30.3)	5.5 (78.7)	5.0 (74.7)	4.1 (70.0)	4.4 (74.0)
VII. Freedom of Exchange in Financial Markets	**5.5**	**6.0**	**5.9**	**7.9**	**8.4**	**8.5**	**8.8**
(a) Private Ownership of Banks	10.0 (95-100)	10.0 (95-100)	10.0 (95-100)	10.0 (95-100)	8.0 (75-95)	8.0 (75-95)	8.0 (75-95)
(b) Extension of Credit to Private Sector	6.7 (67.1)	6.2 (61.5)	5.6 (55.5)	6.4 (63.8)	7.5 (75.2)	8.1 (81.1)	9.3 (92.6)
(c) Avoidance of Negative Interest Rates		6.0	6.0	10.0	10.0	10.0	10.0
(d) Capital Transactions with Foreigners	0.0	2.0	2.0	5.0	8.0	8.0	8.0

OMAN

Summary Ratings	1970	1975	1980	1985	1990	1995	1999
Summary Ratings			6.4	7.4	6.9	7.4	7.6
Rank			23	13	29	31	29

Components of Economic Freedom

	1970	1975	1980	1985	1990	1995	1999
I. Size of Government	**4.7**	**4.8**	**4.8**	**4.6**	**4.7**	**5.5**	**6.2**
(a) Government Consumption	0.1 (39.8)	0.0 (66.6)	0.0 (47.4)	0.0 (45.5)	0.0 (58.8)	1.2 (36.0)	2.7 (30.9)
(b) Transfers and Subsidies	9.3 (3.2)	9.7 (1.7)	9.6 (2.0)	9.3 (3.1)	9.3 (2.9)	9.8 (1.3)	9.7 (1.6)
II. Structure of the Economy and Use of Markets	**6.1**	**6.1**	**6.1**	**6.1**	**5.4**	**5.4**	**5.4**
(a) Government Enterprises	0.0 (65.9)	2.0 (43.7)	2.0 (58.8)	2.0	2.0	2.0	2.0
(b) Price Controls					4.0	4.0	4.0
(c) Top Marginal Tax Rate	10.0	10.0	10.0 (0)	10.0 (0)	10.0 (0)	10.0 (0)	10.0 (0)
(d) Conscription	10.0	10.0	10.0	10.0	10.0	10.0	10.0
III. Monetary Policy and Price Stability	**8.2**	**4.7**	**3.4**	**8.9**	**6.8**	**8.9**	**9.3**
(a) Annual Money Growth		4.6 (27.1)	7.8 (11.1)	8.8 (6.1)	8.9 (-5.4)	9.9 (-0.6)	8.9 (-5.6)
(b) Inflation Variability	7.6 (6.1)	0.0 (75.6)	2.2 (19.4)	8.1 (4.8)	4.5 (13.7)	7.6 (6.1)	9.2 (1.9)
(c) Recent Inflation Rate	8.8 (-6.2)	9.5 (2.4)	0.0 (51.1)	9.9 (-0.5)	6.7 (16.6)	9.3 (3.7)	9.9 (0.4)
IV. Freedom to Use Alternative Currencies	**10.0**	**10.0**	**10.0**	**10.0**	**10.0**	**10.0**	**10.0**
(a) Ownership of Foreign Currency	10.0	10.0	10.0	10.0	10.0	10.0	10.0
(b) Black Market Exchange Rate	10.0 (0.0)	10.0 (0.0)	10.0 (0.0)	10.0 (0.0)	10.0 (0.0)	10.0 (0.0)	10.0 (0.0)
V. Legal Structure and Property Rights				**6.5**	**5.6**	**7.0**	**7.9**
(a) Legal Security				4.8	4.6		
(b) Rule of Law				8.2	6.7	7.0	7.9
VI. International Exchange	**8.4**			**8.6**	**8.0**	**7.7**	**7.9**
(a) Taxes on International Trade							
i. Taxes as a Percentage of Exports and Imports	9.5 (0.8)			9.1 (1.4)	9.3 (1.0)	9.3 (1.1)	9.4 (0.9)
ii. Mean Tariff Rate				9.4 (3.0)		8.9 (5.7)	
iii. Standard Deviation of Tariff Rates						6.3 (9.2)	
(b) Size of Trade Sector	6.2 (93.4)	7.9 (118.2)	6.2 (100.3)	5.9 (87.0)	5.4 (83.3)	4.8 (79.7)	4.8 (79.9)
VII. Freedom of Exchange in Financial Markets			**6.3**	**7.1**	**7.2**	**7.2**	**7.1**
(a) Private Ownership of Banks		5.0 (40-75)	8.0 (75-95)	8.0 (75-90)	8.0 (75-95)	8.0 (75-95)	8.0 (75-95)
(b) Extension of Credit to Private Sector			9.8 (97.8)	9.1 (91.1)	9.3 (93.4)	9.4 (93.5)	8.9 (89.0)
(c) Avoidance of Negative Interest Rates			10.0	10.0	10.0	10.0	10.0
(d) Capital Transactions with Foreigners	2.0	2.0	2.0	2.0	2.0	2.0	2.0

PAKISTAN

Summary Ratings	1970	1975	1980	1985	1990	1995	1999
Summary Ratings	3.5	2.9	3.5	4.2	4.0	5.3	5.0
Rank	55	79	97	85	93	83	97

Components of Economic Freedom	1970	1975	1980	1985	1990	1995	1999
I. Size of Government	**9.2**	**8.9**	**9.1**	**9.0**	**7.8**	**8.7**	**8.7**
(a) Government Consumption	8.5 (11.1)	8.5 (11.2)	8.6 (10.8)	8.0 (12.9)	6.6 (17.5)	7.7 (13.8)	7.4 (14.8)
(b) Transfers and Subsidies	10.0 (0.0)	9.3 (3.0)	9.5 (2.2)	9.9 (0.7)	8.9 (4.4)	9.7 (1.8)	9.9 (0.9)
II. Structure of the Economy and Use of Markets	**0.0**	**0.4**	**2.1**	**1.7**	**2.5**	**3.2**	**4.6**
(a) Government Enterprises	0.0 (49.0)	0.0 (65.4)	0.0 (65.3)	0.0 (53.9)	0.0 (49.4)	0.0 (46.8)	2.0 (33.8)
(b) Price Controls						4.0	4.0
(c) Top Marginal Tax Rate		1.0 (61)	2.0 (55)	1.0 (60)	3.0 (50)	4.0 (45)	7.0 (35)
(d) Conscription	10.0	0.0	10.0	10.0	10.0	10.0	10.0
III. Monetary Policy and Price Stability	**9.2**	**6.8**	**8.0**	**8.9**	**8.6**	**8.2**	**8.4**
(a) Annual Money Growth	9.6 (2.0)	8.5 (7.7)	6.7 (16.4)	8.7 (6.6)	8.1 (9.4)	8.3 (8.7)	8.0 (9.8)
(b) Inflation Variability	9.0 (2.6)	6.6 (8.5)	9.3 (1.7)	9.1 (2.3)	9.0 (2.4)	9.2 (2.0)	8.0 (5.1)
(c) Recent Inflation Rate	9.1 (4.3)	5.2 (24.0)	8.2 (9.1)	9.1 (4.5)	8.7 (6.5)	7.2 (13.8)	9.2 (4.1)
IV. Freedom to Use Alternative Currencies	**0.0**	**3.3**	**2.3**	**4.6**	**6.1**	**7.2**	**3.9**
(a) Ownership of Foreign Currency	0.0	0.0	0.0	0.0	5.0	5.0	0.0
(b) Black Market Exchange Rate	0.0 (134.0)	6.6 (17.0)	4.6 (27.0)	9.2 (4.0)	7.2 (14.0)	9.4 (3.0)	7.8 (11.1)
V. Legal Structure and Property Rights	**1.4**	**0.6**	**1.9**	**3.3**	**2.1**	**7.0**	**3.8**
(a) Legal Security	1.4	0.6	2.2	3.5	2.6		
(b) Rule of Law			1.7	3.1	1.7	7.0	3.8
VI. International Exchange	**1.3**	**1.7**	**1.0**	**1.1**	**0.7**	**1.7**	**4.9**
(a) Taxes on International Trade							
i. Taxes as a Percentage of Exports and Imports	0.3 (14.5)	0.0 (15.3)	0.0 (15.3)	0.2 (14.7)	0.0 (15.2)	2.6 (11.1)	5.0 (7.6)
ii. Mean Tariff Rate	(76.8)	(70.0)	0.0 (77.6)	0.0 (78.0)	0.0 (58.8)	0.0 (61.1)	
iii. Standard Deviation of Tariff Rates				(34.0)	0.0 (34.0)	1.2 (21.9)	
(b) Size of Trade Sector	3.2 (22.4)	5.2 (33.1)	5.2 (36.6)	5.3 (34.0)	5.2 (35.0)	4.8 (35.8)	4.8 (36.0)
VII. Freedom of Exchange in Financial Markets	**4.1**	**2.0**	**3.5**	**4.2**	**3.5**	**3.4**	**3.5**
(a) Private Ownership of Banks	0.0 (0-10)	0.0 (0)	0.0 (0)	0.0 (0)	0.0 (0)	0.0 (0)	0.0 (0)
(b) Extension of Credit to Private Sector	7.7 (76.8)	7.0 (70.0)	6.9 (68.6)	7.9 (79.2)	7.2 (72.2)	6.4 (63.9)	7.0 (70.3)
(c) Avoidance of Negative Interest Rates	8.0	0.0	6.0	8.0	6.0	6.0	6.0
(d) Capital Transactions with Foreigners	2.0	2.0	2.0	2.0	2.0	2.0	2.0

PANAMA

Summary Ratings	1970	1975	1980	1985	1990	1995	1999
Summary Ratings	7.6	7.6	6.7	7.0	6.9	8.2	7.6
Rank	6	6	17	17	29	11	29

Components of Economic Freedom

	1970	1975	1980	1985	1990	1995	1999
I. Size of Government		**6.7**	**6.1**	**6.5**	**6.4**	**6.7**	**6.7**
(a) Government Consumption		4.3 (25.4)	3.5 (28.2)	4.2 (25.8)	4.7 (24.2)	5.1 (22.5)	5.2 (22.2)
(b) Transfers and Subsidies		9.1 (3.8)	8.8 (4.9)	8.8 (4.8)	8.1 (7.4)	8.3 (6.7)	8.1 (7.4)
II. Structure of the Economy and Use of Markets		**4.8**	**4.4**	**4.4**	**4.6**	**7.1**	**7.1**
(a) Government Enterprises	6.0 (26.7)	4.0 (42.9)	4.0 (39.9)	4.0 (31.4)	7.0 (22.1)	8.0 (16.1)	8.0 (17.3)
(b) Price Controls					2.0	4.0	4.0
(c) Top Marginal Tax Rate		4.0 (52)	3.0 (56)	3.0 (56)	3.0 (56)	9.0 (30)	9.0 (30)
(d) Conscription		10.0	10.0	10.0	10.0	10.0	10.0
III. Monetary Policy and Price Stability	**9.5**	**8.5**	**5.7**	**9.6**	**9.8**	**9.0**	**9.4**
(a) Annual Money Growth	9.1 (4.7)	8.9 (5.4)	8.0 (10.0)	9.9 (0.6)	10.0 (-0.3)	7.8 (11.1)	9.0 (4.9)
(b) Inflation Variability	9.7 (0.7)	8.7 (3.2)	5.6 (11.0)	9.0 (2.4)	9.5 (1.2)	9.3 (1.9)	9.4 (1.4)
(c) Recent Inflation Rate	9.8 (1.1)	8.0 (10.3)	3.3 (33.7)	9.8 (0.8)	9.9 (0.6)	9.9 (0.5)	9.7 (1.3)
IV. Freedom to Use Alternative Currencies	**10.0**	**10.0**	**10.0**	**10.0**	**10.0**	**10.0**	**10.0**
(a) Ownership of Foreign Currency	10.0	10.0	10.0	10.0	10.0	10.0	10.0
(b) Black Market Exchange Rate	10.0 (0.0)	10.0 (0.0)	10.0 (0.0)	10.0 (0.0)	10.0 (0.0)	10.0 (0.0)	10.0 (0.0)
V. Legal Structure and Property Rights			**2.8**	**3.3**	**3.6**	**7.0**	**3.8**
(a) Legal Security			4.0	3.5	3.9		
(b) Rule of Law			1.7	3.1	3.3	7.0	3.8
VI. International Exchange	**6.4**	**7.6**	**8.6**	**7.7**	**6.2**	**7.8**	**7.3**
(a) Taxes on International Trade							
i. Taxes as a Percentage of Exports and Imports	6.9 (4.7)	7.9 (3.2)	7.9 (3.1)	7.3 (4.1)	8.8 (1.8)	9.1 (1.4)	7.3 (4.0)
ii. Mean Tariff Rate					2.0 (40.0)	5.6 (22.0)	8.2 (9.2)
iii. Standard Deviation of Tariff Rates							7.6 (5.9)
(b) Size of Trade Sector	5.5 (79.3)	7.0 (101.3)	10.0 (186.9)	8.7 (128.2)	10.0 (165.4)	10.0 (198.8)	4.4 (76.9)
VII. Freedom of Exchange in Financial Markets	**8.1**	**8.1**	**8.3**	**8.2**	**8.8**	**9.4**	**9.4**
(a) Private Ownership of Banks	8.0 (75-90)	8.0 (75-90)	8.0 (75-90)	8.0 (75-90)	8.0 (75-95)	8.0 (80-95)	8.0 (80-95)
(b) Extension of Credit to Private Sector	9.7 (97.3)	8.4 (84.4)	8.9 (89.4)	8.7 (86.6)	9.3 (93.4)	9.9 (98.9)	9.9 (98.9)
(c) Avoidance of Negative Interest Rates					10.0	10.0	10.0
(d) Capital Transactions with Foreigners	8.0	8.0	8.0	8.0	8.0	10.0	10.0

PAPUA NEW GUINEA

	1970	1975	1980	1985	1990	1995	1999
Summary Ratings		4.2	4.6	6.2	6.1	5.9	4.3
Rank		60	69	31	41	68	114

Components of Economic Freedom	1970	1975	1980	1985	1990	1995	1999
I. Size of Government	**2.3**	**0.5**	**3.5**	**6.8**	**6.1**	**6.0**	**3.3**
(a) Government Consumption	2.3 (32.1)	0.5 (38.5)	3.5 (28.1)	4.1 (25.9)	3.1 (29.6)	6.0 (19.6)	3.3 (28.9)
(b) Transfers and Subsidies				9.5 (2.5)	9.1 (3.8)		
II. Structure of the Economy and Use of Markets					**6.3**	**6.3**	**6.3**
(a) Government Enterprises				4.0 (34.0)	7.0 (20.3)	8.0 (18.7)	7.0 (22.9)
(b) Price Controls							
(c) Top Marginal Tax Rate					4.0 (45)		4.0 (47)
(d) Conscription	10.0			10.0	10.0	10.0	10.0
III. Monetary Policy and Price Stability	**9.2**	**8.5**	**8.3**	**8.8**	**8.8**	**7.2**	**7.3**
(a) Annual Money Growth			9.3 (5.5)	9.5 (2.7)	8.8 (5.8)	7.8 (10.9)	8.0 (9.9)
(b) Inflation Variability	9.4 (1.4)	7.5 (6.2)	6.9 (7.6)	7.2 (6.9)	8.4 (4.0)	7.5 (6.2)	6.8 (8.0)
(c) Recent Inflation Rate	8.9 (5.7)	9.5 (2.3)	8.6 (7.1)	9.7 (1.6)	9.2 (4.1)	6.1 (19.7)	7.0 (14.9)
IV. Freedom to Use Alternative Currencies	**0.0**	**0.0**	**0.0**	**4.6**	**4.3**	**4.3**	**0.0**
(a) Ownership of Foreign Currency	0.0	0.0	0.0	0.0	0.0	0.0	0.0
(b) Black Market Exchange Rate				9.2 (4.0)	8.6 (7.0)	8.6 (7.0)	0.0 (66.7)
V. Legal Structure and Property Rights				**6.4**	**7.1**	**7.0**	**3.8**
(a) Legal Security				6.1	5.9		
(b) Rule of Law				6.6	8.3	7.0	3.8
VI. International Exchange		**7.9**	**8.0**	**7.6**	**7.2**	**6.8**	**5.3**
(a) Taxes on International Trade							
i. Taxes as a Percentage of Exports and Imports		7.7 (3.4)	7.8 (3.3)	6.1 (5.9)	5.3 (7.1)		
ii. Mean Tariff Rate				8.6 (7.0)	8.6 (7.0)	6.0 (6.0)	5.9 (20.7)
iii. Standard Deviation of Tariff Rates						7.0 (7.5)	2.3 (19.2)
(b) Size of Trade Sector	6.3 (72.4)	8.4 (86.1)	8.4 (96.5)	8.8 (94.6)	7.9 (89.6)	8.1 (102.8)	10.0 (138.4)
VII. Freedom of Exchange in Financial Markets		**4.2**	**4.0**	**4.3**	**4.3**	**4.7**	**5.1**
(a) Private Ownership of Banks		5.0 (40-60)	5.0 (40-60)	5.0 (40-60)	5.0 (40-60)	5.0 (45-55)	5.0 (45-55)
(b) Extension of Credit to Private Sector		8.5 (85.3)	7.7 (77.4)	8.8 (87.5)	8.9 (88.6)	6.3 (62.8)	6.2 (62.1)
(c) Avoidance of Negative Interest Rates				0.0	0.0	8.0	10.0
(d) Capital Transactions with Foreigners	0.0	0.0	0.0	0.0	0.0	0.0	0.0

PARAGUAY

Summary Ratings	1970	1975	1980	1985	1990	1995	1999
Summary Ratings			6.1	5.4	6.3	7.4	7.3
Rank			27	50	37	31	38

Components of Economic Freedom

Component	1970	1975	1980	1985	1990	1995	1999
I. Size of Government	**9.2**	**9.5**	**9.6**	**9.5**	**9.6**	**8.9**	**9.2**
(a) Government Consumption	8.7 (10.4)	9.5 (7.7)	9.6 (7.4)	9.5 (7.9)	9.6 (7.4)	8.5 (11.2)	9.2 (8.8)
(b) Transfers and Subsidies	9.7 (1.6)	9.6 (2.0)	9.6 (2.0)	9.6 (2.1)	9.6 (1.8)	9.3 (3.0)	
II. Structure of the Economy and Use of Markets				**5.0**	**6.0**	**6.8**	**5.8**
(a) Government Enterprises	6.0 (27.0)	7.0 (21.1)	8.0 (17.8)	4.0 (31.4)	8.0 (13.3)	7.0 (23.2)	4.0 (34.9)
(b) Price Controls					4.0	6.0	6.0
(c) Top Marginal Tax Rate				8.0 (30)	8.0 (30)	10.0 (0)	10.0 (0)
(d) Conscription	0.0	0.0	1.0	0.0	0.0	0.0	0.0
III. Monetary Policy and Price Stability	**9.3**	**7.6**	**6.9**	**6.7**	**4.9**	**7.0**	**7.7**
(a) Annual Money Growth	9.2 (4.0)	7.2 (14.0)	6.1 (19.6)	8.3 (8.7)	3.6 (32.1)	5.6 (22.2)	7.8 (11.1)
(b) Inflation Variability	9.1 (2.2)	7.0 (7.5)	7.9 (5.2)	6.8 (7.9)	8.6 (3.6)	8.3 (4.3)	6.7 (8.2)
(c) Recent Inflation Rate	9.6 (1.9)	8.7 (6.6)	6.7 (16.7)	5.0 (25.2)	2.7 (36.3)	7.4 (13.0)	8.6 (6.8)
IV. Freedom to Use Alternative Currencies	**8.3**	**8.7**	**9.3**	**5.0**	**7.4**	**8.7**	**8.9**
(a) Ownership of Foreign Currency	10.0	10.0	10.0	10.0	10.0	10.0	10.0
(b) Black Market Exchange Rate	6.6 (17.0)	7.4 (13.0)	8.6 (7.0)	0.0 (213.0)	4.8 (26.0)	7.4 (13.0)	7.8 (11.1)
V. Legal Structure and Property Rights			**3.6**	**3.9**	**4.6**	**4.1**	**3.8**
(a) Legal Security			5.4	4.8	5.9		
(b) Rule of Law			1.7	3.1	3.3	4.1	3.8
VI. International Exchange	**2.9**	**3.3**	**3.0**	**4.2**	**6.5**	**7.4**	**7.3**
(a) Taxes on International Trade							
i. Taxes as a Percentage of Exports and Imports	3.3 (10.1)	4.1 (8.8)	6.0 (6.0)	8.5 (2.2)	7.8 (3.3)	8.6 (2.1)	7.1 (4.4)
ii. Mean Tariff Rate			0.0 (71.0)	0.0 (71.7)	6.8 (16.0)	8.1 (9.3)	8.1 (9.5)
iii. Standard Deviation of Tariff Rates					4.9 (12.7)	7.2 (6.9)	7.4 (6.5)
(b) Size of Trade Sector	2.1 (31.0)	1.6 (31.9)	3.2 (44.0)	4.4 (48.4)	6.4 (72.7)	3.5 (47.8)	5.9 (73.4)
VII. Freedom of Exchange in Financial Markets					**5.4**	**9.3**	**9.1**
(a) Private Ownership of Banks					9.9 (99.4)	9.8 (97.5)	9.3 (92.8)
(b) Extension of Credit to Private Sector					2.0	8.0	8.0
(c) Avoidance of Negative Interest Rates							
(d) Capital Transactions with Foreigners	5.0	5.0	5.0	5.0	5.0	10.0	10.0

PERU

	1970	1975	1980	1985	1990	1995	1999
Summary Ratings	4.3	3.3	3.3	2.3	3.8	7.2	7.6
Rank	47	72	99	109	97	37	29

Components of Economic Freedom

	1970	1975	1980	1985	1990	1995	1999
I. Size of Government	**8.5**	**8.6**	**8.4**	**8.8**	**9.0**	**8.9**	**8.8**
(a) Government Consumption	7.4 (14.7)	7.6 (14.3)	7.3 (-5.3)	8.0 (12.7)	8.7 (10.5)	8.8 (10.2)	8.5 (11.2)
(b) Transfers and Subsidies	9.5 (2.3)	9.6 (1.9)	9.6 (1.9)	9.6 (1.8)	9.3 (3.0)	9.1 (3.9)	9.2 (3.4)
II. Structure of the Economy and Use of Markets		**3.5**	**2.7**	**2.0**	**4.3**	**6.6**	**7.3**
(a) Government Enterprises	6.0 (24.3)	4.0 (36.8)	4.0 (28.1)	4.0 (33.9)	8.0 (16.9)	8.0 (17.0)	8.0 (15.5)
(b) Price Controls				0.0	2.0	6.0	8.0
(c) Top Marginal Tax Rate		4.0 (51)	2.0 (65)	0.0 (65)	4.0 (45)	8.0 (30)	8.0 (30)
(d) Conscription	0.0	0.0	0.0	0.0	0.0	0.0	0.0
III. Monetary Policy and Price Stability	**7.7**	**6.4**	**1.8**	**0.0**	**0.0**	**2.5**	**6.6**
(a) Annual Money Growth	6.6 (16.9)	6.3 (18.6)	2.2 (39.1)	0.0 (98.5)	0.0 (690.3)	0.0 (58.2)	3.5 (32.4)
(b) Inflation Variability	8.5 (3.7)	7.7 (5.9)	3.1 (17.3)	0.0 (37.9)	0.0 (2341.4)	0.0 (127.5)	7.3 (6.8)
(c) Recent Inflation Rate	8.1 (9.3)	5.4 (23.2)	0.0 (55.9)	0.0 (167.8)	0.0 (6134.8)	7.6 (12.2)	9.3 (3.5)
IV. Freedom to Use Alternative Currencies	**3.6**	**0.0**	**3.2**	**0.0**	**5.9**	**10.0**	**10.0**
(a) Ownership of Foreign Currency	0.0	0.0	0.0	0.0	5.0	10.0	10.0
(b) Black Market Exchange Rate	7.2 (14.0)	0.0 (56.0)	6.4 (18.0)	0.0 (51.0)	6.8 (16.0)	10.0 (0.0)	10.0 (0.0)
V. Legal Structure and Property Rights	**0.3**	**0.0**	**3.6**	**1.5**	**2.5**	**7.0**	**4.9**
(a) Legal Security	0.3	0.0	4.0	1.6	3.2		6.0
(b) Rule of Law			3.3	1.4	1.7	7.0	3.8
VI. International Exchange	**4.2**	**3.9**	**2.2**	**2.3**	**3.2**	**6.4**	**6.9**
(a) Taxes on International Trade							
i. Taxes as a Percentage of Exports and Imports	4.1 (8.9)	3.7 (9.5)	2.9 (10.6)	4.5 (8.3)	7.4 (3.9)	6.3 (5.5)	6.6 (5.2)
ii. Mean Tariff Rate			0.0 (57.0)	0.0 (64.0)	2.8 (36.0)	6.5 (17.6)	7.4 (13.2)
iii. Standard Deviation of Tariff Rates				1.2 (22.0)	0.0 (25.0)	8.2 (4.4)	8.8 (2.9)
(b) Size of Trade Sector	4.3 (33.9)	4.4 (32.8)	5.1 (41.8)	5.3 (39.4)	1.7 (23.6)	2.3 (28.1)	2.5 (28.7)
VII. Freedom of Exchange in Financial Markets			**2.5**	**2.3**	**2.0**	**7.7**	**8.8**
(a) Private Ownership of Banks							8.0 (92)
(b) Extension of Credit to Private Sector	5.6 (56.1)	4.0 (40.3)	5.9 (58.9)	5.4 (54.3)	4.2 (42.1)	9.4 (93.8)	9.0 (89.8)
(c) Avoidance of Negative Interest Rates	0.0		0.0	0.0	0.0	6.0	8.0
(d) Capital Transactions with Foreigners	0.0	2.0	2.0	2.0	2.0	8.0	10.0

PHILIPPINES

Summary Ratings	1970	1975	1980	1985	1990	1995	1999
Summary Ratings	5.3	4.7	5.0	5.0	5.6	7.2	7.6
Rank	41	53	60	63	51	37	29

Components of Economic Freedom	1970	1975	1980	1985	1990	1995	1999
I. Size of Government	**9.1**	**8.7**	**9.0**	**9.5**	**9.0**	**8.9**	**7.3**
(a) Government Consumption	8.2 (12.3)	7.5 (14.7)	8.1 (12.4)	9.0 (9.4)	8.1 (12.4)	7.8 (13.3)	7.3 (15.2)
(b) Transfers and Subsidies	10.0 (0.4)	9.9 (0.8)	9.8 (1.1)	10.0 (0.2)	9.9 (0.9)	9.9 (0.7)	
II. Structure of the Economy and Use of Markets		**4.5**	**3.7**	**5.6**	**7.9**	**6.6**	**6.3**
(a) Government Enterprises	7.0 (17.1)	6.0 (21.4)	6.0 (27.4)	8.0 (19.5)	8.0 (18.2)	8.0 (19.7)	7.0 (24.0)
(b) Price Controls					4.0	4.0	4.0
(c) Top Marginal Tax Rate		3.0 (56)	1.0 (70)	1.0 (60)	7.0 (35)	7.0 (35)	7.0 (33)
(d) Conscription	3.0	3.0	3.0	10.0	10.0	10.0	10.0
III. Monetary Policy and Price Stability	**9.0**	**7.2**	**7.9**	**6.2**	**5.2**	**8.2**	**8.3**
(a) Annual Money Growth	8.9 (5.7)	7.2 (13.9)	7.8 (11.0)	8.4 (7.9)	0.0 (118.7)	7.5 (12.5)	7.7 (11.7)
(b) Inflation Variability	9.6 (1.0)	6.4 (9.1)	8.8 (2.9)	3.5 (16.4)	8.7 (3.3)	8.6 (3.5)	8.6 (3.5)
(c) Recent Inflation Rate	8.4 (7.9)	8.1 (9.3)	7.2 (14.3)	6.5 (17.6)	7.4 (13.0)	8.5 (7.6)	8.7 (6.7)
IV. Freedom to Use Alternative Currencies	**0.0**	**3.7**	**4.7**	**4.3**	**4.3**	**10.0**	**10.0**
(a) Ownership of Foreign Currency	0.0	0.0	0.0	0.0	0.0	10.0	10.0
(b) Black Market Exchange Rate	0.0 (73.0)	7.4 (13.0)	9.4 (3.0)	8.6 (7.0)	8.6 (7.0)	10.0 (0.0)	10.0 (0.0)
V. Legal Structure and Property Rights	**4.9**	**3.8**	**2.7**	**1.8**	**1.8**	**4.1**	**6.3**
(a) Legal Security	4.9	3.8	3.6	2.2	1.9		6.8
(b) Rule of Law			1.7	1.4	1.7	4.1	5.8
VI. International Exchange	**5.6**	**2.1**	**4.3**	**5.3**	**5.9**	**6.4**	**7.6**
(a) Taxes on International Trade							
i. Taxes as a Percentage of Exports and Imports	4.7 (7.9)	1.1 (13.4)	5.5 (6.8)	5.9 (6.2)	5.6 (6.6)	5.7 (6.4)	7.6 (3.6)
ii. Mean Tariff Rate		1.2 (44.0)	2.4 (38.0)	4.5 (27.6)	5.1 (24.3)	4.5 (27.6)	8.0 (10.2)
iii. Standard Deviation of Tariff Rates					6.3 (9.2)	8.0 (4.9)	6.1 (9.7)
(b) Size of Trade Sector	7.3 (42.6)	6.2 (48.1)	6.0 (52.0)	5.7 (45.9)	7.1 (60.8)	8.3 (80.5)	10.0 (115.6)
VII. Freedom of Exchange in Financial Markets		**5.5**	**5.3**	**4.5**	**6.2**	**7.6**	**7.6**
(a) Private Ownership of Banks		5.0 (40-75)	5.0 (40-75)	5.0 (70-75)	8.0 (88)	8.0 (90)	8.0 (90)
(b) Extension of Credit to Private Sector	6.3 (62.9)	7.9 (78.6)	6.8 (67.8)	7.5 (75.0)	7.1 (70.9)	7.6 (76.2)	7.8 (77.8)
(c) Avoidance of Negative Interest Rates		8.0	8.0	4.0	8.0	10.0	10.0
(d) Capital Transactions with Foreigners	0.0	2.0	2.0	2.0	2.0	5.0	5.0

POLAND

Summary Ratings	1970	1975	1980	1985	1990	1995	1999
Summary Ratings				3.6	4.6	6.3	5.7
Rank				96	80	54	85

Components of Economic Freedom	1970	1975	1980	1985	1990	1995	1999
I. Size of Government		7.2	8.2	5.3	3.0	4.2	5.4
(a) Government Consumption		7.2 (15.6)	8.2 (12.1)	8.0 (13.0)	3.3 (28.7)	5.0 (23.0)	7.1 (16.0)
(b) Transfers and Subsidies				2.7 (27.4)	2.7 (27.4)	3.5 (24.4)	3.7 (23.5)
II. Structure of the Economy and Use of Markets						3.4	2.9
(a) Government Enterprises	0.0 (40.7)	0.0	0.0	0.0	0.0 (58.8)	0.0 (55.8)	0.0 (43.7)
(b) Price Controls						7.0	4.0
(c) Top Marginal Tax Rate						4.0 (45)	5.0 (40)
(d) Conscription	0.0	0.0	0.0	0.0	0.0	1.0	3.0
III. Monetary Policy and Price Stability		9.3	8.6	4.3	0.0	4.7	6.8
(a) Annual Money Growth		9.0 (2.4)	9.2 (2.0)	5.9 (20.5)	0.0 (110.4)	3.8 (30.9)	6.2 (19.2)
(b) Inflation Variability		9.5 (2.4)	8.0 (9.8)	0.0 (37.4)	0.0 (167.6)	5.9 (10.2)	5.6 (11.0)
(c) Recent Inflation Rate				6.8 (15.8)	0.0 (435.7)	4.4 (28.2)	8.5 (7.3)
IV. Freedom to Use Alternative Currencies		2.5	2.5	2.5	9.1	10.0	7.5
(a) Ownership of Foreign Currency		5.0	5.0	5.0	10.0	10.0	5.0
(b) Black Market Exchange Rate		0.0 (3786.0)	0.0 (298.0)	0.0 (301.0)	8.2 (9.0)	10.0 (0.0)	10.0 (0.0)
V. Legal Structure and Property Rights				5.1	7.0	10.0	7.1
(a) Legal Security				3.5	7.3		6.2
(b) Rule of Law				6.6	6.7	10.0	7.9
VI. International Exchange				5.3	6.5	6.1	5.0
(a) Taxes on International Trade							
i. Taxes as a Percentage of Exports and Imports				4.3 (8.6)	6.0 (6.0)	5.9 (6.1)	8.2 (2.7)
ii. Mean Tariff Rate				7.3 (13.6)	7.7 (11.7)	6.3 (18.4)	6.5 (17.6)
iii. Standard Deviation of Tariff Rates					6.4 (8.9)	6.9 (7.8)	0.0 (28.1)
(b) Size of Trade Sector			5.7 (59.2)	3.1 (35.1)	4.9 (50.2)	4.5 (50.5)	5.5 (61.6)
VII. Freedom of Exchange in Financial Markets				0.0	0.3	4.2	5.5
(a) Private Ownership of Banks	0.0 (0-10)			0.0 (0-10)	0.0 (0-10)	2.0 (10-20)	2.0 (20-40)
(b) Extension of Credit to Private Sector			0.0 (4.8)	0.0 (7.6)	1.3 (13.1)	3.8 (38.1)	5.4 (54.2)
(c) Avoidance of Negative Interest Rates				0.0	0.0	6.0	10.0
(d) Capital Transactions with Foreigners	0.0		0.0	0.0	0.0	5.0	5.0

PORTUGAL

Summary Ratings	1970	1975	1980	1985	1990	1995	1999
Summary Ratings	5.8	3.3	5.6	5.6	6.4	7.9	7.8
Rank	36	72	40	46	36	18	24

Components of Economic Freedom

	1970	1975	1980	1985	1990	1995	1999
I. Size of Government	**7.0**	**6.7**	**6.3**	**5.7**	**5.9**	**6.0**	**5.4**
(a) Government Consumption	7.0 (16.4)	7.3 (15.3)	6.8 (16.8)	6.6 (17.6)	6.0 (19.8)	5.5 (21.4)	4.8 (23.6)
(b) Transfers and Subsidies		6.2 (14.6)	5.7 (16.3)	4.8 (19.5)	5.9 (15.5)	6.5 (13.4)	5.9 (15.4)
II. Structure of the Economy and Use of Markets	**2.1**	**1.0**	**1.0**	**2.0**	**4.2**	**5.5**	**5.5**
(a) Government Enterprises	2.0 (41.8)	2.0 (39.7)	2.0 (42.2)	4.0 (30.5)	4.0 (29.9)	6.0 (23.2)	6.0
(b) Price Controls					5.0	6.0	6.0
(c) Top Marginal Tax Rate	3.0 (58)	0.0 (82)	0.0 (84)	0.0 (69)	5.0 (40)	5.0 (40)	5.0 (40)
(d) Conscription	0.0	0.0	0.0	0.0	0.0	3.0	3.0
III. Monetary Policy and Price Stability	**9.5**	**7.4**	**7.4**	**7.4**	**7.6**	**8.7**	**9.1**
(a) Annual Money Growth	9.7 (1.5)	7.5 (12.4)	7.6 (11.9)	7.6 (12.2)	6.8 (16.0)	8.3 (8.7)	8.2 (9.0)
(b) Inflation Variability	9.1 (2.1)	7.9 (5.2)	8.7 (3.3)	8.9 (2.6)	8.5 (3.7)	9.0 (2.6)	9.6 (1.1)
(c) Recent Inflation Rate	9.6 (2.0)	6.8 (16.2)	5.8 (20.9)	5.7 (21.7)	7.4 (12.8)	9.0 (5.2)	9.5 (2.3)
IV. Freedom to Use Alternative Currencies	**5.0**	**0.8**	**4.8**	**4.8**	**4.7**	**10.0**	**10.0**
(a) Ownership of Foreign Currency	0.0	0.0	0.0	0.0	0.0	10.0	10.0
(b) Black Market Exchange Rate	10.0 (0.0)	1.6 (42.0)	9.6 (2.0)	9.6 (2.0)	9.4 (3.0)	10.0 (0.0)	10.0 (0.0)
V. Legal Structure and Property Rights	**8.3**	**0.3**	**9.5**	**6.9**	**9.2**	**10.0**	**8.1**
(a) Legal Security	8.3	0.3	9.0	5.5	10.0		8.2
(b) Rule of Law			10.0	8.2	8.3	10.0	7.9
VI. International Exchange	**6.9**	**5.9**	**7.3**	**8.0**	**7.9**	**8.2**	**8.1**
(a) Taxes on International Trade							
i. Taxes as a Percentage of Exports and Imports	7.9 (3.2)	6.9 (4.6)	8.6 (2.1)	9.2 (1.2)	9.1 (1.3)	9.8 (0.3)	9.7 (0.5)
ii. Mean Tariff Rate					8.5 (7.4)	8.7 (6.7)	8.9 (5.6)
iii. Standard Deviation of Tariff Rates					7.1 (7.2)	7.6 (5.9)	7.6 (5.9)
(b) Size of Trade Sector	4.9 (50.2)	3.7 (48.2)	4.6 (63.0)	5.7 (71.5)	5.7 (76.2)	5.0 (73.9)	4.5 (67.5)
VII. Freedom of Exchange in Financial Markets	**3.2**	**3.3**	**3.5**	**4.8**	**5.4**	**6.7**	**8.0**
(a) Private Ownership of Banks	0.0 (0-10)	0.0 (0-10)	0.0 (5-10)	0.0 (0-10)	2.0 (15)	2.0 (20-40)	5.0 (40-60)
(b) Extension of Credit to Private Sector	9.0 (89.5)	9.1 (90.7)	9.3 (92.6)	8.5 (84.9)	7.3 (72.8)	7.3 (72.6)	9.3 (93.3)
(c) Avoidance of Negative Interest Rates			4.0	10.0	8.0	10.0	10.0
(d) Capital Transactions with Foreigners	2.0	2.0	2.0	2.0	5.0	8.0	8.0

ROMANIA

Summary Ratings

	1970	1975	1980	1985	1990	1995	1999
Summary Ratings				3.6	4.2	4.2	3.8
Rank				96	90	106	118

Components of Economic Freedom

	1970	1975	1980	1985	1990	1995	1999
I. Size of Government			**7.9**	**8.9**	**5.9**	**6.5**	**6.7**
(a) Government Consumption			9.4 (8.0)	9.9 (6.5)	6.8 (16.8)	6.8 (16.8)	6.7 (17.4)
(b) Transfers and Subsidies			6.3 (14.1)	8.0 (7.9)	5.1 (18.6)	6.2 (14.6)	6.7 (12.7)
II. Structure of the Economy and Use of Markets					**0.0**	**2.3**	**2.5**
(a) Government Enterprises	0.0	0.0		0.0	0.0	0.0 (60.7)	0.0 (57.0)
(b) Price Controls					0.0	6.0	6.0
(c) Top Marginal Tax Rate			1.0			1.0 (60)	1.0 (60)
(d) Conscription	0.0	0.0		0.0	0.0	1.0	3.0
III. Monetary Policy and Price Stability			**8.8**	**9.3**	**7.8**	**1.0**	**0.3**
(a) Annual Money Growth			7.8 (11.2)	9.8 (1.2)	8.3 (8.7)	0.0 (97.9)	0.0 (62.5)
(b) Inflation Variability		9.8 (0.4)	8.8 (3.1)	8.1 (4.7)	7.9 (5.3)	0.0 (68.3)	0.0 (55.3)
(c) Recent Inflation Rate			9.9 (0.6)	9.9 (0.4)	7.3 (13.7)	2.9 (35.3)	0.8 (45.8)
IV. Freedom to Use Alternative Currencies	**0.0**	**0.0**	**0.0**	**0.0**	**2.5**	**4.7**	**3.9**
(a) Ownership of Foreign Currency	0.0	0.0	0.0	0.0	5.0	0.0	0.0
(b) Black Market Exchange Rate	0.0 (521.0)	0.0 (596.0)	0.0 (628.0)	0.0 (1246.0)	0.0 (416.0)	9.4 (3.0)	7.8 (11.1)
V. Legal Structure and Property Rights				**3.9**	**7.1**	**7.0**	**5.8**
(a) Legal Security				4.8	5.9		
(b) Rule of Law				3.1	8.3	7.0	5.8
VI. International Exchange					**7.7**	**6.7**	**5.6**
(a) Taxes on International Trade							
i. Taxes as a Percentage of Exports and Imports					9.7 (0.4)	8.2 (2.7)	8.5 (2.3)
ii. Mean Tariff Rate						6.2 (18.8)	6.1 (19.4)
iii. Standard Deviation of Tariff Rates						0.0	2.8 (18.1)
(b) Size of Trade Sector			6.7 (75.3)	3.7 (41.6)	3.6 (42.9)	4.9 (59.4)	4.5 (55.5)
VII. Freedom of Exchange in Financial Markets	**0.0**		**0.0**	**0.0**	**0.0**	**0.5**	**1.2**
(a) Private Ownership of Banks	0.0 (0)	0.0 (0)	0.0 (0)	0.0 (0)	0.0 (0)	2.0 (10-40)	0.0 (0-10)
(b) Extension of Credit to Private Sector	0.0 (0.0)	0.0 (0.0)	0.0 (0.0)	0.0 (0.0)	0.0 (0.0)	0.0 (0.0)	5.5 (55.4)
(c) Avoidance of Negative Interest Rates					0.0	0.0	0.0
(d) Capital Transactions with Foreigners	0.0	0.0	0.0	0.0	0.0	0.0	0.0

RUSSIA

Summary Ratings	1970	1975	1980	1985	1990	1995	1999
Summary Ratings		1.6	1.6	1.6	1.5	4.8	3.9
Rank		83	108	112	115	100	117

Components of Economic Freedom

	1970	1975	1980	1985	1990	1995	1999
I. Size of Government		2.2	2.5	2.3	2.5	5.8	5.2
(a) Government Consumption		2.5 (31.5)	3.0 (29.7)	2.6 (31.0)	3.0 (29.8)	3.7 (27.3)	5.2 (22.4)
(b) Transfers and Subsidies		2.0 (30.0)	2.0 (30.0)	2.0 (30.0)	2.0 (30.0)	7.9 (8.2)	
II. Structure of the Economy and Use of Markets		0.0	0.0	0.0	0.0	2.8	3.0
(a) Government Enterprises	0.0	0.0	0.0	0.0	0.0 (90.0)	2.0 (45.0)	4.0 (35.0)
(b) Price Controls					0.0	5.0	5.0
(c) Top Marginal Tax Rate		0.0 (100)	0.0 (100)	0.0 (100)	0.0 (80)	2.0 (54)	0.0 (61)
(d) Conscription	0.0	0.0	0.0	0.0	0.0	0.0	0.0
III. Monetary Policy and Price Stability		8.9	8.6	8.7	7.9	0.0	0.0
(a) Annual Money Growth		8.3 (8.3)	7.9 (10.6)	8.1 (9.6)	8.1 (9.7)	0.0 (401.4)	0.0 (141.9)
(b) Inflation Variability		9.6 (1.1)	9.3 (1.8)	9.4 (1.4)	8.9 (2.7)	0.0 (522.9)	0.0 (125.9)
(c) Recent Inflation Rate				8.5 (7.3)	6.8 (15.9)	0.0 (170.7)	0.0 (85.7)
IV. Freedom to Use Alternative Currencies	0.0	0.0	0.0	0.0	0.0	7.5	3.2
(a) Ownership of Foreign Currency	0.0	0.0	0.0	0.0	0.0	5.0	5.0
(b) Black Market Exchange Rate	0.0 (606.0)	0.0 (391.0)	0.0 (359.0)	0.0 (637.0)	0.0 (1969.0)	10.0 (0.0)	1.4 (42.9)
V. Legal Structure and Property Rights							4.2
(a) Legal Security							4.7
(b) Rule of Law							3.8
VI. International Exchange						6.8	7.3
(a) Taxes on International Trade							
i. Taxes as a Percentage of Exports and Imports						7.1 (4.4)	6.6 (5.1)
ii. Mean Tariff Rate						7.7 (11.5)	7.5 (12.6)
iii. Standard Deviation of Tariff Rates						5.0 (12.4)	6.6 (8.4)
(b) Size of Trade Sector						7.7 (47.7)	9.4 (58.5)
VII. Freedom of Exchange in Financial Markets		0.0	0.0	0.0	0.0	4.1	2.7
(a) Private Ownership of Banks	0.0 (0)	0.0 (0)	0.0 (0)	0.0 (0)	0.0 (0)	2.0 (32)	2.0 (22)
(b) Extension of Credit to Private Sector					0.0 (5.0)	5.0 (50.4)	5.2 (51.5)
(c) Avoidance of Negative Interest Rates		0.0	0.0	0.0	0.0	8.0	2.0
(d) Capital Transactions with Foreigners	0.0	0.0	0.0	0.0	0.0	2.0	2.0

RWANDA

	1970	1975	1980	1985	1990	1995	1999
Summary Ratings	2.1		3.6		3.8	3.9	4.4
Rank	82		93		97	112	110

Components of Economic Freedom

	1970	1975	1980	1985	1990	1995	1999
I. Size of Government	**9.1**	**8.3**	**8.9**	**8.2**	**8.9**	**9.5**	**9.3**
(a) Government Consumption	9.1 (9.0)	6.6 (17.6)	7.9 (13.0)	8.2 (12.3)	8.6 (10.8)	9.4 (8.0)	9.3 (8.5)
(b) Transfers and Subsidies		10.0 (0.6)	9.9 (0.8)		9.2 (3.5)	9.5 (2.2)	
(c) Top Marginal Tax Rate							
(d) Conscription	10.0	10.0	10.0	10.0	10.0	10.0	10.0
II. Structure of the Economy and Use of Markets	**6.0**				**2.9**	**2.9**	**2.0**
(a) Government Enterprises	6.0	6.0 (16.9)	4.0 (39.4)	4.0 (42.4)	4.0	4.0	2.0
(b) Price Controls			0.0		0.0	0.0	0.0
III. Monetary Policy and Price Stability	**6.0**	**2.6**	**8.1**	**8.9**	**8.2**	**3.0**	**6.4**
(a) Annual Money Growth	7.9 (10.5)	7.3 (13.4)	7.1 (14.5)	9.5 (-2.4)	9.9 (0.8)	5.4 (22.9)	6.3 (18.5)
(b) Inflation Variability	2.0 (20.0)	0.0 (33.5)	8.0 (5.0)	8.0 (5.1)	7.3 (6.7)	3.3 (16.8)	3.4 (16.5)
(c) Recent Inflation Rate	8.0 (9.9)	0.0 (88.0)	9.4 (3.1)	9.1 (4.6)	7.3 (13.5)	0.0 (54.2)	9.5 (-2.4)
IV. Freedom to Use Alternative Currencies	**2.4**	**0.5**	**0.0**	**0.1**	**2.2**	**7.2**	**2.5**
(a) Ownership of Foreign Currency		0.0	0.0	0.0	0.0	5.0	5.0
(b) Black Market Exchange Rate	2.4 (38.0)	1.0 (45.0)	0.0 (57.0)	0.2 (49.0)	4.4 (28.0)	9.4 (3.0)	0.0 (100.0)
V. Legal Structure and Property Rights							
(a) Legal Security							
(b) Rule of Law							
VI. International Exchange		**0.0**	**1.1**		**0.4**	**1.0**	
(a) Taxes on International Trade							
i. Taxes as a Percentage of Exports and Imports		0.0 (16.5)	1.1 (13.3)		0.5 (14.2)	0.3 (14.6)	
ii. Mean Tariff Rate						3.0 (34.8)	
iii. Standard Deviation of Tariff Rates						0.0 (33.1)	
(b) Size of Trade Sector	0.0 (26.7)	0.0 (26.9)	1.0 (40.8)	0.0 (30.7)	0.0 (19.6)	0.0 (35.7)	0.0 (28.4)
VII. Freedom of Exchange in Financial Markets	**1.5**	**1.4**	**3.4**	**3.6**	**3.8**	**1.8**	**3.8**
(a) Private Ownership of Banks	0.0 (0)	0.0 (0)	0.0 (0)	0.0 (0-10)	0.0 (0-10)	0.0 (0-10)	0.0 (0-10)
(b) Extension of Credit to Private Sector	5.5 (54.8)	5.0 (50.2)	9.0 (90.2)	7.8 (77.8)	6.5 (64.8)	8.5 (85.4)	8.8 (87.6)
(c) Avoidance of Negative Interest Rates			6.0	8.0	10.0	0.0	8.0
(d) Capital Transactions with Foreigners	0.0	0.0	0.0	0.0	0.0	0.0	0.0

SENEGAL

Summary Ratings

	1970	1975	1980	1985	1990	1995	1999
Summary Ratings			4.9	4.6	4.7	3.7	4.8
Rank			63	75	72	116	100

Components of Economic Freedom

	1970	1975	1980	1985	1990	1995	1999
I. Size of Government	**7.4**	**8.3**	**7.5**	**7.0**	**7.0**	**7.7**	**7.9**
(a) Government Consumption	7.4 (14.9)	7.2 (15.5)	6.1 (19.3)	7.0 (16.3)	7.0 (16.1)	7.7 (13.9)	7.9 (13.0)
(b) Transfers and Subsidies	9.4	9.4 (2.6)	9.0 (4.2)				
II. Structure of the Economy and Use of Markets				**2.3**	**3.0**	**2.6**	**3.3**
(a) Government Enterprises	6.0 (22.3)	4.0 (33.9)	4.0 (36.7)	4.0 (36.2)	6.0 (30.1)	6.0	6.0
(b) Price Controls					0.0	2.0	4.0
(c) Top Marginal Tax Rate				1.0 (65)	4.0 (48)	0.0 (64)	0.0 (64)
(d) Conscription	0.0	0.0	0.0	0.0	0.0	0.0	0.0
III. Monetary Policy and Price Stability	**9.4**	**7.6**	**8.1**	**8.8**	**9.5**	**7.7**	**7.9**
(a) Annual Money Growth	9.7 (1.7)	7.1 (14.8)	7.8 (11.2)	9.0 (5.0)	9.6 (-2.0)	8.6 (6.9)	7.5 (12.4)
(b) Inflation Variability	9.0 (2.6)	8.0 (5.1)	8.9 (2.6)	9.4 (1.6)	9.0 (2.5)	5.7 (10.9)	6.4 (9.0)
(c) Recent Inflation Rate	9.6 (2.0)	7.7 (11.6)	7.7 (11.5)	8.1 (9.3)	9.8 (1.2)	8.8 (5.9)	9.8 (0.8)
IV. Freedom to Use Alternative Currencies	**4.8**	**4.8**	**4.8**	**4.9**	**4.6**	**4.9**	**4.8**
(a) Ownership of Foreign Currency	0.0	0.0	0.0	0.0	0.0	0.0	0.0
(b) Black Market Exchange Rate	9.6 (2.0)	9.6 (2.0)	9.6 (2.0)	9.8 (1.0)	9.2 (4.0)	9.8 (1.0)	9.6 (2.0)
V. Legal Structure and Property Rights			**3.1**	**3.9**	**3.9**	**0.0**	**3.8**
(a) Legal Security			4.6	4.8	4.6	0.0	
(b) Rule of Law			1.7	3.1	3.3	0.0	3.8
VI. International Exchange	**2.9**	**5.1**	**3.6**	**3.9**	**3.1**	**2.9**	**4.4**
(a) Taxes on International Trade							
i. Taxes as a Percentage of Exports and Imports	1.7 (12.4)	4.2 (8.7)	2.4 (11.4)	4.5 (8.3)	2.1 (11.8)	1.3 (13.0)	0.6 (14.1)
ii. Mean Tariff Rate				2.2 (39.0)	3.0 (35.0)	3.2 (34.2)	7.4 (12.8)
iii. Standard Deviation of Tariff Rates							
(b) Size of Trade Sector	5.4 (59.4)	7.1 (78.4)	5.9 (72.3)	6.3 (70.6)	5.0 (58.9)	5.3 (68.6)	5.6 (71.3)
VII. Freedom of Exchange in Financial Markets			**4.5**	**4.0**	**4.5**	**3.3**	**3.7**
(a) Private Ownership of Banks	2.0 (10-40)	2.0 (10-40)	2.0 (10-40)	2.0 (10-40)	2.0 (10-40)	2.0 (10-40)	2.0 (10-40)
(b) Extension of Credit to Private Sector			9.4 (93.6)	9.6 (95.6)	9.6 (95.9)	8.5 (85.2)	8.1 (81.4)
(c) Avoidance of Negative Interest Rates			8.0	6.0	8.0	4.0	6.0
(d) Capital Transactions with Foreigners	0.0	0.0	0.0	0.0	0.0	0.0	0.0

SIERRA LEONE

Summary Ratings	1970	1975	1980	1985	1990	1995	1999
Summary Ratings		4.0	4.2	3.4	3.6	3.8	3.5
Rank		64	79	99	102	114	119

Components of Economic Freedom	1970	1975	1980	1985	1990	1995	1999
I. Size of Government		**9.0**	**9.3**	**9.6**	**9.0**	**8.3**	**8.6**
(a) Government Consumption		8.3 (11.8)	9.3 (8.4)	9.1 (8.9)	8.3 (11.8)	7.7 (13.8)	8.1 (12.3)
(b) Transfers and Subsidies		9.7 (1.6)		10.0 (0.6)	9.7 (1.6)	9.0 (4.3)	9.0 (4.2)
II. Structure of the Economy and Use of Markets					**2.1**	**3.9**	**3.9**
(a) Government Enterprises	6.0 (14.0)	4.0 (33.3)	2.0 (61.6)	0.0 (81.4)	0.0	0.0	0.0
(b) Price Controls					2.0	6.0	6.0
(c) Top Marginal Tax Rate							
(d) Conscription		10.0	10.0	10.0	10.0	10.0	10.0
III. Monetary Policy and Price Stability	**9.3**	**7.5**	**7.7**	**0.6**	**0.0**	**2.5**	**3.7**
(a) Annual Money Growth	9.7 (1.7)	7.5 (12.6)	6.4 (18.1)	1.6 (41.8)	0.0 (73.0)	4.0 (29.9)	5.2 (24.2)
(b) Inflation Variability	8.8 (3.1)	7.2 (6.9)	8.9 (2.8)	0.0 (26.1)	0.0 (29.2)	0.0 (26.1)	2.7 (18.2)
(c) Recent Inflation Rate	9.5 (-2.7)	7.8 (11.0)	8.0 (9.9)	0.0 (85.1)	0.0 (89.2)	3.3 (33.5)	3.2 (34.1)
IV. Freedom to Use Alternative Currencies	**9.6**	**0.0**	**0.0**	**0.0**	**0.0**	**7.3**	**5.0**
(a) Ownership of Foreign Currency		0.0	0.0	0.0	0.0	5.0	5.0
(b) Black Market Exchange Rate	9.6 (2.0)	0.0 (53.0)	0.0 (52.0)	0.0 (206.0)	0.0 (165.0)	9.6 (2.0)	5.0 (25.0)
V. Legal Structure and Property Rights				**5.7**	**5.8**	**0.0**	**3.8**
(a) Legal Security				4.8	3.2		
(b) Rule of Law				6.6	8.3		3.8
VI. International Exchange		**3.6**	**3.4**	**4.2**	**5.9**	**3.6**	**0.0**
(a) Taxes on International Trade							
i. Taxes as a Percentage of Exports and Imports		3.1 (10.4)	1.1 (13.3)	2.1 (11.9)	7.4 (4.0)	4.1 (8.8)	0.0 (15.8)
ii. Mean Tariff Rate		4.8 (25.8)	4.8 (25.8)	4.8 (25.8)		4.8 (25.8)	
iii. Standard Deviation of Tariff Rates							
(b) Size of Trade Sector	4.7 (61.9)	4.7 (61.5)	5.0 (73.1)	7.2 (96.9)	2.9 (49.1)	0.0 (38.8)	0.0 (24.3)
VII. Freedom of Exchange in Financial Markets		**2.6**	**3.3**	**1.1**	**2.0**	**2.3**	**1.6**
(a) Private Ownership of Banks		2.0 (10-40)	2.0 (10-40)	2.0 (10-40)	2.0 (10-40)	2.0 (10-40)	2.0 (10-40)
(b) Extension of Credit to Private Sector	7.9 (79.2)	6.7 (66.7)	6.0 (60.1)	2.4 (24.0)	6.8 (68.1)	5.8 (57.5)	2.6 (25.7)
(c) Avoidance of Negative Interest Rates		6.0	6.0	0.0	0.0	2.0	2.0
(d) Capital Transactions with Foreigners	0.0	0.0	0.0	0.0	0.0	0.0	0.0

SINGAPORE

	1970	1975	1980	1985	1990	1995	1999
Summary Ratings	7.8	7.6	8.0	8.4	9.0	9.4	9.3
Rank	10	6	5	5	2	2	2

Components of Economic Freedom	1970	1975	1980	1985	1990	1995	1999
I. Size of Government	8.5	8.6	8.5	7.2	7.9	8.3	7.8
(a) Government Consumption	7.3 (15.0)	7.4 (14.9)	7.1 (15.9)	4.7 (24.0)	6.5 (18.1)	6.9 (16.5)	5.8 (20.2)
(b) Transfers and Subsidies	9.6 (1.8)	9.8 (1.4)	9.8 (1.1)	9.6 (1.8)	9.4 (2.6)	9.6 (1.8)	9.8 (1.4)
II. Structure of the Economy and Use of Markets	5.4	4.9	4.9	6.0	7.5	7.9	7.9
(a) Government Enterprises	8.0 (19.4)	7.0 (25.0)	7.0 (24.2)	6.0 (34.7)	8.0 (18.6)	8.0	8.0
(b) Price Controls					8.0	9.0	9.0
(c) Top Marginal Tax Rate	4.0 (55)	4.0 (55)	4.0 (55)	8.0 (40)	9.0 (33)	9.0 (30)	9.0 (28)
(d) Conscription	0.0	0.0	0.0	0.0	0.0	0.0	0.0
III. Monetary Policy and Price Stability	9.6	8.8	8.6	9.6	9.0	9.5	9.3
(a) Annual Money Growth	9.3 (3.3)	9.0 (5.2)	9.4 (3.3)	9.9 (0.3)	9.1 (4.4)	9.6 (2.2)	9.1 (-4.3)
(b) Inflation Variability	9.8 (0.5)	7.9 (5.2)	8.6 (3.6)	8.9 (2.8)	8.9 (2.7)	9.4 (1.5)	9.0 (2.6)
(c) Recent Inflation Rate	9.8 (0.9)	9.6 (2.2)	7.7 (11.5)	9.8 (-1.1)	9.0 (4.9)	9.5 (2.7)	9.9 (0.4)
IV. Freedom to Use Alternative Currencies	4.9	5.0	5.0	7.5	10.0	10.0	10.0
(a) Ownership of Foreign Currency	0.0	0.0	0.0	5.0	10.0	10.0	10.0
(b) Black Market Exchange Rate	9.8 (1.0)	10.0 (0.0)	10.0 (0.0)	10.0 (0.0)	10.0 (0.0)	10.0 (0.0)	10.0 (0.0)
V. Legal Structure and Property Rights	9.1	7.6	9.7	8.5	8.5	10.0	9.8
(a) Legal Security	9.1	7.6	9.4	8.7	8.6		9.5
(b) Rule of Law			10.0	8.2	8.3	10.0	10.0
VI. International Exchange	9.4	9.7	9.9	9.9	9.7	9.7	9.9
(a) Taxes on International Trade							
i. Taxes as a Percentage of Exports and Imports	9.1 (1.3)	9.6 (0.6)	9.7 (0.4)	9.8 (0.3)	9.9 (0.1)	9.9 (0.1)	9.9 (0.1)
ii. Mean Tariff Rate			9.9 (0.3)	9.9 (0.3)	9.9 (0.4)	9.9 (0.4)	9.9 (0.4)
iii. Standard Deviation of Tariff Rates					9.3 (1.8)	8.9 (2.7)	
(b) Size of Trade Sector	10.0 (231.6)	10.0 (302.5)	10.0 (439.6)	10.0 (338.5)	10.0 (386.4)	10.0 (355.6)	10.0 (287.3)
VII. Freedom of Exchange in Financial Markets	8.9		9.2	9.8	9.7	9.7	9.6
(a) Private Ownership of Banks	10.0 (95-100)	10.0 (95-100)	10.0 (95-100)	10.0 (100)	10.0 (95-100)	10.0 (95-100)	10.0 (95-100)
(b) Extension of Credit to Private Sector	8.0 (79.5)	8.7 (86.7)	8.9 (89.0)	9.0 (89.9)	8.8 (87.6)	8.8 (87.5)	8.3 (82.9)
(c) Avoidance of Negative Interest Rates			10.0	10.0	10.0	10.0	10.0
(d) Capital Transactions with Foreigners	5.0		8.0	10.0	10.0	10.0	10.0

SLOVAK REPUBLIC

Summary Ratings

	1970	1975	1980	1985	1990	1995	1999
Summary Ratings					3.8	6.3	6.3
Rank					97	54	68

Components of Economic Freedom

	1970	1975	1980	1985	1990	1995	1999
I. Size of Government		**3.9**	**3.7**	**2.9**	**1.5**	**3.2**	**3.3**
(a) Government Consumption		3.9 (26.6)	3.7 (27.3)	2.9 (30.1)	3.0 (29.9)	3.2 (29.2)	2.9 (30.1)
(b) Transfers and Subsidies					0.0 (37.2)		3.6 (23.9)
II. Structure of the Economy and Use of Markets					**1.0**	**2.4**	**3.3**
(a) Government Enterprises	0.0	0.0	0.0	0.0	0.0	0.0 (75.1)	2.0
(b) Price Controls					0.0	4.0	4.0
(c) Top Marginal Tax Rate					4.0 (55)	4.0 (42)	4.0 (54.6)
(d) Conscription	0.0	0.0	0.0	0.0	0.0	1.0	3.0
III. Monetary Policy and Price Stability				**9.4**	**8.8**	**7.3**	**8.6**
(a) Annual Money Growth				9.4 (3.0)	9.9 (0.4)	7.3 (13.4)	9.1 (4.7)
(b) Inflation Variability				9.1 (2.2)	8.4 (4.0)	6.4 (9.0)	8.7 (3.3)
(c) Recent Inflation Rate		9.9 (0.7)	9.4 (2.9)	9.7 (1.7)	8.1 (9.5)	8.1 (9.7)	7.9 (10.6)
IV. Freedom to Use Alternative Currencies	**0.0**	**0.0**	**0.0**	**0.0**	**0.0**	**7.5**	**7.5**
(a) Ownership of Foreign Currency	0.0	0.0	0.0	0.0	0.0	5.0	5.0
(b) Black Market Exchange Rate	0.0 (525.0)	0.0 (359.0)	0.0 (387.0)	0.0 (423.0)	0.0 (61.0)	10.0 (0.0)	10.0 (0.0)
V. Legal Structure and Property Rights				**7.8**	**8.5**	**10.0**	**7.3**
(a) Legal Security				7.4	8.6		6.6
(b) Rule of Law				8.2	8.3	10.0	7.9
VI. International Exchange						**8.0**	**8.3**
(a) Taxes on International Trade							
i. Mean Tariff Rate							
ii. Mean Tariff Rate					7.3 (4.0)	8.8 (6.1)	8.8 (6.0)
iii. Standard Deviation of Tariff Rates							
(b) Size of Trade Sector						6.5 (124.7)	7.2 (138.5)
VII. Freedom of Exchange in Financial Markets					**0.0**	**4.4**	**5.6**
(a) Private Ownership of Banks	0.0 (0)	0.0 (0)	0.0 (0)	0.0 (0)	0.0 (0)	5.0 (40-75)	2.0 (10-20)
(b) Extension of Credit to Private Sector						5.0 (50.0)	5.7 (57.3)
(c) Avoidance of Negative Interest Rates						6.0	10.0
(d) Capital Transactions with Foreigners	0.0	0.0	0.0	0.0	0.0	2.0	5.0

SLOVENIA

Summary Ratings

	1970	1975	1980	1985	1990	1995	1999
Summary Ratings						5.9	6.2
Rank						68	72

Components of Economic Freedom

	1970	1975	1980	1985	1990	1995	1999
I. Size of Government					**4.1**	**2.6**	**2.4**
(a) Government Consumption					4.1 (25.9)	4.2 (25.8)	3.8 (27.0)
(b) Transfers and Subsidies						1.1 (33.2)	1.0 (33.7)
II. Structure of the Economy and Use of Markets						**3.0**	**4.6**
(a) Government Enterprises						0.0 (75.1)	2.0
(b) Price Controls						6.0	8.0
(c) Top Marginal Tax Rate							4.0 (50)
(d) Conscription						3.0	3.0
III. Monetary Policy and Price Stability						**2.4**	**6.7**
(a) Annual Money Growth						0.0 (57.5)	4.6 (26.9)
(b) Inflation Variability						0.0 (79.6)	6.9 (7.7)
(c) Recent Inflation Rate						7.5 (12.6)	8.7 (6.6)
IV. Freedom to Use Alternative Currencies					**2.5**	**7.5**	**6.4**
(a) Ownership of Foreign Currency					5.0	5.0	5.0
(b) Black Market Exchange Rate					0.0 (106.0)	10.0 (0.0)	7.8 (11.1)
V. Legal Structure and Property Rights						**10.0**	**7.9**
(a) Legal Security							
(b) Rule of Law						10.0	7.9
VI. International Exchange						**6.5**	**7.3**
(a) Taxes on International Trade							
i. Taxes as a Percentage of Exports and Imports						7.5 (3.7)	8.2 (2.7)
ii. Mean Tariff Rate							7.9 (10.6)
iii. Standard Deviation of Tariff Rates							7.0 (7.4)
(b) Size of Trade Sector						4.4 (109.6)	4.7 (114.8)
VII. Freedom of Exchange in Financial Markets						**6.1**	**6.5**
(a) Private Ownership of Banks						5.0 (40-75)	5.0 (57.1)
(b) Extension of Credit to Private Sector						6.5 (65.0)	7.5 (75.1)
(c) Avoidance of Negative Interest Rates						8.0	9.0
(d) Capital Transactions with Foreigners	0.0			0.0	0.0	5.0	5.0

SOUTH AFRICA

Summary Ratings	1970	1975	1980	1985	1990	1995	1999
Summary Ratings	7.5	6.2	6.0	5.6	5.5	6.0	7.0
Rank	13	22	31	46	54	63	46

Components of Economic Freedom

Component	1970	1975	1980	1985	1990	1995	1999
I. Size of Government	**8.1**	**7.6**	**7.4**	**6.7**	**6.6**	**6.6**	**6.9**
(a) Government Consumption	6.9 (16.6)	6.0 (19.6)	5.6 (20.9)	4.6 (24.4)	4.5 (24.8)	4.5 (24.7)	4.7 (24.0)
(b) Transfers and Subsidies	9.3 (3.0)	9.2 (3.4)	9.3 (3.2)	8.8 (4.8)	8.8 (4.8)	8.7 (5.3)	9.0 (4.2)
II. Structure of the Economy and Use of Markets	**1.8**	**1.8**	**1.7**	**2.5**	**3.8**	**5.9**	**6.2**
(a) Government Enterprises	2.0 (43.3)	2.0 (48.2)	2.0 (50.9)	2.0 (42.2)	4.0 (34.2)	6.0 (26.2)	6.0 (27.3)
(b) Price Controls						6.0	7.0
(c) Top Marginal Tax Rate		1.0 (66)	2.0 (60)	4.0 (50)	5.0 (45)	4.0 (43)	4.0 (45)
(d) Conscription	3.0	3.0	0.0	0.0	0.0	10.0	10.0
III. Monetary Policy and Price Stability	**9.4**	**8.2**	**7.1**	**7.0**	**7.6**	**8.1**	**8.1**
(a) Annual Money Growth	9.4 (2.9)	8.2 (8.9)	7.8 (11.0)	6.3 (18.6)	6.5 (17.3)	6.8 (16.0)	7.0 (15.0)
(b) Inflation Variability	9.5 (1.2)	8.5 (3.8)	8.1 (4.7)	8.5 (3.7)	9.5 (1.3)	9.3 (1.8)	8.6 (3.6)
(c) Recent Inflation Rate	9.4 (3.0)	7.8 (10.9)	5.2 (24.1)	6.4 (18.1)	7.0 (15.1)	8.2 (8.8)	9.0 (5.2)
IV. Freedom to Use Alternative Currencies	**4.5**	**4.4**	**4.4**	**2.5**	**4.7**	**5.0**	**7.5**
(a) Ownership of Foreign Currency	0.0	0.0	0.0	0.0	0.0	0.0	5.0
(b) Black Market Exchange Rate	9.0 (5.0)	8.8 (6.0)	8.8 (6.0)	5.0 (25.0)	9.4 (3.0)	10.0 (0.0)	10.0 (0.0)
V. Legal Structure and Property Rights	**8.7**	**6.2**	**7.0**	**4.6**	**2.5**	**4.1**	**5.1**
(a) Legal Security	8.7	6.2	7.0	6.1	3.2		8.6
(b) Rule of Law				3.1	1.7	4.1	1.7
VI. International Exchange	**8.0**	**8.7**	**8.4**	**8.6**	**7.1**	**5.6**	**8.0**
(a) Taxes on International Trade							
i. Taxes as a Percentage of Exports and Imports	8.7 (2.0)	8.7 (2.0)	9.2 (1.2)	9.1 (1.4)	8.5 (2.2)	9.3 (1.0)	9.9 (0.1)
ii. Mean Tariff Rate			8.1 (9.4)	8.8 (6.0)	7.8 (11.0)	6.1 (19.7)	8.6 (7.2)
iii. Standard Deviation of Tariff Rates					5.5 (11.3)	1.2 (21.9)	6.0 (10.0)
(b) Size of Trade Sector	6.8 (47.6)	8.9 (58.6)	7.5 (74.3)	7.2 (66.9)	6.0 (60.1)	5.8 (67.2)	7.1 (84.6)
VII. Freedom of Exchange in Financial Markets	**6.7**	**6.7**	**6.0**	**7.2**	**7.2**	**7.7**	**7.7**
(a) Private Ownership of Banks	10.0 (100)	10.0 (100)	10.0 (100)	10.0 (100)	10.0 (100)	10.0 (100)	10.0 (100)
(b) Extension of Credit to Private Sector	8.5 (84.6)	8.5 (84.7)	8.4 (84.2)	9.2 (92.4)	9.2 (92.1)	9.3 (92.9)	9.2 (91.6)
(c) Avoidance of Negative Interest Rates			4.0	8.0	8.0	10.0	10.0
(d) Capital Transactions with Foreigners	2.0	2.0	2.0	2.0	2.0	2.0	2.0

SOUTH KOREA

	1970	1975	1980	1985	1990	1995	1999
Summary Ratings	6.3	5.7	5.8	5.8	6.3	7.0	7.1
Rank	31	33	36	41	37	43	43

Components of Economic Freedom

	1970	1975	1980	1985	1990	1995	1999
I. Size of Government	**9.2**	**8.7**	**8.4**	**8.5**	**8.2**	**8.2**	**8.1**
(a) Government Consumption	8.5 (11.2)	7.8 (13.5)	7.3 (15.2)	7.4 (14.7)	7.1 (15.9)	7.0 (16.2)	7.0 (16.3)
(b) Transfers and Subsidies	9.9 (1.0)	9.6 (2.0)	9.6 (2.0)	9.5 (2.2)	9.3 (2.9)	9.3 (2.9)	9.1 (3.7)
II. Structure of the Economy and Use of Markets	**4.2**	**4.2**	**3.4**	**4.2**	**3.0**	**3.2**	**3.5**
(a) Government Enterprises	6.0 (25.3)	7.0 (21.1)	7.0 (22.6)	7.0 (25.4)	7.0 (19.2)	6.0 (25.5)	6.0
(b) Price Controls					0.0	0.0	1.0
(c) Top Marginal Tax Rate		2.0 (63)	0.0 (89)	2.0 (65)	3.0 (60)	5.0 (48)	5.0 (44)
(d) Conscription	0.0	0.0	0.0	0.0	0.0	0.0	0.0
III. Monetary Policy and Price Stability	**6.6**	**5.9**	**6.7**	**8.6**	**8.6**	**8.6**	**8.9**
(a) Annual Money Growth	4.4 (28.1)	5.7 (21.6)	6.2 (18.8)	8.6 (7.1)	8.6 (7.0)	7.8 (10.8)	8.8 (-5.8)
(b) Inflation Variability	9.3 (1.8)	7.3 (6.8)	8.8 (3.0)	8.0 (4.9)	9.2 (1.9)	9.3 (1.9)	8.1 (4.7)
(c) Recent Inflation Rate	6.2 (19.1)	4.8 (26.0)	5.0 (24.9)	9.1 (4.6)	8.0 (9.9)	8.9 (5.6)	9.8 (0.8)
IV. Freedom to Use Alternative Currencies	**3.0**	**4.8**	**3.9**	**3.9**	**4.9**	**7.5**	**7.5**
(a) Ownership of Foreign Currency	0.0	0.0	0.0	0.0	0.0	5.0	5.0
(b) Black Market Exchange Rate	6.0 (20.0)	9.6 (2.0)	7.8 (11.0)	7.8 (11.0)	9.8 (1.0)	10.0 (0.0)	10.0 (0.0)
V. Legal Structure and Property Rights	**6.5**	**5.2**	**7.5**	**4.2**	**6.0**	**7.0**	**6.8**
(a) Legal Security	6.5	5.2	6.6	6.1	8.6		7.7
(b) Rule of Law			8.3	2.3	3.3	7.0	5.8
VI. International Exchange	**7.1**	**7.7**	**7.0**	**6.8**	**7.3**	**7.7**	**7.7**
(a) Taxes on International Trade							
i. Taxes as a Percentage of Exports and Imports	8.3 (2.5)	7.9 (3.1)	7.3 (4.1)	7.6 (3.6)	7.7 (3.4)	8.7 (2.0)	8.8 (1.8)
ii. Mean Tariff Rate			5.9 (20.4)	5.4 (23.0)	7.3 (13.3)	7.7 (11.5)	8.1 (9.4)
iii. Standard Deviation of Tariff Rates					7.3 (6.7)	7.4 (6.6)	7.0 (7.6)
(b) Size of Trade Sector	4.6 (37.3)	7.4 (64.1)	8.6 (63.6)	8.2 (55.4)	6.3 (45.2)	6.2 (49.5)	6.4 (50.3)
VII. Freedom of Exchange in Financial Markets	**3.9**		**4.3**	**6.3**	**7.2**	**7.2**	**8.0**
(a) Private Ownership of Banks		5.0 (68)	5.0 (63)	5.0 (59)	5.0 (58)	5.0 (58)	5.0 (62)
(b) Extension of Credit to Private Sector	10.0 (99.5)	9.7 (97.1)	9.4 (93.9)	9.3 (93.1)	9.5 (94.8)	9.7 (97.4)	9.5 (94.7)
(c) Avoidance of Negative Interest Rates	0.0	2.0	4.0	10.0	10.0	10.0	10.0
(d) Capital Transactions with Foreigners	0.0	0.0	0.0	2.0	5.0	5.0	8.0

SPAIN

	1970	1975	1980	1985	1990	1995	1999
Summary Ratings	6.7	5.9	6.1	6.3	6.9	8.0	7.6
Rank	25	31	27	27	29	14	29

Components of Economic Freedom

	1970	1975	1980	1985	1990	1995	1999
I. Size of Government	**8.2**	**7.6**	**6.9**	**5.9**	**5.8**	**5.3**	**5.1**
(a) Government Consumption	8.0 (12.8)	7.7 (13.9)	6.9 (16.5)	6.3 (18.7)	5.9 (20.0)	5.5 (21.2)	5.0 (23.1)
(b) Transfers and Subsidies	8.4 (6.4)	7.5 (9.5)	6.8 (12.3)	5.5 (16.9)	5.8 (16.0)	5.1 (18.5)	5.2 (18.2)
II. Structure of the Economy and Use of Markets		**4.6**	**2.5**	**2.5**	**4.7**	**4.1**	**4.6**
(a) Government Enterprises	6.0	6.0 (17.3)	4.0 (27.1)	4.0 (30.2)	4.0 (33.5)	4.0	4.0
(b) Price Controls					7.0	6.0	6.0
(c) Top Marginal Tax Rate		4.0 (55)	1.0 (66)	1.0 (66)	3.0 (56)	2.0 (56)	4.0 (48)
(d) Conscription	0.0	1.0	1.0	1.0	3.0	3.0	3.0
III. Monetary Policy and Price Stability	**9.1**	**7.3**	**7.8**	**8.6**	**8.2**	**9.4**	**9.3**
(a) Annual Money Growth	9.2 (4.2)	6.9 (15.7)	7.6 (12.2)	8.3 (8.3)	6.8 (16.0)	9.8 (1.2)	8.6 (6.8)
(b) Inflation Variability	9.5 (1.4)	8.5 (3.7)	8.6 (3.5)	9.2 (2.1)	9.2 (2.0)	9.5 (1.3)	9.7 (0.8)
(c) Recent Inflation Rate	8.8 (5.9)	6.6 (16.8)	7.3 (13.4)	8.5 (7.7)	8.5 (7.3)	9.0 (4.8)	9.5 (2.3)
IV. Freedom to Use Alternative Currencies	**4.4**	**4.8**	**5.0**	**4.8**	**4.8**	**10.0**	**10.0**
(a) Ownership of Foreign Currency	0.0	0.0	0.0	0.0	0.0	10.0	10.0
(b) Black Market Exchange Rate	8.8 (6.0)	9.6 (2.0)	10.0 (0.0)	9.6 (2.0)	9.6 (2.0)	10.0 (0.0)	10.0 (0.0)
V. Legal Structure and Property Rights	**8.3**	**5.5**	**7.2**	**7.3**	**8.4**	**10.0**	**7.5**
(a) Legal Security	8.3	5.5	6.1	8.1	10.0		9.1
(b) Rule of Law			8.3	6.6	6.7	10.0	5.8
VI. International Exchange	**4.9**	**6.3**	**7.2**	**7.6**	**7.6**	**8.1**	**8.3**
(a) Taxes on International Trade							
i. Taxes as a Percentage of Exports and Imports	5.5 (6.7)	5.9 (6.1)	8.2 (2.7)	8.0 (3.0)	9.0 (1.5)	9.9 (0.2)	9.7 (0.5)
ii. Mean Tariff Rate		8.1 (9.4)	8.2 (8.8)	8.5 (7.5)	8.5 (7.4)	8.7 (6.7)	8.9 (5.6)
iii. Standard Deviation of Tariff Rates					7.1 (7.2)	7.6 (5.9)	7.6 (5.9)
(b) Size of Trade Sector	3.6 (27.5)	3.2 (30.9)	3.0 (35.8)	5.0 (43.5)	3.9 (37.5)	4.5 (46.9)	5.6 (56.8)
VII. Freedom of Exchange in Financial Markets		**6.0**	**6.7**	**7.4**	**8.2**	**8.2**	**8.5**
(a) Private Ownership of Banks		8.0 (80-90)	8.0 (80-90)	8.0 (92)	8.0 (80-95)	8.0 (85-95)	8.0 (85-95)
(b) Extension of Credit to Private Sector	7.7 (77.2)	8.5 (85.4)	8.1 (81.0)	6.8 (67.9)	6.8 (68.1)	6.7 (66.6)	7.8 (78.4)
(c) Avoidance of Negative Interest Rates			6.0	10.0	10.0	10.0	10.0
(d) Capital Transactions with Foreigners	2.0	2.0	5.0	5.0	8.0	8.0	8.0

SRI LANKA

Summary Ratings	1970	1975	1980	1985	1990	1995	1999
Summary Ratings			4.3	4.6	4.3	6.2	5.8
Rank			77	75	88	57	81

Components of Economic Freedom	1970		1975		1980		1985		1990		1995		1999	
I. Size of Government	7.8		8.4		8.4		8.6		8.5		8.2		8.6	
(a) Government Consumption	7.6	(14.1)	8.8	(10.2)	8.9	(9.6)	8.4	(11.4)	8.4	(11.4)	7.8	(13.5)	8.2	(12.0)
(b) Transfers and Subsidies	8.0	(7.8)	7.9	(8.1)	7.8	(8.4)	8.7	(5.1)	8.5	(6.0)	8.5	(5.9)	8.9	(4.4)
II. Structure of the Economy and Use of Markets					2.3		2.3		4.7		5.3		5.3	
(a) Government Enterprises	4.0	(37.0)	2.0	(40.5)	2.0	(53.5)	2.0	(54.3)	4.0	(39.2)	4.0		4.0	
(b) Price Controls									4.0		4.0		4.0	
(c) Top Marginal Tax Rate					0.0	(60.5)	0.0	(60.5)			7.0	(35)	7.0	(35)
(d) Conscription	10.0		10.0		10.0		10.0		10.0		10.0		10.0	
III. Monetary Policy and Price Stability	9.1		8.3		6.8		8.3		7.2		8.7		9.0	
(a) Annual Money Growth	9.6	(-1.8)	9.0	(-4.8)	5.9	(20.6)	8.0	(9.8)	7.6	(12.1)	8.1	(9.3)	9.0	(5.1)
(b) Inflation Variability	8.5	(3.8)	6.9	(7.8)	8.6	(3.6)	7.0	(7.5)	8.0	(5.0)	9.8	(0.5)	9.0	(2.4)
(c) Recent Inflation Rate	9.0	(5.2)	8.9	(5.4)	6.0	(20.0)	9.9	(0.6)	5.9	(20.3)	8.1	(9.3)	9.1	(4.7)
IV. Freedom to Use Alternative Currencies	0.0		0.0		4.1		3.0		2.6		4.8		5.0	
(a) Ownership of Foreign Currency	0.0		0.0		0.0		0.0		0.0		0.0		0.0	
(b) Black Market Exchange Rate	0.0	(104.0)	0.0	(92.0)	8.2	(9.0)	6.0	(20.0)	5.2	(24.0)	9.6	(2.0)	10.0	(0.0)
V. Legal Structure and Property Rights					3.9		3.1		1.6		7.0		3.8	
(a) Legal Security					4.6		4.8		3.2					
(b) Rule of Law					3.3		1.4		0.0		7.0		3.8	
VI. International Exchange	1.9		3.8		3.1		4.1		3.4		5.1		5.9	
(a) Taxes on International Trade														
i. Taxes as a Percentage of Exports and Imports	0.3	(14.6)	2.6	(11.1)	2.2	(11.7)	2.9	(10.6)	4.1	(8.8)	7.0	(4.5)	7.6	(3.5)
ii. Mean Tariff Rate					1.7	(41.3)	4.2	(29.0)	4.6	(26.9)	4.8	(26.1)	6.0	(20.0)
iii. Standard Deviation of Tariff Rates									0.0	(25.5)	2.8	(18.1)	3.8	(15.4)
(b) Size of Trade Sector	5.2	(54.1)	6.2	(62.4)	7.7	(87.0)	6.1	(64.0)	6.1	(68.2)	6.5	(81.6)	6.2	(78.4)
VII. Freedom of Exchange in Financial Markets					3.7		5.0		4.7		6.1		5.1	
(a) Private Ownership of Banks			5.0	(40-75)	5.0	(40-75)	5.0	(40-75)	5.0	(40-75)	5.0	(40-75)	5.0	(52)
(b) Extension of Credit to Private Sector					6.4	(63.8)	7.9	(79.1)	6.7	(66.7)	8.4	(84.2)	8.0	(80.2)
(c) Avoidance of Negative Interest Rates					4.0		8.0		8.0		10.0		6.0	
(d) Capital Transactions with Foreigners	0.0		0.0		0.0		0.0		0.0		2.0		2.0	

SWEDEN

Summary Ratings	1970	1975	1980	1985	1990	1995	1999
Summary Ratings	5.7	5.6	6.1	6.7	7.3	7.9	7.9
Rank	37	35	27	21	22	18	20

Components of Economic Freedom	1970	1975	1980	1985	1990	1995	1999
I. Size of Government	**3.2**	**2.9**	**2.3**	**2.2**	**1.7**	**1.4**	**2.0**
(a) Government Consumption	3.2 (29.0)	2.4 (31.8)	1.1 (36.3)	1.4 (35.3)	1.5 (34.9)	2.1 (33.0)	1.5 (34.8)
(b) Transfers and Subsidies		3.3 (25.0)	3.4 (24.7)	3.1 (26.0)	2.0 (29.9)	0.8 (34.1)	2.4 (28.4)
II. Structure of the Economy and Use of Markets	**2.1**	**2.7**	**2.4**	**3.3**	**4.2**	**5.2**	**5.7**
(a) Government Enterprises	2.0 (46.2)	4.0 (38.1)	4.0 (41.2)	6.0 (28.0)	6.0 (22.8)	6.0 (28.3)	6.0
(b) Price Controls					6.0	8.0	9.0
(c) Top Marginal Tax Rate	2.0 (61)	1.0 (70)	0.0 (87)	0.0 (80)	0.0 (72)	1.0 (58)	2.0 (56)
(d) Conscription	3.0	3.0	3.0	3.0	3.0	3.0	3.0
III. Monetary Policy and Price Stability	**9.2**	**8.2**	**8.4**	**9.0**	**8.8**	**9.4**	**9.8**
(a) Annual Money Growth		8.6 (7.0)	8.3 (8.7)	8.9 (5.5)	8.7 (6.6)	9.8 (0.9)	9.7 (1.4)
(b) Inflation Variability	9.4 (1.5)	8.8 (2.9)	9.4 (1.5)	9.5 (1.3)	9.4 (1.4)	9.1 (2.2)	9.7 (0.8)
(c) Recent Inflation Rate	9.0 (5.2)	7.1 (14.5)	7.7 (11.7)	8.7 (6.6)	8.2 (8.8)	9.3 (3.7)	9.9 (0.5)
IV. Freedom to Use Alternative Currencies	**4.5**	**7.4**	**7.0**	**7.4**	**7.5**	**10.0**	**10.0**
(a) Ownership of Foreign Currency	0.0	5.0	5.0	5.0	5.0	10.0	10.0
(b) Black Market Exchange Rate	9.0 (5.0)	9.8 (1.0)	9.0 (5.0)	9.8 (1.0)	10.0 (0.0)	10.0	10.0
V. Legal Structure and Property Rights	**7.4**	**4.5**	**7.6**	**8.7**	**10.0**	**10.0**	**9.5**
(a) Legal Security	7.4	4.5	5.2	7.4	10.0		9.0
(b) Rule of Law			10.0	10.0	10.0	10.0	10.0
VI. International Exchange	**7.9**	**8.1**	**8.2**	**8.8**	**8.4**	**8.2**	**8.4**
(a) Taxes on International Trade							
i. Mean Tariff Rate	9.2 (1.3)	9.3 (1.0)	9.5 (0.7)	9.8 (0.3)	9.7 (0.4)	9.7 (0.4)	9.8 (0.3)
iii. Standard Deviation of Tariff Rates		8.4 (8.0)	8.5 (7.5)	9.2 (4.1)	9.1 (4.7)	8.7 (6.7)	8.9 (5.6)
(b) Size of Trade Sector	5.4 (48.2)	5.0 (55.9)	4.8 (60.8)	5.8 (68.9)	4.8 (59.5)	5.5 (75.5)	6.0 (81.3)
VII. Freedom of Exchange in Financial Markets	**5.6**	**5.2**	**6.1**	**6.5**	**8.9**	**9.2**	**8.7**
(a) Private Ownership of Banks		8.0 (79)	8.0 (78)	5.0 (75)	8.0 (78)	8.0 (76)	8.0 (79)
(b) Extension of Credit to Private Sector	7.4 (73.8)	7.1 (71.2)	6.8 (67.5)	6.2 (62.1)	7.2 (71.7)	8.6 (86.1)	9.1 (91.0)
(c) Avoidance of Negative Interest Rates	8.0	4.0	8.0	10.0	10.0	10.0	10.0
(d) Capital Transactions with Foreigners	2.0	2.0	2.0	5.0	10.0	10.0	8.0

SWITZERLAND

	1970	1975	1980	1985	1990	1995	1999
Summary Ratings	8.8	7.9	8.3	8.6	8.4	8.3	8.5
Rank	4	5	4	3	4	9	6

Components of Economic Freedom

	1970	1975	1980	1985	1990	1995	1999
I. Size of Government	**7.3**	**6.8**	**6.7**	**6.5**	**5.9**	**5.6**	**5.7**
(a) Government Consumption	7.3 (15.1)	6.8 (17.0)	6.9 (16.7)	6.5 (17.8)	6.0 (19.6)	6.1 (19.2)	6.0 (19.5)
(b) Transfers and Subsidies			6.5 (13.4)	6.5 (13.2)	5.8 (16.0)	5.0 (18.9)	5.5 (17.2)
II. Structure of the Economy and Use of Markets		**7.2**	**7.2**	**7.2**	**7.4**	**7.1**	**7.4**
(a) Government Enterprises	8.0	8.0	8.0	8.0	8.0	8.0	8.0
(b) Price Controls					7.0	6.0	7.0
(c) Top Marginal Tax Rate		7.0 (38-42)	7.0 (31-44)	7.0 (33-46)	8.0 (33-43)	8.0 (35-39)	8.0 (31-40)
(d) Conscription	5.0	5.0	5.0	5.0	5.0	5.0	5.0
III. Monetary Policy and Price Stability	**9.5**	**9.2**	**9.3**	**9.5**	**9.6**	**9.5**	**9.2**
(a) Annual Money Growth	9.7 (1.4)	9.3 (3.4)	9.0 (5.1)	9.8 (1.0)	9.9 (0.6)	9.5 (2.3)	8.2 (9.2)
(b) Inflation Variability	9.6 (0.9)	9.6 (1.1)	9.5 (1.1)	9.3 (1.8)	9.8 (0.6)	9.3 (1.7)	9.7 (0.7)
(c) Recent Inflation Rate	9.1 (4.7)	8.6 (7.1)	9.5 (2.7)	9.5 (2.4)	9.1 (4.3)	9.8 (1.1)	9.8 (0.8)
IV. Freedom to Use Alternative Currencies	**10.0**	**10.0**	**10.0**	**10.0**	**10.0**	**10.0**	**10.0**
(a) Ownership of Foreign Currency	10.0	10.0	10.0	10.0	10.0	10.0	10.0
(b) Black Market Exchange Rate	10.0	10.0	10.0	10.0	10.0	10.0	10.0
V. Legal Structure and Property Rights	**10.0**	**10.0**	**9.7**	**10.0**	**10.0**	**10.0**	**9.8**
(a) Legal Security	10.0	10.0	9.4	10.0	10.0		9.5
(b) Rule of Law			10.0	10.0	10.0	10.0	10.0
VI. International Exchange	**7.1**	**7.3**	**7.8**	**8.0**	**7.1**	**7.0**	**8.1**
(a) Taxes on International Trade							
i. Taxes as a Percentage of Exports and Imports	7.4 (3.9)	7.7 (3.5)	8.4 (2.4)	8.7 (2.0)	8.7 (1.9)	8.5 (2.3)	9.8 (0.3)
ii. Mean Tariff Rate		8.8 (5.8)	9.1 (4.6)	9.1 (4.4)	9.1 (4.4)	9.3 (3.6)	9.5 (2.4)
iii. Standard Deviation of Tariff Rates					4.8 (13.0)	5.4 (11.6)	7.0 (7.4)
(b) Size of Trade Sector	6.5 (66.5)	3.2 (59.4)	4.0 (76.2)	4.5 (76.9)	3.9 (72.0)	2.7 (66.1)	3.8 (76.7)
VII. Freedom of Exchange in Financial Markets		**5.3**	**7.5**	**8.5**	**8.5**	**8.5**	**8.5**
(a) Private Ownership of Banks		5.0 (40-75)	5.0 (40-75)	5.0 (51)	5.0 (67)	5.0 (40-75)	5.0 (40-75)
(b) Extension of Credit to Private Sector	8.8 (87.8)	8.9 (89.1)	9.1 (90.6)	9.2 (92.4)	9.5 (94.5)	9.2 (92.3)	9.3 (92.7)
(c) Avoidance of Negative Interest Rates		6.0	6.0	10.0	10.0	10.0	10.0
(d) Capital Transactions with Foreigners	2.0	2.0	10.0	10.0	10.0	10.0	10.0

SYRIA

Summary Ratings	1970	1975	1980	1985	1990	1995	1999
Summary Ratings	4.3	5.3	3.7	2.9	2.7	3.5	4.3
Rank	47	44	90	106	113	118	114

Components of Economic Freedom	1970	1975	1980	1985	1990	1995	1999
I. Size of Government	**7.9**	**6.7**	**5.8**	**3.9**	**6.8**	**7.1**	**7.6**
(a) Government Consumption	6.1 (19.3)	4.7 (24.1)	4.2 (25.8)	3.9 (26.8)	6.8 (17.0)	7.1 (15.7)	7.6 (14.1)
(b) Transfers and Subsidies	9.7 (1.7)	8.6 (5.5)	7.4 (10.2)				
II. Structure of the Economy and Use of Markets				**0.0**	**0.0**	**0.0**	**0.0**
(a) Government Enterprises	0.0 (74.2)	0.0 (74.4)	0.0 (70.2)	0.0 (66.3)	0.0 (55.6)	0.0	0.0
(b) Price Controls				0.0	0.0	0.0	0.0
(c) Top Marginal Tax Rate							
(d) Conscription	0.0	0.0	0.0	0.0	0.0	0.0	0.0
III. Monetary Policy and Price Stability	**8.8**	**6.7**	**7.3**	**8.0**	**7.3**	**8.5**	**9.2**
(a) Annual Money Growth	8.3 (8.3)	6.8 (16.1)	6.8 (15.8)	6.9 (15.5)	7.1 (14.5)	8.1 (9.6)	9.4 (3.1)
(b) Inflation Variability	8.6 (3.6)	5.1 (12.3)	8.6 (3.6)	7.9 (5.2)	8.7 (3.1)	8.6 (3.5)	8.3 (4.3)
(c) Recent Inflation Rate	9.4 (3.0)	8.2 (8.8)	6.5 (17.5)	9.2 (4.1)	6.1 (19.3)	8.9 (5.4)	9.9 (-0.5)
IV. Freedom to Use Alternative Currencies	**3.3**	**9.9**	**6.5**	**0.0**	**0.0**	**0.0**	**0.0**
(a) Ownership of Foreign Currency	0.0	10.0	10.0	0.0	0.0	0.0	0.0
(b) Black Market Exchange Rate	6.6 (17.0)	9.8 (1.0)	3.0 (35.0)	0.0 (251.0)	0.0 (301.0)	0.0 (301.0)	0.0 (400.0)
V. Legal Structure and Property Rights			**0.9**	**2.7**	**2.6**	**4.1**	**7.9**
(a) Legal Security			0.0	2.2	1.9		
(b) Rule of Law			1.7	3.1	3.3	4.1	7.9
VI. International Exchange	**3.7**	**4.5**	**3.9**	**4.8**	**4.7**	**6.8**	**6.9**
(a) Taxes on International Trade							
i. Taxes as a Percentage of Exports and Imports	3.8 (9.3)	4.3 (8.5)	5.3 (7.1)	6.3 (5.6)	8.1 (2.9)	7.1 (4.3)	7.6 (3.7)
ii. Mean Tariff Rate			2.5 (37.3)	4.6 (27.0)	5.9 (20.4)	7.0 (14.8)	
iii. Standard Deviation of Tariff Rates					0.0 (27.7)		
(b) Size of Trade Sector	3.4 (38.6)	4.9 (55.4)	4.2 (53.7)	2.4 (37.2)	4.7 (55.1)	5.6 (71.4)	5.5 (69.2)
VII. Freedom of Exchange in Financial Markets	**1.1**	**0.4**	**0.5**	**0.5**	**0.5**	**0.6**	**0.6**
(a) Private Ownership of Banks	0.0 (0)	0.0 (0)	0.0 (0)	0.0 (0)	0.0 (0)	0.0 (0)	0.0 (0)
(b) Extension of Credit to Private Sector	3.7 (37.4)	1.5 (14.8)	1.6 (16.3)	2.6 (25.6)	2.3 (23.3)	2.8 (27.5)	2.9 (28.8)
(c) Avoidance of Negative Interest Rates				0.0	0.0	0.0	0.0
(d) Capital Transactions with Foreigners	0.0	0.0	0.0	0.0	0.0	0.0	0.0

TAIWAN

	1970	1975	1980	1985	1990	1995	1999
Summary Ratings	7.0	6.0	6.8	7.1	7.4	7.4	7.3
Rank	19	28	16	16	20	31	38

Components of Economic Freedom

	1970	1975	1980	1985	1990	1995	1999
I. Size of Government		7.5	7.1	6.9	6.8	7.2	7.5
(a) Government Consumption		5.4 (21.7)	4.8 (23.6)	4.7 (24.0)	4.7 (23.9)	5.8 (20.3)	6.5 (17.8)
(b) Transfers and Subsidies		9.5 (2.2)	9.4 (2.6)	9.2 (3.6)	8.9 (4.7)	8.5 (5.9)	8.5 (6.1)
II. Structure of the Economy and Use of Markets		2.1	2.1	2.1	3.9	4.4	4.4
(a) Government Enterprises	2.0 (43.1)	2.0 (46.1)	2.0 (44.3)	2.0 (43.0)	2.0 (44.3)	2.0 (47.2)	2.0
(b) Price Controls					6.0	6.0	6.0
(c) Top Marginal Tax Rate		3.0 (60)	3.0 (60)	3.0 (60)	5.0 (50)	7.0 (40)	7.0 (40)
(d) Conscription	0.0	0.0	0.0	0.0	0.0	0.0	0.0
III. Monetary Policy and Price Stability	9.0	6.1	7.2	9.2	8.6	9.6	9.6
(a) Annual Money Growth	8.6 (6.9)	6.2 (19.0)	7.5 (12.5)	10.0 (-0.2)	7.4 (12.8)	9.6 (-2.0)	9.2 (-4.0)
(b) Inflation Variability	9.2 (2.0)	3.1 (17.2)	7.8 (5.6)	7.5 (6.2)	9.3 (1.7)	9.8 (0.5)	9.5 (1.2)
(c) Recent Inflation Rate	9.3 (3.4)	9.0 (5.2)	6.2 (19.0)	10.0 (-0.2)	9.2 (4.1)	9.4 (3.0)	10.0 (0.2)
IV. Freedom to Use Alternative Currencies	9.7	9.5	9.9	9.7	10.0	10.0	10.0
(a) Ownership of Foreign Currency	10.0	10.0	10.0	10.0	10.0	10.0	10.0
(b) Black Market Exchange Rate	9.4 (3.0)	9.0 (5.0)	9.8 (1.0)	9.4 (3.0)	10.0 (0.0)	10.0 (0.0)	10.0 (0.0)
V. Legal Structure and Property Rights	9.1	5.8	9.3	8.5	8.5	7.0	7.2
(a) Legal Security	9.1	5.8	8.6	8.7	8.6		8.6
(b) Rule of Law			10.0	8.2	8.3	7.0	5.8
VI. International Exchange	5.7	7.1	8.0	8.2	8.1	8.2	7.4
(a) Taxes on International Trade							
i. Taxes as a Percentage of Exports and Imports	5.7 (6.4)	6.8 (4.8)	7.6 (3.6)	8.1 (2.8)	8.6 (2.1)	8.9 (1.7)	9.1 (1.3)
ii. Mean Tariff Rate					8.1 (9.7)	8.4 (8.0)	8.1 (9.7)
iii. Standard Deviation of Tariff Rates						5.6 (11.0)	5.6 (11.0)
(b) Size of Trade Sector	5.7 (60.7)	7.7 (82.5)	8.7 (106.3)	8.5 (97.8)	7.1 (88.5)	6.6 (95.6)	6.3 (94.5)
VII. Freedom of Exchange in Financial Markets	2.8	4.2	4.2	5.3	6.2	6.2	6.1
(a) Private Ownership of Banks	0.0 (0-5)	0.0 (3)	0.0 (10)	2.0 (12)	2.0 (16)	2.0 (15-25)	2.0 (15-25)
(b) Extension of Credit to Private Sector	7.4 (73.9)	8.0 (79.7)	7.8 (77.8)	8.2 (82.2)	8.6 (86.2)	8.5 (85.0)	8.3 (82.9)
(c) Avoidance of Negative Interest Rates		8.0	8.0	10.0	10.0	10.0	10.0
(d) Capital Transactions with Foreigners	2.0	2.0	2.0	2.0	5.0	5.0	5.0

TANZANIA

	1970	1975	1980	1985	1990	1995	1999
Summary Ratings	4.3	3.2	4.2	3.2	3.6	4.9	5.8
Rank	47	75	79	103	102	96	81

Components of Economic Freedom

	1970	1975	1980	1985	1990	1995	1999
I. Size of Government	**10.0**	**8.1**	**8.8**	**7.6**	**6.7**	**7.0**	**9.3**
(a) Government Consumption		6.2 (18.9)	7.5 (14.5)	6.4 (18.1)	6.7 (17.1)	7.0 (16.1)	9.3 (8.5)
(b) Transfers and Subsidies	10.0 (0.2)	10.0 (0.1)	10.0 (0.0)	8.7 (5.2)			
II. Structure of the Economy and Use of Markets	**1.0**	**1.3**	**1.3**	**0.0**	**0.8**	**4.2**	**3.5**
(a) Government Enterprises	2.0 (47.3)	0.0 (49.0)	0.0 (53.8)	0.0 (53.5)	0.0	0.0	0.0
(b) Price Controls					0.0	4.0	4.0
(c) Top Marginal Tax Rate	0.0 (70)	0.0 (80)		0.0 (95)	3.0 (50)	8.0 (30)	5.0 (36)
(d) Conscription	0.0	10.0	10.0	0.0	0.0	10.0	10.0
III. Monetary Policy and Price Stability	**9.3**	**6.5**	**5.5**	**6.6**	**6.1**	**5.0**	**6.9**
(a) Annual Money Growth		7.0 (15.1)	5.9 (23.3)	7.9 (10.4)	4.0 (30.0)	4.5 (27.6)	7.2 (14.0)
(b) Inflation Variability	9.4 (1.6)	7.8 (5.6)	6.5 (8.7)	8.4 (3.9)	8.7 (3.3)	6.4 (9.1)	5.2 (12.1)
(c) Recent Inflation Rate	9.3 (3.5)	4.8 (26.1)	4.0 (30.2)	3.3 (33.3)	5.6 (21.8)	4.2 (28.9)	8.4 (7.9)
IV. Freedom to Use Alternative Currencies	**1.9**	**0.0**	**0.0**	**0.0**	**0.0**	**7.4**	**8.9**
(a) Ownership of Foreign Currency	0.0	0.0	0.0	0.0	0.0	5.0	10.0
(b) Black Market Exchange Rate	3.8 (31.0)	0.0 (203.0)	0.0 (224.0)	0.0 (259.0)	0.0 (78.0)	9.8 (1.0)	7.8 (11.1)
V. Legal Structure and Property Rights			**6.9**	**6.5**	**5.6**	**4.1**	**7.9**
(a) Legal Security			5.5	4.8	4.6	4.1	7.9
(b) Rule of Law			8.3	8.2	6.7		
VI. International Exchange	**6.1**	**5.6**	**4.8**	**4.1**	**4.8**	**5.5**	**4.2**
(a) Taxes on International Trade							
i. Taxes as a Percentage of Exports and Imports	5.8 (6.3)	5.1 (7.3)	4.9 (7.7)	5.8 (6.3)	5.0 (7.5)	4.6 (8.1)	2.1 (11.9)
ii. Mean Tariff Rate				3.6 (32.0)	4.1 (29.7)	6.1 (19.5)	5.6 (22.1)
iii. Standard Deviation of Tariff Rates						5.1 (12.3)	4.4 (13.9)
(b) Size of Trade Sector	6.7 (52.5)	6.5 (49.2)	4.7 (39.5)	1.9 (23.5)	6.1 (48.6)	7.2 (62.9)	5.0 (43.4)
VII. Freedom of Exchange in Financial Markets	**1.2**	**0.4**	**1.0**	**0.0**	**2.5**	**2.0**	**2.0**
(a) Private Ownership of Banks	0.0 (0)	0.0 (0)	0.0 (0)	0.0 (0)	0.0 (0-5)	0.0 (0-5)	0.0 (0-5)
(b) Extension of Credit to Private Sector	4.2 (42.3)	1.3 (13.2)	0.0 (9.3)	0.0 (8.9)	7.2 (72.0)	4.7 (46.9)	4.7 (47.4)
(c) Avoidance of Negative Interest Rates		4.0	4.0	0.0	4.0	4.0	4.0
(d) Capital Transactions with Foreigners	0.0	0.0	0.0	0.0	0.0	0.0	0.0

THAILAND

Summary Ratings	1970	1975	1980	1985	1990	1995	1999
Summary Ratings	6.4	5.6	5.8	6.0	6.6	7.3	6.8
Rank	27	35	36	37	34	36	52

Components of Economic Freedom

	1970	1975	1980	1985	1990	1995	1999
I. Size of Government	**8.8**	**9.0**	**8.5**	**8.2**	**8.7**	**8.5**	**8.3**
(a) Government Consumption	7.7 (13.9)	8.0 (12.9)	7.1 (15.8)	6.5 (17.9)	7.6 (14.3)	7.2 (15.6)	6.8 (16.8)
(b) Transfers and Subsidies	10.0 (0.5)	10.0 (0.6)	9.9 (0.7)	9.8 (1.2)	9.9 (1.0)	9.8 (1.1)	9.8 (1.3)
II. Structure of the Economy and Use of Markets		**4.1**	**3.1**	**2.7**	**4.6**	**5.7**	**4.9**
(a) Government Enterprises	4.0 (30.0)	6.0 (19.3)	4.0 (30.9)	4.0 (31.4)	7.0 (15.1)	7.0 (20.3)	4.0 (33.7)
(b) Price Controls					4.0	5.0	3.0
(c) Top Marginal Tax Rate		3.0 (60)	3.0 (60)	2.0 (65)	4.0 (55)	7.0 (37)	7.0 (37)
(d) Conscription	0.0	0.0	0.0	0.0	0.0	0.0	10.0
III. Monetary Policy and Price Stability	**9.1**	**8.3**	**8.2**	**9.3**	**8.7**	**9.1**	**9.0**
(a) Annual Money Growth	10.0 (0.2)	9.0 (5.0)	8.3 (8.7)	9.4 (-3.0)	8.0 (10.0)	8.9 (5.3)	9.4 (2.9)
(b) Inflation Variability	8.2 (4.5)	6.7 (8.4)	8.9 (2.9)	9.0 (2.5)	9.3 (1.7)	9.6 (1.0)	7.6 (5.9)
(c) Recent Inflation Rate	9.0 (-5.0)	9.3 (3.5)	7.5 (12.7)	9.6 (2.2)	8.8 (5.8)	8.8 (6.0)	9.9 (0.3)
IV. Freedom to Use Alternative Currencies	**5.0**	**4.8**	**4.5**	**4.7**	**7.5**	**10.0**	**5.0**
(a) Ownership of Foreign Currency	0.0	0.0	0.0	0.0	5.0	10.0	0.0
(b) Black Market Exchange Rate	10.0 (0.0)	9.6 (2.0)	9.0 (5.0)	9.4 (3.0)	10.0 (0.0)	10.0 (0.0)	10.0 (0.0)
V. Legal Structure and Property Rights	**6.5**	**4.8**	**7.5**	**6.5**	**7.3**	**7.0**	**7.7**
(a) Legal Security	6.5	4.8	6.6	4.8	8.0		7.4
(b) Rule of Law			8.3	8.2	6.7	7.0	7.9
VI. International Exchange	**4.6**	**4.3**	**5.0**	**5.1**	**4.1**	**5.3**	**7.4**
(a) Taxes on International Trade							
i. Taxes as a Percentage of Exports and Imports	4.4 (8.4)	5.3 (7.0)	5.4 (6.9)	5.7 (6.5)	6.4 (5.4)	7.7 (3.5)	9.0 (1.5)
ii. Mean Tariff Rate		2.6 (37.0)	3.5 (32.3)	3.8 (31.2)	1.8 (40.8)	2.8 (36.0)	4.5 (27.6)
iii. Standard Deviation of Tariff Rates					1.4 (21.5)	3.2 (16.9)	
(b) Size of Trade Sector	4.9 (34.4)	6.0 (41.3)	7.1 (54.5)	6.8 (49.2)	9.9 (75.5)	10.0 (89.6)	10.0 (101.3)
VII. Freedom of Exchange in Financial Markets		**5.7**	**5.4**	**6.9**	**6.5**	**7.1**	**6.3**
(a) Private Ownership of Banks		8.0 (75-95)	8.0 (75-95)	8.0 (75-95)	8.0 (80-90)	8.0 (90-95)	5.0 (73)
(b) Extension of Credit to Private Sector	7.7 (76.7)	7.5 (75.0)	8.0 (80.1)	8.0 (79.5)	8.8 (87.7)	9.2 (92.2)	9.3 (93.2)
(c) Avoidance of Negative Interest Rates			4.0	10.0	8.0	10.0	10.0
(d) Capital Transactions with Foreigners	2.0	2.0	2.0	2.0	2.0	2.0	2.0

TOGO

	1970	1975	1980	1985	1990	1995	1999
Summary Ratings			4.1	5.7	4.6	5.1	4.5
Rank			84	42	80	91	107

Components of Economic Freedom	1970	1975	1980	1985	1990	1995	1999
I. Size of Government	**5.5**	**4.0**	**3.2**	**8.5**	**6.9**	**7.7**	**8.2**
(a) Government Consumption	5.5 (21.3)	4.0 (26.3)	3.2 (29.1)	7.6 (14.2)	6.9 (16.6)	7.7 (13.8)	8.2 (12.3)
(b) Transfers and Subsidies				9.5 (2.4)			
II. Structure of the Economy and Use of Markets					**0.0**	**0.9**	**0.9**
(a) Government Enterprises	0.0 (54.2)	0.0 (50.2)	0.0 (52.5)	2.0 (40.0)	0.0 (54.8)	0.0 (51.7)	0.0
(b) Price Controls					0.0	2.0	2.0
(c) Top Marginal Tax Rate							
(d) Conscription				0.0	0.0	0.0	0.0
III. Monetary Policy and Price Stability	**9.1**	**6.8**	**6.7**	**8.7**	**9.4**	**6.7**	**6.9**
(a) Annual Money Growth	8.8 (5.9)	7.8 (11.1)	6.7 (16.5)	8.8 (6.2)	9.4 (-2.9)	7.9 (10.6)	5.7 (21.6)
(b) Inflation Variability	8.9 (2.8)	3.3 (16.7)	5.6 (11.1)	8.0 (4.9)	9.4 (1.6)	4.5 (13.7)	5.2 (11.9)
(c) Recent Inflation Rate	9.7 (-1.6)	9.1 (-4.3)	7.9 (10.5)	9.3 (3.4)	9.4 (3.0)	7.6 (12.2)	10.0 (-0.1)
IV. Freedom to Use Alternative Currencies	**4.8**	**4.8**	**4.8**	**4.9**	**4.6**	**4.9**	**4.8**
(a) Ownership of Foreign Currency	0.0	0.0	0.0	0.0	0.0	0.0	0.0
(b) Black Market Exchange Rate	9.6 (2.0)	9.6 (2.0)	9.6 (2.0)	9.8 (1.0)	9.2 (4.0)	9.8 (1.0)	9.6 (2.0)
V. Legal Structure and Property Rights			**3.0**	**4.3**	**4.6**	**7.0**	**3.8**
(a) Legal Security			2.8	5.5	5.9		
(b) Rule of Law			3.3	3.1	3.3	7.0	3.8
VI. International Exchange	**5.8**		**3.5**	**5.3**	**4.4**		
(a) Taxes on International Trade							
i. Taxes as a Percentage of Exports and Imports	5.2 (7.2)		1.7 (12.4)	4.3 (8.6)	3.9 (9.2)		
ii. Mean Tariff Rate							
iii. Standard Deviation of Tariff Rates							
(b) Size of Trade Sector	6.2 (88.4)	6.9 (97.1)	6.9 (-07.4)	7.4 (105.5)	5.3 (78.8)	4.6 (74.6)	4.6 (74.1)
VII. Freedom of Exchange in Financial Markets			**4.5**	**4.6**	**4.6**	**4.5**	**4.5**
(a) Private Ownership of Banks			2.0 (10-40)	2.0 (10-40)	2.0 (10-40)	2.0 (10-40)	2.0 (10-40)
(b) Extension of Credit to Private Sector			9.3 (92.5)	9.8 (98.1)	9.8 (97.6)	9.1 (91.4)	9.1 (91.2)
(c) Avoidance of Negative Interest Rates			8.0	8.0	8.0	8.0	6.0
(d) Capital Transactions with Foreigners	0.0		0.0	0.0	0.0	0.0	2.0

TRINIDAD & TOBAGO

Summary Ratings	1970	1975	1980	1985	1990	1995	1999
Summary Ratings		4.4	4.8	4.7	5.5	6.8	7.0
Rank		59	64	74	54	48	46

Components of Economic Freedom

Component	1970	1975	1980	1985	1990	1995	1999
I. Size of Government	**6.5**	**5.2**	**7.1**	**4.6**	**7.1**	**7.6**	**5.6**
(a) Government Consumption	6.5 (17.9)	5.2 (22.4)	5.6 (20.8)	3.1 (29.5)	6.8 (16.8)	6.7 (17.1)	5.6 (20.8)
(b) Transfers and Subsidies			8.5 (6.0)	6.1 (14.9)	7.4 (10.0)	8.4 (6.2)	
II. Structure of the Economy and Use of Markets				**3.8**	**5.3**	**5.4**	**5.9**
(a) Government Enterprises	2.0 (45.9)	2.0 (45.8)	2.0 (47.6)	2.0 (40.6)	4.0 (34.6)	4.0	4.0
(b) Price Controls					4.0	6.0	6.0
(c) Top Marginal Tax Rate				4.0 (50)	7.0 (35)	5.0 (38)	7.0 (35)
(d) Conscription	10.0	10.0	10.0	10.0	10.0	10.0	10.0
III. Monetary Policy and Price Stability	**9.1**	**5.3**	**5.4**	**7.8**	**8.1**	**7.9**	**8.6**
(a) Annual Money Growth	10.0 (0.2)	6.7 (16.4)	5.7 (21.4)	8.8 (5.8)	9.5 (2.7)	8.2 (9.2)	8.7 (6.7)
(b) Inflation Variability	8.2 (4.5)	3.1 (17.3)	5.9 (10.3)	6.7 (8.3)	7.8 (5.5)	6.4 (9.0)	8.1 (4.7)
(c) Recent Inflation Rate	9.2 (4.0)	6.0 (20.1)	4.5 (27.5)	8.0 (10.1)	6.9 (15.5)	9.3 (3.8)	8.9 (5.6)
IV. Freedom to Use Alternative Currencies	**7.2**	**0.7**	**0.1**	**1.1**	**1.0**	**9.7**	**10.0**
(a) Ownership of Foreign Currency		0.0	0.0	0.0	0.0	10.0	10.0
(b) Black Market Exchange Rate	7.2 (14.0)	1.4 (43.0)	0.2 (49.0)	2.2 (39.0)	2.0 (40.0)	9.4 (3.0)	10.0 (0.0)
V. Legal Structure and Property Rights			**5.9**	**5.1**	**7.0**	**4.1**	**5.8**
(a) Legal Security			5.2	3.5	7.3		
(b) Rule of Law			6.7	6.6	6.7	4.1	5.8
VI. International Exchange		**6.9**	**6.5**	**5.4**	**5.6**	**6.5**	**4.8**
(a) Taxes on International Trade							
i. Taxes as a Percentage of Exports and Imports		8.3 (2.6)	7.9 (3.2)	6.2 (5.7)	8.2 (2.7)	8.9 (1.7)	3.2 (10.2)
ii. Mean Tariff Rate				6.6 (17.0)	6.3 (18.6)	7.2 (14.1)	6.1 (19.3)
iii. Standard Deviation of Tariff Rates					3.9 (15.3)	4.9 (12.7)	5.4 (11.4)
(b) Size of Trade Sector	3.9 (84.4)	4.3 (88.2)	3.7 (89.4)	1.4 (61.0)	2.2 (70.9)	3.7 (97.1)	3.7 (97.7)
VII. Freedom of Exchange in Financial Markets		**4.2**	**4.3**	**5.9**	**5.3**	**7.5**	**8.5**
(a) Private Ownership of Banks		5.0 (40-75)	5.0 (40-75)	8.0 (75-90)	8.0 (75-90)	8.0 (75-90)	8.0 (75-90)
(b) Extension of Credit to Private Sector	8.4 (84.2)	8.4 (84.3)	8.8 (88.0)	8.1 (81.1)	7.7 (77.0)	7.8 (77.5)	8.0 (79.9)
(c) Avoidance of Negative Interest Rates				8.0	6.0	6.0	10.0
(d) Capital Transactions with Foreigners	0.0	0.0	0.0	0.0	0.0	8.0	8.0

TUNISIA

Summary Ratings	1970	1975	1980	1985	1990	1995	1999
Summary Ratings	4.3	4.5	4.5	4.2	4.7	5.4	6.0
Rank	47	57	71	85	72	80	78

Components of Economic Freedom

	1970	1975	1980	1985	1990	1995	1999
I. Size of Government	**7.3**	**7.8**	**7.4**	**6.7**	**6.7**	**6.8**	**6.9**
(a) Government Consumption	5.7 (20.7)	5.9 (19.8)	6.2 (19.0)	5.2 (22.5)	5.7 (20.5)	5.6 (21.1)	5.6 (20.8)
(b) Transfers and Subsidies	9.0 (4.2)	9.6 (1.9)	8.6 (5.6)	8.3 (6.8)	7.7 (9.0)	8.1 (7.3)	8.3 (6.9)
II. Structure of the Economy and Use of Markets			**1.1**	**2.1**	**3.0**	**3.9**	**3.9**
(a) Government Enterprises	0.0 (58.3)	0.0 (52.1)	0.0 (53.1)	2.0 (48.6)	2.0 (49.5)	2.0 (49.3)	2.0 (49.0)
(b) Price Controls					4.0	6.0	6.0
(c) Top Marginal Tax Rate			2.0 (62.3)	2.0 (62.3)			
(d) Conscription	3.0	3.0	3.0	3.0	3.0	3.0	3.0
III. Monetary Policy and Price Stability	**8.9**	**7.7**	**8.2**	**8.4**	**9.3**	**9.3**	**9.3**
(a) Annual Money Growth		7.3 (13.3)	8.5 (7.5)	7.7 (11.5)	9.6 (1.8)	9.4 (2.9)	8.8 (6.1)
(b) Inflation Variability	9.2 (2.1)	6.9 (7.8)	8.6 (3.4)	8.3 (4.4)	9.2 (2.0)	9.6 (0.9)	9.6 (0.9)
(c) Recent Inflation Rate	8.7 (6.6)	9.0 (5.0)	7.4 (12.8)	9.3 (3.6)	9.1 (4.5)	9.0 (5.2)	9.5 (2.7)
IV. Freedom to Use Alternative Currencies	**2.0**	**3.9**	**3.2**	**3.8**	**4.2**	**4.9**	**5.0**
(a) Ownership of Foreign Currency	0.0	0.0	0.0	0.0	0.0	0.0	0.0
(b) Black Market Exchange Rate	4.0 (30.0)	7.8 (11.0)	6.4 (13.0)	7.6 (12.0)	8.4 (8.0)	9.8 (1.0)	10.0 (0.0)
V. Legal Structure and Property Rights	**3.6**	**3.0**	**5.2**	**3.3**	**3.3**	**4.1**	**7.9**
(a) Legal Security	3.6	3.0	2.2	3.5	3.2		
(b) Rule of Law			8.3	3.1	3.3	4.1	7.9
VI. International Exchange	**3.8**	**3.6**	**4.7**	**3.6**	**3.3**	**4.9**	**4.6**
(a) Taxes on International Trade							
i. Taxes as a Percentage of Exports and Imports	3.5 (9.7)	2.9 (10.7)	4.0 (9.0)	1.1 (13.3)	3.7 (9.5)	4.0 (9.0)	4.1 (8.9)
ii. Mean Tariff Rate			4.7 (26.4)	5.2 (24.0)	4.5 (27.5)	4.5 (27.5)	4.0 (29.9)
iii. Standard Deviation of Tariff Rates					0.0 (37.4)	5.3 (11.7)	4.9 (12.8)
(b) Size of Trade Sector	4.2 (46.7)	5.0 (64.0)	6.0 (65.8)	5.4 (70.2)	7.0 (94.2)	6.3 (93.4)	6.0 (88.0)
VII. Freedom of Exchange in Financial Markets	**3.2**	**3.3**	**3.4**	**3.9**	**5.7**	**5.9**	**5.8**
(a) Private Ownership of Banks	2.0 (10-40)	2.0 (10-40)	2.0 (10-40)	2.0 (35)	5.0 (40-60)	5.0 (40-60)	5.0 (40-60)
(b) Extension of Credit to Private Sector	8.9 (88.9)	9.3 (93.2)	8.7 (86.7)	8.7 (87.4)	8.9 (88.7)	9.7 (96.5)	9.3 (93.1)
(c) Avoidance of Negative Interest Rates	0.0	0.0	4.0	6.0	8.0	8.0	8.0
(d) Capital Transactions with Foreigners			0.0	0.0	2.0	2.0	2.0

TURKEY

Summary Ratings	1970	1975	1980	1985	1990	1995	1999
Summary Ratings	3.1	3.3	3.6	5.0	5.4	6.2	6.2
Rank	57	72	93	63	58	57	72

Components of Economic Freedom

	1970	1975	1980	1985	1990	1995	1999
I. Size of Government	**8.1**	**7.8**	**7.8**	**7.9**	**8.4**	**7.9**	**8.3**
(a) Government Consumption	6.8 (16.9)	7.1 (15.7)	7.1 (15.9)	8.4 (11.4)	7.7 (13.8)	7.9 (13.3)	7.2 (15.5)
(b) Transfers and Subsidies	9.5 (2.4)	8.5 (6.0)	8.5 (6.0)	7.3 (10.4)	9.1 (3.9)		9.3 (3.0)
II. Structure of the Economy and Use of Markets		**1.0**	**1.0**	**1.7**	**5.1**	**5.4**	**6.1**
(a) Government Enterprises	2.0 (44.0)	2.0 (47.1)	2.0 (40.0)	2.0 (45.5)	4.0 (31.8)	8.0 (17.5)	7.0 (23.7)
(b) Price Controls					8.0	5.0	6.0
(c) Top Marginal Tax Rate		0.0 (68)	0.0 (75)	2.0 (63)	4.0 (50)	4.0 (55)	7.0 (40)
(d) Conscription	0.0	0.0	0.0	0.0	1.0	1.0	1.0
III. Monetary Policy and Price Stability	**5.3**	**6.4**	**0.7**	**3.1**	**1.1**	**0.9**	**0.0**
(a) Annual Money Growth	0.0 (-64.6)	5.7 (21.6)	1.9 (40.6)	3.7 (31.7)	0.2 (49.0)	0.0 (61.9)	0.0 (76.6)
(b) Inflation Variability	8.2 (4.5)	7.6 (6.0)	0.0 (27.8)	5.7 (10.7)	3.1 (17.2)	2.8 (17.9)	0.0 (45.2)
(c) Recent Inflation Rate	8.2 (8.8)	5.9 (20.5)	0.0 (85.0)	0.0 (52.2)	0.0 (58.2)	0.0 (87.0)	0.0 (64.9)
IV. Freedom to Use Alternative Currencies	**0.0**	**3.9**	**3.4**	**4.7**	**9.8**	**9.8**	**9.9**
(a) Ownership of Foreign Currency	0.0	0.0	0.0	0.0	10.0	10.0	10.0
(b) Black Market Exchange Rate	0.0 (55.0)	7.8 (11.0)	6.8 (16.0)	9.4 (3.0)	9.6 (2.0)	9.6 (2.0)	9.8 (1.0)
V. Legal Structure and Property Rights	**4.5**	**2.3**	**6.1**	**6.5**	**4.6**	**4.1**	**5.7**
(a) Legal Security	4.5	2.3	4.0	4.8	5.9		7.7
(b) Rule of Law			8.3	8.2	3.3	4.1	3.8
VI. International Exchange	**0.0**	**0.3**	**2.8**	**5.9**	**4.4**	**7.8**	**5.6**
(a) Taxes on International Trade							
i. Taxes as a Percentage of Exports and Imports	0.0 (20.7)	0.5 (14.3)	5.8 (6.3)	8.0 (3.0)	8.1 (2.8)	9.0 (1.5)	9.4 (0.9)
ii. Mean Tariff Rate			1.2 (44.0)	4.7 (26.6)	5.5 (22.7)	8.2 (9.0)	7.3 (13.5)
iii. Standard Deviation of Tariff Rates					0.0 (35.7)	7.7 (5.7)	0.0 (25.4)
(b) Size of Trade Sector	0.0 (10.3)	0.0 (15.0)	0.0 (17.1)	4.3 (34.8)	3.4 (30.9)	4.9 (44.2)	5.9 (53.0)
VII. Freedom of Exchange in Financial Markets		**3.9**	**3.0**	**5.0**	**4.0**	**6.2**	**5.9**
(a) Private Ownership of Banks		8.0 (75-90)	8.0 (75-90)	8.0 (82)	8.0 (75-90)	8.0 (75-90)	8.0 (75-90)
(b) Extension of Credit to Private Sector	6.0 (60.4)	5.9 (58.9)	4.0 (39.8)	4.0 (39.6)	6.2 (62.1)	7.3 (73.4)	5.8 (57.9)
(c) Avoidance of Negative Interest Rates		2.0	0.0	8.0	2.0	8.0	8.0
(d) Capital Transactions with Foreigners	0.0	0.0	0.0	0.0	0.0	2.0	2.0

UGANDA

	1970	1975	1980	1985	1990	1995	1999
Summary Ratings			2.6	2.7	2.7	4.9	7.1
Rank			105	107	113	96	43
Components of Economic Freedom							
I. Size of Government				**7.2**	**9.6**	**8.7**	**8.7**
(a) Government Consumption				7.2 (15.5)	9.6 (7.5)	8.7 (10.5)	8.7 (10.4)
(b) Transfers and Subsidies							
II. Structure of the Economy and Use of Markets				**2.3**	**2.3**	**4.9**	**5.5**
(a) Government Enterprises	4.0 (31.5)	2.0 (42.8)	2.0	2.0 (26.4)	2.0 (47.6)	2.0	2.0
(b) Price Controls				0.0	0.0	4.0	6.0
(c) Top Marginal Tax Rate				0.0 (70)	3.0 (50)	8.0 (30)	8.0 (30)
(d) Conscription	10.0	10.0	10.0	10.0	10.0	10.0	10.0
III. Monetary Policy and Price Stability		**4.7**	**1.6**	**0.0**	**0.4**	**5.4**	**8.5**
(a) Annual Money Growth		5.5 (22.5)	3.1 (34.4)	0.0 (76.2)	0.0 (410.0)	3.7 (31.5)	7.5 (12.3)
(b) Inflation Variability		3.8 (15.5)	0.0 (35.8)	0.0 (40.8)	0.0 (52.4)	4.4 (14.1)	9.3 (1.8)
(c) Recent Inflation Rate	1.7 (41.6)			0.0 (120.4)	1.1 (44.4)	8.2 (9.2)	8.7 (6.4)
IV. Freedom to Use Alternative Currencies	**1.9**		**0.0**	**2.5**	**1.0**	**4.7**	**8.9**
(a) Ownership of Foreign Currency	0.0	0.0	0.0	0.0	0.0	0.0	10.0
(b) Black Market Exchange Rate	3.8 (31.0)	0.0 (390.0)	0.0 (360.0)	5.0 (25.0)	2.0 (40.0)	9.4 (3.0)	7.8 (11.1)
V. Legal Structure and Property Rights			**2.2**	**2.5**	**1.8**	**4.1**	**5.8**
(a) Legal Security			2.8	3.5	1.9		
(b) Rule of Law			1.7	1.4	1.7	4.1	5.8
VI. International Exchange		**0.0**	**6.7**	**2.9**	**2.9**	**4.9**	
(a) Taxes on International Trade							
i. Taxes as a Percentage of Exports and Imports		0.0 (20.4)	7.9 (3.1)	2.3 (11.6)	2.8 (10.8)	3.2 (10.2)	
ii. Mean Tariff Rate				4.0 (30.0)	4.0 (30.1)	6.6 (17.1)	
iii. Standard Deviation of Tariff Rates						6.4 (9.1)	
(b) Size of Trade Sector	5.5 (43.5)	0.0 (19.6)	4.3 (45.5)	1.6 (28.7)	0.6 (26.6)	1.6 (32.4)	0.9 (30.0)
VII. Freedom of Exchange in Financial Markets	**2.3**		**1.8**	**1.8**	**2.2**	**3.0**	**6.4**
(a) Private Ownership of Banks		2.0 (10-40)	2.0 (10-40)	2.0 (10-40)	2.0 (10-40)	2.0 (10-40)	2.0 (10-40)
(b) Extension of Credit to Private Sector	7.6 (76.3)	5.7 (56.6)	5.8 (58.3)	5.7 (57.3)	7.7 (76.9)	6.9 (68.5)	5.8 (57.9)
(c) Avoidance of Negative Interest Rates	0.0	0.0	0.0	0.0	0.0	4.0	8.0
(d) Capital Transactions with Foreigners	0.0	0.0	0.0	0.0	0.0	0.0	10.0

UKRAINE

Summary Ratings	1970	1975	1980	1985	1990	1995	1999
Summary Ratings						2.8	4.6
Rank						121	106

Components of Economic Freedom	1970	1975	1980	1985	1990	1995	1999
I. Size of Government			4.6	4.4	5.2	3.6	2.5
(a) Government Consumption			4.6 (24.2)	4.4 (25.0)	5.2 (22.4)	3.6 (27.8)	2.5 (31.7)
(b) Transfers and Subsidies							
II. Structure of the Economy and Use of Markets						1.8	3.0
(a) Government Enterprises						0.0	0.0
(b) Price Controls					0.0	4.0	6.0
(c) Top Marginal Tax Rate							4.0 (42.5)
(d) Conscription						0.0	0.0
III. Monetary Policy and Price Stability						0.0	2.1
(a) Annual Money Growth							0.0 (106.5)
(b) Inflation Variability						0.0 (1158.3)	0.0 (378.2)
(c) Recent Inflation Rate					6.7 (16.3)	0.0 (415.5)	6.6 (17.2)
IV. Freedom to Use Alternative Currencies		0.0	0.0	0.0	2.5	7.2	6.4
(a) Ownership of Foreign Currency					5.0	5.0	5.0
(b) Black Market Exchange Rate		0.0 (391.0)	0.0 (359.0)	0.0 (637.0)	0.0 (1969.0)	9.4 (3.0)	7.8 (11.1)
V. Legal Structure and Property Rights							5.3
(a) Legal Security							4.8
(b) Rule of Law							5.8
VI. International Exchange							7.2
(a) Taxes on International Trade							
i. Taxes as a Percentage of Exports and Imports							
ii. Mean Tariff Rate							8.0 (10.0)
iii. Standard Deviation of Tariff Rates							5.6 (10.9)
(b) Size of Trade Sector						9.9 (97.3)	8.4 (82.7)
VII. Freedom of Exchange in Financial Markets						0.9	3.7
(a) Private Ownership of Banks					0.0 (0)	0.0 (0-10)	0.0 (0-10)
(b) Extension of Credit to Private Sector						1.7 (17.2)	7.9 (79.3)
(c) Avoidance of Negative Interest Rates						0.0	6.0
(d) Capital Transactions with Foreigners	0.0		0.0	0.0	0.0	2.0	2.0

UNITED ARAB EMIRATES

Summary Ratings	1970	1975	1980	1985	1990	1995	1999
Summary Ratings			6.1	6.8	7.7		7.0
Rank			27	20	14		46

Components of Economic Freedom	1970	1975	1980	1985	1990	1995	1999
I. Size of Government		**1.6**	**0.4**	**0.0**	**6.4**	**6.9**	**4.1**
(a) Government Consumption		1.6 (34.4)	0.4 (38.7)	0.0 (41.8)	2.9 (30.1)	3.9 (26.8)	4.1 (26.0)
(b) Transfers and Subsidies					9.8 (1.2)	9.9 (1.0)	
II. Structure of the Economy and Use of Markets							**8.0**
(a) Government Enterprises							6.0
(b) Price Controls					8.0	8.0	8.0
(c) Top Marginal Tax Rate							10.0 (0)
(d) Conscription			3.0	10.0	10.0	10.0	10.0
III. Monetary Policy and Price Stability			**7.2**	**9.0**	**9.4**		**8.3**
(a) Annual Money Growth			5.5 (22.7)	9.8 (-0.9)	9.7 (1.5)	7.2 (13.8)	9.1 (4.3)
(b) Inflation Variability			8.1 (4.3)	8.1 (4.8)	9.3 (1.7)		7.4 (6.4)
(c) Recent Inflation Rate		6.2 (19.0)	8.2 (9.1)	9.1 (4.5)	9.2 (4.1)		
IV. Freedom to Use Alternative Currencies		**10.0**	**10.0**	**10.0**	**10.0**	**10.0**	**10.0**
(a) Ownership of Foreign Currency		10.0	10.0	10.0	10.0	10.0	10.0
(b) Black Market Exchange Rate		10.0 (0.0)	10.0 (0.0)	10.0 (0.0)	10.0 (0.0)	10.0 (0.0)	10.0 (0.0)
V. Legal Structure and Property Rights			**1.3**	**6.5**	**6.4**	**4.1**	**5.8**
(a) Legal Security			0.8	4.8	4.6	4.1	5.8
(b) Rule of Law			1.7	8.2	8.3		
VI. International Exchange		**8.6**	**8.8**	**8.8**	**8.8**		
(a) Taxes on International Trade							
i. Taxes as a Percentage of Exports and Imports		10.0 (0.0)	10.0 (0.0)	10.0 (0.0)	10.0 (0.0)		
ii. Mean Tariff Rate				9.2 (4.0)			
iii. Standard Deviation of Tariff Rates							
(b) Size of Trade Sector		5.8 (103.2)	6.3 (112.4)	5.6 (89.7)	6.5 (107.3)	8.0 (141.8)	
VII. Freedom of Exchange in Financial Markets		**7.9**	**7.8**	**5.7**	**5.8**	**5.8**	**6.0**
(a) Private Ownership of Banks		5.0 (40-75)	5.0 (40-75)	5.0 (40-75)	5.0 (40-75)	5.0 (40-75)	5.0 (40-75)
(b) Extension of Credit to Private Sector		9.1 (90.8)	8.7 (87.0)	7.3 (73.4)	8.0 (79.7)	7.7 (77.2)	8.4 (84.2)
(c) Avoidance of Negative Interest Rates							
(d) Capital Transactions with Foreigners		10.0	10.0	5.0	5.0	5.0	5.0

UNITED KINGDOM

Summary Ratings	1970	1975	1980	1985	1990	1995	1999
Summary Ratings	6.4	6.3	6.6	7.9	8.4	8.7	8.8
Rank	27	18	19	7	4	4	4

Components of Economic Freedom

	1970	1975	1980	1985	1990	1995	1999
I. Size of Government	**5.1**	**5.0**	**4.9**	**4.7**	**5.3**	**4.8**	**5.5**
(a) Government Consumption	5.1 (22.6)	3.9 (26.6)	3.9 (26.6)	4.2 (25.9)	4.5 (24.6)	4.4 (25.2)	5.4 (21.8)
(b) Transfers and Subsidies		6.0 (15.0)	5.8 (15.8)	5.3 (17.9)	6.1 (14.9)	5.3 (17.7)	5.6 (16.5)
II. Structure of the Economy and Use of Markets		**2.3**	**3.3**	**5.0**	**7.8**	**7.8**	**7.7**
(a) Government Enterprises	2.0 (43.4)	2.0 (41.8)	4.0 (29.1)	6.0 (23.5)	8.0 (15.3)	8.0 (16.4)	8.0 (14.5)
(b) Price Controls					9.0	9.0	8.0
(c) Top Marginal Tax Rate		0.0 (83)	0.0 (83)	2.0 (60)	5.0 (40)	5.0 (40)	6.0 (40)
(d) Conscription	10.0	10.0	10.0	10.0	10.0	10.0	10.0
III. Monetary Policy and Price Stability	**9.0**	**6.7**	**7.8**	**8.5**	**7.4**	**9.3**	**9.7**
(a) Annual Money Growth	8.0	8.0 (9.8)	8.0 (9.9)	7.8 (10.9)	4.3 (28.7)	9.0 (4.9)	9.6 (2.2)
(b) Inflation Variability	9.4 (1.5)	7.2 (7.0)	9.0 (2.4)	9.0 (2.5)	9.4 (1.4)	9.3 (1.7)	9.8 (0.6)
(c) Recent Inflation Rate	8.5 (7.3)	4.7 (26.3)	6.2 (18.8)	8.8 (5.9)	8.7 (6.4)	9.5 (2.4)	9.7 (1.6)
IV. Freedom to Use Alternative Currencies	**5.0**	**5.0**	**5.0**	**10.0**	**10.0**	**10.0**	**10.0**
(a) Ownership of Foreign Currency	0.0	0.0	0.0	10.0	10.0	10.0	10.0
(b) Black Market Exchange Rate	10.0 (0.0)	10.0 (0.0)	10.0 (0.0)	10.0 (0.0)	10.0 (0.0)	10.0 (0.0)	10.0 (0.0)
V. Legal Structure and Property Rights	**9.6**	**10.0**	**8.2**	**7.6**	**9.2**	**10.0**	**9.9**
(a) Legal Security	9.6	10.0	6.4	8.7	10.0		9.8
(b) Rule of Law	10.0		10.0	6.6	8.3	10.0	10.0
VI. International Exchange	**3.6**	**8.2**	**8.1**	**8.4**	**7.9**	**8.1**	**8.2**
(a) Taxes on International Trade							
i. Taxes as a Percentage of Exports and Imports	2.1 (11.9)	9.5 (0.7)	9.5 (0.7)	9.6 (0.6)	9.6 (0.6)	9.6 (0.6)	9.7 (0.5)
ii. Mean Tariff Rate		8.1 (9.4)	8.2 (8.8)	8.5 (7.5)	8.5 (7.4)	8.7 (6.7)	8.9 (5.6)
iii. Standard Deviation of Tariff Rates					7.1 (7.2)	7.6 (5.9)	7.6 (5.9)
(b) Size of Trade Sector	6.8 (45.2)	5.8 (53.6)	5.0 (52.3)	5.9 (56.6)	5.1 (51.5)	5.2 (57.7)	4.9 (54.1)
VII. Freedom of Exchange in Financial Markets	**6.6**	**5.8**	**8.1**	**9.8**	**10.0**	**9.9**	**10.0**
(a) Private Ownership of Banks	10.0 (100)	10.0 (100)	10.0 (100)	10.0 (100)	10.0 (100)	10.0 (100)	10.0 (100)
(b) Extension of Credit to Private Sector	6.5 (65.3)	7.3 (72.5)	8.0 (79.9)	9.1 (91.1)	9.8 (97.8)	9.7 (97.0)	9.9 (98.5)
(c) Avoidance of Negative Interest Rates	8.0	4.0	4.0	10.0	10.0	10.0	10.0
(d) Capital Transactions with Foreigners	2.0	2.0	10.0	10.0	10.0	10.0	10.0

UNITED STATES

	1970	1975	1980	1985	1990	1995	1999
Summary Ratings	7.7	8.0	8.4	8.5	8.8	8.7	8.7
Rank	11	4	3	4	3	4	5

Components of Economic Freedom

	1970	1975	1980	1985	1990	1995	1999
I. Size of Government	**5.1**	**6.2**	**6.3**	**6.1**	**6.2**	**6.3**	**6.5**
(a) Government Consumption	5.1 (22.6)	5.2 (22.2)	5.5 (2-.2)	5.5 (21.5)	5.7 (20.8)	6.2 (19.0)	6.5 (18.0)
(b) Transfers and Subsidies		7.1 (11.1)	7.2 (10.9)	6.7 (12.5)	6.7 (12.7)	6.3 (14.0)	6.5 (13.4)
II. Structure of the Economy and Use of Markets	**3.4**	**4.8**	**5.3**	**6.8**	**8.3**	**7.8**	**8.1**
(a) Government Enterprises	7.0 (23.8)	7.0 (21.7)	8.0 (17.2)	8.0 (17.3)	8.0 (20.0)	8.0 (14.6)	10.0 (14.2)
(b) Price Controls					9.0	9.0	8.0
(c) Top Marginal Tax Rate	0.0 (70-75)	0.0 (70-75)	0.0 (70-75)	4.0 (50-59)	7.0 (33-42)	5.0 (42-49)	5.0 (42-49)
(d) Conscription	0.0	10.0	10.0	10.0	10.0	10.0	10.0
III. Monetary Policy and Price Stability	**9.4**	**9.0**	**8.9**	**9.1**	**9.4**	**9.6**	**9.6**
(a) Annual Money Growth	9.7 (1.5)	9.4 (3.1)	9.0 (5.1)	8.9 (5.5)	9.4 (2.9)	9.3 (3.3)	9.7 (-1.4)
(b) Inflation Variability	9.6 (0.9)	9.3 (1.7)	9.5 (1.2)	9.0 (2.4)	9.7 (0.7)	9.7 (0.6)	9.5 (1.2)
(c) Recent Inflation Rate	9.0 (5.1)	8.2 (9.2)	8.1 (9.5)	9.3 (3.5)	9.1 (4.3)	9.6 (2.0)	9.6 (2.2)
IV. Freedom to Use Alternative Currencies	**10.0**	**10.0**	**10.0**	**10.0**	**10.0**	**10.0**	**10.0**
(a) Ownership of Foreign Currency	10.0	10.0	10.0	10.0	10.0	10.0	10.0
(b) Black Market Exchange Rate	10.0 (0.0)	10.0 (0.0)	10.0 (0.0)	10.0 (0.0)	10.0 (0.0)	10.0 (0.0)	10.0 (0.0)
V. Legal Structure and Property Rights	**10.0**	**9.4**	**10.0**	**10.0**	**10.0**	**10.0**	**9.8**
(a) Legal Security	10.0	9.4	10.0	10.0	10.0		9.6
(b) Rule of Law			10.0	10.0	10.0	10.0	10.0
VI. International Exchange	**6.2**	**7.6**	**8.1**	**7.9**	**7.8**	**7.9**	**7.5**
(a) Taxes on International Trade							
i. Taxes as a Percentage of Exports and Imports	8.4 (2.4)	9.0 (1.5)	9.3 (1.1)	8.9 (1.7)	9.0 (1.5)	9.2 (1.2)	9.4 (0.9)
ii. Mean Tariff Rate		7.9 (10.3)	8.5 (7.3)	8.7 (6.6)	8.8 (6.2)	8.8 (5.9)	9.0 (4.8)
iii. Standard Deviation of Tariff Rates					6.9 (7.7)	7.2 (7.0)	5.4 (11.6)
(b) Size of Trade Sector	1.6 (11.4)	4.2 (16.4)	4.9 (21.1)	4.3 (17.6)	5.0 (21.2)	5.1 (24.1)	5.0 (23.8)
VII. Freedom of Exchange in Financial Markets	**9.0**	**8.6**	**9.2**	**9.1**	**9.2**	**9.2**	**9.3**
(a) Private Ownership of Banks	10.0 (100)	10.0 (100)	10.0 (100)	10.0 (100)	10.0 (100)	10.0 (100)	10.0 (100)
(b) Extension of Credit to Private Sector	8.0 (80.0)	8.3 (83.1)	8.5 (85.4)	8.4 (83.9)	8.9 (89.2)	8.8 (87.8)	9.3 (92.9)
(c) Avoidance of Negative Interest Rates	10.0	8.0	10.0	10.0	10.0	10.0	10.0
(d) Capital Transactions with Foreigners	8.0	8.0	8.0	8.0	8.0	8.0	8.0

URUGUAY

Summary Ratings

	1970	1975	1980	1985	1990	1995	1999
Summary Ratings	6.2	6.2	6.2	6.5	6.8	6.9	6.8
Rank	22	22	26	26	32	46	52

Components of Economic Freedom

	1970	1975	1980	1985	1990	1995	1999
I. Size of Government	7.1	6.9	7.6	7.0	6.8	6.5	5.9
(a) Government Consumption	6.8 (17.0)	6.9 (16.6)	7.6 (14.1)	6.6 (17.4)	6.8 (16.8)	7.5 (14.5)	7.0 (16.2)
(b) Transfers and Subsidies	7.4 (10.0)	6.9 (11.8)	7.7 (9.1)	7.4 (10.0)	6.9 (12.0)	5.4 (17.3)	4.8 (19.5)
II. Structure of the Economy and Use of Markets		5.9	7.1	7.1	6.7	7.4	7.4
(a) Government Enterprises	6.0 (25.9)	4.0 (34.9)	4.0 (31.7)	4.0 (36.2)	6.0 (28.5)	6.0 (28.8)	6.0 (28.0)
(b) Price Controls					4.0	6.0	6.0
(c) Top Marginal Tax Rate		7.0 (41)	10.0 (0)	10.0 (0)	10.0 (0)	10.0 (0)	10.0 (0)
(d) Conscription	10.0	10.0	10.0	10.0	10.0	10.0	10.0
III. Monetary Policy and Price Stability	3.5	0.0	1.7	1.5	1.6	0.9	5.7
(a) Annual Money Growth	0.7 (46.5)	0.0 (60.5)	0.0 (58.2)	2.6 (36.9)	0.0 (74.7)	0.0 (54.3)	5.6 (21.8)
(b) Inflation Variability	0.0 (40.6)	0.0 (32.6)	5.3 (11.8)	1.9 (20.4)	5.0 (12.4)	1.1 (22.3)	2.8 (18.1)
(c) Recent Inflation Rate	9.9 (0.7)	0.0 (66.0)	0.0 (54.8)	0.0 (74.0)	0.0 (100.4)	1.6 (42.0)	8.9 (5.7)
IV. Freedom to Use Alternative Currencies	9.7	10.0	10.0	10.0	10.0	10.0	10.0
(a) Ownership of Foreign Currency	10.0	10.0	10.0	10.0	10.0	10.0	10.0
(b) Black Market Exchange Rate	9.4 (3.0)	10.0 (0.0)	10.0 (0.0)	10.0 (0.0)	10.0 (0.0)	10.0 (0.0)	10.0 (0.0)
V. Legal Structure and Property Rights			6.2	5.9	7.1	7.0	3.8
(a) Legal Security			4.1	3.5	5.9		
(b) Rule of Law			8.3	8.2	8.3	7.0	3.8
VI. International Exchange	4.6	5.9	3.0	4.7	5.5	6.8	6.7
(a) Taxes on International Trade							
i. Taxes as a Percentage of Exports and Imports	6.9 (4.7)	7.7 (3.4)	4.1 (8.9)	6.1 (5.8)	6.3 (5.6)	8.2 (2.7)	8.2 (2.7)
ii. Mean Tariff Rate				3.8 (31.0)	3.9 (30.5)	8.1 (9.3)	7.6 (12.2)
iii. Standard Deviation of Tariff Rates					7.6 (5.9)	7.2 (7.1)	6.8 (7.9)
(b) Size of Trade Sector	0.1 (30.1)	2.2 (37.1)	0.9 (35.7)	3.7 (47.9)	3.1 (46.3)	0.6 (38.3)	1.9 (44.4)
VII. Freedom of Exchange in Financial Markets			7.0	7.7	7.7	7.4	7.5
(a) Private Ownership of Banks		5.0 (40-75)	5.0 (40-75)	5.0 (40-75)	5.0 (40-75)	5.0 (40-75)	5.0 (40-75)
(b) Extension of Credit to Private Sector				7.9 (79.0)	7.9 (79.1)	8.7 (87.1)	9.3 (92.7)
(c) Avoidance of Negative Interest Rates	8.0		6.0	8.0	8.0	6.0	6.0
(d) Capital Transactions with Foreigners		8.0	10.0	10.0	10.0	10.0	10.0

VENEZUELA, REPUBLIC

Summary Ratings	1970	1975	1980	1985	1990	1995	1999
Rating	7.5	6.6	7.0	6.1	5.7	4.2	6.1
Rank	13	16	13	34	48	106	77

Components of Economic Freedom

	1970	1975	1980	1985	1990	1995	1999
I. Size of Government	**8.2**	**7.9**	**8.1**	**8.2**	**8.4**	**8.8**	**8.4**
(a) Government Consumption	6.6 (17.6)	6.2 (19.0)	6.6 (17.7)	7.5 (14.4)	8.3 (11.9)	9.0 (9.3)	9.0 (9.4)
(b) Transfers and Subsidies	9.8 (1.1)	9.5 (2.3)	9.6 (2.0)	8.9 (4.5)	8.6 (5.8)	8.5 (6.0)	7.7 (8.8)
II. Structure of the Economy and Use of Markets		**5.7**	**3.6**	**4.7**	**2.6**	**1.8**	**3.4**
(a) Government Enterprises	7.0 (21.1)	4.0 (33.6)	2.0 (45.6)	4.0 (35.8)	0.0 (65.2)	0.0 (58.3)	0.0 (46.1)
(b) Price Controls					5.0	0.0	5.0
(c) Top Marginal Tax Rate	7.0	10.0 (20)	7.0 (45)	7.0 (45)	7.0 (45)	7.0 (34)	7.0 (34)
(d) Conscription	0.0	0.0	0.0	1.0	0.0	0.0	0.0
III. Monetary Policy and Price Stability	**9.6**	**5.9**	**6.4**	**7.7**	**2.7**	**2.2**	**1.7**
(a) Annual Money Growth	9.4 (3.0)	4.8 (26.0)	7.3 (13.6)	7.3 (13.3)	6.1 (19.7)	2.9 (35.8)	0.0 (64.3)
(b) Inflation Variability	9.6 (1.1)	4.0 (15.1)	7.0 (7.4)	7.9 (5.2)	0.0 (30.2)	3.8 (15.6)	0.0 (27.6)
(c) Recent Inflation Rate	9.7 (1.3)	9.0 (5.1)	4.8 (25.0)	7.9 (10.4)	1.7 (41.7)	0.0 (51.9)	5.3 (23.6)
IV. Freedom to Use Alternative Currencies	**10.0**	**10.0**	**10.0**	**7.5**	**10.0**	**0.8**	**10.0**
(a) Ownership of Foreign Currency	10.0	10.0	10.0	10.0	10.0	0.0	10.0
(b) Black Market Exchange Rate	10.0 (0.0)	10.0 (0.0)	10.0 (0.0)	5.0 (25.0)	10.0 (0.0)	1.6 (42.0)	10.0 (0.0)
V. Legal Structure and Property Rights	**4.5**	**2.3**	**7.0**	**5.7**	**6.3**	**4.1**	**5.7**
(a) Legal Security	4.5	2.3	5.8	4.8	5.9		5.6
(b) Rule of Law			8.3	6.6	6.7	4.1	5.8
VI. International Exchange	**6.9**	**7.1**	**7.2**	**3.9**	**4.6**	**7.4**	**6.9**
(a) Taxes on International Trade							
i. Taxes as a Percentage of Exports and Imports	8.1 (2.9)	7.5 (3.7)	8.0 (3.0)	3.9 (9.1)	8.5 (2.2)	7.9 (3.1)	6.7 (4.9)
ii. Mean Tariff Rate				3.4 (32.9)	3.9 (30.6)	7.3 (13.4)	7.6 (12.0)
iii. Standard Deviation of Tariff Rates					0.2 (24.4)	8.1 (4.8)	7.6 (6.1)
(b) Size of Trade Sector	4.6 (37.8)	6.2 (50.8)	5.6 (50.6)	4.9 (40.8)	6.9 (59.6)	5.1 (48.3)	4.1 (40.1)
VII. Freedom of Exchange in Financial Markets		**7.4**	**6.5**	**6.4**	**4.7**	**4.1**	**5.8**
(a) Private Ownership of Banks		5.0 (63)	5.0 (75)	8.0 (95)	8.0 (94)	8.0 (91)	8.0 (92)
(b) Extension of Credit to Private Sector	9.7 (96.7)	9.8 (97.6)	9.3 (92.5)	8.8 (87.6)	5.7 (57.4)	2.7 (27.0)	8.4 (84.3)
(c) Avoidance of Negative Interest Rates			4.0	4.0	0.0	0.0	2.0
(d) Capital Transactions with Foreigners	8.0	8.0	8.0	5.0	5.0	5.0	5.0

ZAMBIA

	1970	1975	1980	1985	1990	1995	1999
Summary Ratings		4.2	4.7	3.3	2.9	4.9	6.3
Rank		60	66	101	110	96	68

Components of Economic Freedom

	1970		1975		1980		1985		1990		1995		1999	
I. Size of Government	**6.3**		**5.0**		**5.1**		**6.3**		**6.9**		**8.4**		**9.2**	
(a) Government Consumption	3.4	(28.3)	1.8	(34.0)	2.5	(31.6)	3.6	(27.8)	5.0	(23.1)	7.3	(15.2)	8.4	(11.5)
(b) Transfers and Subsidies	9.1	(3.8)	8.2	(7.0)	7.8	(8.7)	9.0	(4.2)	8.9	(4.5)	9.4	(2.6)	10.0	(0.0)
II. Structure of the Economy and Use of Markets	**1.3**		**1.3**		**1.3**		**1.3**		**0.9**		**3.3**		**3.6**	
(a) Government Enterprises	0.0	(85.9)	0.0	(94.0)	0.0	(77.1)	0.0	(90.7)	0.0	(44.0)	0.0		0.0	
(b) Price Controls									0.0		2.0		2.0	
(c) Top Marginal Tax Rate			0.0	(70)	0.0	(70)	0.0	(80)	0.0	(75)	7.0	(35)	8.0	(30)
(d) Conscription	10.0		10.0		10.0		10.0		10.0		10.0		10.0	
III. Monetary Policy and Price Stability	**6.4**		**6.8**		**8.1**		**4.4**		**0.1**		**0.9**		**3.1**	
(a) Annual Money Growth	6.9	(15.7)	7.9	(10.3)	8.4	(8.1)	6.3	(18.4)	0.0	(58.6)	0.0	(77.1)	3.4	(33.1)
(b) Inflation Variability	4.5	(13.7)	5.1	(12.3)	8.2	(4.6)	5.0	(12.6)	0.4	(23.9)	0.0	(49.2)	1.0	(22.6)
(c) Recent Inflation Rate	7.7	(-11.4)	7.2	(-14.2)	7.6	(11.8)	1.8	(41.1)	0.0	(106.4)	2.6	(36.9)	4.9	(25.5)
IV. Freedom to Use Alternative Currencies	**0.0**		**0.0**		**0.0**		**1.2**		**0.0**		**4.7**		**7.5**	
(a) Ownership of Foreign Currency	0.0		0.0		0.0		0.0		0.0		0.0		10.0	
(b) Black Market Exchange Rate	0.0	(56.0)	0.0	(140.0)	0.0	(70.0)	2.4	(38.0)	0.0	(212.0)	9.4	(3.0)	5.0	(25.0)
V. Legal Structure and Property Rights					**6.9**		**3.9**		**3.5**		**7.0**		**5.8**	
(a) Legal Security					5.4		4.8		4.6					
(b) Rule of Law					8.3		3.1		2.5		7.0		5.8	
VI. International Exchange			**8.8**		**8.4**		**5.1**		**6.1**		**6.4**		**6.8**	
(a) Taxes on International Trade														
i. Taxes as a Percentage of Exports and Imports			8.3	(2.6)	8.4	(2.4)	5.7	(6.4)	6.8	(4.8)	7.5	(3.8)	7.1	(4.3)
ii. Mean Tariff Rate							3.0	(34.8)	4.9	(25.6)	4.9	(25.6)	7.3	(13.6)
iii. Standard Deviation of Tariff Rates											5.8	(10.6)	6.3	(9.3)
(b) Size of Trade Sector	10.0	(90.5)	10.0	(92.8)	8.5	(86.8)	7.9	(73.6)	7.5	(72.5)	8.5	(91.0)	6.4	(67.7)
VII. Freedom of Exchange in Financial Markets			**3.6**		**3.4**		**1.7**		**2.2**		**3.0**		**7.3**	
(a) Private Ownership of Banks			2.0	(10-40)	2.0	(10-40)	2.0	(10-40)	2.0	(10-40)	5.0	(40-75)	5.0	(40-75)
(b) Extension of Credit to Private Sector	7.3	(73.2)	7.1	(71.3)	6.1	(61.2)	3.1	(31.0)	5.2	(51.7)	5.0	(50.2)	5.9	(59.0)
(c) Avoidance of Negative Interest Rates			4.0		4.0		0.0		0.0		0.0		8.0	
(d) Capital Transactions with Foreigners	2.0		2.0		2.0		2.0		2.0		2.0		10.0	

ZIMBABWE

Summary Ratings

	1970	1975	1980	1985	1990	1995	1999
Summary Ratings			4.3	4.1	4.6	5.4	5.4
Rank			77	88	80	80	89

Components of Economic Freedom

	1970	1975	1980	1985	1990	1995	1999
I. Size of Government	**7.8**	**7.1**	**6.3**	**6.0**	**6.6**	**7.0**	**7.4**
(a) Government Consumption	7.8 (13.5)	7.1 (15.8)	5.6 (21.1)	4.5 (24.6)	4.8 (23.6)	5.4 (21.6)	6.3 (18.5)
(b) Transfers and Subsidies			7.0 (11.4)	7.4 (10.0)	8.4 (6.2)	8.6 (5.7)	8.4 (6.2)
II. Structure of the Economy and Use of Markets			**3.0**	**2.3**	**1.8**	**3.9**	**3.6**
(a) Government Enterprises	2.0 (40.1)	2.0 (39.3)	2.0 (32.5)	2.0 (53.6)	2.0	2.0	2.0
(b) Price Controls					2.0	4.0	4.0
(c) Top Marginal Tax Rate			5.0 (45)	0.0 (63)	1.0 (60)	4.0 (45)	3.0 (50)
(d) Conscription	3.0	3.0	1.0	10.0	3.0	10.0	10.0
III. Monetary Policy and Price Stability	**7.6**	**8.5**	**8.4**	**8.3**	**7.5**	**6.1**	**4.8**
(a) Annual Money Growth			7.8 (11.2)	8.6 (7.2)	7.0 (14.9)	3.4 (32.9)	3.9 (30.3)
(b) Inflation Variability	7.5 (6.2)	8.9 (2.7)	8.7 (3.1)	7.7 (5.8)	8.4 (4.1)	7.3 (6.8)	7.0 (7.6)
(c) Recent Inflation Rate	7.6 (-12.1)	8.1 (9.5)	8.7 (6.6)	8.7 (6.5)	7.1 (14.8)	7.9 (10.7)	3.6 (31.8)
IV. Freedom to Use Alternative Currencies	**3.6**	**0.0**	**0.0**	**0.8**	**3.5**	**4.9**	**6.1**
(a) Ownership of Foreign Currency	0.0	0.0	0.0	0.0	0.0	0.0	5.0
(b) Black Market Exchange Rate	7.2 (14.0)	0.0 (54.0)	0.0 (34.0)	1.6 (42.0)	7.0 (15.0)	9.8 (1.0)	7.2 (14.0)
V. Legal Structure and Property Rights			**2.5**	**2.7**	**3.9**	**4.1**	**6.1**
(a) Legal Security			3.4	2.2	4.6		6.4
(b) Rule of Law			1.7	3.1	3.3	4.1	5.8
VI. International Exchange	**7.9**		**7.8**	**6.4**	**5.8**	**7.1**	**5.1**
(a) Taxes on International Trade							
i. Taxes as a Percentage of Exports and Imports	8.6 (2.1)		8.9 (1.7)	4.7 (8.0)	3.9 (9.2)	5.4 (6.9)	5.1 (7.3)
ii. Mean Tariff Rate			8.0 (10.0)	8.3 (8.7)	8.0 (10.1)	8.2 (9.2)	5.6 (22.2)
iii. Standard Deviation of Tariff Rates					5.3 (11.8)		2.9 (17.8)
(b) Size of Trade Sector	6.4 (60.2)		5.3 (55.6)	5.8 (55.6)	6.4 (63.6)	8.3 (91.2)	8.6 (93.7)
VII. Freedom of Exchange in Financial Markets			**3.7**	**3.9**	**4.5**	**5.3**	**5.0**
(a) Private Ownership of Banks		2.0 (10-40)	2.0 (10-40)	2.0 (14)	2.0 (10-40)	5.0 (40-75)	5.0 (40-75)
(b) Extension of Credit to Private Sector			5.4 (53.5)	4.0 (39.5)	6.7 (66.5)	6.9 (68.6)	7.5 (75.2)
(c) Avoidance of Negative Interest Rates			6.0	8.0	8.0	8.0	6.0
(d) Capital Transactions with Foreigners			2.0	2.0	2.0	2.0	2.0